Critical Business Skills for Success

Various Professors

PUBLISHED BY:

THE GREAT COURSES
Corporate Headquarters
4840 Westfields Boulevard, Suite 500
Chantilly, Virginia 20151-2299
Phone: 1-800-832-2412
Fax: 703-378-3819
www.thegreatcourses.com

Copyright © The Teaching Company, 2015

Michael A. Roberto, D.B.A.
Trustee Professor of Management
Bryant University

Professor, Critical Business Skills: Strategy

Professor Michael A. Roberto is the Trustee Professor of Management at Bryant University in Smithfield, Rhode Island, where he has taught since 2006. Before joining Bryant, Professor Roberto served as a faculty member at Harvard Business School and as a visiting professor at New York University. He earned a bachelor's degree in Economics from Harvard College, as well as an M.B.A. with high distinction and a doctorate in Business Administration from Harvard Business School.

Professor Roberto's research focuses on organizational and team decision-making processes. He has focused extensively on the decision-making breakdowns that lead to large-scale organizational failures. His next book will focus on the challenges that established organizations face as they try to embrace the design thinking approach to creative problem solving and innovation.

The M.B.A. students at Bryant University have chosen Professor Roberto for the Excellence in Teaching Award on eight occasions. He also earned the Allyn Young Prize for Teaching at Harvard on two occasions. Professor Roberto's innovations in teaching with technology have earned several major awards. The *Everest Leadership and Team Simulation* won top prize in the eLearning category at the 16th Annual MITX Interactive Awards. This competition recognizes achievements in the creation of web and mobile innovations and emerging applications produced and developed in New England. Professor Roberto's multimedia case study about the 2003 space shuttle accident, titled *Columbia's Final Mission*, earned the software industry's prestigious CODiE Award in 2006.

i

Professor Roberto is the author of two books: *Why Great Leaders Don't Take Yes for an Answer: Managing for Conflict and Consensus* and *Know What You Don't Know: How Great Leaders Prevent Problems before They Happen*. He has published articles in the *Harvard Business Review*, *MIT Sloan Management Review*, and *California Management Review*. Professor Roberto also has taught two previous Great Courses: *The Art of Critical Decision Making* and *Transformational Leadership: How Leaders Change Teams, Companies, and Organizations*. ■

Thomas J. Goldsby, Ph.D.

Harry T. Mangurian Jr. Foundation Professor
of Business and Professor of Logistics
The Ohio State University,
Fisher College of Business

Professor, Critical Business Skills: Operations

Professor Thomas J. Goldsby is the Harry T. Mangurian Jr. Foundation Professor of Business and Professor of Logistics at The Ohio State University's Fisher College of Business. He has held previous faculty appointments at the University of Kentucky, The Ohio State University, and Iowa State University. Professor Goldsby holds a B.S. in Business Administration from the University of Evansville, an M.B.A. from the University of Kentucky, and a Ph.D. in Marketing and Logistics from Michigan State University.

Professor Goldsby is coeditor in chief of *Transportation Journal*, the oldest academic journal in the field of business logistics; coeditor in chief elect of the *Journal of Business Logistics*, and co–executive editor of *Logistics Quarterly* magazine. He also serves as associate director of the Center for Operational Excellence, a research fellow of the National Center for the Middle Market, and a research associate of the Global Supply Chain Forum, all housed at Ohio State's Fisher College of Business. His research interests include logistics strategy, supply chain integration, and the theory and practice of lean and agile supply chain strategies.

Professor Goldsby has published more than 50 articles in academic and professional journals. He is recognized as one of the most productive researchers in the field of logistics management. Professor Goldsby is a recipient of the Best Paper Award at the *Transportation Journal* (2012–2013) and the Bernard J. LaLonde Award at the *Journal of Business Logistics* (2007). In addition, he has twice received the Accenture Award for Best Paper published in *The International Journal of Logistics Management* (1998 and 2002). He has received recognition for excellence in teaching at Iowa State University, The Ohio State University, and the University of Kentucky. Professor Goldsby has supervised more than 100 Lean/Six Sigma supply chain projects with industry partners; chaired six Ph.D. dissertations; and served as an investigator on five federally funded research projects, exceeding $2 million in grant proceeds. He has fulfilled visiting professor assignments at the Politecnico di Milano (Italy), WHU-Otto Beisheim School of Management (Germany), and the Copenhagen Business School (Denmark).

Professor Goldsby is the coauthor of four books: *The Design and Management of Sustainable Supply Chains*; *The Definitive Guide to Transportation: Principles, Strategies, and Decisions for the Effective Flow of Goods and Services*; *Global Macrotrends and Their Impact on Supply Chain Management: Strategies for Gaining Competitive Advantage*; and *Lean Six Sigma Logistics: Strategic Development to Operational Success*. Professor Goldsby is a member of the selection committees for several industry awards, including Gartner's Supply Chain Top 25, the Council of Supply Chain Management Professionals' Supply Chain Innovation Award, *Logistics Quarterly*'s Sustainability Study and Awards Program, and the University of Kentucky's Corporate Sustainability Awards. ■

Eric Sussman, M.B.A.
Senior Lecturer, Accounting and Real Estate
University of California, Los Angeles,
Anderson School of Management

Professor, Critical Business Skills:
Finance and Accounting

Professor Eric Sussman is a Senior Lecturer in Accounting and Real Estate at the University of California, Los Angeles (UCLA), Anderson School of Management, where he has taught since 1995. He received his M.B.A. from Stanford University with honors in 1993, after graduating summa cum laude from UCLA in 1987. He is a licensed CPA in the state of California.

Professor Sussman has received 13 Teaching Excellence Awards, voted on by Anderson's M.B.A. students, as well as the Citibank Teaching Award and the Neidorf "Decade" Teaching Award, both voted on by a committee of faculty members. In 2011, *Bloomberg Businessweek* recognized him as one of the 10 Most Popular Profs at Top Business Schools, and he has been named one of the 20 Most Influential Business Professors Alive Today by *Top Business Degrees*, a website devoted to business school rankings. In addition, Professor Sussman has advised numerous full-time and fully employed M.B.A. field study teams and has led student travel groups to Brazil, China, Dubai, Saudi Arabia, and Abu Dhabi. He teaches cost/ managerial accounting, financial accounting (beginning through advanced), financial statement analysis, equity valuation, corporate financial reporting, and real estate investment and finance to undergraduate, graduate, and executive education students.

Professor Sussman has consulted for large and small firms, nationally and globally, and is a frequent lecturer on varied topics in financial, accounting, and corporate reporting. In addition, he created Insight FSA, an analytical software tool that automatically measures, evaluates, and reports on the financial accounting and corporate reporting risk for all public companies via EDGAR Online. He also has served as an expert witness and consultant for commercial litigation involving matters of corporate financial reporting and disclosure, audit effectiveness, valuation, real estate due diligence and related practices, and overall damage analyses.

Professor Sussman is President of Amber Capital, Inc.; Manager of Fountain Management, LLC, and Clear Capital, LLC; and Managing Partner of Sequoia Real Estate Partners, LLC, and the Pacific Value Opportunities Funds, which have acquired, rehabilitated, developed, and managed more than 2 million square feet of residential and commercial real estate in the past 20 years. The firms' portfolio currently consists of industrial, multifamily residential, single-family residential, and retail properties.

He is Chairman of the Board of Trustees of Causeway Capital Management's group of funds (which collectively have in excess of $6 billion in assets); sits on the Board of Directors of Pacific Charter School Development and Bentley Forbes Group, LLC; and is former Chairman of the Presidio Fund and former Audit Committee Chair of Atlantic Inertial Systems, Inc., a producer and manufacturer of electromagnetic sensors. ■

Clinton O. Longenecker, Ph.D.
Stranahan Professor of Leadership and
Organizational Excellence
Distinguished University Professor
The University of Toledo, College of Business
and Innovation

Professor, Critical Business Skills:
Organizational Behavior

Professor Clinton O. Longenecker is a Distinguished University Professor and the Stranahan Professor of Leadership and Organizational Excellence in the College of Business and Innovation at The University of Toledo, where he has taught since 1984. He holds a B.B.A. in Marketing and an M.B.A. in Management from The University of Toledo, as well as a Ph.D. in Management from The Pennsylvania State University. Professor Longenecker also has served as a Visiting Lecturer at The University of the West Indies at Cave Hill, Barbados, and has lectured extensively in Poland, Hungary, and Russia.

Professor Longenecker's teaching, research, and consulting interests are in high-performance leadership and the creation of great organizations. He has published more than 180 articles and papers in leading academic and professional journals, including the *MIT Sloan Management Review*, *Industrial Management*, *Business Horizons*, *The European Business Review*, *Organizational Dynamics*, and others. He is a frequent media source, and his research has been featured in *The Wall Street Journal* and *Investor's Business Daily*, on MSNBC and NPR, and in a wide variety of other outlets.

Professor Longenecker is an active management consultant, educator, and executive coach. His clients represent a broad range of Fortune 500 firms and entrepreneurial organizations, including Harley-Davidson, ConAgra Foods, the SSOE Group, ProMedica Health Systems, Whirlpool Corporation, Eaton Corporation, Cooper Tire & Rubber Company, Dana Holding Corporation, the Howard Hughes Medical Institute, and O-I, Inc., among others. Professor

Longenecker has been described by Career Publications as "one of the top motivational speakers in the U.S. who can blend cutting edge research, common sense, humor and conviction into a real and inspiring call for better performance that can help us all!"

Professor Longenecker has received more than 40 outstanding teaching, service, and research awards and is the only professor in the history of The University of Toledo to have been the recipient of the university's Outstanding Teacher, Outstanding Researcher, and Outstanding Service awards. In addition, he has received numerous industry awards, including the Ernst & Young Entrepreneur of the Year Award, a Toastmasters International Leadership Award, and a Jefferson Award for outstanding public service. He has been recently recognized by *The Economist* as one of the top 15 business professors in the world.

Professor Longenecker's best-selling book, *Getting Results: Five Absolutes for High Performance* (coauthored with Jack Simonetti), describes the best practices of more than 2,000 high-performance managers and how they achieve outstanding performance; the book has been translated into nine languages. His latest book is *The Two-Minute Drill: Lessons for Rapid Organizational Improvement from America's Greatest Game*, published with Greg Papp and Tim Stansfield. The book chronicles the keys to rapid performance improvement from the authors' research on more than 1,000 organizational improvement initiatives. Professor Longenecker is also featured in a number of educational videos, including the award-winning CRM training film *Effective Performance Appraisal* and *Continuous Improvement in Manufacturing*, based on his research.

Professor Longenecker is an active community servant and a Bible study leader and Christian speaker. He has spent extensive time working in the country of Haiti, managing several missionary schools and hospital construction projects. He is happily married to the former Cindy Breese and has three children. ∎

Ryan Hamilton, Ph.D.
Associate Professor of Marketing
Emory University, Goizueta Business School

Professor, Critical Business Skills: Marketing

Professor Ryan Hamilton is an Associate Professor of Marketing at Emory University's Goizueta Business School, where he has taught since 2008. He received his Ph.D. in Marketing from Northwestern University's Kellogg School of Management. He also has a B.S. in Applied Physics from Brigham Young University, where he participated in proton-induced X-ray emission research using a Van de Graaff proton accelerator.

Professor Hamilton is a consumer psychologist, whose research investigates shopper decision making: how brands, prices, and choice architecture influence decision making at the point of purchase. His research generally fits within the school of behavioral decision theory, examining how contextual factors produce decision biases and irregularities. In 2013, he was recognized by the Marketing Science Institute as being among the most productive young scholars in his field.

Professor Hamilton has received multiple teaching excellence awards from his M.B.A. students at Emory and, in 2011, was named one of "The World's Best 40 B-School Profs under the Age of 40" by *Poets & Quants*, an online magazine that covers the world of M.B.A. education.

Professor Hamilton's research findings have been published in some of the most prestigious peer-reviewed journals in marketing and management, including the *Journal of Consumer Research*, the *Journal of Marketing Research*, the *Journal of Marketing*, *Management Science*, and *Organizational Behavior and Human Decision Processes*. His findings also have found an audience in the popular press, having been covered by *The New York Times*, *The Wall Street Journal*, *TIME*, *USA TODAY*, *The Financial Times*, *New York* magazine, and CNN Headline News.

Professor Hamilton is the proud father of five young children, which means that he spends much of his time exhausted and slightly rumpled. He is also a former amateur sketch and stand-up comedian and performed in that capacity in clubs and on college campuses across the country. ■

Table of Contents

Table of Contents

Critical Business Skills: Operations

Table of Contents

Disciaimer

The financial information provided in these lectures is for informational purposes only and not for the purpose of providing specific financial advice. Financial investing carries an inherent risk that you will lose part or all of your investment. Investors must independently and thoroughly research and analyze each and every investment prior to investing. The consequences of such risk may involve but are not limited to federal/state/municipal tax liabilities, loss of all or part of the investment capital, loss of interest, contract liability to third parties, and other risks not specifically listed herein. Use of these lectures does not create any financial advisor relationship with The Teaching Company or its lecturers, and neither The Teaching Company nor the lecturer is responsible for your use of this educational material or its consequences. You should contact a financial advisor to obtain advice with respect to any specific financial investing questions. The opinions and positions provided in these lectures reflect the opinions and positions of the relevant lecturer and do not necessarily reflect the opinions or positions of The Teaching Company or its affiliates. Pursuant to IRS Circular 230, any tax advice provided in these lectures may not be used to avoid tax penalties or to promote, market, or recommend any matter therein.

The Teaching Company expressly DISCLAIMS LIABILITY for any DIRECT, INDIRECT, INCIDENTAL, SPECIAL, OR CONSEQUENTIAL DAMAGES OR LOST PROFITS that result directly or indirectly from the use of these lectures. In states that do not allow some or all of the above limitations of liability, liability shall be limited to the greatest extent allowed by law.

Critical Business Skills: Strategy

Michael A. Roberto, D.B.A.

Critical Business Skills: Strategy

Scope:

Successful businesses formulate a clear competitive strategy. They make the tough choices about how and where to compete. These firms do not try to be all things to all people. Instead, they select their target markets carefully, and they choose what not to do. By making clear trade-offs, they develop a distinctive position in the marketplace, and they make it quite difficult for established rivals to engage in successful imitation.

In this section of the course, we will explore the fundamental question: Why do some firms perform better than others? To answer this question, we will examine two factors: industry attractiveness and competitive advantage. We will learn that some industries earn much higher returns on investment than others. In the first six lectures, we will introduce a framework for analyzing industry structure and explaining the substantial differences in profitability across industries. Of course, companies can earn higher returns than their competitors by building competitive advantage within whichever industry they choose to compete. We will examine how firms establish a distinctive competitive position and create competitive advantage over rivals. Moreover, we will analyze how firms can sustain that competitive advantage against a variety of external and internal threats. Most firms cannot sustain advantage for a lengthy period of time. We will try to understand why and how leading companies lose their competitive edge.

The second six lectures shift focus from business strategy to corporate strategy. The latter topic emphasizes the strategic choices faced by diversified, multi–business unit companies. We will examine why these firms choose to expand their horizontal and vertical scope. In this section, we ask the fundamental question: Is the whole worth more than the sum of the parts? In other words, how can companies create (or destroy) value by choosing to own and operate multiple business units competing in different product markets? This section of the course closes by examining the role of the entrepreneur. We examine how start-ups can use a lean approach to launching a new business, while applying many of the strategic concepts introduced in these lectures.

Throughout the lectures, we will use a wide variety of case studies to introduce key concepts from the field of competitive strategy. For instance, we will examine the dynamics of such industries as airlines, personal computers, and pharmaceuticals. We will look at how such firms as Apple have positioned themselves to succeed in challenging competitive environments. We will explore how Trader Joe's made a series of trade-offs to establish a position that others could not imitate easily, and we will analyze the competitive battle between Blockbuster and Netflix. We will also explore the diversification and vertical integration strategies used by such firms as Disney and Zara. As we examine these case studies, we will see how the core ideas of business strategy work in practice, not just in theory. ■

Strategy Is Making Choices
Lecture 1

A ndy Grove, the CEO of Intel, has noted that in business, only the paranoid survive. As proof of this idea, consider what has happened in just a few industries in recent years: The movie rental business Blockbuster has been toppled by Netflix; record stores have given way to music-streaming services, such as Spotify; and taxicabs may soon be supplanted by Uber. In each of these industries, a disruptive rival has emerged and threatened or eliminated the incumbent players. In this section of the course, we will try to understand how you can sustain a competitive advantage in your industry or how, as a new entrant, you can plot a strategy to knock off the top players.

The Field of Business Strategy
- The field of business strategy might be said to have emerged from an ancient Chinese military treatise, *The Art of War*, written by Sun Tzu. Many in business have used this text to formulate ideas on how companies can build and sustain competitive advantage.

- In the 1950s and 1960s, leading business schools began to explore the idea of competitive strategy. In the early 1960s, the business historian Alfred Chandler studied some of America's great 20th-century corporations. He noted that as those firms changed their strategies, they also had to change their organizational structures, systems, and processes. For this reason, he argued that strategy drives structure in large organizations.

- But in 1970, Joseph Bower at Harvard Business School turned that argument on its head. He didn't disagree with Chandler, but he argued that in some companies, structure can also drive strategy. The choices a firm makes regarding systems, organizational structures, processes, measurements, and so on can drive the firm's future. Such choices are behind the kinds of ideas that bubble up from below about new products and services and reach top management.

- The modern field of strategy was initiated by Ken Andrews and his colleagues at Harvard Business School. They argued that strategy is a pattern of choices that reveals the purpose and goals of an organization.

- Economics has also influenced the field of strategy. Michael Porter was one of the early economists who began to fuse ideas from economics with ideas from the field of business management.

Organizational Performance

- The fundamental question we'll try to answer in these lectures on strategy is simple: Why do some firms perform better than others? To answer this question, we must look at two factors: industry attractiveness and competitive advantage.

- Industry attractiveness simply means that some industries are more profitable than others. In those environments, there are more opportunities for more companies to make healthy returns. In other industries, it's much more difficult for firms to make money. Thus, one part of explaining a firm's performance is understanding the environment in which it competes.

- But we also then have to understand how a firm competes against its rivals. Does it have an advantage over rivals? Is it able to generate returns above the industry average? And can it do so year after year? That's what we mean by competitive advantage.

- We can also identify two key questions related to competitive advantage: (1) How do you establish a distinctive competitive position and create advantage over your rivals? (2) How do you sustain that advantage against a variety of external and internal threats?
    - We live in a world where information is readily available and moves quickly. Anyone can get on the Internet and learn about competitors. Consultants can be hired to help benchmark a firm against the competition.

- ○ Without question, if you've proven that you have a successful product or service, if your customers are happy and your investors are getting attractive returns, others will try to imitate you. They will look for a slightly better way to do what you're doing—and they won't stop.

- ○ For this reason, understanding how to sustain competitive advantage is crucial to business strategy.

Strategic Planning

- Porter has argued for the importance of having an explicit process for formulating strategies, for understanding the goals of a corporation and how they will be achieved. But some have been much more skeptical and critical of the idea of strategic planning in organizations. For example, management professor Russell Ackoff said, "Most corporate planning is like a ritual rain dance. It has no effect on the weather that follows, but it makes those who engage in it feel that they are in control."

In many corporate strategic planning processes, discussions focus more on financial targets and budgets than about where and how to compete.

- It's important to note that Ackoff is criticizing the strategic planning process as it occurs in many companies. That process, especially in large organizations, tends to be bureaucratic and cumbersome. It takes a great deal of time, and it tends to focus on budgeting rather than strategy. In contrast, strategy formulation should focus on where and how to compete.

- Some have also criticized the field the strategy by arguing that it's simply not appropriate to talk about establishing and sustaining competitive advantage in today's turbulent environment.
  - Rita McGrath at Columbia has said that competitive advantage is transient. It's simply too difficult, she says, for firms to establish an advantage and sustain it over a long period of time.

  - According to McGrath, firms must adapt constantly, managing a pipeline of initiatives, not just one strategy. Any organization should experiment, iterate, and learn. Adapting is what great firms do, not plotting a distinctive position and trying to sustain it.

- Roger Martin from the University of Toronto disagrees with McGrath. Strategy, he says, should not be confused with strategic planning processes. Yes, your organization should adapt and iterate, but you must begin with a clear set of choices. You must know the direction in which you're headed. From there, you can adapt. But many managers, according to Martin, embrace the adaptive view because they don't want to make hard choices.

- Both Martin and McGrath fundamentally agree that strategy ultimately comes down to making choices about what to do and what not to do. And Martin would agree with McGrath that competitive advantage is more fleeting today than it was decades ago. But Martin believes an organization must start with a clear direction; from there, managers must scan the market, the customer, and the competition and be ready to flex the strategy appropriately.

- It's generally not the case that strategy formulation is explicit, conscious, and purposeful. It's more often the true that strategy emerges and evolves over time. It's important to think about strategy as a pattern in a stream of decisions and actions; it's not an event but a process.

- The authors of *Playing to Win* have noted five key questions to ask yourself when plotting strategy:
  - What's your winning aspiration? In other words, what are you trying to achieve?

  - Where will you play—in what product markets, segments, and geographies?

  - How are you going to win? That is, what are you going to do that will give you an advantage over the competition?

  - What capabilities must be in place to execute your strategy?

  - What management systems are required to implement your strategy?

Competition
- Four facts about competition will set the stage for our analysis of competitive environments as we move through these lectures. First, industries vary widely in their profitability. That is, in some businesses, it will be difficult to make money no matter how smart the management team or how great the strategy.

- Second, the industry you're in matters a great deal; in other words, sometimes there are forces beyond your control driving your profitability. Those in the newspaper business, for example, have learned this lesson as the Internet has grown.

- Third, competitive advantage may be fleeting.

- Fourth, industry structure varies widely around the world. It's true that we live in a more global world today, but competitive environments can look very different in different parts of the world for a variety of reasons, from consumer tastes and culture to government regulation and institutions.

Industry Structure and Competitive Advantage

- In 2013, the return on assets for Pfizer, a pharmaceutical company, was 12.8%. For Alaska Airlines, it was 8.7%. Can we conclude that Pfizer is a better-managed firm than Alaska Airlines? No, we can't look only at absolute financial returns to make conclusions about these two companies.
  - The pharmaceuticals industry is high profit, while the airlines industry is low profit. If we look more deeply, we would learn that Alaska Airlines outperforms rivals in its industry.

  - That's the key comparison we need to make. We're looking for companies that generate excess returns relative to the industry average; that's competitive advantage.

- As we look across industries, we also see that in some industries, the leader in one year is much more likely to stay on top than the leader in other industries. In other words, competitive advantage is fleeting, but it's more fleeting in some industries than others.

- The fact that you're in an industry that's low profit doesn't mean you can't make money.
  - In the supermarket business, many firms generate returns on assets in the low single digits, but if we look at the major competitors, we still see variation in returns. For example, in 2012, Whole Foods generated an 8% return on assets, while Kroger generated 2.6%. Even though the industry as a whole generates thin margins, we see wide variation across major competitors.

○ This tells us that Whole Foods has found a way to build a strong competitive advantage in an otherwise structurally unattractive business. In the coming lectures, we'll look at a number of companies that have done just that. As we'll see, we can learn more about strategy by studying companies in tough businesses to identify how they achieved a distinctive position than we can by looking at companies that compete with many other players that also generate healthy earnings.

Suggested Reading

Arbesman, "Fortune 500 Turnover and Its Meaning."

Lafley and Martin, *Playing to Win*.

McGrath, *The End of Competitive Advantage*.

Questions to Consider

1. Should firms establish a long-term strategy, or should they embrace a more adaptive approach to management?

2. Why do many strategic planning processes fail to produce positive results?

3. Why is it so difficult for firms to sustain high performance?

Strategy Is Making Choices
Lecture 1—Transcript

Imagine that you are working in or leading a very successful company. You've been featured in leading newspapers and magazines. They herald your innovative products and services. Your investors are enjoying attractive returns. You're producing strong earnings, and you have competitive advantage over your rivals. I have a harsh truth to share with you. You're unlikely to be on top a decade from now. It's very difficult to sustain competitive advantage. It's hard to stay on top. That's what the evidence shows when we look at companies in a wide variety of industries.

In fact, the Kauffman Foundation did an interesting analysis several years ago of the Fortune 500. Fortune magazine, each year, starting back in the 1950s, produces a list of the 500 largest firms by revenue. Now, what the Kauffman Foundation did is look at how many of those firms remain on the list as time transpires. So they looked at the original list produced in 1955 and asked how many firms remained on the list 30 years later. Well, three decades after the original list was published, we had about 250 of the original 500 firms still among the 500 largest firms in the country, in other words, half of the firms, no longer on the list.

But then the Kauffman Foundation looked at firms that were on the list in 1995 and looked ahead. How quickly did firms fall off the list in the last couple of decades? Interestingly, they found that it took less than 15 years to get to a point where there are only 250 survivors on the list. In other words, the attrition rate had increased considerably. Put another way, they examined the turnover, year by year, on the Fortune 500 list, and what they found is, while there have been some fluctuations over time, there's been, overall, a trend, a steady increase in turnover, over the last few decades among these leading companies. It's really hard to stay on top.

You know, some years ago, Andy Grove, the longtime CEO at Intel, a leading microprocessor company, he wrote a book in which he talked about the notion that only the paranoid survive. He said, as a leader, you have to always be ready to confront new competitive threats and be ready to scan your environment and spot the new, emerging rival that might knock you off. If you're not paranoid, you won't stay on top.

Let's take a look at what's been happening in just a few industries in recent years. In the movie-rental business, Blockbuster used to dominate, and Netflix toppled them. In music, we used to go to stores, like Tower Records, to purchase CDs, or even albums many years ago. Today, young people stream music on a service called Spotify. Most of us, when we're thinking about traveling to another city, we think about getting a hotel room. And yet, many people today are using the service called Airbnb, and they're finding a room or an apartment that someone owns and is willing to rent for a short period of time to them in that city.

And what about when you're travelling in a city and you need to get from one place to the other and you hop in that Yellow Cab? Well today, many people are using the service called Uber—controversial, but so far, very successful. Only the paranoid survive. In each of these industries, we've seen a disruptive threat come and emerge and knock off, or at least threaten, the incumbent players who were so successful some years ago.

In this course, we'll be trying to understand how, as a new entrant, as an entrepreneur, how do you plot a strategy to knock off the top players in your industry? But we'll also be looking at the perspective of the incumbent firm. If you're on top and you have competitive advantage, how do you sustain it? How do you avoid being Netflixed? How do you avoid becoming your industry's Blockbuster?

Strategy, that's the topic of this course. How do you define strategy? What does it mean to talk about business strategy? Well, several years ago, A. G. Lafley, the CEO of Procter & Gamble, collaborated with the University of Toronto's business school dean, Roger Martin. They wrote a book called *Playing to Win*, and they defined strategy. They argued that strategy is all about making choices—choices about where and how you will compete. And that really involves three things. What will you as a company do? And what will you not do? And how will you create advantage over the competition? It's as simple as that, and yet at the same time, so challenging to actually formulate and execute.

Why is it important to have a strategy, to be crystal clear about it? They argued that it's important because resources are limited. They're scarce. You can't do everything. And so you have to be very clear about how you're going to use your resources in the most efficient way possible to serve the customers you intend to serve and serve better than anyone else in your business.

Now, where did the field of business strategy emerge from? How did it originate? Well really, you go back centuries to military strategy to understand the concept, right? You have an ancient Chinese military treatise by Sun Tzu, called *The Art of War*, in which he talked about strategy from a military perspective. Many in the field of business have looked to that text and begun to use it to formulate ideas on how companies can build and sustain competitive advantage. How do they beat their "enemies," their competitors?

Strategy in the business context is really only a few decades old. We can go back to the 1950s and '60s at leading business schools, such as Wharton and Harvard, where you began to see people talking about the idea of a competitive strategy. And in fact, interestingly, it was a great business historian who wrote extensively on the topic and began to grow the field. Alfred Chandler was a business historian, and he wrote a classic book in the early 1960s. His thesis? Strategy drives structure in large organizations.

He studied the history of some of America's great corporations of the 20th century, and he noted that as those firms changed their strategies, they also had to change their organizational structure, their systems, and their processes. And he argued, therefore, that strategy really drove structure in the way firms operated.

But then in 1970, Joseph Bower at the Harvard Business School turned that argument on its head. He didn't disagree with Chandler, but he argued that in some companies, structure can also drive strategy. The choices you make about the systems and the organizational structure and the processes and the measurements and reward systems, well, those choices can drive where the firm might go in the future, because they drive the kind of ideas that bubble up from below and get to top management about new products and services that they might offer.

The modern field the strategy was really initiated by Ken Andrews and his colleagues at Harvard Business School, and they argued that strategy was a pattern of choices that revealed the purpose and goals of an organization. Later, we began to see the influence of industrial organization economics on the field of strategy. Michael Porter was one of those early economists who began to fuse ideas from economics with ideas from management, and he began to introduce other young scholars into the field, and they begin to shape our ideas around how we formulate effective strategies, how we build competitive advantage, and how we sustain it.

So what's the fundamental question we're going to try to answer in this course? I would argue it's very simple; it's why do some firms perform better than others? To answer this question, we have to look at two factors, and they become a bit more complex. We have to look at industry attractiveness and competitive advantage.

Industry attractiveness, some industries are more profitable than others. In those environments, there are more opportunities for more companies to make healthy returns. Other industries, it's really difficult for firms to make money. So one part of explaining a firm's performance is understanding the environment in which they compete. But we also then have to understand how they compete against their rivals. And do they have advantage over their rivals? Are you able to generate returns above the industry average? That's what we mean by competitive advantage. And can you do that year after year?

Now, there are two key questions related to competitive advantage. First, how do you establish that distinctive competitive position and create that advantage over your rivals? But then, the second part, in a way, is much more challenging. How do you sustain that advantage against a variety of external and internal threats? We're in a world where information is readily available; It moves very quickly, and we can get on the internet and learn about our competitors so easily. We have consultants out there helping us benchmark against the competition.

What that means is, if you've proven that you have a successful product or service, if your customers are happy and your investors are generating attractive returns, guess what? Others are going to try to imitate you. They're going to try to find what you're doing and find a little bit better way of doing it. And they won't stop. Others will try as well, and people will also offer alternative products and services, slightly different than your own, that might attract some customers. People are coming after you. They're trying to imitate and undermine your business. And so understanding how to sustain that advantage is crucial when we talk about business strategy.

Now, there are two views of strategic planning. Porter's view is that strategic planning is a crucial process in organizations. He argues for the importance of having an explicit process for formulating strategies, for understanding what the goals are of the corporation, and how you intend to achieve them.

But some have been much more skeptical and critical of the idea of strategic planning in organizations. Russell Ackoff has a wonderful quote that describes his view and his cynicism about corporate strategic planning. He says, "Most corporate planning is like a ritual rain dance: It has no effect on the weather that follows, but it makes those who engage in it feel that they are in control."

Now, it's important to note here that Ackoff is criticizing the strategic planning process in many companies, and I would agree with him. Those processes, especially in large organizations, tend to be very bureaucratic and cumbersome; they take a lot of time; they actually aren't really about formulating strategy.

What happens in the strategic planning process in many firms? Well, there are lots of arguments about exactly what the financial target should be. What should we be trying to achieve? What market share will we have next year? What earnings will we generate? How much revenue should we set out to achieve? But that's not strategic planning; that's really budgeting, or the programming of a strategy. Strategy formulation is about making tough choices about how to compete and where to compete. And unfortunately,

Ackoff is right. In many corporate strategic planning processes, they don't actually talk about making those tough choices. They argue over financial targets and budgets, and that's not strategy.

Some have also criticized the field the strategy by arguing that it's simply not appropriate to talk about establishing and sustaining competitive advantage in today's turbulent environment. Rita McGrath at Columbia has argued that competitive advantage is transient. It's not something you can sustain. It's simply too difficult, she says, for firms to establish an advantage and sustain it over a long period of time. In other words, she says, you have to adapt constantly. You have to manage a pipeline of initiatives, not one set strategy. You have to experiment. You have to iterate. You have to learn. Adapting is what great firms do, not plotting a distinctive position and trying to sustain it.

Now, Roger Martin from the University of Toronto, he disagrees with McGrath. He says, "Don't confuse strategy with strategic planning processes." Yes, you have to adapt and iterate, but you have to begin with a clear set of choices. You have to know what direction you're headed in. Now from there, you can adapt, but managers, he says, sometimes embrace this adaptive view, because they don't want to make hard, and perhaps, uncomfortable choices. But a great strategist makes those tough choices, and they know where they're headed. Now, they're open to adapting, but they start with a clear sense of direction.

Now, Martin and McGrath actually don't disagree as much as some have noted that they do. If you actually look at what they're saying, they both fundamentally agree that strategy ultimately is about making choices about what to do and what not to do. And Martin would agree with McGrath that competitive advantage is more fleeting today than it was decades ago. It's harder to stay on top. He just thinks we can't start with a view that you're constantly adapting; you should start with a view that says, here is the clear direction I intend to go in. But then I'm going to listen to the market and to the customer, and I'm going to scan the competition and be ready to flex that strategy appropriately.

Now, you might ask, can I go into a company, and can I find a document that says, here's how Dell intends to compete in the computer market, or here's how Ford Motor Company intends to compete in the automobile market? Is the strategy written down somewhere? And can I find it, read it, and understand it?

In other words, is strategy formulation always explicit, conscious, and purposeful? Did Michael Dell have it all figured out in his dorm room when he began to enter the computer market as a young man and dropped out of college to build his company? Did each of these entrepreneurs that we might look at in the course, did they all have it figured out in advance? Did Sam Walton know exactly where he was headed when he launched Walmart stores? I would argue that in many cases, they did not. Yes, we can find some entrepreneurs who had a business plan, who wrote down exactly what they intended to do, and they executed it. But in most cases, we see a lot of adaptation and change, and not everything was thought through in advance.

You know, James Bryant Quinn of Dartmouth once wrote that he went out and studied a large automobile manufacturer, and he talked to a senior executive there who said to him, when I was younger, I always conceived of a room where all these strategic concepts were worked out for the whole company. Later, I didn't find any such room. The strategy may not even exist in the mind of one man. I certainly don't know where it's written down. It's simply transmitted in the series of decisions made. I think you'll find that in a lot of companies, that you can't actually find the strategy written down. You may find a strategic plan, but again, that looks more like a budget and a set of targets, not a clear description of what we will do, what we will not do, and how we will compete.

In other words, what we can argue here is that sometimes strategy is very deliberate. Sometimes we know exactly where we're headed, and we've got everyone executing that strategy. Sometimes if you look today at where a firm is, you actually realize that the strategy emerged and evolved over time. In fact, some of the ideas may have bubbled up from below, not been generated in the executive suites. Some strategies are clear at the outset, and others go through many iterations.

It's not right or wrong to pursue a deliberate strategy. It's not right or wrong to have emergent strategy. It's simply the reality that sometimes strategy formulation is very explicit and purposeful and conscious, and sometimes it's much more evolutionary. It's important to think about strategy as a pattern in a stream of decisions and actions, something that unfolds over time. It's not an event, but a process.

Now throughout the course, we'll actually look at two levels of strategy. In the first series of lectures, we'll be talking about business-unit strategy. We'll be looking at a particular company and how it tries to beat its rivals in a particular product market, how to compete to win. But then we'll also, later in the course, beginning with a case study about Disney, be looking at the concept of corporate strategy. Here, we'll be looking at what we call multi-business unit corporations, diversified companies that operate in a variety of product markets, and we'll be looking at the choices being made at the corporate office, not the level of the business unit.

We'll be asking, where did they choose to compete? Why did Disney choose to compete in theme parks and movies and retail stores and consumer products? In the early part of course, it's all about how to compete. How does the theme park business defeat its rivals? On the corporate strategy question it's, why that portfolio of businesses is all under one roof?

Martin and Lafley say, as you plot this strategy, you really have to ask yourself five key questions. What's your winning aspiration? What are you trying to achieve? What's the vision here? Number two, where will you play, in what product markets, in what segments of those markets, in what geographies, and what's your target market? What customer are you trying to serve?

Third, how are you going to win? What is it that you're going to do that's going to give you an advantage over the competition, fundamentally, that's going to make you different? And then, the last two questions are about how you're going to get there. The fourth question they ask is, what capabilities must be in place? What's it going to take to execute this strategy?

A strategy that's just a great idea in the heads of men and women at the top of a corporation is not going to lead to high performance. You have to have the processes, the systems, and the capabilities to get there. And so the fifth question is: What management systems are required to implement this strategy? How will you measure performance? What kind of technological systems will you have? How are you going to monitor and control different parts of the organization? Those management systems are crucial to getting things done.

Ultimately, the winner in the marketplace is not the one with the best ideas or even necessarily the best product; it's the one who can plot that strategy and then implement it very efficiently and in a timely manner—because markets move fast, and if you can't act quickly and execute that strategy in a timely fashion, you won't win.

Now I want to turn to four key facts about competition that will set the stage for our analysis of competitive environments and of the companies that are trying to win in those environments, as we move through the course. Here are the four facts. The first, industries vary widely in their profitability. This is a really important point. You know, Warren Buffett once said, when an industry with a reputation for tough economics meets a manager with a reputation for excellent performance, it's usually the industry that keeps its reputation intact. In other words, if you're in a really tough business, it's going to be difficult to make money no matter how smart the management team is, and even if you think you have a great strategy, because frankly, for many years, that business has been one where the fundamental economic forces are causing profitability to be low.

So industries vary widely in their profitability. In fact, some studies show that the median return on invested capital across all industries is probably in the low teens, maybe 12–14%. But the distribution, well, it's really interesting. There are some industries that over time generate virtually no returns. That's not one company; that's all companies in the industry are looking at cumulative profit of virtually zero. On the other hand, we can find some industries where they're generating incredible returns on invested capital year after year. So this first factor is really important: Industries vary widely in their profitability.

And the second, related, fact is that the industry you're in matters a great deal. What does that mean? That means sometimes there are forces beyond your control driving your profitability. So if you're in the newspaper business today, as the web has grown, and as the business has fundamentally transformed, well, no matter how smart your strategy and how capable your management team, your profitability is being driven in large part by greater forces beyond your firm at the industry level in your competitive environment. So industry matters a great deal. There are often things beyond your company's strategy that will drive profitability.

The third key fact, competitive advantage certainly may be fleeting. And we've argued that it's really hard to stay on top. If you look at a ranking of the top firms in an industry, and by top, I don't mean the highest market share; I mean the highest profitability. Well, if you look at that today, and then look at it five years from now, the list may look quite different, and the leader may very well not be the leader any longer. But what about industry structure? If we look at which industries are really profitable today and then look 5 years ago, or 10 years ago, or 20 years ago, we see the industry structure tends to be much more stable. The high-profit industries tend to be high-profit industries over time. And the low-profit industries, they don't tend to turn it around very quickly. And the structure, how concentrated the industry is, in other words, is the industry one where a few firms dominate or not? That structure tends to be more stable than competitive advantage. Competitive advantage—that can change really quickly.

And finally, the fourth fact, industry structure varies widely around the world. You don't have situations where industries look identical in country after country. Yes, we live in a more global world, and yet, there are profound differences. So we see some industries that look very fragmented in one country and highly consolidated in others. So be careful when people talk about a global industry. Yes, global trade occurs, but industries in competitive environments can look very different in different parts of the world for a variety of reasons, stretching from consumer tastes and culture, to government regulation and institutions, and even forms of government.

Now, let's take a look at an example to understand these two drivers of profitability, industry structure, and competitive advantage. If we looked at the financials for two companies, we'd see something interesting. Let's take Pfizer, a pharmaceutical company, and Alaska Air, an airline company. In 2013, the return on assets for Pfizer, 12.8%; for Alaska Air, 8.7%. Can we conclude from that that Pfizer is a better-managed firm than Alaska Air? Be careful. You cannot. You can't just look at the absolute financial returns for these two companies.

Why? Pharmaceuticals is a high-profit business. Airlines are a low-profit industry. So if you actually look more deeply, what you'd find is that Alaska Air is outperforming rivals within its industry. That's the key comparison you want to make. Alaska Air has competitive advantage. No, it's not as profitable as Pfizer, but it's in a much tougher environment. It's like a football team playing in a much tougher division. And that's what we have to remember; we're looking for companies that generate excess returns relative to the industry average. That's competitive advantage.

So two fundamental drivers of superior, long-run returns on investment, an attractive industry structure, an environment where the forces are such that profits are there to be made, and competitive advantage. Can we beat our rivals? Can we have a distinctive competitive advantage, a position that we can defend? Now, this is not to say that economics and financial returns are the be-all and end-all for companies. Yes, we have other goals as a company; we want to serve our customers and have an engaged workforce. We want to do things that preserve and protect our environment. There may be other goals. But if we don't make money, it's hard to achieve those other goals. And so we will be talking about financial returns throughout the course.

Now, one other note about industries that's really important, as we look across industries, we also see that in some industries, the leader in one year is much more likely to stay on top than in other industries. What do I mean by that? In other words, competitive advantage is fleeting, but it's more fleeting in some industries than others. If you're in semiconductors or computers or electronic components, fast-moving technological industries, well, the chances that someone who's on top today will be on top five years from now are much lower than if you're in a more mature, low-tech business, say, like beverages or cigarettes or paper mills. So there's real differences in the persistence of high profits in certain industries. We have to be aware of that. Are we in a turbulent environment or a more stable environment? And that will dictate how quickly we have to be ready to adapt our strategy.

Remember what Martin and McGrath were arguing about. You know, how important is it to adapt, to evolve, to iterate, to experiment? Well, in certain industries it's much more important to do that, because it's much harder to stay on top than in others. This is not to say that any firm should become complacent. Everybody has to be scanning their competitive environment looking for the next new threat. We're going to give you some tools in this course for how to do just that.

Now, I may have made some of you think, my gosh, I'm in a really tough business. I'm in one of those industries that the professor mentioned are very low profit and have been for many years. Does that mean I should just throw up my arms and go home? Do I need to find another job or exit this industry? You don't. In fact, you can make money in lousy industries.

Let's take the supermarket business. It's not exactly a high-earnings business. Many firms flight to scrape by, to generate very thin, low, single-digit returns on assets. So, it's a tough industry. But does that mean everyone is facing the same predicament? Not at all. If we look at major competitors in the business, we still see variation returns. Whole Foods Market in 2012 generated an 8% return on assets; Kroger, 2.6%; Supervalu, it lost a lot of money. It was in deep trouble. So even though the industry as a whole is generating thin margins, we see wide variation across major competitors.

What does this tell us? Whole Foods has found a way to build a strong competitive advantage in an otherwise structurally unattractive business. Well that's really neat, and as we go through the course, we'll want to look at some companies who have done just that, because we can learn a lot more about strategy by studying companies in really tough businesses and understanding how they achieved a distinctive position, and won, than we can by looking at companies where lots of other players are generating healthy earnings as well. In other words, let's go to the extreme, to the tough businesses, and let's find the winners.

Now, we won't only do that, but we will do that in a number of cases, because it will help us. But remember, it's hard to stay on top. The winners today are not likely to be the winners a decade from now. So we'll use some examples of successful companies throughout the course. But I'm not at all promising they will be successful 5 or 10 years now. In fact, I'm predicting they won't be. So we have to be careful about the lessons we draw and about assuming that companies that are successful today can continue that record of success.

So what's coming next in the course? We're going to dig into a framework for how to analyze an industry and understand its profitability. We've noted that there are these big differences between certain businesses, that some industries are more profitable than others. But we haven't explained why that is. And we need to do that. And importantly, we're going to help introduce a framework through case studies of several industries that help us explain why some industries are very high profit and others are not. That framework will be simple, yet powerful. And we'll have you practicing that framework and applying it within just one lecture.

And it will have more uses than just understanding why some industries are more profitable than others. The framework will help us formulate strategy. Why? Because it will help us identify threats and opportunities in our environment. It will help us understand what the barriers are to making good earnings. And it will help us think about how we might position our firm within a segment of a business where maybe there's more money to be made, or how we can buttress our firm against some of those really prevailing headwinds that could threaten us, and that's important.

So, you have an assignment. At the end of each lecture, in fact, in the course, I'm going to give you a small assignment. In order to really learn these ideas, you need to practice them. Learning by doing is more powerful than just listening to what I have to say. So I'd like you to take the ideas and apply them at the end of each lecture, a few moments to listen, to integrate and synthesize what you've heard, and then go out and look at some case studies and try to apply the ideas.

So before the next lecture, consider two industries, the airline business and pharmaceuticals, and ask yourself the following question. Why might it be that airlines have been so unprofitable over many, many years? And why is the pharmaceutical business so incredibly profitable, and it has been for decades? You don't know yet how to answer that question, but you can begin to tackle that question, and in the lectures to come, we'll give you the frameworks and concepts to help you distinguish industries that look like airlines from those that look like pharmaceuticals. We look forward to some great discussions ahead.

How Apple Raises Competitive Barriers
Lecture 2

Richard Branson, the British entrepreneur and successful founder of the Virgin Group, once joked that it's rather easy to become a millionaire; you simply start as a billionaire, then go into the airline business. Warren Buffett, in his analysis, found that the airline industry as a whole has lost money for the last 100 years. What explains the difference between the notoriously low-profit airline industry and high-profit industries, such as pharmaceuticals? In this lecture, we'll look at Michael Porter's seminal work on the five forces that shape strategy, which offers a comprehensive framework to help understand these differences in profitability across industries.

The Five Forces

- The first of Michael Porter's five forces shaping strategy is barriers to entry. As Porter argued, high barriers to entry improve the profitability of an industry.

- The second force is the threat of substitutes, that is, alternative products or services that fulfill the same need. These may not always be direct rivals but, in some cases, quite different products or services than the ones you're selling. For example, substitutes for fitness centers might include home workout equipment, diet plans, video game systems for exercising, and even local bars, because some people join fitness centers for social purposes.

- The third force shaping strategy is the bargaining power of suppliers. Who provides the key inputs and components for your product or your firm, and do those suppliers have leverage over you? Can they extract some of the profits you might otherwise make?

- The fourth force shaping strategy is the bargaining power of the customer. Again, who has the leverage in the buyer-seller relationship?

- Finally, the fifth force is rivalry among existing competitors. In particular, it's important to consider whether firms in the industry compete hard on price. Are there frequent price wars in the industry, or is the environment one of friendly competition, perhaps one in which competitors engage in mutually beneficial activities?

Applying the Framework: Airlines
- At first glance, barriers to entry might seem high in the airline industry, yet over the past few decades, the industry has seen many new players. In fact, the barriers aren't as high as they initially appear. A new entrant can lease old planes rather than buying new ones. In addition, entrants don't have to fight for slots at large, expensive airports but can easily gain access to regional airports, where states and counties are trying to draw traffic for economic development and tourism.

- However, buyer power in the airline industry is high. Customers don't see much differentiation in airlines and aren't particularly loyal. Moreover, air travel customers are highly price sensitive, and they can look for bargains on travel websites, which offer perfect price transparency.

- Supplier power is also high. Airbus and Boeing provide jumbo jets and a few other players provide regional jets, but there aren't many alternatives when it comes to buying planes. As for labor, airlines have to negotiate with powerful unions. And the price of fuel is driven by OPEC.

- These days, there are also numerous substitutes for air travel, including other forms of transportation, such as cars or trains, and technology, such as video conferencing, which allows businesspeople to avoid traveling to meetings.

- Finally, the airline business has a unique characteristic that drives intense price competition: The business has very high fixed costs and virtually no variable or marginal costs.

- Getting the plane in the sky involves all fixed costs; there is very little expense that varies depending on how many passengers are on the plane.

- In that situation, anything an airline receives above zero is what's called *contribution margin*—dollars that could go toward covering fixed costs or toward profitability. Thus, there is intense price competition to try to fill seats.

• As you can see, the five forces framework is useful for examining the competitive environment in a systematic fashion. If, for example, consumer tastes or technology are changing in a substantial way, the framework can be used to help understand the potential impact of those changes on profitability.

With the drive to reduce obesity, fitness centers have been seen as an attractive business, but in fact, overall, this industry hasn't generated much profit.

- You can also use the framework to think about how you might position your company to deal with threats. In a tough industry, can you find a segment that is, perhaps, a little more profitable, allowing your business to thrive when others are losing money?

- Finally, you might be able to think about how your firm, as a leading company in the industry, might shape a more favorable industry structure. Can you, perhaps, raise barriers to entry, thereby increasing your own profitability and making the environment better for all?

The Spectrum of Competition

- Economists, such as Porter, typically examine the behavior of firms in the economy by building models of perfect competition. These models usually encompass the following assumptions: There is free entry and exit into the business; there are many buyers and sellers, all of which are relatively small and equal in size; complete information is available about the goods and services; the goods are homogeneous; and each firm is trying to maximize profits. Economists argue that the result of perfect competition is maximum social welfare.

  o Economic profits in this world of perfect competition equal zero, although that's not to say that firms make no accounting profits.

  o Accounting profits do not include opportunity costs for the labor and the capital that are deployed in a firm, while economic profits account for opportunity costs.

- In the past, economists who studied industrial organization tended to examine markets characterized by imperfect competition from the perspective of the consumer. They were looking for antitrust issues. Were there instances of imperfect competition where firms might be engaging in behavior that harms consumers or diminishes social welfare?

- Porter, however, looked at markets from the perspective of a company and found that businesses want imperfect competition. They don't want economic profits to be zero, but they also don't want to create antitrust concerns. Thus, he reversed the assumptions of perfect competition.

- According to Porter, CEOs should look for businesses where there are barriers to entry and exit. Further, the goods should not be homogeneous but differentiated. Those who can find these imperfections in an industry—or help shape them—can drive economic profits higher. And that's what you're looking for as you shape strategy.

- Of course, what we're thinking about here is really a spectrum of competition. On one end, we have many buyers and sellers, homogeneous goods, and no barriers to entry. On the other end, we have one firm with 100% market share. In between, we might have a number of situations, including fragmented markets with buyers and sellers of different sizes; an oligopoly, with three or four dominant players in an industry; and so on.

Steps in a Five Forces Analysis

- The first step in a five forces analysis is to define the industry you wish to analyze.

- The next step is to identify the players, including the buyers, suppliers, and rivals. When you're looking at buyers, remember to think about all the buyers, not just the end user but the distributor, retailer, and others along the supply chain.

- Next, you should assess the strength of each force using quantitative evidence. Look at the profitability of other companies in the business.

- Finally, you can't look to the past only; you must look forward, trying to understand the critical trends within the business. How can you project, based on your assessment of the environment, where each of the forces will be in the years ahead?

Crafting Strategy with the Five Forces

- One of the applications for the five forces framework is to craft a strategy that mitigates the negative forces in an industry. Consider, for example, Apple, which is in an industry with low barriers to entry, high buyer and supplier power, intense rivalry, and multiple substitutes.

- One way Apple mitigated these negative forces was to construct its own operating system. This step made it difficult for others to enter Apple's market and become direct competitors.

- Further, the Apple operating system fundamentally differentiates the company's products, making the products easier to use. And the operating system mitigates the power of Microsoft; Apple is not dependent on buying Windows, as other PC makers are.

- Apple also established its own stores, which mitigates the power of the big-box retail chains and online retailers.

- As for substitutes, Apple has been willing to cannibalize itself—to build tablets and smartphones. The company has gotten into the substitute business for its own products, rather than letting others do so.

Common Mistakes with the Framework

- One common mistake in five forces analysis is to apply the framework to a company, rather than an industry. In addition, management teams may not define the industry clearly when they begin to do their analysis.

- It's also common for managers to spend too much time looking back, rather than trying to understand the trends that might affect the future. Some managers might also ignore the full range of substitutes.

- Note, too, that you can't give equal weight to all five forces, thinking that if four of the five are in your favor, your business is in good shape. Even one negative force can cause harm.

- As we said, you can't presume that industry structure is the same around the world. For example, in Australia, several firms dominate the wine business, while in France, there are more than 200,000 independent wineries. It would be difficult to do a single five forces analysis for the global wine industry.

- Finally, it's important to take into account the limitations of the framework: It works primarily for industries where there are clear boundaries, it provides limited tools and techniques for understanding the nature of rivalry, and it doesn't address the issue of complements—a product or service that adds value to the original product offering when the two are used together.
  - Gillette pioneered the business model of complements. The company sells razors at a low cost because it knows that if customers like the razor, they'll buy blades forever.

  - Apple turned this traditional razors-and-blades strategy around when it entered the iPod, iPhone, and iPad market.

  - Before the iPhone, people paid very little for phones. How, then, has Apple induced customers to pay $400 or more for phones? Ask yourself: How do you get people to buy expensive peanut butter? By giving them lots of cheap jelly. And that's what Apple has done with its free and low-cost apps.

Suggested Reading

Brandenburger and Nalebuff, *Co-opetition.*

Porter, *Competitive Strategy.*

Questions to Consider

1. Why do some industries generate much higher profits than others?

2. What types of strategies can firms use to mitigate negative aspects of industry structure?

3. What are some examples of firms for which complements are a crucial element of strategy?

How Apple Raises Competitive Barriers
Lecture 2—Transcript

Richard Branson, the British entrepreneur and successful founder of the Virgin Group, once joked that it's rather easy to become a millionaire. How do you do it? You start as a billionaire and then you go enter the airline business.

Warren Buffett has actually analyzed the airline industry. He added all the profits and losses of the various airlines that have competed in the United States over the last century, and he got a negative number. The industry as a whole has lost money for 100 years. He, too, joked about the industry. He said, it would have been the reasonable financial, if not moral, move to simply shoot down the Wright brothers on that day a century ago when they got an airplane into the sky.

If you actually look back at the airline industry in the United States in the early 1980s and peruse the names of the brands, you notice that many of them are gone. In fact, of the top 15 airlines, all but one have either gone bankrupt or been acquired since that time. Which one has stood out? Southwest Airlines. It not only still exists as an independent company, but it's been profitable every year for four decades.

The airline industry represents one of the lowest-profit industries that we see. Now of course, as you recall from the prior lecture, there are some industries that make a lot of money as a whole, pharmaceuticals, chewing gum, carbonated soft drinks, distilled spirits. There are others, like the restaurant business, personal computers, and airlines that are very low in profitability on a consistent basis. What explains the difference?

Well, the key is that you cannot find one factor that explains the differences in industry profitability. Michael Porter's seminal work on the five forces that shape strategy offered us a comprehensive framework for helping us understand the differences in profitability across industries. Now, Michael first published his work in the Harvard Business Review in the late 1970s, and his framework, the five forces, became one of the most widely used, and frankly, misused, management frameworks in subsequent decades.

The five forces, what are they? Porter started by looking at barriers to entry, and he argued that if you have high barriers to entry, it improves the profitability of your industry. In other words, can you build a moat around your castle? Can you keep new entrepreneurs and new entrants from coming in and grabbing a share of your profits? Some industries have very high barriers, others, very low. He then turned to the question of the threat of substitutes. What's a substitute? It's an alternative product or service that fulfills the same basic human need. It's not a direct rival; it's a very different product or service, but, it can be a replacement for the product or service that you're selling.

What's an example? Let's take a look at fitness centers. What are some substitutes for fitness centers? Well, you might have some equipment in your home, in your basement, like a treadmill. You might be on a diet plan. You may actually have something like the Nintendo Wii Fit to work out in your home. You may have an alternative at work where you can work out. You may go to a bar to meet people. It's another thing that happens in a fitness center. It's another service or another need that you could fulfill in other ways. There are many substitutes for the fitness center.

Then Porter looked at the bargaining power of suppliers. Who is providing the key inputs and components for your product, for your firm? And do these suppliers have leverage over you? Do they have power? And can they extract some of the profits that you otherwise might make? He also looked at the bargaining power of the customer. Who are your customers? Who buys from you? Do they have leverage? Are they able to extract profits? Or do you have leverage over them?

And finally, he looked at the rivalry among existing competitors. How intense is it? And in particular, do the firms in the industry compete hard on price? Do we see frequent price wars? Or do we see something that looks more like friendly competition, not quite so vicious, perhaps something where there's mutually beneficial work being done by competitors?

These are the five forces, then, that shape strategy, that shape the profitability of an industry. You'd love to be in an industry where there's high barriers to entry, low power for suppliers and customers, where there aren't many alternatives, attractive substitutes, and where price wars are very infrequent or nonexistent. So let's take a look at the airline industry again and see if we can apply this framework.

Let's start with barriers to entry. At first glance, you might think it's very difficult to enter this business; it's got to be expensive and challenging. And yet, if you look over the past few decades, you see that many new players have entered this business. Therefore, we must conclude that the barriers cannot be so formidable. Why is it easy to enter the business, or at least, moderately easy?

Well, let's start with planes. Do you need to go out and buy new planes? You don't. You can lease old planes, and there are many of them available, because frankly, many companies are going bankrupt in this business every year. Pilots, the military trains them for you. And so you have people that you don't have to train from scratch. Airports, well, do you have to fight for a slot, an expensive one, at an airport like LAX or JFK in New York? You don't. You can go to smaller, regional airports, where states and counties are trying to draw traffic for economic development and tourism, and you can get access to a slot and start flying your planes. Barriers to entry are not so high.

What about buyer power? Well, who are the buyers, the end users, the customers, like you and me, who fly? Well, we look at the product, and we don't see much differentiation. Frankly, we aren't very loyal because there isn't really a difference between United and American, between any of the airlines that we look at. They look rather homogeneous. Moreover, there are travel sites, like Expedia and Travelocity, that offer us perfect price transparency. We can compare and look for the best bargain, and we often buy on price. We're highly price sensitive when it comes to air travel.

Who are the suppliers, and do they have power? Airbus and Boeing provide jumbo jets. A couple more players provide regional jets. But there aren't many alternatives when it comes to getting planes. As for labor, you've got to negotiate with powerful unions. And as for fuel, well, OPEC is a cartel that's going to drive the price of oil. So suppliers and buyers, they're powerful in this business.

How about the threat of substitutes? Well, what do we have as substitutes for air travel? We certainly have other forms of transportation, like the car, and the train, and other forms that we might use. But also, we have things like video conferencing and the internet that provide us an alternative, so a business person doesn't have to go from New York to Shanghai on a plane; they might be able to get the work done in other ways using technology.

And do they compete on price? Well, you betcha they do. There's not much differentiation. It's a homogeneous product. But there's also a very unique characteristic of the airline business that drives intense price competition. There are very high, fixed costs in this business and virtually no variable or marginal costs. What do I mean by that? Well, what's the incremental expense to put you on a plane in that next seat that's vacant? It's virtually nothing. You might say, it's peanuts, literally. As for the fixed costs, well getting the plane in the sky is all fixed costs. There's very little expense that varies depending on how many passengers are on the plane.

Well, what happens when you have high fixed costs and virtually no variable costs? Well, anything the airline receives above 0 is what we call contribution margin. It's dollars that could go toward covering those fixed expenses, and if we cover them all, could go toward profitability. So there's an intense price competition to try to fill the seats. Moreover, the seats are perishable. That's is to say, when that plane takes off, you can never sell that seat on that flight again. So you're dying to fill the plane to be able to be as profitable as possible. And it leads to price wars.

It's a five-star terrible industry. The forces are all working to diminish profitability. So, you see that the framework can be powerful, but why do we need it in general? Why do we need such a conceptual understanding to help us plot strategy as a company? Well, the competitive environment is really complex and messy. And I think managers find it helpful to use this type of framework to examine their competitive environment in a systematic fashion.

Now, like all frameworks, this one is a simplified version of reality. It's not perfect. It's not even correct in any sense, but it's very useful. As Milton Friedman said about any theory or conceptual framework, the question really isn't whether it's right; the question is, can it be useful to people so they can understand the world around them and make better decisions? And the five forces can definitely help us do that.

So, one key thing to remember about this framework, though, is that it's useful not just to help us understand why some industries are profitable and others are not; we can use the framework to help us with other key strategic choices. Do I want to enter a particular market? Do I want to launch a venture, or perhaps, as an established company, move into an adjacent market? Do I want to exit? Might I want to get out of this business? Understanding the five forces and the attractiveness of that industry helps us with the entry and exit decision.

What if consumer tastes or technology or government regulation are changing in a substantial way? Can I use the five forces to understand the impact on my profitability moving forward? You also can use the framework to think about how you might position your company to deal with some of the real threats that you face. How can you find a segment within what might be a really tough industry, where a segment, perhaps, is a little more profitable, and you might be able to thrive, whereas in the industry as a whole, many are losing money?

And finally, you might be able to think about how you as a leading company in the industry might shape a more favorable industry structure. Can you do some things that perhaps raise barriers to entry and lift all boats, not just increase your profitability, but make the environment better for all?

Now, where did this framework come from? As I say, Michael Porter first wrote about this in the 1970s. He was trained as an economist, but he was working at Harvard Business School training managers who were going to go out and launch careers in the workplace. Now, economists typically begin by examining the behavior of firms in the economy by building models of what they call perfect competition. Now, there are certain assumptions that are embedded in these models of perfect competition.

Here are those assumptions: Free entry and exit, it's easy to get in and out of the business. There are many buyers and sellers, and they're all relatively small and equal in size. There's complete information about the goods and services, the costs of producing them, and delivering them. The goods themselves, they're homogeneous; they're relatively undifferentiated, and each firm is trying to maximize profits. What's the result of this perfect competition? Economists argue that this leads to maximum social welfare, and that's why they always start with this model of how the world works.

What's the profit level for companies in that world, though? Well, economic profits equal zero. Now, this is not to say that firms make no accounting profits. What's the difference between accounting profits and economic profit? Well, accounting profits do not include opportunity costs for the labor and the capital that are deployed in a firm. Economic profits also account for those opportunity costs. And when you do so, in a perfectly competitive world, economic profits equal zero in these fundamental economic models that have been built and used by economists for many decades.

Now, economists who studied industrial organization, in history, they tended to examine markets characterized by imperfect competition from the perspective of the consumer. They were looking for antitrust issues. Were there instances of imperfect competition where firms might be engaging in behavior that harms consumers, that diminishes social welfare?

Now, Porter looked at markets and said, from the perspective of a company, though, you'd like to be in a business where imperfect competition exists. You don't want economic profits to be zero. You want high earnings. Now, you don't want to create antitrust concerns, so you'd like to be imperfect, but not so imperfect that the government sues you. So what he did is begin to turn the assumptions of perfect competition on their head. He said, as a CEO, you should be looking for businesses where there are barriers to entry and berries to exit, where it's not easy to get in or out. You'd like your goods not to be homogeneous, but differentiated. And if you can find these imperfections, or help shape them, you can drive economic profits higher and higher. And that's what you're looking for as you shape strategy.

Of course, the decision or the framework, we should be thinking about is not one of perfect competition or monopoly; it's really a spectrum. At one end, we have many, many buyers and sellers, homogeneous goods, and no barriers to entry. At the other, we have one firm with 100% market share. Of course, there's things that are in between that. We have fragmented markets with many buyers and sellers, but they're not all tiny.

But we also have something we call oligopoly. This is where you have three or four dominant players in an industry. And many of those industries, like chewing gum or carbonated soft drinks, we see some firms with significant market share, and we tend to see some high profits. So as we go through the course, we'll look at some oligopolies, and we'll try to understand how they operate.

So what are the typical steps in this kind of a Five-Forces analysis, analyzing an industry structure? First step, you have to define the industry that you wish to analyze. What do I mean by that? Well, suppose that you were working at Coca-Cola and you wanted to analyze your industry and you brought your management team together. You have to think about, well, what's the unit of analysis? Are we talking about carbonated soft drinks, all soft drinks, all beverages? There's no right answer there, but it's important that all of the members of the management team, they're all speaking the same language, that they're all focused on the same unit of analysis.

Then you have to identify the players. Who are the buyers? Who are the suppliers? Who are our main rivals? Who are the substitutes? And it's important when you're looking at something like buyers that you think about all the buyers, not just the end user, but the distributor, the retailer, everyone along the supply chain with whom you interact.

And then you're going to assess the strength of each force. Is buyer power high or low? Is supplier power high or low? But then you've got to look at the quantitative evidence. What do I mean by that? You have to look at the profitability of companies in the business. If you've done your five forces and concluded that things look great, but then you turn to the profitability of companies and you see very low margins, well, there's a fundamental disconnect there. You haven't done an appropriate analysis. You've got to look to the quantitative evidence and try to explain why you're seeing the profit margins that exist in your particular business.

And lastly, you can't just look back; you've got to look forward. You have to understand the critical trends within your business. You don't want to just conclude that in the last five years, firepower has been low. What you want to understand is, where will it be five years from now? And how can I project, based on my assessment of the environment, where these forces will be in the years ahead?

So let's practice for a moment. Let's think about the pharmaceutical business, which historically has been very high profit. Are there barriers to entry? They're incredibly high. There's huge economies of scale. It's very expensive to get in this business. Just to develop one new drug can cost over $1 billion. There's strong intellectual property rights. You can patent your inventions and protect them against the competition. There are federal regulations that make it difficult to get a new drug on the market. There are formidable barriers to entry.

What about the threat of substitutes? Well, think about that. What's the substitute to taking the prescription drug that your doctor has advised you to take? Surgery, death, homeopathic solutions—not very attractive substitutes. How about the buyer? As an end user, do we have power? We don't. We don't even make the decision. The doctor makes the decision for us in many cases. And do we even know the price that we're paying? Most of us do not. We're paying a copayment when we go to the pharmacy to pick up our drug. We don't actually understand or know the underlying price.

Suppliers, do they have any power? Well, who are the suppliers? They are companies that provide the compounds, right, the organic compounds that are then used and combined to create the prescription drug. But those are commodities. The real value lies with the companies, the pharma companies that actually combine those commodities using science to alleviate a particular condition, to provide us treatment. The products, the components themselves that they buy from suppliers, they're simply commodities. They can buy them from anyone.

And lastly, is there intense rivalry in this business? Not at all. They don't compete on price as long as the patents are in effect. Once they are and they have intellectual property that they can defend, they don't have to compete on price. And the customer, after all, isn't shopping around on price at that point, because they have few choices, and insurance is covering a big chunk of the cost. So the pharma business is a wonderful business. The five forces look great.

But contrast that with personal computers. So let's set Apple aside and look at what we call the Wintel world. The market for assembling and selling personal computers that operate off the Windows platform and largely off of Intel microprocessors. Are there barriers to entry in that business? What do you need to get into the business of assembling personal computers? Where did HP, Dell, and Apple start? HP and Apple started in a garage, and Dell started in a dorm room in Texas. There couldn't have been formidable barriers to entry if they could start so easily. In fact, all you need is a screwdriver, and you're in the business of assembling personal computers. The components are modular, and you can buy them from anywhere. In fact, in emerging markets, white boxes, non-branded products, account for a substantial share of the marketplace. There are low barriers to entry.

Buyers, do we have power? It's a homogeneous product. If we're looking at Windows, it's basic operating system for all these machines, can we even tell what brand of computer we're working on if we don't look for the logo? Suppliers, do they have power? Incredible. Not all of them, but two in particular, Microsoft and Intel, because Microsoft dominates the operating system market, and Intel dominates the market for buying microprocessors. Substitutes, are they available? Tablets, smartphones, other forms of technology have begun to arise that are key substitutes for your laptop.

And lastly, are there price wars in this business? You bet. They're intense. It's a homogeneous product. There isn't a lot of differentiation between Dell and HP. Moreover, the products become rapidly obsolete. Every year we have new models coming to market, and once the customer knows a new model is coming, their willingness to pay for existing models, it falls. And so what do retailers do? They begin to cut price. They're dying to get rid of that inventory before it becomes totally obsolete. So the personal-computer business, despite high growth, actually looks quite unattractive from the perspective of the five forces. And in fact, Microsoft and Intel, over the last few decades, have made more money than the entire global personal computer business combined.

So what's interesting about the five forces, as I mentioned earlier, is that it's not just a measure or a framework for helping us understand whether an industry is profitable or not. We can also use it to help us shape strategy. We can think about the negative forces in a business and ask ourselves, how can we craft a strategy that mitigates some of those negative forces? So let's think about Apple for a moment. If this industry is so unprofitable, and remember, yes, Dell has made quite a bit of money in this business, but think about all the personal computer businesses that have gone bankrupt over the years, so many brands that have gone by the wayside. It's been a tough business.

But Apple, what have they done? How have they raised barriers to entry, reduced buyer and supplier power, cut rivalry, and mitigated the threat of substitutes? Well, they built their own operating system. It cost a billion dollars or more to do so. So it's expensive. It's hard for others to enter and compete directly with them. And their operating system fundamentally differentiates their product. It makes it easier for users to use an Apple product, and they've mitigated the power of Microsoft; they're not dependent on buying Windows, as the other PC makers are.

They built their own stores. Why is that important? That's mitigated the power of the big box retail chains and other online retailers, so that's been key as well. And as for substitutes, well, Apple has been willing to cannibalize themselves, to build tablets, to build smartphones. They've gotten into the substitute business rather than letting others eat their lunch. The lesson? The framework is useful for thinking about how a firm can position itself well in a very tough industry and make money, which Apple has done.

Are there some common mistakes we see as people use this framework? I think sometimes we see managers applying this to their company, not realizing it's really a tool for understanding your industry, not your company. And we see management teams not defining the industry clearly when they begin to do their analysis. We also see people looking back and not looking forward and not trying to understand the trends, but spending too much time looking at what's happened before. And they ignore the full range of substitutes. So if you're in the fitness center business, they're not thinking about the bar down the street or necessarily thinking about diet plans or even surgery as alternatives to a fitness center. Thinking about the full range of substitutes is crucial if you want to sustain your advantage.

We also can't pay equal attention all the forces. Four of the five can look great, but if barriers to entry are collapsing in your business, look out. You may see a real hit to your profit margins. This is not a simple linear edition of the Five, and you can say check, check, check, check. Four of these look great. I'm in good shape. One negative force can harm you.

And finally, industry structure is not the same around the world, and some people presume that it is at times. What do I mean by that? Well, suppose you were going to analyze the wine business, that you were Gallo or another leading wine brand. Could you do an industry analysis of the wine business? You'd have to be careful, because in Australia, several firms dominate the whole business. It's an oligopoly. In France, there are over 200,000 independent wineries, each of them very small. It's an incredibly fragmented market. So the industry has a fundamentally different structure in these two parts of the world. It's very hard to do one five forces for the entire global industry.

Now, the framework is not perfect. There are clearly limitations. And I want to talk about five of them. First, boundaries, as technology has changed and the world has changed, it's become more difficult to draw clear industry boundaries in many cases. We've seen industries converge. And so when you look at firms like Google and Amazon, it's not even clear what industries they compete with or who their rivals are, because they seem to be competing in many different spaces in different ways.

Globalization is also an interesting issue. As we said, it's dangerous to apply the five forces on a global basis, when despite globalization, we see dramatic differences in markets around the world. How much of an impact does industry structure have on profitability? Some studies have shown that it has a big impact. Others, academics, have argued, no, not as much of an impact. I think that academic debate misses a key point, which is, managers are simply worried about is this important and does it help shape competition and affect my margins? Exactly how much it affects profitability? That's less relevant to a manager.

Rivalry, this framework provides limited tools and techniques for understanding the nature of rivalry, and I think the framework in its original conceptualization wasn't crystal clear on the differences between price rivalry and non-price competition. Price wars are really bad for profitability. Non-price competition, creative advertising campaigns and merchandising and retailers, well, that kind of competition can actually lift all boats. It can grow the overall market and build primary demand for your product. Coke and Pepsi were rivals, but they didn't get into price wars in the 20th century; they engaged in non-price competition that actually increased the market for soft drinks overall and was beneficial to both parties.

And finally, there's the issue of complements. Industry analysis in its original form did not explicitly address the nature and the importance of complements. What's a complement? Some have called it the sixth force that needs to be considered. A complement is a product or service that adds value to the original product offering when the two are used together, peanut butter and jelly, computer hardware and software.

Adam Brandenburger is one of the first scholars who began to point to the importance of complements, and why did he think this was crucial for helping us understand our competitive environment? Well he coined the term *coopetition*. He said, there are instances, many of them, when competitors are also cooperating to achieve strategic objectives, and this can be quite tricky, when you have someone who is both your rival and someone who's producing a complement to your product. Samsung and Google, Samsung makes the phone, and Google makes the Android operating system, but Google is also competing directly with Samsung in the phone market at times, so you have this interesting dynamic of the rival and the complementer being one in the same.

When it comes to complements, it's really important to understand the business model and how it works. So let's take razors and blades, two complements. Gillette pioneered this model. How do they make money?

Printers + Ink cartridges
is another example

Gillette is not making money off the razor; they want to get that razor into your hands, even if it costs them money to get it into your hands. Why? Because if you like the razor, you'll be buying blades forever, and you're buying pretty expensive blades, and they're making a lot of money.

What's interesting, of course, is we have another firm that's sort of flipped that business model on its head. In Apple's case, they went to a blades-and-razors strategy when they entered the iPod and the smartphone and the iPad market. Blades and razors, what do I mean by that? Well, how do you get someone to pay $400 for a smartphone? I mean, before the Apple iPhone, were you and I paying for a phone? A few dollars, often nothing. How do you go from that to $400? Well, how do you get someone to buy really expensive peanut butter? You give them a lot of really cheap jelly. And that's what Steve Jobs did. He gave us $0.99 songs on iTunes. He gave us a lot of free apps. And by doing that, all that cheap, really cool, tasty jelly, we went out and bought really expensive peanut butter. We called it the iPhone, for $400, or the iPad. Razors and blades? No, blades and razors at Apple.

So, what are some of the lessons that surprise us from this lecture in thinking about industry and the structure that differs across industries? Number one, sexy industries are not necessarily the high-profit industries. Airlines have also always been something featured in films, and they've attracted the macho entrepreneurs who want to enter and be in the skies and dominate the business. Fitness centers have been a "sexy business" in that we've seen a drive to reduce obesity and to try to get more fit. It's been a growing phenomenon in the United States and other countries. Yet these industries, which look like they're attractive, haven't generated much profit.

Moreover, the second lesson that surprises is high growth doesn't equal high profits. Personal computers grew dramatically in the '80s and '90s but didn't generate a lot of earnings. The third lesson is that stable, relatively low-growth industries can be very profitable. Who knows much about the industrial gas market? Yet it's been a wildly profitable business for many years. And our final lesson is that with the appropriate competitive positioning, firms can mitigate negative forces and make healthy earnings even in a tough industry. It's difficult to do, but some have done it.

So, what's your assignment? We want you to practice the five forces. Take the fitness center industry and compare it to the chewing gum industry. The chewing gum business has been highly profitable in recent decades, and it's not a fragmented business. It's an oligopoly. Several firms dominate the business. So your assignment, take the Five Forces, work through them for chewing gum, and try to explain why this business has been so profitable in contrast to fitness centers.

The Danger of Straddling
Lecture 3

W hat's different about the competitive strategies of Dell, Mercedes, and JCPenney? Dell tries to be the low-cost player in the personal computer market, while Mercedes tries to be a differentiated player in the automobile market. JCPenney seems to be stuck in the middle—achieving neither a low-cost strategy nor a differentiation strategy. As we've discussed, strategy involves understanding your competitive environment, then positioning yourself for success in that environment. In the last lecture, we saw how to understand the environment by conducting a five forces analysis. In this lecture, we'll try to understand the resources and capabilities that will enable you to succeed in that environment.

Creating Economic Value
- Professor Robert Grant wrote that strategy is concerned with matching a firm's resources and capabilities to the opportunities that arise in the external environment. As you do this—as you plot your strategy and try to position yourself—you're trying to create a competitive advantage relative to your rivals. To do that, you must create more economic value than your rivals.

- What does it mean to create economic value? When you produce and sell a good or service, customers have a certain perceived value for that good and service. There is also a cost, of course, for you to deliver that product or service to customers. The perceived value less the total cost equals the economic value created.

- Of course, the company that provides a good doesn't get all of the economic value created. That value is split between the company and the consumer.
  - Anything consumers pay that's less than what they're willing to pay—less than what they perceive as the value for that good—is surplus to them. That's part of the economic value that they get.

○ Any price or revenue that the company can achieve that's higher than the cost of producing and delivering the good is surplus, or profit. And the goal of a firm is to generate more economic value than the competition. That's what we mean by achieving competitive advantage.

Fundamental Strategy Choices

- There are three basic types of competitive advantage that firms can strive to achieve: low cost, differentiated, or dual.

- In addition, competitive scope can be categorized into two basic types:
  ○ A firm might be a *niche competitor*, competing with a fairly narrow product line and focusing on a particular geography and a small target market.

  ○ A firm might also choose to be a *broad competitor*, offering a wide array of products, competing in an expansive geographical setting, and serving a wider target market.

- These are the fundamental choices that firms must make as they choose strategy: What type of advantage does the firm seek, and how focused or broad will it be in terms of product, geography, and customer?

Competitive Advantage

- In thinking about competitive advantage, we start with the average competitor in an industry and the amount of economic value it creates. What is the gap between the willingness to pay for this competitor's product and the cost to deliver that product to customers? In trying to achieve competitive advantage, you want to generate a larger gap between willingness to pay and cost than your competition.

- For example, Mercedes tries to generate much higher willingness to pay than Chevrolet. Of course, costs for Mercedes are higher than they are for the firm's competition. If Mercedes wants to be a successful differentiated player, it will seek a much higher willingness to pay but only slightly higher costs, so that the gap between willingness to pay and cost is higher than it is for the competition.

- A successful low-cost player tries to drive its costs much lower than those of its rivals. In the process, the low-cost player sacrifices a bit of willingness to pay.

- A third way to achieve competitive advantage is the dual strategy, with both a higher perceived value and a lower cost structure than the competition. This dual advantage is extremely difficult to achieve.
  - A firm that's trying to achieve higher willingness to pay and create more perceived value will have higher costs. It will to have to invest in research and development, branding, and high-quality components. It's difficult to have much lower costs than the competition if you're trying to create a premium product.

  - Likewise, if you're trying to bring your costs down significantly, it may be difficult to command the same brand image and position in the market and be able to achieve the same pricing.

  - With a dual strategy, players that are focused on either differentiation or low cost may be able to attack you. If you're trying to sell a vehicle at a high price, yet you're trying to achieve lower costs than the competition, Mercedes may critique the quality of your vehicles. Similarly, another player may have a strong cost position and be able to undercut you on price.

© fiphoto/iStock/Thinkstock.

A high-end clothing store might generate high gross margins, have higher expenses, and accept lower inventory turnover than a more mainstream retailer.

- Interestingly, a firm's financials often tell us what type of competitive advantage it's trying to achieve. For example, consider the financials of Walmart relative to Target.
  - Walmart has much lower gross margins than Target; lower overhead costs; and lower selling, general, and administrative expenses, but it has much higher asset turnover than Target.

  - Target's high gross margins and lower turns paint a picture of a typical differentiation strategy. Target has higher margins because it has chosen to sell slightly higher-quality goods—more fashionable items—and sets higher prices in some categories. Target has lower inventory turns because it sells fewer of the basics than Walmart.

Competitive Strategies

- Thus far, we can see that there are four generic competitive strategies:
  - Broad differentiated, used by Starbucks, for example. Here, we see a firm with a wide target market, competing in many geographies with a premium-priced (differentiated) product.

  - Focused differentiated, used by the motorcycle manufacturer Ducati. This Italian firm serves a narrow target market with a limited selection of products.

  - Broad low cost, used by Walmart, which serves a wide range of customers in many geographies with many products and services.

  - Focused low cost, used by the Irish airline Ryanair. This carrier serves certain geographies with a well-defined product set and a much narrower target market than major airlines.

- None of these strategies is "the best"; the mistake firms make in choosing strategies is to be unclear about where the firm is situated—to be stuck in the middle. This situation can occur when firms fail to choose a strategy, try to shift strategy but don't make the shift successfully, or react inappropriately to the emergence of a new competitor.

Competitive Advantage as a System

- We need to think of competitive advantage as an integrated, self-reinforcing system of capabilities, resources, and choices. With this mindset, crafting an effective strategy means that your firm must be different; you can't simply copy the assortment of resources and capabilities that your rivals have achieved.

- The idea behind thinking of competitive advantage as a system is that one choice you make enhances the value of other choices, and one capability you develop creates stronger capabilities elsewhere. If these capabilities and choices fit together well, not only can you create a powerful advantage, but it can also be difficult for others to copy your system.

- Consider, for example, some of the early choices made by Walmart: an everyday low-price strategy, little national advertising, a focus on rural locations, a network of stores built around distribution centers, frugal travel policies, and no regional offices. Each of these choices reinforced other choices. For example, having an everyday low-price strategy fits well with not doing much national advertising.

- Competitors often look at what they think a firm does best and try to emulate that one part of the system. For example, a competitor might try to emulate Walmart's supply chain or logistics, but there are two mistakes inherent in this approach.
    - First, it isn't one thing that Walmart does that's a silver bullet. It's how Walmart's logistics plan and system fit with everything else it does that creates advantage.

    - Second, any potential competitor has its own system of activities that's quite different than Walmart's. Choosing one element of Walmart's system and trying to drop it into another system won't achieve the same advantage.

- Even a firm with a well-integrated, successful system may face difficulties if it tries to move into a new segment. This has been the case with Walmart's attempt to move into the wholesale club business with Sam's Club. Although Sam's Club is profitable, it is outperformed by Costco because Sam's Club is too tied to the legacy of Walmart to truly serve the different set of customers who shop at wholesale clubs.

- Another problem firms face when they have successfully tailored their activities to a particular environment is rigidity. They become committed to past choices and unable to adapt if the environment changes.
  - Because core capabilities can become rigid, successful entrants to an industry are often able to use the incumbent's strengths against it. Dell used this *judo strategy* when it took on IBM.

  - IBM had tremendous manufacturing capability to produce high volumes of its standardized products at low cost. It also had well-developed relationships with its distribution channel— retailers, wholesalers, and value-added resellers.

  - Dell built its strategy in such a way that these strengths of IBM became liabilities. IBM couldn't go direct and sell online because if it did, it would alienate many of its wholesalers and retailers. Further, IBM's factories weren't configured to build customized products.

Threats to Competitive Advantage
- The ability to be successful as a firm, to be more profitable than your rivals, is about not just achieving advantage but sustaining it. And to sustain advantage, you have to address three major external threats: imitation, substitution, and holdup (gaining leverage) by buyers and suppliers.

- Internally, firms face the threat of not perceiving and reacting adequately to threats. Incumbent players sometimes don't see a threat early enough, don't know how to respond, or can't motivate their organizations to respond quickly enough when threats emerge.

- One final threat is the risk of engaging in herd behavior. In many markets, companies aren't trying to be as different as they could be. This stems from risk aversion on the part of executives. If strategy is about identifying different activities and different positions in the marketplace, herd behavior is the antithesis of great strategy.

Suggested Reading

Ghemawat and Rivkin, "Creating Competitive Advantage."

Montgomery, *The Strategist*.

Porter, *Competitive Advantage*.

Yoffie and Kwak, *Judo Strategy*.

Questions to Consider

1. How and why do firms end up "stuck in the middle" in terms of competitive positioning?

2. Why is it so difficult for rivals to copy such a firm as IKEA?

3. Why do successful firms sometimes struggle when they move into adjacent markets?

The Danger of Straddling
Lecture 3—Transcript

What's different about the competitive strategies of these three firms, Dell, Mercedes, and JCPenney? At Dell, they're trying to be the low-cost player in the personal computer market. Mercedes, a very different strategy, Mercedes, offering luxury automobiles; they're trying to be a differentiated player. They have a high premium price, and they're proud of it. They're selling you a luxury product and asking you to pay a price commensurate with the quality that they offer.

And then what about JCPenney? Where do they stand? Hmm, a little more difficult to understand precisely what that strategy is all about. They are stuck in the middle, neither successfully achieving that low-cost strategy, like Dell or Walmart, nor successfully achieving a differentiation strategy, like Mercedes or Apple. Strategy is all about understanding your competitive environment and then positioning yourself for success in that environment.

Now, we looked in the last lecture about understanding your environment by doing the Five Forces. Now we try to understand what is it about the resources and the capabilities that you build as a firm that enable you to succeed in that environment? How do you position yourself in that environment? Robert Grant wrote that strategy is concerned with matching a firm's resources and capabilities to the opportunities that arise in the external environment. As you do this, as you plot your strategy and try to position yourself, you're trying to create a competitive advantage relative to your rivals. To do that, you have to create more economic value than your rivals.

What does it mean to create economic value? Well, when you produce a good or service and sell it, there's a certain perceived value for that good and service. Customers have some perception of what they're willing to pay for that product. There's also the cost, of course, for you to deliver that product or service to them. What is the cost of producing, distributing, and selling that item? The perceived value, less the total cost, equals the economic value created. Of course, you as the company that provides that good, you don't get all of that economic value created. That value is then split between you and your consumer.

For the consumer, anything that they pay that's less than what they're willing to pay, less than what they perceive is the value for that good, well that's surplus to them. That's part of the economic value that they get. For you as the company, any price or any revenue that you can achieve higher than the cost of producing and delivering that good, that's the surplus. That's the profit for you. And your goal as a firm is to generate more economic value than your competition. That's what we mean by achieving competitive advantage.

Now, in terms of competitive positioning, there are two real questions that you have to ask yourself as you plot your strategy. First, what type of advantage do I seek? What type of competitive advantage am I trying to achieve as I look at my strategy relative to my competitors? And there really are three types of competitive advantage that you can strive to achieve. First, you can try to be the low-cost player, like T.J. Maxx or Dell. Or, you could be a differentiated player, like Mercedes. And finally, you may try to achieve what's called dual advantage, having very low cost and somehow achieving a premium price, a rather difficult task that we'll look at in a moment, but it is a possibility at least, in terms of a strategy—low cost, differentiated, dual advantage.

But it's not just about what type of advantage you seek. It's also the question of what is the scope of your firm? What is your competitive scope? And here, you could think about being a very focused firm, what we call a niche competitor, where you've chosen a particular product category in which to compete with a fairly narrow product line. You've focused on a particular geography and you have a fairly narrow customer segment that you're trying to serve, what we call a narrow target market. But you don't have to be a focused competitor; you could choose to be a broad competitor. You could offer a wide array of products. You could compete in an expansive geographical setting, perhaps even be a global player. And you could serve a wider target market with many customers of demographic background, of different income, etc.

So, what type of advantage do you seek, that low cost differentiation choice, and what's your scope? How focused or how broad are you in terms of product, geography, and customer? These are the fundamental choices that every firm must make as it chooses its strategy, as it chooses, how do I want to position myself within my external environment to mitigate any negative forces and to take advantage of the opportunities there, so that I can achieve more economic value, create more of that than my competition?

So let's go into this in a little more detail. When we think about competitive advantage, we always start with: Who is the average competitor in my industry, and how much economic value are they creating? What is the gap between the willingness to pay for their product and the cost for that firm to deliver that product to their customers? What kind of wedge is there between willingness to pay and cost for the average firm in my industry?

Now what am I trying to achieve if I want competitive advantage? Well, I'm trying to generate a higher wedge, a larger wedge, between willingness to pay and cost than my competition. I'm trying to generate more economic value. How can I do that? Well, let's start by looking at how a differentiated firm does that. How does Mercedes do that? Well, they're trying to create much higher perceived value. They're trying to generate much higher willingness to pay than Chevrolet.

But what about their costs? Well, their costs are going to be slightly higher than a brand like Chevrolet. It's going to cost more for that quality German engineering, for the luxurious look and feel of the automobile. So their costs are going to be higher than the competition. But the goal, if they want to be a successful differentiated player, is to have much higher willingness to pay but only slightly higher costs, such that the wedge between willingness to pay and cost is higher than the competition, is larger than the competition.

What does a successful low-cost player do? Well, they're trying to drive their costs much lower than their rivals. Now, they're going to sacrifice a little bit of willingness to pay; they're not going to be able to charge the same prices that the competition is charging. But hopefully, they're not sacrificing too much on price, and they're driving costs much, much lower. If they can do that, they have achieved a larger gap, a larger wedge between willingness to pay and cost. They've generated more economic value than their rivals. So two paths to creating that larger wedge between willingness to pay and cost—differentiation and low cost.

Well, there is a third way to achieve competitive advantage. That's what we call dual advantage. That's where you both have a higher perceived value and a lower-cost structure than your competition. Well, is that easy to achieve? Well, Michael Porter in his seminal work on strategy argued that dual advantage was very, very difficult to achieve, if not impossible. And I would concur, not saying impossible, but it's very unlikely. Why is it so difficult to do? Well, because if you're trying to achieve that higher willingness to pay and create more perceived value, well, it's going to cost you some money. You're going to have to invest in research and development, in branding, in quality components. It's hard to have much lower costs than your competition if you're trying to create a premium product.

Likewise, if you're trying to bring your costs down significantly, you're going to find that it may be difficult to still command the same brand image and the same position in the market and be able to achieve the same pricing. And players that are very focused on either differentiation or low cost may be able to really attack you. You know, if you're trying to sell this vehicle and you're saying it's a premium vehicle at a high price, and yet you're trying to have lower costs than the competition, Mercedes may come in there and really attack you and start to critique the quality of your vehicles.

Similarly, there may be a player that comes in and undercuts you on price, and they're able to do that because they have such a strong cost position. So the players who are focused on either differentiation or low cost tend to be able to attack people trying to achieve dual advantage; it's why dual advantage is so difficult to achieve, not impossible, but a dangerous place to try to play, particularly for a firm that has many, very tough, competitors in their market.

Now interestingly, the financials tell us a story when we're analyzing the company. We can actually look at the financial statements and perceive or pick out from that precisely what type of competitive advantage they're trying to achieve. Let's take Walmart and Target, two major players in the mass-merchandising business in retail in the United States, and for Walmart, around the globe. If you look at Walmart's financials relative to Target, you'll notice some really interesting and stark differences. Walmart has much lower gross margins than Target. They have lower overhead costs, lower selling, general, and administrative expenses. But, they have much higher asset turnover than Target. They utilize their fixed assets more efficiently. They turn their inventory much more quickly than Target.

When we look at these real differences in financial measures, are we simply saying, well, is one firm better than the other? It turns out both Target and Walmart generate very strong returns for their shareholders, or have over the last few decades. But what's interesting when we look at the financials is we notice they've taken a very different path to achieving success. Both successful firms, but very different approaches.

What does that mean? Well, Target, high gross margins, lower turns, a typical differentiation strategy. Why do they have higher margins? They've chosen to sell a slightly higher quality good, sell more fashionable items, try to set some higher prices in some of those categories. For example, when they produce apparel collections in collaboration with famous designers, they're trying to bring a slightly premium price to that category in the mass-merchandising business. But they have lower inventory turns. Why? They sell fewer of the basics than Walmart. They sell a few more of these fashion forward items. And so those items may not sell as frequently as some of the very basic low-price items that Walmart sells.

On the other hand, for Walmart, a lower margin business, always trying to have rock bottom prices, but very high turns. They're good at selling staples, basic products that you buy every day. You're going to go into that store very often, and so they're going to turn that inventory very quickly. Moreover, they're going to pack items in the store. The aisles aren't going to be quite as wide, the layout not quite as clean. It's more "stack 'em high and let 'em fly" at Walmart. And that is reflected in the higher inventory turns and the higher asset utilization that we see.

What's the point? The financials tell us a story. They tell us not just which firms are better than others, they also tell us what kind of strategy is that firm trying to achieve, and is it doing so successfully? So if we looked at Nordstrom in the retail business, and compared its financials to TJX, the parent company of Marshalls and T.J.Maxx, we also would see a very different story, one generating high gross margins; having higher selling, general, and administrative expenses though; and perhaps accepting lower inventory turnover. That would be Nordstrom. And then we'd see TJX, very low expenses, but lower gross margins, charging lower prices, but turning their assets, utilizing their assets very efficiently, and therefore, achieving high profitability in that way, different paths to success.

So if we put together what we've learned so far, we can see that there are four basic what Porter calls generic competitive strategies. There's the broad differentiated strategy, Starbucks, a wide target market competing in many geographies with a differentiated product, a premium priced product in the coffee business. Ducati, on the other hand, they're a focused differentiator. Ducati in the motorcycle business, based in Italy, serving a very narrow target market with a limited selection of products, very much a niche player in the motorcycle business.

Contrast this then with the low-cost strategies we might employ, either broad or focused. A broad, low-cost player would be Walmart, serving a wider range of customers in many geographies with many products and services. On the other hand, in the focused, low-cost category, we'd have a firm like Irish-based airline Ryanair, serving certain geographies with a very well defined product set and very much a narrower target market than major airlines, like British Airways or Alitalia. So which is the best of these four generic strategies? Which should we pursue? Well, the answer is there is no one best strategy. But there is one place you don't want to be, and that's stuck in the middle, like JCPenney. Unclear as to whether you're really a differentiated player or a low-cost player, whether you're a niche player or a broad player. That's the real danger that we want to avoid.

Well, how do you become stuck in the middle? Well, first is you simply fail to choose; you're trying to be all things to all people. And we certainly know some companies trying to do that. They're so desperate for growth, for top-line growth in terms of revenue, that they are expanding and moving and trying to be everything to all their customers, and they're not clear on their strategy. Well, you also can have the issue of trying to move from one box to the other. Shifting your strategy may cause you to not actually achieve the shift, but end up straying and stuck in the middle.

Consider Starbucks in the period from, say, 2000 to 2008. Starbucks began, of course, as a niche player, a focused differentiator. They set out to grow and become more of a broad differentiator, but as they did that, they lost a little of their soul; they diluted their brand a bit. Howard Schultz, the founder, was no longer CEO at the time. But in 2008, he saw the writing on the wall; he saw the dangerous place that Starbucks found itself in. He stepped back in as CEO, and he noticed, he said, I don't think we're about coffee any more. He noticed, for example, that when he walked into the stores, there were lots of other items in the stores besides coffee crowding the identity of the store, pushing coffee to the side to some extent. He even didn't smell coffee, he said, when he went into the store. In an effort to become a broader player, to serve the mass market, they diluted the brand. And of course, what's interesting is Schultz brought them back to the coffee roots, and they've had more success in recent years.

But there are other examples of companies trying to move from one box to the other that get into trouble. Pierre Cardin and Gucci, both focused differentiators, also as they tried to grow, found themselves diluting their brand to some extent in certain periods of their history.

And finally, the third way you might find yourself stuck in the middle is you're trying to react to the emergence of a new competitor, and you end up straddling different competitive positions because you're moving in many different directions trying to adapt to a really tough new rival in your market who may be taking market share and profits away from you.

So let's take a look at this issue of straddling, this idea of finding yourself caught between two fundamentally different competitive positions and how it happens. An example will really help us. So let's take a look at the airline business again. And what's interesting about this is to look at the legacy carriers, mainline carriers like Delta, United, Continental, and British Airways. How did they react to the emergence of new, low-cost rivals, like Southwest Airlines in the U.S., or like Ryanair or EasyJet in Europe? Well interestingly, many of the legacy carriers decided to create new subsidiaries, low-cost subsidiaries that would compete directly with companies like Southwest or like Ryanair.

So Delta created a unit called Song. United created a unit called Ted. Continental created Continental Lite. And British created a subsidiary, British Airways did, called Go. What were they trying to achieve with each of these units? Well, they were trying to compete aggressively with this low-cost rival without having to change their fundamental business model for their main airline. And so they created these units, gave them a little bit of independence, but not complete independence, and let them try to compete.

But did they really create something that was as effective as these rivals that had entered their market? Did Delta really create something that was as good as Southwest? Did British Airways really create something that was as good as EasyJet or Ryanair? In fact, what you found in each of those cases is they straddled; they created something that had elements of their old model and elements of the new model the competitors had used. But in creating something that was a bit of a hybrid, it was neither as effective as the old model nor as effective as these new upstarts that had entered the market.

So we had British Airways, for example, with Go. Well, they weren't willing to go quite so far as to not have assigned seats, the way Ryanair didn't. They weren't willing to eliminate food altogether; they would offer good food, but try to charge for it. So they were making these compromises, creating a model that was neither as good as what they had or what had entered the market to compete with them. They straddled. And as a result, all of those new units established by legacy airlines, they all failed. None of them were successful.

We see the same issue with how IBM reacted to the emergence of Dell in the personal computer business. IBM was selling standardized products through a massive distribution channel, both at the retailer and wholesaler level. They had large factories achieving economies of scale, pumping out huge volumes of the same products. Dell, creating customized products, mass customization, if you will, selling them only over the phone or online, not selling through retailers or wholesalers at all.

Two very different strategies. How did IBM initially react to the emergence of Dell? Did they create a separate unit to strictly sell computers over the phone or on the internet? No, They tried to create a hybrid; they tried to ship partially assembled computers out to their wholesalers, who then could perhaps customize for some of their corporate clients. They straddled. They created something neither as effective as their old model, nor quite as effective as that new model that Dell had founded in a dorm room in Texas. They straddled.

So competitive advantage is an interesting thing. It's not about doing one thing well. It's not about what you often hear of as the term core competence. Competitive advantage is about a whole system of capabilities, an integrated self-reinforcing system of activities that enable you to achieve advantage, a collection, an interconnected set of capabilities, resources, and choices. So crafting an effective strategy means you have to be different, not just copy the assortment of resources and capabilities that your rivals have achieved. You've either got to perform activities differently or perform different activities. That's the key if you want to achieve advantage. There is no silver bullet, no one thing that you can do better than the competition and therefore achieve long-term advantage.

Why is this idea of interconnectedness or fit among your choices so important? Well, the idea is that one choice you make enhances the value of other choices you make. One capability you develop creates a stronger capability elsewhere in the organization. If these capabilities and choices fit together well, not only can you create a powerful advantage, it can be really hard for others to copy that system of activities.

To understand this in a little more detail, let's take a look at Walmart's value chain. Looking back at their original strategy, what are some of the key choices that they made as they grew in the 1960s and '70s and '80s to be the most formidable retailer in the world? Well, they had an everyday low-price strategy. Very few sales, everything always at low prices. They had little national advertising. They weren't doing a lot of new stores in urban areas. They were focused in rural locations. They had satellite technology to connect their corporate office in Bentonville, Arkansas with the stores in these rural areas. They grew not by hopscotching around the country, but instead, by creating a dense network of stores built around distribution centers that they had opened. They had very frugal travel policies and no regional offices, as many of their competitors did.

So, think about that for a moment. Each of those choices they made reinforced other choices. So having an everyday low-price strategy fit very well with not doing a lot of national advertising. No need to advertise sales if you don't run a lot of sales, if you operate with everyday low prices. You want to have a highly efficient logistics system and distribution system? Well, everyday low pricing creates very predictable demand, and therefore, it's much easier to run a very powerful and seamless integrated logistics system. So each of these choices fit together.

Now think about what would happen if a competitor, like Kmart, tried to emulate Walmart. What competitors often do is they look at what you do and they look at what they think you do best, and they emulate one part of the system. Oh, Walmart is really good at supply chain; they're really good at logistics; and they try to copy that. Two mistakes inherent in that attempt by a firm like Kmart, number one, it isn't the one thing that Walmart does that's a silver bullet; it's how their logistics plan and system fits with everything else they do that creates advantage.

But secondly, you at Kmart, you have your own system of activities that's quite different than Walmart's. So taking one thing out of a Walmart system and trying to drop it into your system, you can't achieve the same power, the same advantage. You end up with some things that don't fit together quite so nicely.

So if you think about why this is so important, this idea of fit and how these activities fit together, it's important because rivals, first of all, sometimes face what we call causal ambiguity. They don't really understand how all these activities fit together to create advantage. Secondly, they try to copy one piece of what you do, instead of understanding the need to copy the whole thing. They also have made very different commitments than you have and very different trade offs than you have. Therefore, it's difficult for them to alter those. Historical commitments are often rigid, and that rigidity prevents them from copying you. So fit is a great thing if you can create this really well aligned, self-reinforcing system of activities.

Of course, the challenge is, if you've done that very well and you've tailored your activities to one set of customers in one market, what if you try to grow? What if you try to move into a new segment? Will you now face the problem that your strategy and your system activities don't actually fit so well in this new market that you're trying to enter? This is a problem many companies face, and we'll take a look in a moment at how Walmart faced that when they moved from their normal retailing business into the wholesale club business.

But first, a little note about IKEA, a very successful company in the furniture business. What's interesting about that is one of their CEOs at one point said that many competitors had tried to copy one or two of the things IKEA did well. And the problem is they didn't try to understand the totality of the system that enabled IKEA to perform so effectively. So they tried to copy Scandinavian design, or they tried to copy the store experience, or they tried to copy the idea of having the customer assemble the furniture at home. They didn't understand that it's how all of those things fit together that created such an advantage for IKEA.

So let's take a look at a company that was successful in one market that moved into another and found that that very system of activities, which was so well interconnected, so well aligned, now suddenly didn't fit the external opportunity in front of them. So you have to ask the question, why has Costco outperformed Walmart in the wholesale club business? Now, Walmart has a very good business. Sam's Club is very effective and profitable, but it's not nearly as profitable and successful as Costco. Why did Walmart, who had this great value chain, this great system activities, why did they struggle when they tried to apply it to a business that's also about selling things at low prices, isn't it? Isn't the wholesale-club business actually quite similar to what Walmart had thrived and succeeded in so well over the years?

Turns out, maybe not. Actually, the customer in the wholesale-club business is a little different than in the basic Walmart business. It's a little higher-wealth customer. Now why would that be? Why does Costco attract people of higher income than a typical Walmart store? What's different about the wholesale-club business?

Well, you have to pay a fee each year to be able to shop there. And when you shop there, while things might be great values, you have to spend more on each trip, more of a total cash outlay because you're buying in bulk. And how do you get those goods home? Well, you need a big vehicle to get them home, and then you need to live in a big house to be able to store all those products. So put that all together, the annual fee and the bulk buying and the big house and the large car, and you see where, suddenly, the typical customer at Costco isn't quite the same as at Walmart.

And what did Costco do well? They built a system of activities tailored to the customer driving the Volvo or the BMW, not the Chevy. They built a store experience that was different than Sam's Club because they understood it was a different customer. Sam's Club was too tied down by the legacy of Walmart to truly serve in a unique way this different set of customers. You see, here is the problem. It's difficult to create a great value chain and to create a great system of activities that's well connected. But it's also difficult to move that to a new market at times.

The other problem you face, of course, is you've tailored your activities to a particular environment. You've done really well, and then the world changes. And now suddenly, your strategy, which fit very well in the environment and was successful, now you're the one that's become rigid. You've got capabilities and choices you've made and commitments you've made that are hard to undo. The idea of historical commitments that become rigid is a fundamental one, because it's often our explanation for why incumbent players aren't nimble enough, flexible enough, to adapt to a changing environment.

This leads us to an important concept to close out our lecture called judo strategy. Judo strategy. Because core capabilities can become rigid, successful entrepreneurs, successful entrants, often are able to use the incumbent's strengths against them. That's a key principle in judo, using the strength of your competitor against them. Consider the case of Dell versus IBM. What were IBM's strengths? Well, it had tremendous manufacturing capability to produce high volumes of the standardized product at low cost. It also had tremendous relationships with the distribution channel, with retailers, with wholesalers, with value-added resellers.

Well, what did Dell do? By building its strategy, very differently, now this very strength that IBM had became a liability. IBM couldn't go direct and sell online. If it did so, it would alienate many of the wholesalers it had been working with and many of the retailers. So IBM was hesitant to go online as quickly as Dell did. IBM's factories weren't configured to build customized products every day based on customer demand. They were configured to produce large batches of standardized products as efficiently as possible. So IBM's strengths now became liabilities as they tried to adapt to this nimble new entrant. Judo strategy. Take advantage of the strengths of your competitor and turn them against that rival.

There are many threats that come to a competitive advantage if you achieve it successfully. The ability to be successful as a firm, to be more profitable than your rivals, is about not just achieving advantage, but sustaining it. And to sustain it, you have to be worried about three major external threats. Can someone imitate what you're doing, but do it better than you? Can a substitute emerge, an alternative product or service that undermines your position? So, can a tablet computer supplant the laptop for many consumers?

And hold up. What is hold up? Hold up is when your buyers and suppliers gain leverage over you and grab more of the profit pie. It's like a convenience store hold up. They've got a gun to your head. They have leverage. And they're able to extract some profit from you, like Microsoft did from the personal-computer makers by having such a powerful position in the operating-system market.

So imitation, substitution, and hold up are the three main external threats. From an internal basis, of course, we can shoot ourselves in the foot if we don't perceive and react to threats in an adequate fashion. And incumbent players sometimes don't see the threat early enough, or they don't know how to respond, or they can't motivate their organization to respond quickly enough when threats emerge.

One thing you'll note about strategies in many markets is that we actually aren't trying to be as different as we should in many companies. If strategy is about identifying different activities and different positions in the marketplace, what we see in many markets is strategies converging. We see herd behavior, companies simply imitating one another. Why is that? It's safe to follow the herd. There's risk aversion on the part of many executives. Being really different can be risky. Benchmarking is widespread, so people are constantly looking at their competitors and trying to identify what they do well, and then they copy them. And, as growth slows in the market and we compete for market share, we're no longer going after new customers but trying to steal old ones from our rivals, we start to do things that are similar to our rivals. So herd behavior, unfortunately, is chronic, and exists in many industries, even though it's the antithesis of a great competitive strategy.

I'll close with a couple of quotes. There's one great quote from Alan Jay Lerner, who wrote, "You write a hit the same way you write a flop." Success sows the seeds of its own destruction. A firm that's been really successful in one market, that's built a great system of activities, can see those same strengths become a liability because the commitments they've made become rigid, and they're unable to change as the environment changes around them.

Well, John Maynard Keynes also wrote something very interesting that pertains to the issue of strategy, though he was an economist. He said, "The difficulty lies, not in the new ideas, but in escaping from the old ones, which ramify, for those brought up as most of us have been, into every corner of our minds." It's hard to change the way you think, and for many companies, they've got one way they think about how to make money in a business, and they can't shake that when someone comes along with a new model, as we'll see in upcoming lectures.

So your assignment, look at the annual reports of two companies before our next lecture, Whole Foods and Kroger, both in the supermarket business. Take a look at the financial statements. How do their key ratios differ? Things like the return on assets, their net income margin, their gross margin, their inventory turnover. And how do those differences reflect the contrasting strategies of these two firms? Which firm is pursuing a differentiation strategy and which is pursuing the low-cost strategy?

What Trader Joe's Doesn't Do
Lecture 4

S uppose that several decades ago, a Stanford M.B.A. named Joe Coulombe asked you to invest in his new grocery retailer. He planned to open small stores in low-rent strip malls, offer a limited selection of goods, and do very little advertising. You probably would have made the mistake of turning down that investment, as many others did. But Coulombe went on to open a chain called Trader Joe's that became one of the most successful grocery retailers in the last few decades. In this lecture, we'll explore how Coulombe created a business where people want to work, customers want to shop, and investors want to put their money.

The Importance of Trade-Offs
- Unlike most other grocery stores, Trader Joe's doesn't offer many branded products; almost all of its products are private label. Its stores don't have large parking lots or wide aisles. It doesn't offer self-checkout, accept coupons, or have a loyalty card. It doesn't really run sales, doesn't advertise on television, and doesn't have a large selection of items. Finally, there is no stable product line at Trader Joe's.

- As Michael Porter once wrote, "The essence of strategy is choosing what not to do." You can't be all things to all people, which means that you have to choose not just what you will do but what you won't do. You need to have a clear understanding of the things your rivals offer that you choose not to offer. Such trade-offs make your firm distinct from your competitors, make it hard for existing players to imitate you, and can help you mitigate the negative forces in your industry.

- Some of the leading firms in past decades have achieved success by making firm choices about what they would not do and emphasizing those trade-offs.

- o Southwest Airlines, for example, doesn't offer assigned seats, uses smaller regional airports, has only one kind of plane in its fleet, doesn't allow customers to transfer bags to other airlines, and doesn't operate a hub-and-spoke system. Southwest has chosen not to do what many major airlines have done.

- o Likewise, Planet Fitness has positioned itself as a gym for people who aren't fitness nuts, and it emphasizes this trade-off approach in its advertising. By doing so, the firm hopes to attract customers who are more casual about their fitness regimes, those who want to lose a few pounds but don't want to be intimidated by bodybuilders.

Preventing Imitation

- Because of the trade-offs it has made, Trader Joe's has made it difficult for other grocery retailers to become imitators. Consider Kroger, for example, a large supermarket chain. Kroger has made historical commitments that are rigid. It already has large stores with wide aisles, and it can't change that format to mimic Trader Joe's. Kroger also has many branded goods and offers sales each week. It couldn't easily shift to everyday low pricing. To some extent, Kroger is stuck with the choices it has made.

- Moreover, the mindset of people operating a typical grocery store is quite different than the mindset of Trader Joe's leadership, and it's difficult to change mindset, as well. Tesco, a British retailer, tried to set up a separate subsidiary to build a chain of smaller-format stores to compete directly with Trader Joe's. But Tesco ended up stuck in the middle—creating something that was neither as good as Trader Joe's nor as effective as its main business.

Mitigating Negative Forces

- Trader Joe's strategy of making trade-offs has also helped the store mitigate negative forces in terms of industry structure.

- The unique array of private-label products that are unavailable at other retailers diminishes both buyer power and competitive rivalry. When you're not selling the same goods that other stores sell, people can't compare prices, and you don't get dragged into price wars.

- The distinctive in-store experience at Trader Joe's mitigates both buyer power and rivalry, and it helps to counter the threat of substitutions from other retail formats, including e-commerce. The everyday low pricing strategy also minimizes price rivalry and buyer power.

- In addition, Trader Joe's willingness to alter its product mix frequently mitigates supplier power. The store maintains a credible threat with regard to discontinuing products. Because customers don't know who makes the private-label items for Trader Joe's, the firm can also readily change its suppliers to get a better price.

- Finally, locating stores in older strip malls offsets the power of real estate firms and landlords that charge high rents to many retailers.

The Growth Trap

- The *growth trap* is a primary reason that other firms don't make trade-offs. CEOs want to grow revenue, and they believe that trade-offs could constrain growth. Obviously, as you make trade-offs, you narrow your target market, which makes it difficult to grow sales aggressively.

- Publicly traded firms definitely feel pressure to meet Wall Street expectations. But it's also true that large firms get more publicity, and their executives often receive higher compensation. Thus, there are some personal interests driving the obsession with growth for many companies.

- There's also a real challenge when CEOs set aggressive growth targets. What does it mean if a CEO sets a target of 15% or 20% growth per year?

- o Mathematicians have a rule of 72 that helps us think about the growth of any number. If we divide 72 by the growth rate that a firm aspires to achieve, we get the number of years it will take for that firm to reach its target.

- o If a firm is trying to grow at 20% per year, it will take about 3.5 years for that firm to reach its target. How is a firm that might have been around for 40 or 50 years going to achieve 20% growth in such a short period of time? In many cases, it does so by violating key trade-offs it originally made.

- o A firm might have started with a long list of things it didn't plan to do—things that made it distinct but create a narrow target market. To go beyond that market, the firm begins to eliminate a few of the trade-offs.

A Dual Advantage Strategy?

- • Some observers have pointed to Trader Joe's as an example of a firm pursuing a dual advantage strategy, achieving both differentiation and low costs. However, the reference point here is crucial.

- • If we compare Trader Joe's to a typical supermarket, it might seem to have slightly higher prices and lower costs. But in comparison to other organic or natural stores, such as Whole Foods, Trader Joe's prices are clearly lower; therefore, it's hard to argue that the store is a differentiated player.

- • The bottom line is that it's difficult to come to a definitive conclusion about the issue of dual advantage with Trader Joe's because it's not a publicly traded company. We don't have financial data on the company, and because it offers private-label goods, it's difficult to even assess the price level at the firm. We can't tell if Trader Joe's prices are lower than those of a given competitor because the products are not identical in both locations.

- This issue of dual advantage highlights the fact that many people confuse the term *differentiation* with the general notion of being different than the competition. Low-cost players can be highly distinctive, but that doesn't mean they're differentiated in the precise way that Porter initially defined the term. In the original generic strategies framework, *differentiation* meant creating a larger wedge between willingness to pay and costs than the average rival.

Blue Ocean Strategy

- The concept of *blue ocean strategy* was introduced in a book of the same name written by W. Chan Kim and Renée Mauborgne. These authors argued that dual advantage is not only possible, but it's much more prevalent than Porter believed. Kim and Mauborgne claimed that true innovators are able to break the trade-off between low cost and differentiation and create a new value proposition that allows them to deliver both.

- As an example, the authors point to Cirque du Soleil, which is a hybrid of a circus and a Broadway show. The show charges a premium price, yet the authors argue that it has lower costs than a typical circus.

- Southwest Airlines is offered as another example of a blue ocean company, but it doesn't charge premium prices. Southwest is a low-cost player that's different but not differentiated in the sense that it enjoys higher willingness to pay than many of its rivals.

- According to Kim and Mauborgne, a blue ocean firm is created by turning around the strengths and weaknesses of a typical firm in an industry. Can a new firm be great at things that typical firms in the industry aren't doing well? And can a new firm sacrifice or cut down on things in which other firms invest?

- Cirque du Soleil, for example, invests in choreography and the composition of beautiful music—things that a typical circus doesn't have—but it doesn't have animals or star performers. By making those kinds of choices, a new firm can flip the industry on its head and create a different company, one that doesn't have direct competitors.

- Kim and Mauborgne offer what they call the four actions framework to help people think about how they might redefine an industry and come up with a strategy that sets them apart from many competitors. The key questions to ask here are: (1) What can you eliminate that others are doing? (2) What can you reduce? (3) What can you create? (4) What can you enhance?

- Interestingly, this model actually seems to have much in common with Porter's work, particularly with regard to the idea of trade-offs. By eschewing certain activities that are commonplace in an industry, firms can create a distinctive position that's hard to imitate.

Homogenization
- In benchmarking, a firm typically looks for things that it's doing less effectively than the competition and tries to catch up. Unfortunately, benchmarking can lead to the homogenization of strategies. This is not to say that you shouldn't study the competition, but you may want to amplify what you do differently rather than just trying to catch up.

Today, we often see many different brands, flavors, and sizes of certain products, but in the end, the products are just commodities; they're not truly differentiated.

- Youngme Moon, a marketing professor at Harvard Business School, has noted the phenomenon of convergence in many industries, with rivals becoming increasingly alike. In retail stores, Moon sees what she calls heterogeneous homogenizing. In other words, there is diversity on the surface but homogeneity underneath. Companies are spending a great deal of money to create many varieties of the same basic products.

- As we've seen, however, strategy rests on unique activities. And to create a sustainable strategic position, you must make trade-offs. Without making those trade-offs, your ideas can be imitated, and you won't be able to sustain your advantage.

Suggested Reading

Ager and Roberto, "Trader Joe's."

Kim and Mauborgne, *Blue Ocean Strategy*.

Moon, *Different*.

Porter, "What Is Strategy?"

Questions to Consider

1. What is the value of making a series of trade-offs as you formulate a competitive strategy?

2. Why do firms have such a hard time imitating a company that has made a number of trade-offs?

3. Why is it so difficult to achieve dual advantage?

What Trader Joe's Doesn't Do
Lecture 4—Transcript

Suppose you were an investor, and several decades ago, a Stanford MBA named Joe Coulombe came to you and requested an investment in his new grocery retailer. He described the retailer he envisioned operating. There were going to be very small stores, fairly cramped aisles, small parking lots. He envisioned opening these in low-rent, beat-up strip malls, where he could have low rent for his space.

He wanted to offer a limited selection of goods, not nearly as many as the typical supermarket. He didn't want to sell any branded goods; he wanted to only sell private label. He wasn't going to accept coupons and do any television advertising. He didn't envision a loyalty card or any self-checkout lines. He didn't really envision sales. He didn't even want to have inserts in the Sunday newspaper with advertisements about what was on sale that week at his firm. Would you have invested in Joe Coulombe's new grocery retailer? I suspect many of you would not have. And you would have made a big mistake, like many others did at the time, because Joe Coulombe opened a chain named Trader Joe's that went on to become one of the most successful grocery retailers, really, retailers of any kind, over the last few decades.

Now, the Albrecht family of Germany, they believed in Joe Coulombe. They actually bought his firm. The Albrecht family owned a chain of grocers in Germany and other places in Europe called Aldi. And they acquired Trader Joe's, leaving Joe Coulombe to run the stores as the CEO. And great success followed. In fact, this company has passionate fans. It's incredible the lengths to which people will go to demonstrate their love for Trader Joe's. Facebook pages have been created trying to get people at the company to open a store somewhere close to the owner of that Facebook page. There have been people that have gone on Twitter and created accounts describing the "yummy, healthy Trader Joe's items" on their shopping list; that's the @ TraderJoesList Twitter handle. She has more than 55,000 followers.

A customer has created a "if I made a commercial for Trader Joe's" homemade video on their smartphone, and they've accumulated 925,000 people who viewed the video. It's incredible to see the amount of attention that the firm has gotten from these passionate fans. There have even been people who've written cookbooks featuring meals prepared strictly with the firm's products. People wait in line for hours before a new store grand opening.

Joe Coulombe has once said, "I own the cult." He says, "My children say that the Albrechts own the business, but I own the cult." It truly is a cult-like, passionate following. Trader Joe's doesn't have customers; they have fans. And any company would love to have fans, not just customers. It's interesting to watch how the firm has succeeded and how much attention it's gotten for its success. In 2013, they've been ranked highly in a number of measures by a number of different periodicals. They're considered one of the most successful grocers in the United States.

For example, their sales per square foot is said to exceed that of most major grocery chains, even significantly higher than top performers, such as Whole Foods Market. Customers ranked it their favorite supermarket in the U.S. in a 2013 survey. Consumer Reports ranked it as the second best supermarket in the nation. Fast Company gave it high marks for innovation. And Forbes lists the company as one of the top 25 firms to work for in 2013. Trader Joe's claimed that 80% of its customers had attended college. The company described its target market as intelligent, educated, and inquisitive individuals. It had a very clear view of who its customer was and how it wanted to serve that customer.

They focused on people who were health conscious, enjoyed travel, and liked trying new things. Tony Hales, a store captain, as they call their managers, described the clientele. He said, "Our favorite customers are out-of-work college professors. Well-read. Well-traveled. Appreciates a good value." Industry consultant, Kevin Kelly, described the target customer as, quote, "A Volvo-driving professor who could be CEO of a Fortune 100 company if he could get over his capitalist angst."

I seem to see a pattern here. Professors, like me, seem to love Trader Joe's. But I don't love Trader Joe's just because of the in-store experience; I love it because it's a high performer. Not only does it have passionate fans, but it's returned tremendous profits for its investors over the years. It's succeeded by creating a place where people want to work, where customers want to shop, and where investors want to put their money. How have they done it? How has this upstart from California, owned by a German corporate parent, out-competed many formidable rivals in the supermarket business? They've known their customer; they've known them very well. That's certainly one first step.

A little more about the Trader Joe's customer, I think it's interesting, there was a Los Angeles Times article several years ago about them. And it wrote, "These are people who wear sunscreen even over their tattoos; who travel on frequent-flyer miles, and with a Lonely Planet guide, rather than *Frommer's*." It's people who really love to shop there, but who are quirky, who are different. They want something other than the usual supermarket and they've found it in Trader Joe's.

And the cult-like following is demonstrated when they open a new store. People waiting in line overnight in Spokane, Washington. People were there from three o'clock in the morning. People taking days off from work to pitch their tent-like chairs and their set up overnight so they can stay there and wait for the doors to open. People flocking and forming long lines. In certain cities they've even had to bring police in to manage the traffic around a new store, because so many people flood there on the first day. In Manhattan, when they opened a new store, the lines wound around the block. And, again, police had to help manage the flow. And they could only let certain amounts of people in the store at once, because so many wanted to get in at the same time when the doors opened.

Well, what's the secret? How do you create a company that has such a passionate following and that's done so well for its employees, it's customers, and it's investors? Well, let's list for a moment what Trader Joe's does not do. The things that most other grocery stores typically do that Trader Joe's does not: They don't offer many branded products; it's almost all private label. Actually, with very funny names, right? It's Trader Joe's private label; as they produce foods from other countries, they simply translate "Joe" into that language and apply that.

So Trader Jose for Mexican food. Traders Jacques for French food, etc. They don't have spacious parking lots. They don't have spacious stores with wide aisles. They don't offer self checkout or TV ads. They don't accept coupons or have a loyalty card. They don't really run sales and no TV advertisements. And interestingly, they don't have a large selection. A typical Trader Joe's location might have 3,000 or 4,000 items in it. A typical supermarket, like one run by Kroger, might have 30,000 or 40,000 items in it. And, finally, there is not a stable product line at Trader Joe's; products come and go. This week you go there and you love their mango salsa. Next week you go, and it may not be there. Not because they're out of stock, but because they've moved on and they're offering a different item in that space.

Well, what's the lesson from this company that's choosing not to do all these things that a typical grocery store would do? Well, Michael Porter once wrote, "The essence of strategy is choosing what not to do." You can't be all things to all people. And to not be all things to all people it means really identifying not just what you're going to do, but understanding what you're not going to do. Being very clear about the things that rivals are offering that you're choosing not to offer. Why is this is so important? What is the value of this concept of making trade offs?

Well, trade offs offer several key advantages. First, they make you distinct. The more that you've chosen a very different set of activities and a different set of offerings than your competition, the more you're unlike them; the more you're different. And that's important, as we said in prior lectures. But even more than that, making trade offs, choosing carefully what not to do, makes it very hard for existing players to imitate you. And that's important because not only do you have to be able to achieve competitive advantage to generate high returns, you have to sustain that advantage. You can't be easily imitated if you want to have long-term success. And making trade offs, choosing what not to do, could actually make it very difficult for others to emulate you.

And finally, making trade offs can help you mitigate the negative forces in your industry. They can help you deal with high buyer power, or high supplier power, or strong threats from things like substitutes. So choosing what not to do makes you distinct, hard to be imitated, and can help you mitigate negative forces in your industry, all important if you're going to achieve long-term success.

Think about the strategies of some leading firms in past decades, Southwest Airlines, eHarmony, Edward Jones, and Planet Fitness. Southwest succeeding in the tough airline business. eHarmony succeeding in the online dating market, creating a marketplace where people can match and find people they're interested in having a long-term relationship with. Edward Jones, a brokerage house, competing with the likes of Merrill Lynch and others, very successful over the last few decades. And Planet Fitness, in that very difficult fitness center business, they've done very well.

How have these firms done it? Well, take Southwest: no assigned seats; smaller regional airports; not having multiple jets in their fleet, they only have one kind of plane; not offering inter-service, you can't transfer your bags to other airlines; not operating a hub-and-spoke system, instead offering point-to-point service between certain airports. They've chosen to not do what many major airlines have done.

eHarmony, choosing not to be in the business of casual dating matches. They're not trying to find that one-night stand for you; they're not trying to find that person you might date for a month and then move on to find someone else. They're trying to get people married, to establish and help people establish long-term relationships, and they've done some things to actually push away the casual dater from their site.

How about Edward Jones? They don't offer online brokerage services; they don't want you trading online. They don't want to sell initial public offerings, commodities, penny stocks. They don't offer a huge array of investment banking services, as many other brokerage houses also do. They've chosen to be the trusted adviser to conservative clientele who are interested in long-term investing. And they have made a set of tradeoffs to distinguish themselves from the competition.

And finally, Planet Fitness, they're sort of the gym for people who aren't fitness freaks, the gym for people who get put off by fitness centers that cater to people who are incredibly into their regiment. They want people who are just trying to lose a few pounds or get in a little better shape, and they're just interested in a place that's safe that won't make them feel awkward and the like. You see in their ads how they've exemplified in their advertisements this strategy of trade offs. The great ad where this really buff man comes in with bulging muscles, and they ask him what he wants from his fitness center, and he says, I pick things up and I put them down, and he repeats that three or four times. And eventually, they escort him out of the building. They don't want him as a customer.

How many companies do you know create advertisements that say, these are people we don't want as customers. That is the ultimate strategy of making trade offs. But, by doing that they make themselves even more attractive to the person who's casually into a fitness regime, who's trying to lose a few pounds, but who doesn't want to be intimidated by the bodybuilder. So by pushing the bodybuilder away, they bring in the casual fitness person. They've done it very well making trade offs. Really key, but many firms don't do it.

So, could people imitate Trader Joe's? And why do trade offs help make it difficult for others to imitate Trader Joe's? Well, consider the case of Kroger, a large supermarket chain in the United States; they have made historical commitments that are rigid. They can't just change their entire store format to be able to mimic Trader Joe's. They have large stores with wide aisles. They have many branded goods in their stores and relationships with the manufacturers of those branded goods. They have a strategy of offering sales each week; they can't easily shift to everyday low pricing. In other words, it's really hard for them to modify everything they do to imitate Trader Joe's. They're stuck with a set of choices they've made, to some extent. Moreover there's the issue of mindset. The mindset of people operating a typical grocery store, well, that's very different than the mindset of Trader Joe's leadership, and it's hard to change mindset, as well.

Well, you might say maybe the way to imitate Trader Joe's is by setting up a separate subsidiary within one of these large grocery chains and let them begin to build a chain of smaller-format stores to compete directly with Trader Joe's. Well, the large and successful British retailer, Tesco, tried just that. They created a chain called Fresh & Easy; launched it in the western portion of the United States to compete with Trader Joe's, smaller format, limited selection of items, very much in the spirit of Trader Joe's.

But was it as good as Trader Joe's? No. Tesco, like British Airways and United Airlines and like IBM, in our previous lectures, they straddled. They created something neither as good as Trader Joe's, nor as effective as their main business at Tesco. So one of the reasons making trade offs works really well is because you make it very hard to be imitated because of the commitments that companies have made that they cannot easily change. And you tend to increase the chance that your competitors will end up straddling in an attempt to compete more effectively with you.

The Trader Joe's strategy of making trade offs, though, is more than just about making it hard for others to imitate them. It has also helped them mitigate some of the very negative forces in terms of the industry structure. The unique array of private-label products, unavailable at other retailers, diminishes both buyer power and competitive rivalry. When you're not selling the same goods that Stop and Shop and Kroger and others sell, well, then people can't compare on price, and you don't get dragged into price wars.

The distinctive in-store experience mitigates both buyer power and rivalry, and it helps to counter the threat of substitutions from other retail formats, including e-commerce. You know, I asked one executive, when I was running a workshop for a Fortune 500 company, I asked them about Trader Joe's. I was teaching a case study about the firm, and she said to me, I love the store. I go there every Saturday; it's my little Saturday morning vacation. Who would describe going shopping as a vacation? But at Trader Joe's, many customers do view it as an enjoyable experience. And by creating that experience, they've mitigated the threat of substitution from e-commerce, to some extent.

As for the everyday low-pricing strategy, that minimizes price rivalry and buyer power, as well. We're not in the business of having things on sale below cost to drag people in to then convince them to pay higher prices for certain items where we make our profit. They're not in that business, and by having an everyday low-price strategy, they minimize rivalry and buyer power.

Mitigating negative forces is really key, and they do it in another way, as well. Their willingness to alter their product mix frequently mitigates supplier power. Trader Joe's maintains a credible threat with regard to discontinuing products. As customers have come to understand that the product mix is highly dynamic. As a customer, I know that I may not see the same item I saw a month ago, and I've come to accept that as a customer of Trader Joe's. And the chain actually trains its employees to counsel me when I'm worried about the fact or I'm upset about the fact that my item is gone. And they're there to help you sample and try a new item that has replaced it. Suppliers don't have as much power if they know that Trader Joe's simply doesn't have to have their item, because they're willing to change and move to someone else's item over time.

Popular items will come and go, and many suppliers find it difficult to argue customers will be upset if a product disappears from the shelf or if a different manufacturer provides it. But, moreover, the secrecy of the fact that many customers don't know who makes these private-label items for Trader Joe's makes it such that Trader Joe's can offer the very same item under the Trader Joe's moniker, under that brand, change its supplier to get a better price in the negotiating table, and you, the customer, has no knowledge of that.

Finally, locating stores in old strip malls offsets the power of real estate firms and landlords that charge high rents to many retailers. So you can see, by choosing the strategy, as they have done, they've dealt with an industry where the Five Forces, frankly, aren't very good. It's not an attractive industry. It's tough. It's a fight for profits. But their choices have mitigated each of those Five Forces in a way that's enabled them to be successful.

So why don't other firms make trade offs like this? Why is it so hard for firms to make trade offs? We've listed a few that have done it well, like Planet Fitness or eHarmony or Edward Jones. Why don't others do it? I think it's because of the growth trap. CEOs want to grow the top line. They want to grow revenue. And trade offs could constrain growth. They are the one downside. Right?

Because, as you make trade offs, you narrow the scope of the firm. You narrow your target market. And narrowing your target market means it's more difficult to grow that top line to grow sales aggressively. Plus, it's very hard to say no to customers. Making trade offs means, when the customer comes in and wants three or four other items that you don't have, you have to be willing to say, no, we don't carry those items. We don't carry those brands. Sorry, we don't have a loyalty card. That's a tough conversation for many managers to have. They hear the request from the customer, and they want to please them. But by pleasing them, they find themselves moving in many different directions at once, not making the trade offs that enable them to be distinctive from their competition. They follow the herd and become more like their competition, where they're constantly saying yes to new customer requests.

Why are some firms and some CEOs so obsessed with growth, you might ask. Well, for publicly traded firms, there's definitely the pressure to meet Wall Street expectations. But also, you have to note that large firms typically offer higher compensation to their executives. You get more publicity if you run a large firm than a smaller firm. If you're Trader Joe's, you're privately held, you're fairly secretive, you don't see the CEO's face on the cover of Business Week or Fortune magazine. CEOs who become obsessed with growth often do so because it does lead to more publicity, a bigger empire that they get to lead, more compensation, and the like. There are some personal interests driving the obsession with growth for many companies.

You know, there's a real challenge, though, when you offer such high, such aggressive growth targets as a CEO. You have to ask yourself, you know, what does that mean when I say I want to grow at 15, or 20, or 25% a year. Let's think about that for a moment. Mathematicians have this rule of 72 that helps us think about growth of any number. So how long until a firm doubles in size? Well, if you take 72 and divide by the growth rate that firm aspires to achieve, you get the number of years it will take for that firm to double in size.

So if a firm's trying to grow at 20% per year, it's going to take about three and a half years for that firm to double in size. How is a firm that might have been around for 30, 40, 50 years going to double in size in such a short period of time? How are they going to achieve that aggressive target? Well, in many cases, what they begin to do is violate the key trade offs that they originally made. So they began by having a long list of what they weren't going to do, things that made them distinct, but that created a very narrow target market.

So, how do you go beyond that? You begin to say, well let's lop off a few of those trade offs; let's start doing a few things we didn't do in the past in pursuit of growth. Some have said that this is what Southwest Airlines has been doing recently ,beginning to walk away from a few of those trade offs because they saturated the market that they first set out to dominate in the United States, and so, in looking for new growth, they've started to walk away from a few of those trade offs, and maybe that's meant they're not quite as distinct as they used to be. The airline understands this, and they've pushed back on some of that criticism. It's been interesting to watch the dialogue between those who see them as violating some trade offs and the managers there who see themselves as making smart choices to try to continue to grow.

One other point about Trader Joe's that's interesting, some point to them as an example of dual advantage. They are one of the rare cases, perhaps, where they've achieved differentiation and low costs simultaneously. Is that true? Well, I think the reference point here is crucial. If one compares Trader Joe's to a typical supermarket, you might say that they have slightly higher prices, maybe they are premium, and they have lower costs. But if you compare them to other organic or natural stores, like Whole Foods, well, clearly their prices are lower, and therefore it's hard to argue that they are a differentiated player. Perhaps they are low cost, but not differentiated at the same time.

The bottom line is, with Trader Joe's, it's hard to come to a definitive conclusion with regard to this issue of dual advantage because they're not a publicly traded company. We don't have their financial data. Moreover, because they offer private-label goods, it's very hard to even assess the price level at the firm. Are their prices higher or lower than XYZ competitor? We're not quite sure, because the products are not identical in both locations.

This issue of dual advantage is interesting because many people come to a misguided view of the meaning of generic strategies. They confuse the term *differentiation* with the general notion of being different than the competition. It's important to note that low-cost players can be highly distinctive; think Dell in its heyday or Southwest. But that doesn't mean they're differentiated in the precise way that Porter initially defined the firm. In the original generic strategies framework, differentiation meant creating a larger wedge between willingness to pay in costs than the average rival by raising willingness to pay much higher than the average competitor while incurring somewhat higher costs.

So many times people point to a firm and say they're both differentiated and low cost. But, in fact, they're not differentiated; they're not charging a premium price; they're just really different than other firms. And this makes it difficult when people misinterpret the framework. But whether you misinterpret it or not, the bottom line is Trader Joe's is a very interesting firm because, at a minimum, it's a tremendous low-cost player with a unique store experience. And perhaps, there's even a bit of differentiation there as well in some cases.

Now this brings us to an alternative point of view on strategy articulated by Kim and Mauborgne in a book, *Blue Ocean Strategy*. They wrote it in strict contrast to the work of Porter and his view of strategy. They argued that dual advantage is not only possible, it's much more prevalent in the world than Porter came to admit; that true innovators are able to break this trade off between low cost and differentiation. They're able to create a new value proposition, where they can, in fact, deliver both. And they point, for example, at one firm, one innovator, that they claim has done this very well—Cirque du Soleil.

Cirque du Soleil, this hybrid between a circus and a Broadway show, this elaborate production. They charge a premium price. Yet the authors argue they have lower costs than the typical circus. One point, they haven't really articulated the evidence behind that assertion on cost. On the issue of premium price, we all know that they do, in fact, charge a premium price relative to circuses. So Cirque du Soleil is their example of a company they would argue that didn't have to make a choice, that was able to achieve dual advantage.

One weakness is some of their other examples, I think, don't measure up. Southwest, they offered as an example of a Blue Ocean Strategy company, but I would argue that's not dual advantage; there's no premium price there. There's a low-cost player that's different, that's distinct, but not differentiated in the sense that they have higher willingness to pay than many of their rivals.

How do you create this Blue Ocean Strategy firm, this firm that can break the paradigm in an industry and perhaps achieve dual advantage? They argue that what you have to do is think about what the typical firm in the industry is good at and not so good at, and flip that on its head. Can we be great at things that typical firms in the industry aren't doing very well? And can we sacrifice or cut down on things that other firms are investing a lot in? Maybe we won't do that.

So with Cirque du Soleil, we'll invest in choreography and the composition of beautiful music, things that the typical circus doesn't do as much of. But we'll cut back; we won't have animals, and we won't have star performers. And by making those choices, you flip the industry on its head and create a very different kind of company, one that doesn't even have a direct competitor. How beautiful is that? Whether you're Trader Joe's or you're Cirque du Soleil, when you can't even identify a direct competitor very easily, well now you know you have a great strategy.

So, Kim and Mauborgne, in their book, *Blue Ocean Strategy*, ask four questions, they call it the four actions framework, to help people think about how they might redefine an industry, how they might come up with a strategy that sets it apart from many competitors. They say, first ask yourself what can we not do that others are doing? What can we eliminate that others are doing? What can we reduce that others are doing a lot of? We'll do less of. But also we can ask, what can we create and enhance? What are some things that others aren't doing at all that we could do? Or what are they doing a little bit of that we could do a lot more of? So what can we create and enhance? What can we reduce and eliminate? The four key questions, the four key actions, that help us build a truly innovative strategy.

How different is that view actually than Porter? Many people who study strategy think of these two sets of authors as really in direct contrast to one another. But I would argue, in fact, these models have a lot in common. You should recognize rather quickly that trade-offs represent a common element to the work of Porter or the *Blue Ocean Strategy* authors. In their own way, each scholar emphasizes the importance of not doing some key things that many traditional players are doing. By eschewing certain activities that are commonplace in an industry, firms create a distinctive position that's hard to imitate. The Blue Ocean Strategy framework, in short, has much more in common with Porter's perspective than many people recognize initially.

I like the framework from *Blue Ocean Strategy*, because it does ask you good questions. It asks good questions that can help you sharpen your distinctiveness relative to other firms, and in the end, it's all about being distinctive; that's the key. So has Google, for example, have they reduced or eliminated things that other search portals did? They certainly did. They stripped down their homepage to something so simple. But they enhanced the search capability a great deal, and offered something others did not. So in a way, their strategy fits the framework very nicely. So the framework can be helpful at helping us ask good questions to coming up with a better strategy.

And one of the problems, I think, in why firms don't have distinctive strategies, why they end up so much like their competition, is they do a lot of benchmarking. And what happens when you benchmark? You typically look for the things you're doing much less effectively than the competition, and you try to catch up to them. Let's get as good as them on an item where we're lagging behind. Of course, that competitor, they're doing the very same thing. They're benchmarking you. They're looking at where they're behind and trying to catch up. But if you catch up to them on issue A, and they catch up to you on issue C, at the end of the day, the two of you have become much more alike. Benchmarking can lead to the homogenization of strategies. Benchmarking leads to less effective strategies in some cases. Not to say you shouldn't study the competition, but maybe you want to amplify what you do differently more so than you just always want to play catch up.

Youngme Moon is a marketing professor at Harvard Business School, and she has said that she has seen convergence in many industries, rivals becoming more and more alike, and she says, in many cases, what she sees as she walks through the aisles of a grocery store and apparel retailer, she says, I see heterogeneous homogenating. In other words, on the face of it, I see diversity, but underneath it all, I see a lot of homogeneity.

So in the bottled-water market, she says, as I walk down the aisle, I see many different brands, many different flavors of water, many different pack sizes. And at the end of the day, it's all water. It's still a commodity. It's not truly differentiated. But all those things they've done to create many varieties of the same basic product, she says, that's an expensive root to commoditization. It's truly convergence, not distinctiveness.

So what are some of the lessons here for us? Strategy rests on unique activities, and to create a sustainable strategic position, you have to make trade offs. Without making those trade offs, your ideas can be imitated and you won't be able to sustain the advantage. So you have to be able to choose what not to do. That's really crucial. And that's tough, because for many of us, we're not willing to make those tough choices at times, not willing to say no to certain customers, or no to certain activities, in part, because we want to achieve that top-line growth.

So your homework at the end of this lecture, select a firm you think has been very successful in a particular industry, and ask yourself what trade offs has the company made so as to distinguish itself from its rivals? Can you find a firm like Planet Fitness or Trader Joe's and analyze them? But then, turn to a firm that you've seen try to pursue rapid growth, but maybe, who's seen it's distinctiveness erode recently, and ask yourself, what trade offs has that company violated as it's pursued all that revenue growth.

First Movers versus Fast Followers
Lecture 5

First-mover advantage is the competitive advantage established by virtue of the fact that a company has entered a market first and established a position. And it's true that first movers sometimes do achieve tremendous advantage; consider Gillette in razors or Coca-Cola in carbonated soft drinks. But we also have plenty of examples of first movers that did not succeed or were completely eliminated from the market. Before Facebook, for example, there was a social media company called Friendster, and before Google, there was Netscape. In this lecture, we'll challenge the commonly held view that being first is crucial.

Sources of First-Mover Advantage
- First movers gain advantage from four major sources: economies of scale, economies of scope, network effects, and learning effects.

- Economies of scale exist in a business when the costs per unit to produce and distribute a good fall as the business produces more units of the good in any given time period. In other words, the larger you are, the more your costs per unit come down. Scale economies are pronounced in such businesses as Toyota, Bank of America, and FedEx. The higher the volume for any business with high fixed costs, the greater the degree to which those fixed costs can be amortized over many units, bringing the cost per unit down.

- Learning effects also bring about falling costs per unit. In this case, however, the lower costs are not the result of more units being produced in a given time; instead, they're attributed to efficiencies learned from producing the good over an extended period.

- Another source of first-mover advantage is network effect, which has less to do with cost and more to do with perceived value on the part of the user. A network effect is seen when the value per user rises as the total number of users rises. Network effects are in play in such businesses as eBay, LinkedIn, Google, eHarmony, and Amazon. For example, eBay, has value for users because many other buyers and sellers can be found on the site.

o Presumably, the first mover can gather many users and, thus, increase its own value to each user. That creates an advantage over the upstart who comes in with no users and has very little value to offer.

o Many Internet firms that are in businesses where network effects exist have pursued the so-called get-big-fast strategy. The first order of business here is to build a network effect as a defense against others who might come in later and try to compete; it's only after they've built the network that these firms figure out how to make money. In fact, this has been a powerful phenomenon for such firms as Facebook and LinkedIn.

o In markets with network effects, typically, there are high switching costs for users, which results in a lock-in effect. Users are, in effect, stuck with a particular good, service, or platform. From the perspective of the user, that may not be ideal. But from the perspective of a company offering a product or service, switching costs are wonderful.

o In some markets with strong network effects, not only is there a first-mover advantage, but the first mover can also come to be the dominant technology or firm—the so-called standard in the market. This is true of Microsoft Windows, which has 90% of the market share in the operating system market. Keep in mind, though, that with certain products or services, there may also be high demand for variety on the part of the customer. This is the case, for example, with video games, which have a wide array of customers.

Countering Conventional Wisdom

• The speed at which a given market or technology evolves can have a significant bearing on whether a dominant player will emerge with enduring first-mover advantage.

- One product for which there is fairly slow evolution of both technology and the market is Scotch tape. 3M created this product in a very slow-moving space and has been able to achieve enduring first-mover advantage.

- But in the personal computer business, where we've seen rapid technological obsolescence and a great deal of dynamic change over time, it's much more difficult to establish and maintain a first-mover advantage.

- Another reason that first movers don't always win is that there may be high costs involved in blazing a new technological trail. Such costs are known as *pioneering costs*. In particular, educating consumers about an entirely new product category may be expensive, and a great deal of change may take place early in a technology's existence. *Fast followers*—those who come in after a first mover—may be able to take advantage of the fact that you've blazed the trail, then move quickly to supersede you.

- Those who move first may also have to make certain commitments that can become rigid and difficult to change. First movers who have had initial success may become complacent or experience organizational inertia and may not be able to change as the market begins to evolve.

- In addition, first movers may fall into the *sunk cost trap*. They invest heavily in a particular technology or way of doing business, and even if they start to get negative feedback, they can't cut their losses and shift strategy. They become over-committed to an initial course of action and fail to adapt as markets evolve.

- Business researcher Greg Carpenter has noted that in many cases, pioneers in a field are not very well funded. They create a competitive game, but they're unable to dominate it because their resources are simply too limited.

- Despite the disadvantages first movers face, there are a number of situations in which pioneering may be the right strategy: if the expected life of a product category is very short, if the value of the product is highly subjective or intangible, if brand is important, and if the cost of imitation is high.

Economies of Scale
- Although we've said that economies of scale represent a source of first-mover advantage, managers often grossly overestimate the importance of this factor.

- Costs per unit certainly fall over time as volume increases in many businesses, but at some point, that curve begins to rise again. In other words, the costs per unit eventually start to rise again as a company gets too big, complex, and bureaucratic. Organizations grow to a point at which some inefficiency begins to be built in, and smaller firms then gain the advantage.

- In many cases, firms believe that bigger is better because that has been true in the past. For example, scale was a tremendous advantage for General Motors for much of the 20th century. But eventually, the firm's size became a liability. GM became vulnerable, because it wasn't as flexible and nimble as other firms.

Large companies may sometimes overestimate the importance of economies of scale and fail to realize the disadvantages they have relative to start-ups and entrepreneurs.

© gerenme/iStock/Thinkstock.

Learning Curves

- Learning curves can also be a significant source of first-mover advantage, but in some situations, firms may be unable to hold onto their learning or protect their intellectual property. The result is what scholars call *spillover effects*—when the learning a firm has achieved through experience spills out beyond the boundaries of the firm. A second mover can capture those spillovers and can learn from the first mover's mistakes.

- This issue is particularly problematic in economies without strong intellectual property protection, such as China. It's also challenging in situations where labor is very mobile and the knowledge that's being created cannot be easily protected through patents; such was the situation in Silicon Valley, for example.

Network Effects

- It seems that if network effects exist, it would always make sense for a firm to be first and get big fast. But think about social media. If network effects are so crucial in that business, then how is that Facebook was able to supplant early players, such as Friendster and Myspace?

- Misiek Piskorski is a scholar who studied social media platforms, and he concluded that for some certain networks, customers actually prefer a non-crowded space. They want more users—there's value as others use the site—but if too many people use the site, the value starts to turn negative.

- The example Piskorski gives is eHarmony. Users want to be on a dating platform where there is a wide variety of potential partners, but they don't want too many other people on the platform because that eventually causes competition.

- Felix Oberholzer-Gee at Harvard has also looked at possible downsides to the network effect. In social media, the early company Friendster pursued a get-big-fast strategy, trying to get customers in both Asia and North America.

○ But the Asian users generally weren't interested in interacting with American users and vice versa. Thus, spending money to build two giant sets of individuals on the network on two different continents didn't actually add a lot of value.

○ Friendster might have done better if it had focused on building the network in only one region, rather than trying to expend its resources to get big fast across two regions. That waste of resources made the company vulnerable to others—specifically, Facebook—which built a better platform with a more focused strategy.

○ Not only did Facebook focus on only one region, but it also focused initially on only one customer segment—college students. This focus created network effects but in a bounded way.

Diminishing First-Mover Advantage?

- Might there be less first-mover advantage today than there was several decades ago in business? As we've seen, incumbents seem to get toppled much more readily, and firms face much shorter periods of time during which they're able to achieve advantage and hold onto it.

- Some scholars have looked at platforms where users can sign on across multiple platforms and move their contacts easily. They have one profile that they can use on multiple networks and can move with their friends en masse from one platform to another. In these situations, users are not as locked in as they were previously, which means that first movers have less of an advantage.

- One strategy for dealing with situations where network effects exist has been described as the *freemium business model*. Here, a firm might give away a product for free but also have a premium offering that requirements payment. This model is used by LinkedIn, which has two levels of membership. The model makes sense for a firm that's trying to build a network quickly and if there are low marginal costs for adding new users.

- It's important to think carefully about the pluses and minuses of pioneering versus being a fast follower. Understand the sources of first-mover advantage and the limitations of those advantages. As an entrant or a follower, exploit the weaknesses in a pioneer's first-mover status. In short, don't buy the conventional wisdom: Being first is not always as advantageous as we think it is.

Suggested Reading

Anderson, *Free*.

Coughlan, "Leader's (Dis)Advantage."

Shankar and Carpenter, "Late Mover Strategy."

Shapiro and Varian. *Information Rules*.

Suarez and Lanzolla, "The Half-Truth of First Mover Advantage."

Questions to Consider

1. What are the pros and cons of being the first mover?

2. Why do first movers not always succeed, even when learning curves and network effects exist?

3. What are some examples of firms that have used network effects to achieve competitive advantage?

First Movers versus Fast Followers
Lecture 5—Transcript

In this lecture, I would like to challenge an important and commonly held view about strategy. Many entrepreneurs, many companies, believe that being first is crucial. You have to be first to market. They believe there's tremendous advantage from being first to market. Is that true? Should we believe that conventional wisdom? That's what I'd like to look at in this lecture.

What do we mean by first-mover advantage? We mean the competitive advantage established by virtue of the fact that a company has entered a market first and established a position. And yes, first movers sometimes do achieve tremendous advantage. Let's take a few examples: Gillette in razors; Sony in portable stereos with its Walkman product; Coca Cola in carbonated soft drinks; Hoover in vacuum cleaners. Each of those firms was first to market in their category, or early to market in their category, and they seemed to achieve a tremendous advantage by being early to market.

But, it's not always the case that first movers win. We certainly do have plenty of examples of first movers who did not succeed, or even who ended up completely out of the market. Who was the first, or at least one of the early players in social media? It was not Facebook; it was a company called Friendster, one many of you may not even recall. What about the first mover in VCRs, videocassette recorders? That would be Sony, but they bet on beta, and VHS became the technological standard. Sony did not become the winner, despite being the first mover. What about the first mover in Internet retailing? Do you remember eToys? They were very early moving to the web and offering products without any physical stores. What about Internet browsers? Do you remember Netscape? Search, was Google first? No, they were not.

One study, in fact, showed that pioneers were more successful than late movers in just 15 of 50 product categories. That is what research coming out of the Kellogg School of Management at Northwestern has shown. First-mover advantage, where does it come from? What are the causes of the situations where first movers do have advantage? Well, there are four major things that we can think about that help incumbents have advantage:

economies of scale, economies of scope, network effects, and learning effects. We're going to talk about each of those in turn. Let's delve into them a bit.

What does it mean for a firm to have economies of scale? What does it mean to have a learning advantage? What is a network effect? And might there also be some source of first-mover advantage from preempting access to scarce resources or assets? So, maybe you get the key locations or talented employees or key suppliers first. So these are all potential sources of first-mover advantage. If scale matters, if learning matters, if network effects matter, and if getting access to key assets is key, all those might be the basis for first-mover advantage.

What do we mean by economies of scale? Economies of scale exist in the business when the costs per unit to produce and distribute that good falls as you produce more units of the good in any given time period. So, the bigger, the better. The larger you are, the more your costs per unit come down. That's what we mean by economies of scale. And we can think of a number of businesses where such scale economies are pronounced. Toyota, in the automobile business, right? Their size and scale enables them to have lower costs of production than smaller firms. Bank of America in commercial banking, there are certain efficiencies that come from being a large nationwide and global financial institution.

Or even FedEx, for example, which operates a logistics company. Again, there's huge technological investments and infrastructure investments in that business. Any time you see these huge investments that have to be made, these very high fixed costs, well, the higher your volume, the more you're able to amortize those fixed costs over many units and bring your cost per unit down. That's what we mean by economies of scale.

Well, what about the learning curve? How is that different, a learning curve effect, from a scale effect? Well, in the case of a learning curve, what you have is, again, cost per unit falling. But this time, not because you produce more units today, but because you've been producing this good over some extended period of time. And over time, you've become more experienced at producing this good, you've learned how to do it more efficiently, and so your costs per unit fall over time; they fall as the total number of units you've ever produced continues to grow.

And we see this, for example, in the submarine manufacturing business. One of my first jobs in the private sector was at General Dynamics, maker of the Trident 688 and Seawolf submarines when I was there. And what we learned as we were projecting our costs on future summary contracts is, we knew there was a significant learning curve. When we produced the first Trident submarine, the cost to produce that was quite high, but our workers became more and more familiar with the boat, and they were able to bring costs down on each subsequent ship. We learned; our experience gave us great benefit.

So whether it's economies of scale or learning curves, in each case, the incumbent has the advantage. If you can get in there first, you can bring your cost down, because you can get bigger faster, and you can get more experience faster, before other players enter the business.

But there's another key source of competitive advantage, of first-mover advantage, that we need to discuss. And that's what we call network effects. This one is less understood, perhaps, by many business people than the issues of scale economies or learning curves. Network effects have less to do with cost and more to do with the perceived value on the part of the user. What is a network effect? It's when the value per user rises as the total number of users rises.

So let's think for a moment about buying a refrigerator. There's the value to me of a particular brand of refrigerator. Is it at all dependent on whether lots of other people buy that particular brand of refrigerator? The answer is largely, not. The value to each user of that particular refrigerator is independent of how many people use that refrigerator. But now, let's think about some other products and services. Let's think about eBay, LinkedIn, video games, Google, eHarmony, or Amazon. In each of these cases, the users of those products and services find that the value to each user rises as the number of users increases.

Let's see if we can explain this with regard to eBay, because some may not understand quite why and how that works, eBay, of course, the online auction marketplace that has come to be very, very successful since the mid-1990s. Well, what is the value to each user of eBay? Well, let's think about a new online auction marketplace that was to come to be. Suppose an entrepreneur launched an online auction marketplace to compete with eBay. What would the value be to each user?

Well in the early days, with very few users, there would be very little value to each customer. Why? Because each customer would look and say, this is only valuable to me if there are many other people with whom I can buy and sell goods. Without many other people with whom I can interact, this service, as pretty as the website may be, and as cool is the branding campaign may be, this service isn't really valuable to me. But eBay, this is valuable to me. There's great value.

Why? Because I can go on that site and find many other buyers and sellers. If I have an item that I'm looking to sell, there'll be lots of interested parties out there with whom I can transact. And hopefully, I can get a good price as a result. If I'm looking to buy, I'm hoping there's many sellers offering the same good, and I can look for the best price. So there's value to me as more users enter the network.

This is also true with LinkedIn and other social-media platforms. LinkedIn is a professional networking platform, social media platform, for professionals in a variety of fields, including business. What's the value to me of using LinkedIn? Well, it rises significantly as many other colleagues in different institutions join the LinkedIn network, because now I have people with whom I can share ideas, with whom I can network, with whom I can look for jobs, etc.

Google, what's the network effect in the search business? Well, the more people that use Google, the more Google is able to refine its search algorithms, the more it learns and becomes smarter about being able to predict what each of us wants when we go to the site and try to search. So the more people that use the site, the smarter Google becomes, the more value to each of us of the site.

And what about Amazon? Where's the network effect there? Well, many people go to Amazon, and they review products that they've purchased. It began, of course, with their famous book reviews, but now, there are reviews for a whole array of items that Amazon offers on its site. Well, the more people that go to Amazon, the more people review products and services, the more value to me of using Amazon as a service to buy goods. Why? Because more others using the site means more reviews, means more information for me as I try to decide which brand of that particular item that I'd like to purchase.

So each of these examples, the value to each user rises as more users come on board. Why, then, does this phenomenon lead to first-mover advantage? Well, because presumably, the first mover can gather lots of users, and as such, they can increase their value to each user, and that creates an advantage over the upstart who comes in with no users and has very little value to offer. So, many of these new-economy firms, many Internet firms, who are in businesses where network effects exist, have pursued the so-called get-big-fast strategy. Get a lot of users to create that higher value per user. Ultimately, we'll find out how to make money later. Right now, let's build the network effect as a defense against others who choose to come in and try to compete with us. And this has been a powerful, powerful phenomenon with firms like Facebook or LinkedIn, with companies like eBay and Amazon.

In markets with these network effects, you should note that, typically, there are high switching costs for users, and when switching costs are high, users encounter a lock-in effect. They're, in effect, stuck with a particular good or service, or platform. From the perspective of the user, that may not be ideal. But from the perspective of a company offering a product or service, switching costs are a wonderful thing. You'd like your customer to be locked-in to you.

Why are customers locked in to a firm like LinkedIn? Well, let's think about that for a moment. Are there high switching costs if you were to switch to another platform for professional networking? Of course there are, because if I switch, but none of my colleagues at my firm and other firms switch, well then what value is there to me of this new platform? So, I have to be able to get all of my colleagues to switch as well. That's difficult. And recreating my new network, all those contacts, all those interconnections on a new platform, that's going to be very difficult; that's going to be time consuming; that's going to be inefficient. So the switching costs are high; it keeps me locked in to a firm like LinkedIn. And that's true with a number of platforms where network effects exist.

What are the sources of these switching costs? Well, there are many sources. Let me just touch on a couple. First, if there are any durable purchases, if there's any equipment you must buy to use a particular product or service, that locks you in. So in the video-game case, you buy a console to play a particular set of games. That console, whether it's the PlayStation or the Xbox, that's a durable purchase, and now, that's locked you in to buying video games from that same company or its partners.

Brand-specific training can be a source of lock-in; if you've had to do some training so that you know a particular service or a platform, and that, of course, creates switching costs. If there are specialized suppliers, that may also create switching costs, or contractual commitments that you've had to make. Loyalty programs can create switching costs as well, if you have something where you've been rewarded for your loyalty and you will continue to be, you may be reluctant to switch. All of these issues create lock-in and make it good for companies as they try to retain their customers.

So, in some of these markets, where strong network effects exist, not only is there a first-mover advantage, but that first mover can come to be the dominant technology or firm. They can become the so-called standard in that market. We see that in certain cases. Right? Microsoft with Windows becoming a dominant player with 90% market share in the operating system business. So not only did the network effects enable them to have first-mover advantage, but they became the standard, almost completely dominating the market.

But that's not always the case. Why is that? Because in certain products or services, while there may be strong network effects, there's also high demand for variety on the part of the customer. The customer doesn't want only one solution. And so, one dominant standard doesn't come to prevail, but several standards come to co-exist. So let's take video games. In video games, there are strong network effects. Right? There is value to me if other people use the Sony PlayStation. I can share games with them; I can perhaps rent games more easily; I know that if others use the platform, then developers are more likely build cool games for that platform. So there's definitely more value to me if more people use the same platform I'm using.

Network effects exist. But, there's also high demand for variety. There's a wide array of people who play video games, from the casual gamer, to young children, to the hardcore gamer in their 20s who's perhaps the male living in their mother's basement playing video games. There are lots of different people with different tastes and preferences playing, and as a result, despite strong network effects, one player hasn't come to dominate the market. And right now, we're looking at three players who coexist—Xbox, PlayStation, and Nintendo, with its Wii family of products. So, sometimes we see a dominant standard, but if there's high demand for variety and a really heterogeneous customer base, we may see multiple firms come to coexist, and the first mover alone doesn't win.

Now, this leads me to a really important point. Can we identify some characteristics of situations when first movers definitely had the advantage and others where, perhaps, not so much? Well, one framework has looked at the fact that market evolution and technological evolution—the speed at which both the market evolves and technology evolves—that has a great bearing on whether we'll see a standard or a dominant player who moved first see enduring advantage.

So, let's take a market where we've seen fairly slow evolution of both technology and the market itself, like Scotch tape. Right? 3M creates a product, Scotch tape, very, very slow-moving space where they've been able to achieve first-mover advantage, and it has endured. But in the personal computer business, where we've seen rapid technological obsolescence and lots of dynamic changes over time, much harder for someone to establish and maintain a first-mover advantage.

And this is really key—the notion that first movers don't always win, that the conventional wisdom is not correct, that there's a real downside to first-mover advantage. Well, why? First and most importantly, there are high costs in some cases of blazing a new trail technologically. Some people call these pioneering costs. What does that mean? It means sometimes, moving into an entirely new category with a product customers don't know anything about, well, there's a lot of uncertainty there. There's a lot of education of the consumer that needs to take place. There's a lot of change that will happen early in that technology's existence. And so moving first can have its disadvantages, because those fast followers, the people who come in second and third, they can watch the mistakes you've made; they can learn from those; and they can catapult beyond you. They can take advantage of the fact that you've blazed the trail and then moved quickly to supersede you.

There's also a problem, though, that you make certain commitments when you move first. Those commitments, as we've noted, can become rigid, and they could become hard for you to change. If you've had success as a first mover initially, you can become complacent or experience organizational inertia and not be able to change as the market begins to evolve.

And finally, there's the sunk-cost trap. The bottom line is, you begin to invest in a particular technology, in a particular way of doing business; you are the first mover. And now, even if you start to get negative feedback, you can't cut your losses and shift strategy. Instead, you're beholden to what you've already invested, and you throw good money after bad. You become over committed to your initial course of action because of all the emotion, and the money, and the effort you've put into it. That sunk-cost trap definitely inhibits many first movers from adapting as markets evolve, and it's why second movers come in and supersede them in many cases.

Pioneering a new category can be expensive, and it's really interesting to watch how second movers, often large firms, but are agile enough, they have money; they have resources, but they have agility. They can come in and pass you by. And there's a great quote from Greg Carpenter who is a researcher in this field, who's shown that second movers often do better than first movers. He said, "A lot of times, pioneers are not very well funded. They create a competitive game, and then they're unable to dominate it. Their resources are just too limited. So competitors enter quickly and, with more resources, are able to win the game that the pioneer has created." We see this in many situations, right? Where eToys comes in; they're an entrepreneurial upstart. They see the future. They know retailing on the web is going to be a dominant trend, but they don't really have the resources; they don't have it all figured out. So they pioneer the way, but then others pass them by.

Well, when should you pioneer? When is it that that may be the right strategy? Well, if the expected life of a product category is very short, then being first may be important, because, if there's only a short time window, let's take advantage of it. If the value of the product is highly subjective or intangible, it may be important to be the first mover. Right? If brand matters a lot, establishing that brand, because the product is somewhat intangible and its perceived value is very subjective.

And finally, if the cost of imitation is high. Why might it be high? Well, if there's patents or other barriers that second movers will face. If you can protect intellectual property, then the cost of imitating will be high, and so being first can have tremendous advantage. And maybe then, you should pioneer.

But first members don't always win, and in part, it's because they overestimate the importance of economies of scale, learning curves, and network effects. All those things that are sources of first-mover advantage, sometimes we over attribute success to those sources of advantage. We rely on them too much, and therefore we think that being first will lead to great performance and sustainable advantage.

Let's think about economies of scale for a moment. I would argue that managers often grossly overestimate the economies of scale in a business. Why? Well, costs per unit certainly do fall over time as volume increases in many businesses, whether it's automobile manufacturing, or the logistics business at FedEx, and others. But at some point, that curve begins to rise again. In other words, the costs per unit, eventually, start to rise again as you get too big, too complex, too bureaucratic. There is some point where bigger is no longer better, where eventually, you've grown your organization to a point where there's some inefficiency that begins to be built in and where smaller firms now have the advantage over you.

Why do firms overestimate economies of scale? In many cases, they believe bigger is better because that has been true up to a point. So they believe it will continue to be true, and they don't see the limits of those economies. They don't see where it will begin to turn negative for them. If we look at General Motors in the automobile business, scale was a tremendous advantage for them for much of the 20th century. But eventually, they became so big, so bureaucratic, so complex to manage, that it became a liability. They became vulnerable, because they weren't as flexible and nimble as other firms. Leaders like to lead large firms, right? They believe in the power of big if they're the incumbent player, and they don't realize sometimes the liabilities, the disadvantages they have relative to the upstart and the entrepreneur.

Learning curves have an issue, as well, that we have to consider. Learning curves can be a tremendous source of advantage, but what happens if we're in a situation where we can't hold all that learning tight, where we can't protect our intellectual property? Scholars call these spillover effects. What if the learning that we're achieving through experience, through being in the marketplace for some period of time and having produced it, we become and better at producing it over time. What if that learning spills out beyond the boundaries of our firm? And if that's the case, then being first no longer is as much of an advantage. The second mover can capture those spillovers, can learn from us, including from our mistakes, and pass us.

This issue is particularly problematic in economies without strong intellectual property protection. So in Asia, in China, for example, where we don't have those laws that are able to protect the intellectual property, or if we're in situations where labor is very mobile and knowledge that's being created is not the type you can easily protect through patents, think Silicon Valley, for example, in these situations, where we can't protect and hold proprietary what we've learned, the learning curve no longer becomes a source of first-mover advantage. Now the second mover can grab that labor that's mobile, can grab that knowledge that can't be patented, or perhaps, can even grab knowledge that's patentable, because there aren't strong intellectual property protections built into the law. In each of those cases, the learning curve no longer conveys first-mover advantage as much as it does in some cases where you can protect your intellectual property. You can keep learning proprietary.

How about network effects? Surely, that's the one where, if they exist, it will always make sense to be first and to get in fast. Well, maybe not. I mean, let's think about social media, for example. If network effects are so crucial in that business, then how come Facebook came along, and not only did supplant early members like Friendster, but it overwhelmed a company like Myspace as well.

So, even in a case where the network effect exists and where lots of entrepreneurs believing these network effects exist are pursuing get-big-fast strategies, is it right? Are they correct? Well, Misiek Piskorski is a scholar who's looked at social media platforms in great detail. And he's looked and said, sometimes, there are certain networks where the customer actually prefers a non-crowded network. They don't want too many other users on the site. They want more users; there's value as others use the site, but as too many people use the site, the value starts to turn negative again.

The example he gives is eHarmony. He says, we want to be on a dating platform where there are lots of others who post on the platform. We want a variety of other potential partners. But we don't want too many, because eventually we run into competition. We want to date a certain person, but too many others want to date that person as well, and some of them may be more attractive to that other individual than we are. And so, there's some limits to how many other users sometimes we want.

Felix Oberholzer-Gee, at Harvard, has also looked at this issue of might there be some downsides to the network effect? And he looked at why and how Friendster failed in social media and why Facebook survived. He said, Friendster pursued a first come, first served strategy, trying to get big fast. They pursued customers around the world in both Asia and North America. But he said, there was an interesting problem; the Asian users generally didn't really care much about being on the same network and interacting with U.S. users, and vice versa. So spending all the money to build two giant sets of individuals on the network in two different continents didn't actually add a lot of value. They might have done better if they just focused on building the network within one region than trying to expend all those resources to getting big fast across two regions. And that waste of resources made them vulnerable to others who came in and built a better platform with more focus in their strategy.

Who was more focused? Facebook was. What did they do? Not only did Facebook focus on one region, but they also focused, initially, on one customer segment. How did Facebook begin? They began with someone at Harvard who took the physical Facebook that had pictures and backgrounds on all of the members of the first-year class and putting that up on the web. And they began, then—Mark Zuckerberg, the founder—began then creating this network for college students, people who had an e-mail address that ended in .edu. This focus created network effects, but in a bounded way. And Gee, in his scholarship on Friendster and its demise, has argued that indiscriminate growth often undermines the very network effects you're trying to achieve. And he would argue that's what happened at a firm like Friendster. The more focused strategy, still creating value as more users joined Facebook, but with some boundaries, was more successful.

Are there lower switching costs today? Might there be less first-mover advantage today than there was several decades ago in business? This is an interesting question that's been asked recently. You know, as we see, incumbents get toppled much more readily, and firms face much shorter periods of time during which they're able to achieve advantage and hold onto it. Some have begun to ask, maybe it's just easier today to switch to a new rival, to a new upstart, and therefore, first-mover advantage is not as crucial, not as enduring, as it once was.

And this is some interesting scholarship by Eyal and Choudary, where they've argued that as we've moved to things like LinkedIn, where we can move our contacts very easily, where we can log in with universal logins and sign-ons across multiple platforms, as we begin to do this, what's happened is we're not as locked in. We can port our contacts from one platform to the other. We can move en masse with our friends from one platform to the other. We can have one profile that we can now use to log in to multiple networks. As all of that's happened, we're facing a situation where it's easier to switch for customers, and we're not as locked in. And therefore, first movers have less of an advantage.

Now interestingly, one strategy for dealing with situations where network effects exist and where firms are trying to achieve first-mover advantage, one strategy for that is what's been described as the freemium business model. Some firms give away their products for free, and then they have a premium offering for which people can pay. LinkedIn does this, for example. When does that make sense? Well, it makes sense if there are strong network effects. You're trying to build your network as fast as you can. But it only makes sense if, also, we know that there are low marginal costs for adding new users.

If we can add new users without a lot of additional expense, then getting big fast and getting a lot of free people on the site, and then trying to offer premium services, that makes sense. But if there are high marginal costs of any new users, and you can cost yourself a lot of money, and you can get deep in the red and perhaps even go bankrupt trying to get big fast. So freemium can be an effective strategy, but only if there are low marginal costs for adding new users coupled with those strong network effects.

The lessons, then. Think carefully about the pluses and minuses of pioneering versus being a fast follower. Understand the sources of first-mover advantage and the limitations of those advantages. As an entrant or a follower, exploit the weaknesses in a pioneer's first mover status. In short, don't buy the conventional wisdom. Being first, being early, is not always as advantageous as we think it is.

So now, your assignment. Consider Boeing, think about Boeing, one of the leaders in airplane manufacturing. And ask yourself, why did the firm have such powerful first-mover advantage with regard to the jumbo-jet business? What is it, what were the sources of advantage they had by being first? And then contrast that with personal digital assistance. Why were the early the movers in the 1980s and early '90s, such as Apple's Newton product, why were they not successful? What happened that caused the first movers there not to have enduring advantage over time?

When Netflix Met Blockbuster
Lecture 6

In this lecture, we'll go back to 1999 and take a look at the retail chain Blockbuster, which sold and rented videos. At the time, Blockbuster's mainstream customers were 30- to 45-year-old soccer moms, living in the suburbs with their families and looking to rent new movie releases on VHS tapes. In the same year, Netflix began offering its service, which allowed people to rent movies through the mail by subscription. Its mainstream customers were 18- to 29-year-old males who watched DVDs rather than tapes and were interested in cult classics and independent films. In this lecture, we'll look at how Blockbuster reacted to the disruptive innovation in the industry presented by Netflix.

Disruptive versus Incremental Innovation

- In 1999, Blockbuster's market research probably revealed that its customers wanted more copies of hit movies to be available in stores. In response, the company began to guarantee just that—that its stores would have new releases on hand to rent. The "new release" section of the stores changed from a small area to an entire wall and, later, to the entire perimeter of the store.

- However, the potential Netflix customer—the young men who liked cult classics—were dissatisfied with this change. There was no room on the shelves for old movies because new releases had crowded them out. Further, these customers disliked late fees because they didn't have much money and because they liked to keep movies longer and watch them multiple times.

- In making the change, Blockbuster pursued *incremental innovation*. The company conducted focus groups and surveys among its mainstream customers and, in response to their suggestions, offered a small improvement in its service. But Netflix presented a *disruptive innovation*—a fundamentally different product, service, or business model—that undermined Blockbuster's competitive advantage.

- As we've said, there are three main external threats to competitive advantage: imitation, substitution, and holdup. In many ways, substitution is the most serious of these, and that's the threat that Netflix presented. Substitution is often hard to foresee and, perhaps, even harder to respond to.

- Many years ago, the economist Joseph Schumpeter wrote about the need to look beyond your direct rivals when thinking about the principal threat to your competitive advantage. He said that attention is often focused exclusively on competition within a rigid pattern of invariant conditions, methods of production, and forms of industrial organization. But in reality, that kind of competition is not as threatening as the competition from a new commodity, new technology, or new type of organization.

- Earlier in his academic career, Harvard Business School professor Clay Christensen traced the evolution of the disk drive industry from 1976 through 1992, watching as a series of technological innovations came to market and observing what happened to the players in that market.
    - From a technological perspective, the physical size of the disk drive shrank dramatically during that time. Moreover, the cost per megabyte of storage dropped substantially. In this situation, Christensen observed that the incumbent leaders in one generation of technology often were not able to maintain their leadership in the next technological generation.

    - Christensen argued that the incumbent players were intent on pursuing incremental innovation—minor improvements to the attributes that mainstream customers valued. In contrast, disruptive innovators introduced a different package of attributes from the ones that mainstream customers typically valued. Indeed, disruptive innovators often performed significantly worse on certain attributes that mainstream customers valued highly, but their performance trajectory was steep for the disruptive innovations.

○ In our example, Netflix wasn't focused on such attributes as in-store experience or availability of new releases. In fact, Netflix performed significantly worse on some of these attributes. But Netflix was focused on renting older movies, and it came up with a new way of doing business for that purpose. Initially, Netflix didn't perform well, but the company improved at a rapid rate.

Challenges in the Face of Disruption

- In the face of disruptive innovation, incumbent firms often struggle a great deal. According to Christensen and his coauthor, Joseph Bower, the sources of incumbents' problems are traditional market research and traditional resource allocation processes.

- Of course, traditional market research focuses on gathering feedback from customers. But customers tend to think in terms of incremental improvement— minor adjustments a firm might make to increase customer satisfaction. Customers don't think in terms of totally new ways of doing business.

- In addition, incumbent firms tend to have rigorous financial criteria for allocating their investment dollars. If someone has a new idea, the firm looks to cost-benefit analysis or return-on-investment figures

As Blockbuster learned, conducting market research with typical customers tends to result in incremental innovation; it doesn't help you foresee disruptive innovation.

to determine whether the idea makes economic sense. With an idea that's completely new or involves cutting-edge technology, it's difficult to come up with precise financial models. Large firms also often fear that a new product or service will cannibalize an existing one.

- Another reason that incumbent firms struggle so much with disruptive innovation is *mental lock-in*. Such firms get stuck in a particular mental model of how to make money in their markets and don't consider alternatives that may be introduced by disruptive innovations.

    o For example, Polaroid was built on a deeply imbedded razors-and-blades business model: Sell cameras to people at relatively low cost, and they will buy film for many years to come. In fact, Polaroid made most of its money on film.

    o Many people believe that Polaroid simply failed to recognize the revolution in digital photography, but that's not the case. Substantial research and development activity in digital technology took place at Polaroid, but senior executives were strongly resistant to giving this new technology the resources needed to go to market because they were wedded to the old business model.

The Long Tail

- The *long tail* is an idea put forth by Chris Anderson, the former editor of *Wired* magazine. Anderson looked at the largest brick-and-mortar music retailer in the United States, Walmart, which at the time of his study, carried about 4,500 unique CD titles, or about 55,000 songs.

- Most of the activity in the music section of Walmart stores centered on the hits. The top 200 albums—about 5% of the albums in the section—accounted for 90% of Walmart's music sales at any given point in time. In this, Walmart's music business exhibited the usual pattern found in hit-driven businesses (books, movies, and music) before the Internet.

- But Anderson noticed something different when he looked at some of the emerging technologies of entertainment, such as Rhapsody, a digital music service. Rhapsody carried more than 1.5 million songs, and a big chunk of its sales also came from hit songs. But Rhapsody also reported that songs ranked as low as 900,000 on its popularity charts were streamed at least once per quarter.

- Anderson noticed the same phenomenon in other new economy firms: 21% of Netflix's revenue was generated from movies not available at Blockbuster; 40% of Rhapsody's revenue was generated from music not available at Walmart; and 25% of Amazon's book business was generated from books not available in brick-and-mortar stores. The long tail is the idea that a great deal of revenue can be generated from products that are low in popularity.

- According to Anderson, traditional entertainment retailers made all their money from the hits. Hybrid retailers, selling physical goods through catalogs or online sites, could make money from many more items because they could stock more of those items in a distribution center than in a physical store. And purely digital retailers could make money on an even wider array of products. No matter how low in popularity an item is, the cost to add it to a digital library is so low that a digital retailer can make virtually any song or movie available even if there is only one customer who wants it.

- Anderson also noted that social networking, customer reviews, playlists, blogs, and other forms of social media drive demand for these niche products, rather than mass marketing. Beyond that, digital retailers can collect information about customers and build sophisticated algorithms to create customized recommendations for them. Netflix, for example, built a huge customer database, and the predictive power of its algorithms was quite high. When Blockbuster tried to catch up, it wasn't able to capitalize on the same network effect.

Reacting to Disruptive Innovation

- In his work on disruptive innovation, Clay Christensen argued that incumbent firms must create a separate unit or subsidiary to react to an upstart entry and wall this unit off from the mainstream business. This separation is necessary because without it, the mainstream business will squash the innovation in an effort to protect its profit margins.

- Some have critiqued Christensen's theory of disruptive innovation, and in fact, it may be an overused concept. It's a good descriptive tool but not necessarily a good predictive one. In addition, Christensen focuses on the idea of incumbent firms missing a disruptive threat, but he doesn't address the misguided investments firms can make when they misperceive a threat. Creating a new unit to cope with a threat may not always be wise.

- It's also important to consider the competitive advantage that comes from an integrated system of activities. If a firm creates a separate unit to go after a new idea, will it still have an integrated system of activities, or will the firm become disjointed?

Suggested Reading

Anderson, *The Long Tail*.

Christensen, *The Innovator's Dilemma*.

Lepore, "The Disruption Machine."

Questions to Consider

1. How do resource allocation processes in large organizations stifle radical innovation?

2. How have many innovators capitalized on the long-tail phenomenon to build successful businesses?

3. Why has the theory of disruptive innovation become so widely embraced and, perhaps, misused at times?

When Netflix Met Blockbuster
Lecture 6—Transcript

Let's go back to 1999 and take a look at a retail chain called Blockbuster. You remember them. Selling videos, rentals, to Americans. Who was the Blockbuster mainstream customer in 1999? They were a 30- to 45-year-old mom, so-called soccer mom, living in the suburbs, husband, two kids, and a dog, driving a minivan or an SUV, renting VHS tapes at the time. Coming to Blockbuster on a Friday or Saturday night, stopping for take out at the same strip mall or a nearby one at the Blockbuster store. And they were looking for new releases. Recent hits that had just come to the store having been in the theaters several months earlier.

Now contrast that with the original Netflix customer. In 1999, Netflix began offering its service to Americans. Who was that original Netflix customer? Were they the same as the mainstream Blockbuster customer? They were not. They tended to be an 18–29-year-old male. Where were they living? Many of them in their mother's basement or dorm room. They weren't renting VHS tapes; they were trying out a new technology called DVDs. Were they watching on a flat screen television? No, they couldn't afford one. They were watching DVDs on a computer, often on a laptop. And they weren't always renting new releases.

What were they watching? Old, cult classics, independent films, and tried-and-true films, like Caddy Shack and Star Wars, Monty Python movies and The Godfather. They weren't necessarily simply watching new releases, as the families often did when mom brought home the latest and greatest hit that had been in theaters just a few months earlier.

Now, what's interesting about this is to think about Blockbuster's market research at the time in 1999. They were conducting focus groups and surveys with their mainstream customer. They were asking that soccer mom what she liked and disliked about Blockbuster. And what was her main criticism of Blockbuster stores? She wanted more copies of hit movies. Why? Well, she could recall those instances where little Sally, her six-year-old, had cried all the way home because blockbuster didn't have any more copies of *Finding Nemo*. And the store had had posters for weeks saying that on May 1 *Finding Nemo* would be hitting the stores and available for rental.

So what did Blockbuster do? They had to offer more copies. So they began to offer their guarantee that they would have available the movies that were just hitting their stores. And so they went from one area, small area, of new releases to an entire wall of new releases in the store. Soon, it was multiple walls of the store, the entire perimeter, lined with the new releases, sometimes with 50, 60, 70 copies of a particular movie. Well, who is getting more disenchanted with Blockbuster as this is going on? The mom is happy, because now little Sally is not crying. But the 18- to 29-year-old male, they're really upset. Now they can't find Caddy Shack, not because some other young man has rented it, but because Caddy Shack is no longer available at any Blockbuster store. There's no more room on the shelves for certain old movies, because new releases have crowded them out.

What's the young male's other big complaint about Blockbuster? Late fees. You remember those. If you didn't return your movie within 48 hours, they whacked you with a fee, sometimes equal to the amount you paid to rent the movie. Why did the young male hate late fees? He didn't have much money. He was an irresponsible young male who wanted to watch the movie 10 times, never leave his basement, and who always forgot to return the movies when they were due. He wanted to watch that movie often. That was key. That was key. He hated the late fees.

Now, what's a lesson from this story? Lesson from this story is that Blockbuster was pursuing what we call incremental innovation. They were talking to their customer and offering small improvements in their service, in their in-store experience, in the availability of the movies. But along came Netflix with what we call a disruptive innovation, a fundamentally different product and service, in fact, a whole new business model, and it undermined Blockbuster's competitive advantage.

Recall that we talked about the main threats to competitive advantage. We said there were three main external threats to competitive advantage. The first was imitation. When someone does what you're doing but finds a way to do it better. Then there was substitution, where someone comes along with an alternative product or service that fulfills the same human need. And finally, there was hold up, when either your buyers or your suppliers gain leverage over you and begin to extract more of the profit from the value chain.

In many ways, the most serious threat is substitution, and that's what we're seeing here with Netflix offering, really, a substitute to the traditional brick-and-mortar store that rented movies to customers. Why is the most serious threat substitution in many cases? It's because it's so hard to foresee, and perhaps it's even harder to respond to, as we will see with Blockbuster.

You know, Joseph Schumpeter, the great economist, wrote many years ago about the need to look beyond your direct rivals when thinking about the principal threat to your competitive advantage. He said, it is still competition within a rigid pattern of invariant conditions, methods of production, and forms of industrial organization that practically monopolizes attention. But in capitalist reality, as distinct from its textbook picture, it's not that kind of competition which counts, but the competition from the new commodity, new technology, new type of organization. This kind of competition is much more effective than the other as a bombardment is in comparison with forcing the door. Schumpeter was telling us that, in fact, this threat of substitution comes out of left field and often poses the most serious threat.

We have a classic study of this idea of disruptive innovation. In fact, the author who coined this term was a man named Clay Christensen. Clay Christensen had been in the business world for many years and then returned to Harvard Business School to pursue his doctorate in the early 1990s. And he conducted a study for his dissertation on the disk-drive industry. And he traced the evolution of that industry from 1976 through 1992, watching as a series of technological innovations came to market and observing what happened to the players in that market.

From a technological perspective, the physical size of the disk drive shrank dramatically during that time. Moreover, the cost per megabyte of storage dropped substantially. Well, that is what was happening from a technology standpoint. What happened in the market? Well, he observed that the incumbent leaders in one generation of technology often were not able to maintain their leadership in the next technological generation. So we saw a new player emerge as the leader in each subsequent evolution of disk-drive technology.

Now, why was that? What was going on? Well, Christensen argued that the incumbent players were intent on pursuing what he called sustaining or incremental innovation, minor improvements to the attributes that mainstream customers valued. They were doing their market research, listening to those small changes that might enhance customer satisfaction, and implementing them. But what about those disruptive innovators? The people who entered the market and supplanted those leaders. The disruptive innovation was something very different. These innovators were introducing a quite different package of attributes from the ones that mainstream customers typically valued. They often perform significantly worse on certain attributes that the mainstream customers valued a lot, but their performance trajectory was steep for these disruptive innovations.

Think about this in terms of Netflix. They weren't focused on the attributes that Blockbuster was focused on. They had no stores. So, in-store experience, availability of new releases, these were not things they focused on. They performed significantly worse, in fact, on new-release availability. Netflix didn't want to be in the new-release business; they, in fact, were intent on being in the business of renting older movies. Well, for doing that, for renting older movies, they came up with an entire new way of doing business, and they performed, initially not so well, but they were on that steep trajectory, improving at a rapid rate. And while Blockbuster took a while to respond, by the time they did respond, Netflix had improved considerably and now was a formidable competitor.

Well, you might wonder, why do incumbent firms struggle so much? Why did Blockbuster struggle? Why did the incumbent players in the disk-drive industry struggle so much to respond to this disruptive innovation? We'll start with two main reasons that Christensen and his co-author, Joseph Bauer, articulated in an article in the mid-1990s based on this research. They looked to traditional market research and traditional resource allocation processes within the incumbent firms as sources of the problem.

Let's take a look at this. First, traditional market research. Every marketing guru tells companies, you must listen to your customers. You must be more customer centric. Put the customer first. The customer is boss, you hear. But when you ask the customer about your product or service, what type of feedback do you receive? The customer, it turns out, thinks mostly in terms of incremental improvement, the minor adjustments you might make to make them more satisfied, to make them happier. They don't think in terms of totally new ways of doing business. The customer can't see the future in that way in many cases. You know, Steve Jobs said, you don't invent the iPod through a focus group. Steven Spielberg said, you don't come out with a groundbreaking new movie by focus group. So talking to customers is important, but it tends to be good at incremental innovation and not so much at helping you foresee disruptive innovation.

But there's another piece that's important here, and that has to do with resource allocation processes. What do we mean by a resource allocation process? Well, every firm has to have some way of deciding how to allocate scarce investment dollars. So they have to have some way of assessing requests for major capital investments. And how do they do that? Well, incumbent firms tend to have rigorous financial practices for doing so. What do they ask for when someone has an idea? They ask for a model. They ask for an estimate of the return on investment. And employees will use financial techniques, like discounted cash flow, or cost benefit analysis, ROI techniques, other things, to try to understand whether it makes economic sense to pursue this new idea.

But think about it for a moment, if you've got an idea that's really out of left field, that's totally new, that's a cutting-edge technology, can you actually do a very sophisticated financial analysis? To do so, you'd have to be able, with precision, estimate the revenues that you will generate, the size of the market opportunity, the costs of bringing that product or service to market. In a really bleeding-edge technological situation, it's going to be very hard to come up with that kind of precise financial model.

So, there's a bias built in at incumbent firms. That bias is built in, and it tends to lead to the funding of incremental innovation, because an incremental innovation is one that's building just as a minor addition off of the existing product or service. As a result, you can be much more precise in estimating the new revenues you generate or the cost savings that you will produce by implementing this sustaining innovation.

So big firms tend to shuttle their resources toward people who can make a good financial case. And the incremental innovators, well, they can make their case much more effectively than the bleeding-edge technological leaders, who come in there and have to say, I don't know a lot when trying to represent their cost-benefit analysis. Big firms don't want to hear, I don't know. They don't want to hear, it's uncertain. They want to hear, this is what the benefits and costs will be. And so there's a bias to incremental innovation.

There's also a fear of big firms that this new product or service may cannibalize our existing product or service. If we move online at Blockbuster, well, that will take traffic away from our stores. We'll kill the golden goose. We can't do that. So big firms worry about that; they don't want to take revenue away from a product or service that's been so successful and that's profitable in hopes that this new idea could someday, down the road, become as profitable.

But there's other reasons why incumbent firms struggle so much with disruptive innovation. Richard Foster was a long-time partner at McKinsey Consulting. He talked about the idea of mindset. And he said, many large firms end up in a situation of what he called mental lock-in. They get stuck in a particular mental model of how you make money in a particular business. And the problem, he said, is disruptive technologies, well, they not only have a different set of product attributes that they're bringing to market, sometimes they have a fundamentally different business model. And the incumbent firm can't wrap their heads around that new business model, because they're so used to making money in a certain way.

Let's take a look at an example of that. You all remember that, at one point in time, Polaroid was a dominant brand in the world in the field of instant photography. They were a long-time leader not only with a great product, but it was backed by great science and manufacturing and distribution capabilities. Polaroid was built around a deeply held business model. Razors and blades, something that we've talked about. The idea that you got people the camera; you sold it to them at cost, maybe even at a loss. Why? Because once they had that Polaroid camera, they had to buy film, the so-called blades, and they had to buy that film for many years to come.

So Polaroid did not make its money on the hardware, on the camera, they made all their money on the film. And it was incredibly lucrative. Now, the story that many have heard is that they simply failed to see the digital revolution, that they were caught completely off guard, and they never realized the world was going to move to digital. That's actually not the reality. A case study by Tripsas and Gavetti looks in detail at what happened with the demise of Polaroid.

They found that, in fact, substantial research and development activity was taking place going all the way back to the 1980s in the Polaroid labs. They were working on digital technology, but they were very late coming to market with that technology. Why was that? Was it the scientists' fault? Did they not see the future? Tripsas and Gavetti conclude that it was not. They find, in fact, that there was strong resistance from senior management, who did not want to advance the project, did not want to give this new technology, digital cameras, the resources needed to go to market. They were hesitant. Why?

They were wedded to an old business model. Let me see if I can explain that. In Tripsas and Gavetti's research, they interviewed someone who worked in the labs on the research and development with regard to digital cameras. And he said at one point, the catch to our product concept was that you had to be in the hardware business to make money. How could you say that? Where's the film? There's no film. So what we had was a constant fight with the senior executive management in Polaroid for five years. In other words, what he was saying was, the razors-and-blades model didn't fit with regard to digital technology. Now, there was no film, so now you had to make money off of the hardware. You had to generate a strong profit margin from selling the digital camera with no profit to come from the blades, from the film.

Well, that new business model didn't fit at all with the way Polaroid had operated for years, and management was stuck. They had a mental lock-in phenomenon taking place. And they couldn't adapt quickly enough, and they didn't allocate the resources to people working on that new technology in their very own research and development laboratories.

Netflix, too, was bringing a different business model, not just a different product or service, to market. And here, their business model was dependent on something that Chris Anderson, the former editor of Wired Magazine, called the long tail in a great book that he published several years ago. What's the long tail and how does it work? And why was it so different than the traditional Blockbuster model?

Well, in Anderson's book, published several years ago, he took a look, at the time, at the largest brick-and-mortar music retailer in the United States. That was Walmart. And he looked, and he said, he noticed that they carried about 4,500 unique CD titles, or about 55,000 songs. Moreover, most of the activity in the Walmart store in their music section was about the hits. The top 200 albums accounted for 90% of Walmart's music sales at any given point in time. Thus, roughly 5% of the albums on the shelves accounted for 90% of their revenue.

Walmart's music business exhibited the usual pattern found in hit-driven businesses before the Internet. We see this in books, in movies, in music. Entertainment businesses, in general, were hit driven at the time. But he noticed something rather different when you looked at some of the new emerging technologies of entertainment. He took a look at Rhapsody, a digital music service. They carried more than 1.5 million songs, many, many times greater than the number of songs available at a Walmart store. Moreover, a big chunk of the sales, yes, they were accounted for by the hit songs; the most popular songs definitely drove a big portion of Rhapsody's volume, but Rhapsody also reported that songs ranked as low as number 900,000 on their popularity charts were streamed at least once per quarter.

Remember, Walmart only sold 55,000 songs at the time in their stores. Here was Rhapsody, a digital music service, selling many, many more songs, having a huge library available to them. Anderson looked at several different sort of new economy firms and noticed the same phenomenon. At Netflix, 21% of their revenue was generated from movies not available at Blockbuster. Rhapsody, 40% of its revenue generated from music not available in a Walmart store. Amazon, 25% of its revenue in the book business generated from books not available in any Barnes & Noble brick-and-mortar store. The long tail. The idea, then, that you could generate a lot of revenue from products that were low in popularity, so low, that they weren't carried in any of your brick-and-mortar competitors.

This was an interesting phenomenon, a whole new possibility for how to make money. And Netflix was capitalizing it. In fact, they didn't want to be in the new release-business, because that's a difficult business. Yes, you make a lot of money when *Finding Nemo* first hits the store. But if you need many, many copies in order to please all those soccer moms, what you do a month later when everyone has watched *Finding Nemo*? You don't need those copies anymore, and so you have to dump them. You start selling used movies in Blockbuster stores, trying to capture as much revenue as possible from all this excess inventory.

Netflix, they didn't want to be in that business. They wanted to be in the long tail. They wanted to sell less popular movies, but movies that were cheap to acquire and that they could hold in a few distribution centers around the country and then ship at the customer's request. What a better model that they could operate if they could avoid having to keep all of that inventory that would soon be obsolete, the way it was in Blockbuster stores.

So, Chris Anderson wrote that traditional retailers made all their money in these entertainment businesses off of the hits. The top 100 or 200 songs or books or movies at any given point in time. Hybrid retailers, people who operated catalogs or online sites, still selling physical goods, but not distributing them through brick-and-mortar stores, they could make money off of many more items, because they could stalk many more items in a distribution center than Walmart or Barnes & Noble could stock in a physical store.

But then he said, the purely digital retailers, they can make money forever. No matter how low in popularity an item is, because the marginal cost of adding another song to the iTunes or Spotify library was so low, virtually zero, you could make any song available, even if there was only one customer out there who wanted that song. Purely digital retailers could make money on a wide, wide array of products in a way brick-and-mortar retailers simply could not.

And Netflix, as they moved to streaming, they could do that. No longer were they simply a hybrid retailer offering physical products online, with the streaming revolution, they could offer any movie they wanted to any customer, and the cost of putting that movie up was very low in terms of that marginal cost of adding an additional movie.

But what drove demand for these non-hits? How do you get people to rent a movie that's not a major hit in the theaters? How do you create demand from the customer? Well, you do it in a whole new way. What Anderson noted was the traditional way that you got people to go to the theaters to see *Finding Nemo* or rent it at a Blockbuster store, or the traditional way that you might get them to listen to a new song from Taylor Swift for Brad Paisley, well, you used mass marketing. But in this new world, Anderson said, now you saw social networking, customer reviews, playlists, blogs, other forms of social media driving demand for niche products, products that you could never justify running a mass-marketing campaign for. But now you could target and find the people who liked that particular genre, and you could offer them some new information via social media about that, and get them to then come to your service and purchase it.

But even beyond that, what Netflix did in bringing a new business model to the table, was build algorithms, sophisticated, statistical algorithms that used information they were collecting about the customer to create customized recommendations, so that when you logged on to the Netflix site, they would tell you, here's a movie you may never have heard of, but we think you will like, based on people like you, based on your history of renting movies, and based on the reviews you've performed and put up on our site about past movies you viewed.

Think about that. That's a whole new way of operating. Not going to the Blockbuster store and hoping that an associate might be able to offer a recommendation to you, but having personalized recommendations coming to your site all the time. Why couldn't Blockbuster replicate this when they finally went online many years later? Well, that was very, very difficult. By the time they moved to go online, several years after Netflix had already been there, they couldn't build those algorithms as easily. Netflix had been building this huge database for several years, and their predictive power of their statistical algorithms was quite high.

Blockbuster now was playing catch up. They didn't have that network effect going for them. Netflix's algorithms were getting better with each additional user. As more and more users used Netflix, there was more value to each new customer who could go there and say, wow, what a great personalized recommendation I just received. Moreover, as Blockbuster eventually moved online, the customer they were trying to attract was initially the same customer they had catered to in their store, the soccer mom. But she was busy. She was much less likely to review movies or complete surveys as that young male living in his mother's basement. So they couldn't build algorithms as quickly and as effectively as Netflix had. A new business model upended the incumbent, not just a new product or service.

So what should incumbent firms do? How should they react? Clay Christensen argued in his work on disruptive innovation that incumbent firms must separate a new unit trying to react to an upstart entry. They have to create a separate subsidiary, wall them off from the mainstream business, and tell them to go after a new innovative opportunity in the market. Why? He argued that big companies eat their young, that it's very difficult, the mainstream unit will be so worried about protecting its profit margins and not seeing sales bleed off to this new innovation that they will essentially overwhelm this new idea, so separate it out, protect it from the rest of the business, and let them innovate. That was his argument. And he offered examples of this, like IBM, when they moved from the mainstream computer business to personal computers. They set up a separate business unit far away from their headquarters in New York and told them to go after this new opportunity. And at the time, it worked.

Now, interestingly, there has been some criticism of these theories of disruptive innovation. In fact, just recently in 2014, historian Jill Lepore wrote an article in The New Yorker, a harsh critique of Christensen's theory of disruptive innovation. It was a very harsh critique, even personal at times, and it received a lot of attention. But there was some validity. She critiqued some of the research methods and some of the applicability of the theory to a wide range of situations. She argued, in fact, that it had been applied in a wide range of industries, and perhaps it wasn't so widely applicable. Maybe you couldn't generalize quite as much as Christensen had done.

What's my view on the critique? I think we have to be careful about this term, disruptive innovation. We're hearing it all the time; it seems like it's in Fortune magazine and on the Wall Street Journal's pages every day. It's become something like a hammer, and we're looking for a nail to hammer in. It's an overused concept. Moreover, it's a very good descriptive tool. Looking back at a story like Netflix and Blockbuster, we can use the theory to explain Blockbuster's demise. But can we predict the future with the model? It's much more difficult to do.

There's also this issue of two kinds of errors. You know, the error Christensen focuses on is the idea that incumbent firms sometimes miss the disruptive threat; they don't see it coming. But I think there's another kind of error that companies can make. They can make huge misguided investments because they misperceive a threat. They begin to look at every new entrant as a potential disruptive innovator, and they start to throw huge dollars at lots of unproven technologies. That can be just as misguided as the blindness to a new idea that can happen when there's mental lock-in at an incumbent firm.

You know, we have to be careful about the prescription that incumbent firms should separate units that are aiming to cope with a disruptive threat. I think that's the other thing that we have to be very careful about. You know, we talked about competitive advantage coming from an integrated system of activities, but if we separate out this new unit to go after a new idea, are we still going to have this integrated system of activities, or will we have a disjointed firm? Will we have disconnects and not as powerful an advantage as a result? And we saw some of the misguided nature of this with Netflix itself when it perceived streaming as the next disruptive threat that might undermine its mail business. And so it tried to separate itself into two firms, and customers revolted. It was a simplistic response to a much more complicated problem.

Now, what was the ultimate demise of Blockbuster? In fact, Netflix isn't the firm that put the stake through Blockbuster's heart. It was Redbox. Why? Think about what Redbox did. They said, well, interestingly, if Blockbuster is really about new releases, we can do new releases more effectively, more cost efficiently, than Blockbuster can. We don't need a giant brick-and-mortar store to give the customer new releases; we can do it with vending machines in supermarkets and convenience stores. So now Blockbuster was faced with Redbox, a pure play, new release business with vending machines; Netflix, offering old movies via online technology. What was Blockbuster now trying to do in the late 2000s? They were straddling. They were trying to brick and click, be online and in the stores, and could do neither as well as the two pure plays, Redbox and Netflix.

So your assignment, as we close this lecture, I want you to think about two interesting businesses facing some disruptive innovation today. Consider the hotel and the taxi businesses. What's changing about these businesses in the last few years?

Let me give you a hint, think about Uber and Airbnb. If you haven't heard of those firms, go ahead and Google them, and learn a little bit about what Uber and Airbnb are doing to the hotel and the taxi businesses, and ask yourself what makes these firms such an imposing threat to the incumbent players.

Anticipating Your Rival's Response
Lecture 7

In this lecture, we'll try to understand competitive dynamics in more detail. As we'll see, successful firms are able to put themselves in the shoes of their rivals, anticipate how those competitors will react, and use that information to help plot more effective strategies. In particular, we'll look at three well-known historical examples of competitive dynamics in the business world: the story of NutraSweet and its reaction to a new entrant in the market for artificial sweeteners, the case of the upstart Irish airline Ryanair that competed against two dominant incumbent players, and Blockbuster's reaction to Netflix.

Analyzing Competitors

- Analyzing competitors is a multifaceted task that starts with looking at their past and current strategies, understanding what they're trying to accomplish, and identifying how they're trying to position themselves in the marketplace. It also involves trying to understand their goals. What specific financial targets and market-share goals are they trying to achieve? How are they trying to advance the objectives of their shareholders, satisfy their customers more effectively, and keep their employees motivated and engaged?

- It's also important to understand your competitors' capabilities and weaknesses. What is world class about their production, distribution, and research and development, and where do they lag behind?

- Perhaps most importantly, you need to try to get inside the heads of the executives in a rival firm. What industries are they from, what companies did they work for in the past, and how might those experiences shape their decision making? Where have they succeeded in the past, and where have they failed? Is there a certain formula that has worked for them in the past that they are likely to go to again in hopes of achieving another success?

- Anticipating a competitor's actions and potential responses to your actions means understanding four factors:
  - First, you must understand the economic and financial incentives of your competitors—the costs and benefits of a particular action.

  - Second, you must look at the competitor's noneconomic motives, such as making itself a more attractive workplace or, perhaps, forsaking profits in the short term to achieve a more dominant position in the marketplace.

  - The third factor to understand is the biases that may affect your rival's behavior. For example, is your competitor falling into the sunk-cost trap, that is, escalating its commitment to a course of action even if that action is failing?

  - Finally, you need to understand the broader context in which your rival operates. What political and historical factors may affect the rival firm's responses or shape its actions?

Economic Motives

- To understand a rival's economic motives, a simple application of game theory may be helpful. In game theory, one player tries to predict what an opponent might do in various circumstances and bases his or her strategy on that prediction.

- Many researchers have applied game theory to the scenario of an entrepreneur moving into a new market and confronting an incumbent player. Here, the entrant faces a simple choice: whether to move into the market or not. The incumbent also faces a choice: whether to respond aggressively or to accommodate, perhaps even relinquishing a small amount of market share in hopes of maintaining its current pricing, marketing spend, and so on.

- Applying game theory, a new player coming into a market might anticipate that the incumbent would be reluctant to fight a price war, which would mean sacrificing profit by cutting revenue dramatically and, perhaps, saving only a small amount of market share. The better course for the incumbent would be to give up a small piece of the market in exchange for maintaining its current prices. In this situation, the new entrant might conclude that entering the market is a good move. In contrast, if the entrant believes that the incumbent will retaliate aggressively, then entering the market might not be affordable.

- The idea here is to look forward and reason back. Game theorists call this type of thinking *backward induction*. Ask yourself what your rivals will do in the future based on your actions now. From the answer to that question, you decide what to do today.

- Game theory can be helpful for thinking about the potential responses of competitors to your choices, but it's limited in some ways. The real world is different than the realm of game theory because the actors may not be completely rational—they may not care only about maximizing economic profits.

Netflix and Blockbuster
- In 1999, Netflix entered the movie rental market, confronting the incumbent, Blockbuster. In response, Blockbuster had a choice: whether to fight the new player or accommodate.

- Recall that Netflix came into the market with a different pricing model than Blockbuster. Netflix charged a monthly subscription fee, rather than per movie, and it didn't charge late fees. Thus, one important decision that Blockbuster had to make early on was whether to cut its late fees, which generated at least $300 million per year for the company.
  - Keep in mind that in its first few years, Netflix had only a few hundred thousand subscribers, while Blockbuster had millions of customers.

- o For Blockbuster, cutting late fees would destroy the entire profitability of the firm, while saving only a tiny slice of market share. In this situation, Blockbuster chose to accommodate, keeping its late fees and preserving its profitability, while ceding some customers to Netflix.

- In making this decision, Blockbuster's projection was that Netflix was a niche player that would never become mainstream. Of course, Blockbuster was wrong. The company eventually had to cut late fees, but it took years to reach that decision.

Rynair and British Airways

- In the 1980s, when Ryanair entered the European airline industry, it probably believed that British Airways would not cut its prices because doing so would result in a significant hit to the incumbent's profits. At the time, British Airways charged IR£166 for the London-Dublin ticket, while Ryanair planned to charge IR£98. A price war would mean a substantial drop in revenue and profitability for the incumbent.

- Keep in mind, too, that the slice of the market Ryanair sought was tiny. In fact, the company originally had only a few small planes and planned to make just four round trips per day between London and Dublin.

- British Airways faced the choice of destroying its profitability by cutting prices dramatically for that route or giving a few seats to Ryanair and maintaining its pricing. But British Airways also had to think about the entrant's intentions: Will Rynair grow? Will it add capacity, and if so, what effect will that have on the market? Further, if British Airways accommodated Ryanair, would other new players try to come into the industry?

Lessons for Incumbents and Entrants

- Incumbents can learn a number of important lessons from such situations.
  - First, you don't want to ruin the whole market just to save a small slice. But it's also true that you may be able to identify and focus on the customers who are most likely to defect to the new entry. In that situation, you could cut prices or market aggressively to one segment of customers but maintain higher prices for others. Such a strategy would allow you to attack without destroying your own profitability.

  - You should also consider the signals you send by your responses to new entrants. Perhaps fighting aggressively will deter other entrepreneurs from entering your segment.

  - Finally, you should think about how fast entrants may grow. Is this upstart a niche player, or is it focused on taking over the market?

A smart way to analyze the competition is to ask your management team to role-play how a competitor might respond to your firm's actions.

- Potential entrants should also think about a range of factors that might prompt incumbents to make aggressive moves.
  - Is this a slow-growth market? If so, the incumbent might fight hard to preserve its customers.

  - Is this a commodity product? If a product is not highly differentiated, an incumbent might resort to price as its only competitive weapon.

  - Does the incumbent have high fixed costs relative to marginal costs? If so, it might respond aggressively simply to keep its capacity utilization high to cover fixed costs.

  - What kind of resources does the incumbent have to wage a battle?

  - How has the incumbent reacted when other companies have entered the market?

  - Can the incumbent target its fight? Will it have to cut prices across the board, or can it lower prices only for a segment of customers who are most likely to defect?

NutraSweet and Holland Sweetener

- In the 1980s, NutraSweet was the dominant player in the artificial sweetener market, but the company's patents were about to expire, and others were looking to enter the market.

- A potential new entrant, Holland Sweetener, made the mistake of not understanding NutraSweet's powerful cost advantage. In other words, the artificial sweetener industry was highly influenced by economies of scale and a substantial learning curve, and NutraSweet had the advantage in these factors. For Holland Sweetener, that meant that NutraSweet could fight aggressively, cutting its prices significantly while still making money.

- Holland Sweetener also failed to apply game theory to understand NutraSweet's relationship with its two largest customers, Coca-Cola and Pepsi.
  - Holland figured that Coke and Pepsi wouldn't want to be entirely dependent on NutraSweet and would shift some of their volume over to a new entrant in the market, especially if they were offered an attractive price.

  - But Coke and Pepsi were caught in game theory's classic prisoner's dilemma: It would have been in each company's interest to switch some volume and get a better price from Holland, but neither wanted to move first. Each company believed that if it changed an ingredient, its rival would argue to customers that the taste of the product had changed.

  - For this reason, NutraSweet was able to retain its customers, and Holland never made money in the artificial sweetener market.

Suggested Reading

Coughlan, Freier, and Kaiho, "Competitor Analysis."

Dixit and Nalebuff, *The Art of Strategy*.

Rivkin, "Dogfight over Europe."

Questions to Consider

1. Why is game theory useful in conducting competitor analysis?

2. Why do we have to go beyond thinking about the short-term economic motives of our rivals?

3. Why might incumbent firms retaliate aggressively against a new entrant, even at a significant short-term financial cost?

Anticipating Your Rival's Response
Lecture 7—Transcript

In his great treatise on military strategy, Sun Tzu once wrote, "Know your enemy, know yourself, and you can fight 100 battles with no danger of defeat. When you are ignorant of the enemy but know yourself, your chances of winning and losing are equal. If you don't know either your enemy or yourself, you are bound to perish in all battles," he wrote.

Sun Tzu reminded us of the importance of analyzing your enemy, understanding your competitor. This is crucial in business, as well as in the military. In this lecture, we'll try to understand competitive dynamics in more detail. We'll look at several situations where new entrants were doing battle with incumbents. We'll try to say, how might they have put themselves in the shoes of the incumbent player and tried to anticipate how that incumbent might respond to the entry of an entrepreneur into their market?

This is what good firms do. They put themselves in the shoes of their rivals, and they try to anticipate how those competitors will react. And they use that information to help them plot a more effective strategy. Competitor analysis is a crucial tool for any strategist. There are three situations we'll look at in depth in this lecture, three famous historical examples of competitive battles in the field of business.

First, we'll look at the story of NutraSweet and their production of aspartame, an artificial sweetener. NutraSweet, the incumbent player, with strong patents protecting their intellectual property in the 1980s. As the patents were set to expire, a new entrant emerged, Holland Sweetener Company, threatening their dominance, and we'll look at what happened. We'll also take a look at an Irish upstart airline, called Ryanair, that emerged in the late 1980s, entering into the market for the Dublin-London route for air travel. They competed against two dominate incumbent players, British Airways and Aer Lingus.

And finally, we'll look again at Blockbuster the incumbent player in the movie rental business, and how they dealt with an upstart called Netflix. Now, what's interesting about these three situations is that they're not all the same success story. Holland Sweetener faltered badly trying to unseat NutraSweet. Ryanair faltered badly at first, but then turned themselves around, adapted their strategy, and succeeded with flying colors. And finally, Netflix, we know, not only unseated Blockbuster, but drove Blockbuster to bankruptcy.

Analyzing your competitor is a multifaceted task. It starts with looking at their past and their current strategy, understanding what they're trying to accomplish and how they're trying to position themselves in the marketplace. But it also means trying to understand their goals. What specific financial targets are they trying to achieve? What market-share goals are they trying to achieve? How are they trying to advance the objectives of their shareholders, satisfy their customers more effectively, keep their employees motivated and engaged?

But you also have to understand your competitors' capabilities and their weaknesses. What's world class about their production, their distribution, their research and development, and where do they lag behind? In what areas are they substandard? And finally, and perhaps most importantly, you really have to get inside the heads of the executives within that rival firm. You have to understand how they think, what motivates them, what is their background, where did they come from educationally? What industries are they from, what prior companies did they work for, and how might that shape their experience? Where have they succeeded in the past and where have they failed? Is there a certain formula that has worked for them in the past that they are likely to go to again in hopes of achieving another success?

Anticipating the competitor's actions and their potential response to your actions means doing four things really well. First, it starts with understanding the economic and financial incentives of your competitors; that means taking a look at a particular action and trying to understand the cost and the benefits for your rival. So suppose that we thought about their action, taking in and engaging in a price war. What are the costs to their firm of doing that? How much might your rivals' profits fall if they were to launch a price war? What benefits would accrue to them? Might they gain market share? How much market share, and what kind of an increase in revenue and profit might they see by doing that? Understanding the costs and benefits of that particular action, a price war, is crucial to understanding how you might respond or deal with their efforts.

But there's more than that. You can't just understand their economic incentives. You have to understand their are non-economic motives. Beyond maximizing profits, what are the other goals that competitors are striving to achieve? Are they really focused on making themselves a more attractive workplace, trying to engage their employees more effectively? Are they trying to build market share now, perhaps forsaking profits in the short term to establish a more dominant position in the marketplace? Or, are they dealing with intense pressures from Wall Street, and do they have to deliver quarterly earnings? And are they not able to take a hit now to build for the future. So understanding the non-economic motives of the competition, that's crucial. And that means understanding how they think.

But we also have to understand the biases that may affect rivals' behavior. What do I mean by biases? Well, there's certain decision-making traps that we're all vulnerable to that may shape our decision making. For example, we know that many of us, as individuals and as organizations, fall victim to something called the sunk-cost trap. We have a hard time cutting our losses. If we put a lot into something, we tend to not want to walk away. So we end up escalating our commitment to courses of action, even if that course of action is failing. We throw good money after bad.

What does this mean in terms of anticipating your competitor's actions and responses? Well, it means you may look at a situation and say, they really ought to exit that market. They really ought to shut down that product category. And we, therefore, are going to act in a certain way, knowing that we think they're going to exit. But they don't exit. That shouldn't surprise you. If you look more closely, you may realize, they are really committed to that category, and they're going to have a hard time cutting their losses. Their bias is going to be the double down.

Why? Because they're emotionally invested in that, not just financially invested in that, and so they'll have a hard time walking away. And if the product category is really tied to the history and legacy of their firm, all the more recent they may have a hard time walking away. So non-economic motives and biases cause them to stay in, when you may initially thought they were going to exit.

Finally, you've already understood the financial incentives and the non-economic motives and the biases. Now, we have to look at the broader context. What political factors may affect your rivals' response? What contextual factors may shape their behavior? What do I mean by that? Well, let's think again about an anticipation of an exit from a particular product category. You may think your rival is going to get out of a certain segment of the market. But will they?

Suppose your rival is based in France, not in the United States. Can they exit that easily? Or the political context may make it difficult to do so. In France, certain restrictions exist, so it's much harder to downsize your firm, to close a factory, to lay off employees. Understanding that context may cause you to reevaluate your understanding of that rival. And you may say to yourself, they're going to stay in, when initially, looking only at the numbers, I thought they would have gotten out.

So understanding the context. Where does national pride play? What does the history of the company tell us about how they might behave. What does the history of the individuals leading the firm tell us about how they might behave? Understanding these factors are all crucial if we're going to do a good competitor analysis and plot a more effective strategy as a result.

Let's start by understanding the economic motives of our rivals. And here, game theory, a simple application of game theory, can be helpful. Remember, in game theory, you're asking the question, what should I do? But first, you're saying to yourself, let me think about what the opponent might do in various circumstances. Then, based on that prediction, let me figure out my strategy. So you're putting yourself in the rival's shoes, thinking about the different choices they have, trying to understand what they'll do, and then backing into what you might do, what's optimal for you given your expectation of what they will do.

Now, many people have looked at game theory and applied it to business in the simple scenario of an entrant, of an entrepreneur moving into a new market and confronting an incumbent player. The entrant is facing a simple choice. Do we move into this market or not? Do we go find another product market opportunity? The incumbent is also facing a choice. Do we fight? Do we retaliate? Do we aggressively respond to try to crush this entrepreneur and drive them out of the market? Do we protect our market share and our position fiercely?

Or, they could accommodate. What does *accommodate* mean? Accommodate doesn't mean that you're not all trying to defend your position, but you're not as aggressive. You may even see the small amount of market share in hopes of maintaining your current pricing, your current marketing spend, and the like. So you're not going to sacrifice a huge amount of profit to try to crush this rival today; you're going to be a little more accommodating to the new entrepreneur. So you face a choice, fight hard, or maybe less hard. The entrant, do I come in? Or do I not?

Now, you could imagine the scenario where you had a very small entrant, a new player coming in, and likely only to take a very small slice of market share. If they look ahead and try to anticipate what the incumbent will do, well, if they're applying game theory, they might look and say, gosh, if the incumbent fights a price war to protect their market when we're so small, well they may have to sacrifice huge amounts of profit by slicing their revenue dramatically to fight us. But they're only saving a small amount of market share.

Perhaps it might be better for them to keep price where it is, to keep advertising right where it is, and to give us a little piece of the market. Maybe they'll be OK with that, as long as it's not too big of a piece of the market. Maybe they won't retaliate that aggressively. If I know that is the entrant, I might be more likely to enter. If, on the other hand, I thought they were going to retaliate very aggressively, and I understood that was their likely action, then I might look at my own profitability as an entrepreneur and say, I'm going to take a huge loss early on. I cannot afford to enter this market.

The idea, then, in game theory is to look forward and reason back. Game theorists call this backward induction. You ask yourself, what will my rivals do in the future based on my actions now? And based on that answer, you decide what you'll do today. Strategy, ultimately, is about anticipating competitor response whenever you make choices. And that's why game theory can be helpful. But game theory can also be limited. Why?

Well, the real world isn't quite as simple as a game-theory matrix or decision tree. First and foremost, the real world is different, because actors may not be completely rational. What do I mean by that? What I mean is that the opposing firm, the rival, well, they may not only care about maximizing economic profits. And in game theory, we typically think only in terms of the numbers at first. But to really understand your competitor, you have to go beyond that. You need to understand who the people on the other side of the table are, how they think, and what they care about.

Who are the decision makers? And are these folks purely about maximizing short-run profits? Now, in some cases they may very well be. As I said, they may be in a situation where Wall Street is pressing hard on them and demanding that they meet certain quarterly earnings targets. But in other cases, many other factors may be shaping their decisions. And so this is crucial.

Now, let's think about this in the context of Netflix and Blockbuster. Netflix entered the market 1999, confronting the incumbent, Blockbuster. Now, Blockbuster had a choice. How hard do we fight this new player, or do we accommodate? How did that play out in the movie-rental business? Well one important factor, one important decision, that the incumbent, Blockbuster, confronted early on was, do we cut our late fees? Recall that Netflix came in the market with a different pricing model. They weren't charging per movie; they were charging a monthly subscription. You paid a certain fixed amount per month and rented as many movies as you wanted. Within that, you didn't have to return each movie in a prescribed period of time. You could keep the movie for more days than Blockbuster typically allowed their customer to keep the movie. But of course, you couldn't rent new movies unless you eventually returned the movies you had. So there's some limit there, that Netflix imposed. But there were not traditional late fees.

Now, Blockbuster had to decide. Do we cut late fees, which we know some customers really dislike, to compete with this upstart Netflix. And Netflix is thinking, what do we anticipate about what Blockbuster will do? Will they come after us hard? Now, it's interesting to look at the economic motives of Blockbuster, and I'm sure Netflix did, based on my conversations with people in the industry. Blockbuster was generating at least $300 million per year in late fees in the early 2000s. In some years, that was more than the total operating profit of the entire company. They were dependent on late-fee revenue for their profitability.

Now, what about Netflix? Who were they in the beginning? Well, in those first few years, they only had a few hundred thousand subscribers. Blockbuster had millions of customers. So do the math. If you're Blockbuster, and you cut late fees, you destroy the entire profitability of the firm. But what do you gain? You save a tiny slice of market share. So what do you do? Blockbuster chose to accommodate. They said, we'll keep late fees in place. We'll cede a few 100,000 customers to Netflix. But in our interest, we're looking and saying, preserve our profitability today, rather than try to save a bit of market share and sacrifice so much of our profitability.

Of course, you might say that was very shortsighted. What about the long run? What, if Netflix starts to grow and grow rapidly? Blockbuster's estimation, their projection, was that Netflix would not grow that rapidly, that it was a niche player, catering to a certain subset of customers, but it would never go mainstream. So with that expectation, they weren't willing to eliminate late fees to save this tiny slice of the market.

They were wrong, of course. Eventually, they had to cut late fees, but it took them years to come to that decision. And they only did it when the financials began to turn, when the number of customers that Netflix had built up and accumulated became so large that now, the accommodation strategy was costing Blockbuster a great deal of money as well. And now, they finally cut late fees.

Let's take a look at another example of this dynamic between an entrant and an incumbent, one that played out a little differently. The question was, how will British Airways and Aer Lingus react when Ryanair entered the European airline industry? Would they launch a price war to crush this upstart Irish airline in the late 1980s?

And if you're Ryanair, you're thinking and saying, well, if British Airways cuts price, they will take a huge hit to profits, because every dollar that they cut their price, that automatically is one less dollar of profit. And they have a large market share. They have hundreds of thousands of customers, so cutting price significantly will cost them a fortune. And at this point, it was really interesting to see, because British Airways was charging 166 Irish pounds for the London-Dublin ticket. Ryanair was coming in, saying they were going to charge 98 Irish pounds. So a price war would mean a substantial drop in revenue and profitability for the incumbent players.

Now, remember that Ryanair was only looking at taking a tiny slice of the market. In fact, they originally only had a few planes, and they were only planning on running four round trips per day between London and Dublin. And the planes are rather small, so they weren't going to hold a ton of passengers, either. So, if you're British Airways and Aer Lingus, you're looking and saying, do we destroy our profitability by cutting price so dramatically on this route? Or do we give a few seats over to Ryan air and maintain our pricing?

Well, but you have to think about the entrant's intentions. Will Ryanair grow? Will they buy or lease more planes? Will they add capacity? And if they do so, then what effect will this have? Moreover, you have to ask, if we play nice with Ryanair today, will new players come in industry and start attacking us? What precedent will we set by playing nice? Maybe we have to sacrifice profit now and attack aggressively, not only to keep Ryanair from growing, but to keep others out of the market. It's a complicated dynamic.

What are some of the principles that we can learn by looking at this situation? I think one of the key principles, for its incumbents, at least, is, you don't want to ruin your whole market just to save a tiny slice. But what if you could target your attack? What if you could identify and focus on the customers most likely to defect to this new entrant? Well, if you could cut price or market aggressively to them, but keep price higher for other customers who are less price sensitive, then you could attack without destroying your profitability.

This kind of targeted fight is something that many incumbent firms will try to achieve if they can, and we certainly know, on airlines, whenever you get on a plane, you often find the person sitting next to you has not paid the same price for a ticket. So they are trying to split hairs; they're trying to identify which customers are more price sensitive, and how can we adjust price for them to keep them, and keep price higher for others to maintain our profitability?

But there's a few other principles here that we can learn about competitors and how they respond to one another. For the incumbent, one key is, what signal am I sending to other potential entrants by my behavior today? So, not, what is the short-term impact on my profit, but what is the long-term impact on the competitive dynamic? If I play nice, or if I fight? Perhaps if I fight aggressively, I will deter other entrepreneurs from coming into my segment.

And finally, you have to think about how fast the entrant may wish to grow. What are their aspirations? Is this a company set out on taking over the world? Are they truly a niche player that's only going to focus on a small target-customer segment? Understanding that will dictate how you respond.

If you think about what you're trying to do as an incumbent player in these markets, what you'd love to do is be able to take action up front to deter entry before the player even comes in. Could you fight a little preemptively, and therefore, avoid the situation of having to take a huge hit to profits later on to fight them in reality? Could you engage in preemptive action?

Let me give you an example of that. Several years ago, Clorox and Procter & Gamble were in an interesting competitive situation. Procter & Gamble, maker of laundry detergents, like Tide, was thinking about entering the bleach category. This was one area in the laundry detergent aisle that they did not compete in. Clorox was the dominant player. Most Americans use the word Clorox and bleach interchangeably; the brand was the product. Now, Procter & Gamble was planning on test marketing this product in Portland, Maine, their new bleach. Why Portland Maine? It was far from Clorox's headquarters in California. It was a small market, and they were all set with a couponing and sampling strategy for introducing their product and testing it out.

Now, Clorox caught wind of this, and they said to themselves, how might we deter entry by P&G? They launched a preemptive attack. They dropped a gallon of bleach on every doorstep for every household in Portland, Maine. What did Procter & Gamble do? They said to themselves, well, our whole sampling and couponing strategy won't do much good now that everyone has an extra bottle of bleach already on hand. Moreover, we just learned that Clorox is going to fight to the death in this market. This won't be an easy battle. So what did Procter & Gamble do? They never entered the market; they decided to forsake the bleach category. A preemptive strike that deterred entry, a very effective business strategy.

So assessing the competitors' response, as a potential entrant, you're thinking about a range of factors that might suggest aggressive moves coming from the incumbent that could be harmful to you as an entrepreneur. Is this a slow-growth market? Is this a situation where the incumbent is starving for new customers, where there is no growth, and therefore, they might fight to preserve the customers they already have.

Is this a commodity product? Is it not really very differentiated, and therefore, it's going to be really hard for the incumbent to argue their product is better, higher quality, etc. And so might they resort to price as their only competitive weapon? Does the competitor have high fixed costs relative to marginal costs? Are they looking to cover those fixed costs, and might they fight hard simply to keep their capacity utilization high to cover those fixed costs?

Do they have deep pockets? What kind of resources does the incumbent player have available to it? And therefore, with those resources, might they be able to attack us aggressively? And what about their history? What have they done when other entrepreneurs have come after them, or other companies have entered their market? What does their history say about what they might do today?

Understanding each of these factors is crucial if you want to be able to understand whether or not we might be in for a really tough fight when we enter their market. And lastly, can they target their fight? Do they have to cut price across the board to come after us, or, can they identify only a segment of customers most likely to defect to us, and respond only, for those customers, to retain them? The more they can target the fight, the more likely they're going to come after us, and do it in a way that's really cost effective for the incumbent player.

So let's take a look at one final example of an interesting competitive battle. So the 1980s, NutraSweet was the dominant player in the aspartame, or artificial sweetener, market. And their biggest customers were Coke and Pepsi. In fact, Coke and Pepsi accounted for almost half of their sales worldwide. Now, their patents were about to expire, and so people were looking at entering the market. Holland Sweetener was one of those firms thinking about coming in to compete with NutraSweet.

It's really interesting to see how that unfolded. Would NutraSweet retaliate aggressively? How might they respond? Well, Holland Sweetener made a single, big mistake in their efforts to enter this market, and that was, they didn't fully understand how powerful the cost advantage that the incumbent player had on them. What do I mean by that? It turns out, in the aspartame market, we had huge economies of scale and a substantial learning curve. Therefore, NutraSweet had a huge cost advantage over this new player, Holland Sweetener. The learning curve was so powerful that the cost of producing aspartame had been falling significantly for years, as NutraSweet gained more and more experience producing this good.

And there were huge economies of scale. Really, you only needed a few factories to produce enough aspartame to serve the entire worldwide market. Now, if you know this, if you understanding the incumbent player has these cost advantages, what does this mean for Holland Sweetener? It means the incumbent can fight, and fight aggressively, because they can being price way down and still make money because of their cost advantage over us. And Holland Sweetener made a mistake. They had no other way of differentiating their product. It was the same, basic product. With no cost advantage and no differentiation, they were toast.

Moreover, they made one other mistake. They didn't apply a little game theory to understand NutraSweet's behavior with respect to Coke and Pepsi. Holland Sweetener was counting on Coke and Pepsi to shift some of their volume over. They figured Coke and Pepsi don't want to be so dependent on NutraSweet. They'll want to shift some of their volume, especially if we offer them an attractive price.

But Coke and Pepsi were caught in a prisoner's dilemma, explained by NYU Professor Adam Brandenburger. He said Coke and Pepsi were caught in a situation, where, it would have been in their interest to switch some volume and get a better price from Holland Sweetener, but neither wanted to move first. Each looked and said, if we move, will our opponent attack us? Will Pepsi say to Coke, you're changing an ingredient, and it's changing the taste of your soda. Maybe that's not true, but would they try to argue that to the customer, and vice versa. And so, NutraSweet was able to retain those customers. Neither wanted to switch. A story of not fully understand your competitor and getting caught a really difficult situation. And Holland Sweetener never made money in the artificial sweetener market.

There's value, now, in role playing the competition. That's an important lesson that we can learn from sports. What do great football coaches do? They study the film. They look closely at their opponent, and then they have a scout team. What's a scout team? That's a set of backup players that practice and behave as if they are the opponent. They pretend to be the rival before the big game, and that helps the first-team players, the best players, try to understand what they're going to do when they actually get into the game.

There's a great story of this in the 2004 AFC Championship game in the National Football League. The New England Patriots were playing the Indianapolis Colts, Tom Brady against Peyton Manning. And my beloved Patriots won that game and went on to a Super Bowl victory. After the game, Bill Belichick spoke at a press conference. If you've ever seen one of these press conferences, you know they're rather odd events. Belichick doesn't exactly like talking to the media. But here, he crowed about a particular player. He boasted and bragged about the incredible effort of Damon Huard. Damon Huard? Who was he? A backup quarterback who had never stepped foot on the field that day. Why was he being praised by the head coach? It turns out that Huard had pretended to be Peyton Manning, the opponent, all week during practice. He had copied his mannerisms, copied his throwing motions, copied everything that he thought Manning might do in the game.

What did that enable the Patriot defense to do? It enabled them to practice against this perfect copy of Peyton Manning, and to get better as a result. What's the point here? Role playing the competition can be very powerful.

Asking people on your management team, can you put yourself in the rival's shoes, and can you role play how that competitor might respond? Pretend to be them. Will it be helpful? Every management team should have a scout team. You would have some people who are pretending to be the management team of the competition and helping them practice for the real deal in the marketplace.

Now sometimes, this competitive dynamic between an incumbent and an entrant, or between two existing players, can actually not be so vicious; it can be rather cooperative. How come sometimes two rival firms getting up cooperating with one another and not competing aggressively with one another? When does that happen?

Well, cooperative behavior is more likely to emerge when there are only a few competitors and when they've known each other for a long, long period of time. If there are many players in the market, then it's hard to maintain cooperative behavior. There's a greater likelihood that one player will cheat, that they will start cutting price, that they will start doing things aggressively and undermine this sort of tacit agreement to play nice with one another. You say, are there really markets where people play nice with one another? We'll take a look at Coke and Pepsi over the years. They competed hard in terms of their advertising and their marketing, yet they never engaged in price wars with one another. In a sense, it was a friendly war. They grew the overall market together, and they both enjoyed strong profits. But there were only two of them, and they've known each other for 100 years.

Contrast that with other businesses, like the fitness-center business, where there are many, many competitors, where the market is really fragmented, and where the competition is intense. So what are some of the lessons from this lecture? Think ahead, and anticipate. Think about your economic and non-economic motives of your competition. Consider the people. Who are they, and how do they think? Balance the short run and the long run. Think about the hit-to-profits today, but also the long-run implications of your actions and your competitor's actions. And try to put yourself in the rival's shoes. Try to role play the competition to get better at what you do.

So your assignment for Lecture 7. What should you do now to reflect on what we've learned? I want you to suppose you're going to open a new restaurant in the town in which you live. Who are the incumbent players? How are they likely to react to your entry into the market? What are their economic motives, and what about their non-economic motives? How have they reacted to past entries by other players, and how should you adapt your strategy, given your expectations about how those restaurants will react, when you open yours.

Why Did Disney Buy Pixar?
Lecture 8

The Walt Disney Company competes in a number of businesses, including theme parks, a film studio, cable television channels, hotels, retail stores, consumer products, and more. Disney is a multi–business unit corporation, and each of its business units competes in a different product market. Thus far, we've been discussing strategy on the business unit level. How does a company gain advantage over its rivals in a particular product market? In this lecture, however, we'll turn to corporate strategy, asking the question: In what markets does a company choose to compete? With a multi–business unit corporation, such as the Walt Disney Company, why has the firm chosen to build a particular portfolio of businesses?

Horizontal and Vertical Integration

- With horizontal integration, a company chooses to compete in multiple product markets in the hopes of achieving some integration or synergy across those business. Horizontal integration can be divided into two categories: related diversification and unrelated diversification.

  - Of course, *related diversification* applies when a company appears to be competing in related product markets, where there are apparent synergistic possibilities. Examples include Disney and Procter & Gamble.

  - *Unrelated diversification* refers to a situation in which a company appears to be competing in markets that don't have much to do with one another. Examples here include General Electric and the Virgin Group.

- With vertical integration, the company isn't competing in multiple product markets. Instead, it focuses on one particular product market and competes along multiple links of the supply chain. Vertical integration can also be divided into two types: forward integration and backward integration.

- ○ *Backward integration* refers to a company that produces its own components or raw materials.

- ○ *Forward integration* refers to a company that operates its own distribution or retail store network.

- In evaluating corporate strategy, we ask two fundamental questions about each of the businesses that are part of a firm's portfolio: (1) Is each business better off as part of the corporation than it would be by itself? (2) Does each business unit within the corporation outperform comparable focused companies—those that compete in only one product market?

Related Diversification

- Related diversification is focused on the idea of synergy, or what economists call *scope economies*. The related diversification strategy tries to achieve scope economies among businesses competing in similar product markets. Put another way, with a related diversification strategy, the firm tries to share resources or capabilities across multiple businesses, whether those resources are distribution channels, sales forces, R&D facilities, or factories. In Disney's case, the company shares its characters across multiple businesses, leveraging them to enhance the value of its television shows, theme parks, and consumer products.

- Put another way, economies of scope exist when each business unit enjoys either a stronger willingness to pay or lower costs because of its cooperation with sister units. The related diversification

Disney believes that its theme parks are somehow more valuable as part of the Disney family than they would be as an independent company.

strategy is all about strengthening the competitive advantage of each of the business units, making it better off than it would be on its own.

- Disney's theme parks, for example, seem to enjoy higher willingness to pay than competing theme parks largely because Disney's characters are incorporated into the theme parks in multiple ways.

Specialized versus Fungible Resources

- Disney is a powerful example of a company that has leveraged a set of resources and capabilities into a number of different businesses. In particular, Disney's characters are valuable resources because they are highly durable and difficult to imitate. How can a firm leverage such valuable resources across multiple business units? To answer that question, we need to think about specialized versus fungible (general) resources.

- Examples of highly fungible resources or capabilities include brand management expertise, innovation, and risk management—fairly generic capabilities that could apply widely across a range of businesses. A highly specialized capability might be a patented product formula or specific engineering expertise in a narrow discipline.

- A fungible capability can be transferred easily across lines of business. But if it's too general, it won't provide substantial competitive advantage. Highly specialized capabilities can convey powerful competitive advantage, but they may not be as widely applicable.

- In the 1980s, when Michael Eisner arrived at Disney, the company's core capabilities revolved around animated character development and deployment—highly specialized capabilities that constrained growth in some ways. But Eisner redefined Disney's core capabilities more broadly—as creativity management. This definition enabled him to justify the move into a broader range of businesses.

- Interestingly, in Eisner's first decade at Disney, when he was focused on leveraging the characters, the company did incredibly well. But as he stretched the definition of what Disney was good at—moving farther away from its core business into sports teams, films for adults, and so on—performance started to suffer.

- Bob Iger, the chief executive who took over from Eisner, appears to have returned to the formula of leveraging characters and has had great success financially.

Transaction Costs
- Just looking at synergy alone is not enough in thinking about whether multiple businesses should be under one roof. It's also important to ask whether the businesses should be merged or can act as partners.

- There is some cost to bringing two companies together under one roof—costs related to additional bureaucracy, costs of going through a merger, and so on. In some cases, it may be wiser to keep the companies independent but cooperate and achieve economies of scope. Consider this issue is terms of Disney's hotel and consumer products businesses.
  - Disney owns many hotels near its theme parks, but it outsources production of its consumer products, such as toys and games. Consumer products are synergistic with the rest of the Disney family, but the company has chosen not to manufacture those products in house. What's the difference between the hotel business and consumer products?

  - One major difference is that the hotel business offers more of an indefinable experience that's created by Disney, while consumer products lend themselves to a clear design that can be communicated to an outside manufacturer.

- This issue relates to a question asked by Novel Prize winner Ronald Coase in a paper called "The Nature of the Firm": Why do firms exist? If markets are such a great way to coordinate economic activity, why is not all activity conducted through the marketplace with small firms run by entrepreneurs? Why do we need large organizations?
  - Coase refined the questions as follows: Should economic activity be coordinated by the market mechanism or by intra-firm organizational structures and processes? In other words, should you contract with an outside supplier to make components, or should you build and run your own factory?

  - Coase's answer was that it's necessary to look at the transaction costs associated with organizing certain economic activities. For a company deciding whether to contract with an outside manufacturer or handle its own manufacturing, the question becomes: Under which arrangement will the transaction costs be lower?

  - For Disney, it would be difficult to train personnel from an outside hotel chain to create the guest experience that Disney seeks; thus, the firm owns its own hotels and monitors the interaction between employees and guests closely. But consumer products can be monitored from afar, which means that the company can outsource manufacturing to get the best price.

- Three factors drive transaction costs: uncertainty, frequency, and asset specificity.
  - Market coordination becomes very difficult and costly when the potential arises for opportunistic behavior, and such potential exists when economic actors invest heavily in transaction-specific assets—in other words, when factors of production are highly specific to the other party.

- ○ Imagine an oil refinery that has only one way to pump its oil to customers—from a pipeline attached to the refinery. The pipeline has only one use—to pump the oil from that particular refinery. Could the refinery and the pipeline be independent companies and contract with each other? The answer is no.

- ○ Each asset is completely specific to its partner asset; therefore, the two are totally dependent on each other. Problems could arise if one partner reneged on the contract or tried to get a better price from the other. Their codependence makes it difficult for them to operate peacefully through the marketplace; for this reason, the two should operate as one firm.

- Of course, the choice is never simply to own or to contract with an outside supplier. There is a spectrum of choices in between those two options, such as a joint venture, strategic alliance, franchise or licensing arrangement, and so on. Two companies that have the ability to cooperate and achieve synergy may do so as independent companies, through some kind of alliance, or through a merger.

- To close this lecture, let's think about asset specificity and codependence in the context of Disney and its acquisition of Pixar.
  - ○ When Pixar was making its first feature film, *Toy Story*, the firm approached Disney to act as distributor for the movie. Disney agreed under the condition that it would retain the characters that Pixar developed and be able to use them in sequels, in the theme parks, and so on, even if Pixar eventually went on to work with another studio.

  - ○ A decade later, Pixar had achieved remarkable success, but Disney Animation was struggling. Pixar threatened to go to another studio but ultimately didn't because of the earlier agreement that Disney would retain the characters.

o   In the end, Disney acquired Pixar because the two firms had become codependent. They couldn't work together through the market; to achieve synergy, they had to come together in a merger. Today, the Pixar characters are leveraged in the same way that other Disney characters are across a range of businesses. Pixar was more valuable as part of the Disney family because Disney could fully exploit the value of those characters in a way that few other firms could do.

Suggested Reading

Coase, "The Nature of the Firm."

Collis and Montgomery, *Corporate Strategy*.

Williamson, *Markets and Hierarchies*.

Questions to Consider

1. Why do firms diversify, putting multiple business units under one corporate parent?

2. What alternatives exist to horizontal and vertical integration?

3. Why must we consider transaction costs when determining the appropriate corporate strategy?

Why Did Disney Buy Pixar?
Lecture 8—Transcript

Think about the Walt Disney Company for a moment. Consider the businesses in which they've chosen to compete, just a few of them—theme parks, a film studio, cable television channels, hotels, retail stores, and consumer products, just to name a few. Why is Disney choosing to compete in all of these businesses? That is a fundamental question about corporate strategy, our topic for this lecture and subsequent lectures.

Here, with Disney, we're talking about a multi business-unit corporation. We're talking about a company with a corporate office overseeing multiple subsidiaries, and each of these subsidiaries, or business units, is competing in a different product market.

The question, when we look at a firm like this, is, why is the company choosing to compete in a wider range of businesses? Why are they choosing to compete in multiple product markets? And are these businesses somehow better off because they're together? The fundamental question, then, of corporate strategy is, is the whole worth more than the sum of the parts?

For Disney, their hope is that the answer is yes, that somehow, one plus one equals three; that the theme parks are somehow more valuable as part of the Disney family than they would be as an independent company; that the cable television channels, likewise, are more valuable as part of the Disney family than if they were outside the portfolio; that somehow these businesses are stronger, have a more formidable competitive advantage, because they're working in unison.

We often hear the term *synergy* when we talk about that cooperation among multiple business units within a corporation, synergy, the idea that one plus one equals three. Walt Disney captured this beautifully with a quote once. He said, "I only hope that we never lose sight of one thing, that it was all started by a mouse." The mouse, the characters, in fact, are what tie a lot of the units at Disney together. Many of them leverage the power of the characters. Think for a moment about the theme parks. Are we attracted to the theme parks just because there's great rides there? Or do the characters add additional value to the theme park experience, making the theme parks better competitors against theme parks that do not have those famous Disney characters?

There's two levels of strategy, then, that we're covering in this course. Up until now, we've been talking about business-unit strategy. We're talking about how a company chooses to compete. How do they try to gain advantage over their rivals in a particular product market? But now, with corporate strategy, we're not looking at how to compete, we're asking the question, where do you compete? As a multi business-unit corporation, why are you choosing to build this particular portfolio of businesses? Why is Disney choosing to compete in the movie product market, as well as the theme park product market, as well as the cable television product market? Not how do they achieve advantage in any one of those markets? But why are they choosing to compete in that entire set of businesses? That's the question that we want to ask in this lecture, as well as in several moving forward.

Now, there are several types of corporate strategy that we will evaluate, two basic types, horizontal integration and vertical integration. And with each, there are two types within them. So let's start with horizontal integration. That's the idea that a company is choosing to compete in multiple product markets, hopefully, achieving some integration, or synergy, across those businesses. There are two kinds of horizontal integration. There's what we call related diversification and unrelated diversification. Related diversification is when the company appears to be competing in related product markets, products that have something to do with one another, where there are apparent synergistic possibilities. Unrelated diversification is when a company appears to be competing in markets that don't have much to do with one another. Do such firms exist? They do.

Think about General Electric, the Virgin Group, or in the past, a company like Sara Lee, which competed in a wide range of businesses, in products that didn't really have much to do with one another. General Electric, for example, making everything from airplane engines, to plastics, to light bulbs, to appliances, to running a television network for many years—NBC. As for related diversification, examples of that include not only Disney, but a company like Procter & Gamble, which has a wide array of health and beauty aids, as well as laundry detergents and other items that it sells in its portfolio of products. So horizontal integration can involve either related diversification or unrelated diversification.

But then we also have a second type of corporate strategy, and that's what we call vertical integration. Now, it's not about competing in multiple product markets, but it's taking one particular product market and deciding to compete along multiple pieces of the supply chain. Think about this in terms of two types, forward integration and backward. Backward integration is when a company chooses to produce its own components, or raw materials. Forward integration is when a company is choosing to own its own distribution, or retail store network.

So think about Apple choosing to open its own stores; that's an example of forward integration. As for Amazon, think about when Amazon decided to become it's own book publisher. It's not just selling books, but publishing them. That's backward integration. Backward integration is when we're moving back toward the earth and toward raw materials. Forward integration, when we're moving closer to the end user. So corporate strategy involves these two fundamental, broad choices. Do we integrate horizontally? Do we compete in multiple product markets? And, do we integrate vertically? Do we choose to operate at multiple points along the supply chain?

Now, how could we evaluate a corporate strategy? We can ask two fundamental questions about each of the businesses that are part of this family, this portfolio. The first is, is each business better off as part of this corporation than it would be by itself? And the second question we can ask is, does each business unit within this corporation, outperform comparable, focused companies, companies that only compete in that product market and nowhere else? Do they do better than their rivals? If they do, then presumably, they're getting some benefit from being part of this corporate family; it's strengthening their competitive advantage. If not, maybe they should be elsewhere and not part of this portfolio.

So related diversification is all about this idea of synergy, or what economists call scope economies. And related diversification is about trying to achieve these scope economies among businesses competing in similar product markets. Put another way, related diversification is when a firm is trying to share resources or capabilities across multiple businesses, whether it's distribution channels, sales forces, or R & D facilities, or factories. In Disney's case, they're sharing the characters across multiple businesses, leveraging them to enhance the value of their television, of their theme parks, of their consumer products, of their stores.

To define economies of scope more precisely, what we mean is that either a business unit's willingness to pay is higher because the units within a firm are working together, than the willingness to pay would be if these units were independent. And/or each business unit's costs are lower because the units are working together, than the unit's costs would be if these businesses were independent.

So economies of scope exist, in a related diversification strategy, when each unit either has stronger willingness to pay or lower costs because of their cooperation with their sister units. In other words, a good corporate strategy is all about strengthening the competitive advantage of each of these business units, making them better off than they would be on their own. Think, for a moment, about the theme parks at Disney. Do they have higher willingness to pay or lower costs as a result of being part of the Disney family?

I would argue they do. In particular, I want to focus on willingness to pay. Are we willing to pay more to go to a Disney theme park than to generic theme parks operated by competitors, like Six Flags? Many people are. Now, why are they willing to pay more to go to a Disney theme park? Because Disney theme parks are working together with other business units in the Disney family, most specifically, the animation studio. They're drawing the characters in, from the animation studio; building attractions around those characters; bringing the characters themselves into the theme park and having them sign autographs, take photos, eat meals with young children and families. All of this raises the willingness to pay and makes the theme parks a tremendous competitor against more generic rivals. Economies of scope exist.

Now, let's think, for a moment, about Disney's capabilities. Disney represents a powerful example of a company that leveraged a set of resources and capabilities into a number of different businesses, leveraging those characters. And when we think about the characters at Disney, we should point out that these resources are quite valuable, because they're highly durable and hard to imitate. Others can't imitate the Disney characters because Disney has protected that intellectual property; they've patented and copyrighted them. But moreover, the characters are really durable. They last forever. Unlike a factory asset or piece of machinery that depreciates, it seems as though the Disney characters, they appreciate in value over time. Moreover, every few years a new generation of children is born, and their families introduce them to those characters.

And Disney can appropriate the value associated with these resources. In other words, when they create something based on those characters, they can garner much of a profit. As Warren Buffet once said, "The mouse has no agent." Right? We don't have to pay Tom Cruise a big share of the profit for making a movie; we get to keep the profits. It's a wonderful thing.

Now the question, then, is, how can you think about leveraging these valuable resources across multiple business units? A strategist needs to think about how specialized versus how fungible, or general, a resource is. What do I mean by that? A highly fungible resource, or capability, is something like brand management expertise, innovation, risk management, a fairly generic capability that you can apply widely across a range of businesses. A highly specialized capability might be a patented product formula or a specific engineering expertise in a very narrow discipline.

Now, why is it important to distinguish between fungible and more generic capabilities from those that are more specialized? Well, a fungible capability is something you can easily transfer across lines of business. But if it's too general, it's not unique enough, you won't be able to get substantial competitive advantage based on having that resource or capability. On the other hand, highly specialized capabilities can convey powerful competitive advantage. But, you may not be able to transfer them as widely; they're narrower in their applicability. And this is really important. In other words, there are only so many areas in which you can grow based on a highly specialized set of capabilities. What does this have to do with Disney?

Well, think about it. In the 1980s, Michael Eisner arrived at Disney, and the company was in tough shape. It needed a turnaround. And he executed a remarkable turnaround at the time. Disney's core capabilities, that he built and enhanced, revolved around animated character development and deployment. In other words, Disney's capabilities were highly specialized, and they were able to leverage those capabilities to enter new businesses, like the hotel business and the retail-store business. But ultimately, growth was constrained by the very specialized nature of that capability; there's only so many things you can do with animated characters. You don't want to hurt their value in any way by branching out too far.

But Michael Eisner wanted to grow the company, and he had an aggressive growth plan. How can you do that? He wanted to move into more diverse businesses in order to achieve his revenue targets. Now, Disney has to be able to make the case under Eisner that has capabilities that are more fungible, that can be stretched to many more markets. And so Eisner began to talk not just about animated character development, he began to talk about the fact that Disney was excellent at managing creativity. He defined Disney's capabilities more broadly. He didn't want to talk about the specialized capability of animated character development. He wanted to talk about creativity management. It enabled him to justify the move into a broader range of businesses to achieve his growth goals.

Well, there's some challenges associated with defining your capabilities very broadly. It's more difficult to make the case that you're truly unique and superior to all your rivals in that set of capabilities. Is Disney really better at managing creativity than all the other firms that it competes with? It also becomes rather difficult to discriminate among various options for diversification. In other words, how many businesses have something to do with managing creativity? You could argue many, many different kinds of businesses do and begin to articulate a justification to move into things that are pretty far from what you're really good at, from your core.

On the other hand, if you manage and you think about your business in term of developing and deploying family-friendly animated characters, it narrows the kinds of businesses that you're likely to enter. So now, think about it. What happened at Disney during Eisner's tenure? He spent about two decades at the firm. In his first decade, he soared. The company did incredibly well. He was focused around leveraging the characters.

As he stretched his definition of what Disney was good at and began to move further and further away from that core business and started to argue that scope economies existed, between what they were doing in some things that looked really different, like owning a hockey team and a baseball team, or the Miramax Films studio that made adult films, like Pulp Fiction, and doing a wide range of other things, performance started to suffer. And in the second half of Eisner's tenure, the stock lagged the general market, the stock market overall.

Now, think about the recent moves by Bob Iger, the chief executive who took over from Eisner. He's had great success financially, both in terms of profit and stock performance. What's he done strategically? I would point out, interestingly, that Iger appears to have returned to the formula of leveraging characters. He's made three big acquisitions during his tenure. He bought Pixar, which owned characters, like those from *Toy Story*, and *Finding Nemo*, and *The Incredibles*, and *Cars*. He bought Marvel. And most recently, he bought Lucas Film, owner of the Star Wars and Indiana Jones franchises. What do all of those acquisitions have in common? He's back to defining Disney as being in the business of leveraging a specialized capability, character development and deployment, across a range of businesses.

Now, just looking at this issue of synergy alone is not enough in thinking about whether multiple businesses should be under one roof. We also have to ask ourselves, maybe there's synergy between two businesses, but do we have to have them under one roof, or could we operate as partners, two independent firms cooperating with one another, achieving some synergistic value, but maybe we don't have to actually merge our two companies?

And you know, there's some cost to having to bring two companies together under one roof, added bureaucracy, costs of going through a merger. Maybe we could stay independent, cooperate, and achieve economies of scope without having to go through and bring us totally together. Let's think about that question for a moment. Let's think about it back in terms of Disney, in terms of two businesses that they have, a hotel business and a consumer products business.

Why did they initially choose to own many of the hotels near their theme parks? On the other hand, they're in the consumer-product business. But they don't make their own toys and games; they outsource the production of that. So toys and games are synergistic with the rest of the Disney family, but, they've chosen not to actually do all of it in-house. They've outsourced. What's different about the hotel business versus consumer products? Well, initially, it might strike you that the hotel business is much more of an experience, right? We've got families going to breakfast with the characters, the characters walking around, and signing autographs, and taking pictures with these families and these children. It's a really interactive experience. Consumer products, outsourcing the production of that, we can draw a clear diagram, a design of what we want, and we can ask a manufacturer in Asia to make it for us at a low cost, two very different businesses.

So what's the key question we have to ask ourselves if we want to analyze the decision to keep hotels in-house versus outsource the production of certain consumer goods at Disney? We have to go back to a Nobel Prize winner, Ronald Coase, and a famous paper he wrote in 1937 called "The Nature of the Firm." He asked a crucial question. Why do firms exist? Seems like rather odd question. Why do companies exist? Well, he said, if markets are such a great way to coordinate economic activity, why is not all activity conducted through the marketplace with small firms run by entrepreneurs? Why do we need large organizations?

And he refined his question. He said, should economic activity be coordinated by the market mechanism or by intra-firm organizational structures and processes? In other words, should I contract with an outside supplier to make components? Or, should I build and run my own factory? And how do I decide whether to use a contract through the market, or to organize component manufacturing within my own firm, in my own factory.

His answer? You have to look at the transaction costs associated with organizing certain economic activities. Many years later, Oliver Williamson extended Coase's argument. He too was rewarded for his great work. And between Coase and Williamson, they've given us great insights to help us understand corporate strategy.

To help us understand transaction costs, suppose I'm considering signing a contract with an outside supplier for components for a personal computer. There are costs—time, money, effort, risk—associated with conducting transactions with outside parties. Contacting with them may be cumbersome and difficult at times. And there's a risk that one party may renege on the contract, or not fulfill its obligations. On the other hand, there are also transaction costs associated with coordinating that activity within my firm. I have to get my personal computer assembly plant to coordinate with my component manufacturing operation. and they may not exist in the same geographic location.

The question, then, becomes, under which arrangement will the transaction costs be lower? What's more efficient, doing it in-house or outside? To give you an example of this, consider Starbucks and Dunkin' Donuts. You'll note the two have made a very different choice about their restaurants. Starbucks has chosen to own most of its free-standing stores in the United States. Dunkin' Donuts, on the other hand, has chosen to franchise most of its free-standing stores in the country. So, why and how might transaction costs help us understand the contrasting decisions of these two players? Well, think about it. Starbucks is trying to create an experience within their store. Howard Schultz, its founder, talked about the Third Place; there's home. there's work, and then, there's a place where we can gather to work, talk to friends. It's Starbucks. It's an experience. We're not just selling coffee. Dunkin', much more about selling coffee, much more of an easy transaction. Get in there. Get out very quickly.

So, if you were going to contract with an outside party, where is it easier? Is it easier to do at Dunkin' or at Starbucks? The answer's pretty simple. It's much easier to contract with a franchisee at Dunkin'. It's much harder to write into a contract, at Starbucks, how you would want a franchisee to operate that experience, so you keep it in-house. Right? It's too difficult to use the market. And this is something that we see, also, with hotels at Disney. It's rather difficult to tell Goofy how Goofy should behave at breakfast with my child. So you keep Goofy in-house. You run the hotel yourself, and you train that employee on how to interact with children. And you monitor closely how that interaction takes place every day. On the other hand, consumer products produced in Asia, you can outsource that. You can monitor from afar. And you can use the marketplace to get the best price for producing that good for you. So we make this choice.

What drives transaction costs? Well, three big things. Uncertainty, the more uncertainty in the market, the harder it is to use contracts to work with an outside party. No more likely you may move activity in-house. Frequency, the more frequently we have to interact with one another, maybe we might as well just bring our companies together, as opposed to having to constantly work through the marketplace.

And lastly, there's the issue of what we call asset specificity. Market coordination becomes very difficult and costly when the potential arises for what we call opportunistic behavior. Such potential exists when economic actors invest heavily in what we call transaction-specific assets. In other words, when factors of production are really specific to the other party. Let me see if I can explain. Imagine an oil refinery; and it only has one way to pump it's oil out to its customers, and that's a pipeline attached to the refinery. The pipeline has only one use, to pump the oil from that particular refinery. What will happen in that case? Could they be independent companies? And could they simply contract with one another? The answer is no. Each asset is totally specific to its partner asset, and therefore, they're totally dependent on one another.

What's the problem with being highly dependent on another party? Well, now the opportunity for opportunistic behavior arises. One could renege on the contract, put the other in a precarious position. One could say, I want to reopen the contract; I'd like a better price from you. Their co-dependence makes it difficult for them to operate peacefully through the marketplace. Contracting is difficult, so we see them come together in the same firm.

So, this choice, then, this choice is between do it in the market or do it outside of the market. Do it within the company. Well, no it's not quite that. It's really a spectrum. The choice is never simply contracts versus firms; there's a whole spectrum of choices you make with regard to corporate strategy. On the one hand, you could contract with an outside party through the marketplace. On the other hand, you could have two entities, an oil refinery and a pipeline, come together. But there's a whole bunch of choices in between, joint ventures, strategic alliances, franchising, licensing, a whole spectrum of choices. So, you may have two companies that have an ability to cooperate and to achieve synergy. The question is, do they do it as independent companies? Or, do they have to come together more closely through an alliance, through a joint venture? Or, maybe, they have to merge.

So think about this in the context of Disney in its acquisition of Pixar. Think about assets specificity and co-dependence, and consider the correlation to pipelines and refineries. Disney, initially, worked with Pixar back when Steve Jobs was CEO of a young outfit called Pixar. Steve Jobs had bought Pixar from George Lucas, and they were looking at making their first feature film, which turned out to be *Toy Story*.

Now, think about it. You're not Steve Jobs, the legend you are today. You're Steve Jobs the unemployed, former CEO and founder of Apple. You've bought this little outfit, called Pixar, that no one's ever heard of. And you think you're going to make a movie when you've never been in the movie business. Who's going to distribute that movie? Nobody. It's going to be really difficult to distribute that movie. You need help. So you go to Disney. You go to Michael Eisner. And you say, will you help market and distribute this movie? And so they evolved. They came to some agreement. They formed a contract, a partnership. They didn't merge at that time.

But Disney was in the driver's seat. And they extracted some significant concessions from Steve Jobs and Pixar. They said, if the contract ends, and when it ends, we get to retain the characters that we worked on together and continue to use them in sequels and within our theme parks, even if you, Pixar, eventually move on to work with another movie studio. And that was very powerful. Eisner was in the driver's seat. Steve Jobs needed Disney much more than Disney needed Pixar at that time.

But now, what happened a decade later? A decade later, Pixar had had remarkable success. Every one of its movies had gone to number one at the box office. Disney Animation, it was really struggling. It had had some real tough times, some hard years. It had not had repeated successes like Pixar. So here was Jobs threatening to go elsewhere. He wanted to negotiate with Universal, or others, or at least he was threatening to do so. Why did he not go to somewhere else? He didn't really get along with Eisner. Why didn't Pixar go elsewhere? Why did they end up selling to Disney?

Well, you could argue that these two firms had evolved into a co-dependency that made it difficult to work together through a contractual relationship. But the co-dependency made it so that they really needed to come together. They couldn't go their separate ways. Why were they co-dependent? Well, at this point, Disney really needed Pixar in a way they didn't a decade earlier, because Disney Animation had fallen on hard times. They needed a fresh infusion of characters to fuel synergy in the theme parks, and on cable television, and elsewhere.

But, wait. Did Pixar need Disney? Could Pixar really walk away? Remember, the contract concessions originally negotiated by Eisner and Jobs, as John Lasseter, the creative head of Pixar said, "Over my dead body will I see Toy Story 3½ straight to DVD issued by Disney, and we're not part of that. I can't give up my beloved characters." The two companies were co-dependent on one another, much like the oil refinery and the pipeline. And therefore, they couldn't work together through the market. They had to go deeper, and come together in a merger, and achieve that synergy. And now the Pixar characters are leveraged much like the Disney characters across that range of businesses. Pixar was more valuable as part of the Disney family because Disney could fully exploit the value of those characters in a way few other firms could do.

So what are the lessons for us from this lecture? Multi business-unit corporations competing in a wider range of product markets must be able to articulate that the whole is worth more than the sum of the parts, that each business is more valuable, has a stronger competitive advantage because it's part of the family than if it were on its own. Related diversification, then, is all about the logic of economies of scope. The idea that you have higher willingness to pay or lower costs because you're working together with sister companies.

Now, cooperative behavior to produce these mutual benefits, does it all have to happen inside the firm? Perhaps not. Maybe, sometimes, we can outsource part of what we do and work through the market through a contract with an outside party and produce mutual benefits. But sometimes that contracting is cumbersome, and sometimes there's the opportunity for opportunistic behavior, and in an extreme case, so much co-dependency that we need to actually bring it inside the firm and work together as sister companies within one portfolio.

Of course, sometimes there are diseconomies of scope, something we haven't talked about yet, but I'll leave you with. Could it be possible that we get into multiple businesses, and now, trying to manage multiple businesses actually causes us more harm than good? Can it be so difficult to manage different businesses that we actually destroy value, rather then create it? And this is something we're going to talk about in an upcoming lecture. It's a real challenge. And I would simply argue now that executives sometimes overestimate economies of scope. They overestimate synergy to justify their move into new businesses, to support their growth ambitions. And it can get them in trouble.

So now to close, what's your assignment? Select a diversified firm, such as Procter & Gamble, owner of a wide variety of brands, such as Tide, Ivory, Neutrogena, and Swiffer, or Darden Restaurants, owner of multiple restaurant chains, like Olive Garden and LongHorn Steakhouse, and ask yourself, what synergies exist among the business units within these companies? Is the whole worth more than the sum of the parts? And maybe even look and say, how and why have they changed their portfolio businesses in recent years? Perhaps, maybe, executives have reconsidered the extent of the synergies among these units within their company.

The Diversification Discount
Lecture 9

Consider two historical corporations that used to be very successful: Fortune Brands and Sara Lee. Fortune Brands was a large, diversified firm that competed in three segments: golf, liquor, and home hardware. In addition to producing baked goods, Sara Lee owned a chain of supermarkets, the Coach handbag company, Jimmy Dean meats, and other businesses. As we saw in the last lecture, Disney is a related diversified firm seeking to pursue synergies across product markets. In contrast, Fortune Brands and Sara Lee are two classic examples of unrelated diversification. In this lecture, we'll look at why these firms assembled the portfolios they did and why they later sold off these divisions and became much narrower in focus.

Analyzing Diversified Firms
- When looking at a diversified firm, analysts and investors compare its market value to its *breakup value*—that is, the amount each of the firm's divisions would be worth independently. Analysts try to learn whether the sum of those amounts would be more or less than the value of the whole company.

- A *diversification discount* results when the whole is worth less than the proposed sum of the parts. Unfortunately for many diversified firms, particularly unrelated diversifiers in the United States, it's often the case that the whole is worth less than parts, which is why we've seen many corporate breakups in the last few years.

- Research from academics has also demonstrated that firms that focus on one product market tend to do well in the United States. Studies have shown that increases in focus tend to be followed by stock price increases, and decreases in focus are often followed by stock price decreases. Further, both spinoffs and their original parent companies tend to outperform the overall stock market after the separation of the two.

- All this financial evidence has proven to be a powerful rationale for companies to slim down and for fewer companies to pursue a strategy of unrelated diversification. However, it's also important to look at each company individually to understand its strategy. In some cases, a company's management may argue that the firm is pursuing a related diversification strategy, while investors and analysts may think that its business units are unrelated.

Risks of Unrelated Diversification
- There are four invalid reasons for diversification.
  - The first of these is to diversify risk. Management may plan to have some businesses in a firm's portfolio that tend to do well in a strong economy and others that are counter-cyclical. When one of these businesses is doing well, the idea is that it would offset others that are experiencing difficulties. But diversifying risk is an invalid reason for a company to pursue a diversification strategy.

  - A second invalid reason for diversification is known as *cross-subsidization*—that is, having a portfolio of seemingly unrelated businesses at different stages of the business life cycle. Businesses using this strategy are taking the cash that's being generated by profitable but mature businesses and using it to fund growth in newer, high-growth industries.

  - Businesses also sometimes pursue unrelated diversification when they are looking for revenue and profit growth because of problems in the core business.

  - Finally, some companies look to unrelated diversification in an effort to manipulate the stock markets. They try to enhance the valuation of a business that is, perhaps, mature and not growing by acquiring a newer, higher-growth business.

- As individuals, we know it makes good sense to diversify our investment portfolios, but individuals can diversify much more effectively and inexpensively than companies can. The external capital market does a much better job of moving resources around and valuing opportunities than the internal market. In a sense, we can say—and research confirms—that a manager at the top of a corporation is not as smart as the crowd—the entire external market.

- Cross-subsidization—taking money from mature businesses and funding new opportunities—came from a concept introduced by the Boston Consulting Group many years ago, the so-called BCG Matrix. The basic matrix is shown below.

	Low Market Share	High Market Share
Slow Growth	Dog	Cash Cow
Fast Growth	Question Mark	Star

- ○ BCG argued that an unrelated corporation could effectively classify its business units by looking at two basic measures: What kind of market share does the particular business have, high or low? And how fast is the particular industry growing?

- ○ In the matrix, a unit that is in a slow-moving industry and has low market share is a dog. A unit in a slow-moving industry with high market share is a cash cow; it generates a great deal of cash and doesn't have many opportunities to reinvest the money in the business. A unit with a low share in a high-growth industry is a question mark; it may or may not turn out to be profitable. Finally, a unit with a high share in a high-growth industry is a star.

- ○ The idea of the matrix was to divest the dogs and milk the cash cows. Take the excess cash from slow-moving industries and invest in the question marks, even if they were unrelated to the mainstream business.

- ○ Again, this strategy presumes that managers inside the firm can allocate resources better than the external market—that they know where the best new opportunity is and they can beat the market, but this is very difficult to do. The wiser course is often to give the excess cash back to the investors and allow them to find the next opportunity. Let the question marks get their funding from venture capitalists, angel investors, or private equity firms rather than large, complex, and mature corporations.

Governance Economies

- A company is pursuing unrelated diversification when it is operating various businesses independently. Instead of trying to add value to each of its businesses through the realization of synergies—as we saw with related diversification—the idea here is to add value by using a common management system across all the businesses. The premise is that by having a single company controlling operations and by transferring knowledge and best practices among the businesses, all the businesses are managed better together than they could be managed on their own—and they achieve governance economies.

- In this strategy, it's purely management skill that is being leveraged across businesses, not tangible resources and capabilities, such as common distribution channels, common production facilities, and so on.

- The classic example of a firm that has pursued governance economies is General Electric. Throughout the 20th century, GE was a high-performing stock. It was also clearly an unrelated diversifier, operating a television broadcasting network, a jet engine business, an appliance business, a lighting business, and others. However, GE had a management system that spread across the businesses.

- Achieving governance economies is easier to pull off when there's a clear dominant logic or common theme across many businesses. For many years, Emerson Electric was a successful unrelated diversifier, but each of its businesses was in manufacturing, each was in a fairly mature sector, each pursued a low-cost strategy, and each involved a fairly mature technology. Thus, there were common threads, even though the product markets were seemingly unrelated.

- Today, some have begun to question whether GE is still as powerful as it once was in its exercise and execution of governance economies. The spread of knowledge is easy and costless in today's economy, which means that other companies have adopted GE's best practices, and the company may no longer achieve the governance economies it once did.

Unrelated Diversification around the World

- Research by Professor Tarun Khanna has shown that although unrelated diversification may no longer make sense in developed economies, such as the United Kingdom or the United States, the picture may be different in emerging markets, such as India.

- To explain this difference, Khanna pointed to the idea of *institutional voids*. He argued that a capitalist economic system requires the effective functioning of certain institutions that enable parties to enter voluntarily into mutually beneficial transactions. Institutional voids occur when specialized intermediaries are absent.

- *Intermediaries* are economic entities that insert themselves between a potential buyer and a seller in an attempt to bring them together and help them engage in a mutually beneficial transaction.
    - Consider, for instance, a firm pursuing a differentiation strategy in an effort to achieve high willingness to pay.

    - Certain intermediaries, such as *Consumer Reports*, may enable potential buyers to confirm the quality of the firm's products. Other intermediaries, such as a market research firm, may help the company assess consumer tastes. And still other intermediaries, such as government regulatory agencies, may certify high quality.

- There are many intermediaries that help make transactions work in developed economies, such as that in the United States. In the capital markets, there are auditors who verify financial statements. In the labor markets, there are headhunting firms, certification agencies, and business schools that help match candidates with job opportunities. And through all the markets, there is a judiciary system that operates to enforce the rule of law and property rights.

- But these intermediaries may not exist to the same extent in emerging markets. And a large corporation—an unrelated diversifier—may step into that institutional void to provide that value.

- Khanna has shown that the diversification discount we see in the United States does not exist in, for example, India. Family business groups that are in unrelated businesses are ubiquitous in India, while we no longer see many unrelated diversifiers in the United States. And the percentage of conglomerates trading at discount is below 50% in India, while it's much higher than 50% in the United States.

- The House of Tata, or Tata Group, in India comprises more than 100 companies in seven business sectors, and it serves as a specialized intermediary in a number of ways.
  - For example, in an economy where there aren't clear ways to certify the quality of goods and services, Tata putting its name on a product gives the Indian people confidence that the product is of high quality.

  - For companies that are part of the Tata family, talent for a new business can be reallocated from an established business. Capital can also be moved from a successful business into emerging opportunities.

  - By serving as an intermediary in these ways, Tata makes up for inefficiencies in the market; therefore, it adds value to the businesses in its portfolio in a way that an unrelated diversifier could not in the United States.

- In the United States today, many of the unrelated diversifiers that were successful three or four decades ago have been broken up. The reason for this is that product, labor, and capital markets in the United States have become much more efficient. In the 1960s, the U.S. economy bore a closer resemblance to an emerging market, with institutional voids and the opportunity for unrelated diversifiers to fill them. Today, with far fewer institutional voids, we see far fewer unrelated diversifiers.

Suggested Reading

Hitt, Hoskisson, and Ireland, *Competing for Advantage.*

Khanna and Palepu, *Winning in Emerging Markets.*

Stewart, *The Quest for Value.*

Questions to Consider

1. What are some flawed reasons for engaging in unrelated diversification?

2. Why might unrelated diversification make sense in certain emerging markets?

3. What are the limitations and deficiencies of the BCG model of portfolio management?

The Diversification Discount
Lecture 9—Transcript

Consider for a moment two historical corporations that used to be very successful, Fortune Brands and Sarah Lee. Fortune Brands was a large, diversified firm that competed in three segments. They had a large golf business that used to be quite successful. They had a liquor business that sold distilled spirits. And they had a division that sold home hardware products.

Then consider Sarah Lee. Sarah lee did far more, historically, than produce baked goods. They operated the Piggly Wiggly chain of supermarkets. They had Coach handbags, Jimmy Dean meats, Playtex and Hanes undergarments. Chock full o'Nuts coffee, and the Hillshire Farm brand of meats.

What do these two firms have in common, and how are they different than Disney? Disney is a related diversified firm trying to pursue synergies or economies of scope across related product markets. Fortune Brands and Sarah Lee are two classic examples of unrelated diversification. They're competing in a wide range of product markets where there are no apparent economies of scope or synergies. Why, then, have these firms assembled the portfolios that they did? Was there an economic logic to bringing together unrelated subsidiaries in one corporation?

Well, interestingly, these corporations have both broken up. That is to say, today, the conclusion has been that the whole is not worth the sum of the parts. And these companies gradually sold off divisions and became much narrower in their focus. We'll try to understand why that happened. Why did management come to that conclusion? Perhaps at the behest of investors over time.

There's some interesting evidence that has accumulated over the years with regard to diversification, particularly unrelated diversification, in the United States. And I stress the United States because later in the lecture, I'll talk about some key differences between developed nations and emerging markets with regard to the strategy of unrelated diversification.

Numerous academic studies have found that diversified firms trade at a discount to their break-up values, on average. Now, what does that mean? What do we mean by break-up value? Well, what analysts and investors are doing all the time with regard to diversified firms is they're examining what the firm is worth today. What is its market value? And they're comparing that to something they call the break-up value. What does that mean?

Well, let's say a firm has three major divisions. They take a look at a hypothetical scenario. What if this firm broke up? What if the three divisions were independent operating companies? What would each of them be worth independently? And if we add up those three, the sum of the parts, is that worth more or less than the whole is worth today? A diversification discount is when the whole is worth less than the proposed sum of the parts. And, unfortunately, for many diversified firms, particularly unrelated diversifiers in the U.S., the whole seems to be worth less than the sum of the parts, and it's why we've seen many corporate break ups in the last few years.

Not only have Sara Lee and Fortune Brands broken up. But in 2014 we saw some very successful corporations, like HP, Hewlett Packard; or eBay; or the Gannett Corporation, parent company of USA Today, all engage in break ups, each of them splitting in two, Gannett separating its newspaper and publishing business and broadcasting business. Then we saw eBay splitting off PayPal, and HP breaking into two corporations. In each case, analysts looked at it, management analyzed it, and concluded the whole was worth less than the sum of the parts.

Research from academics has also demonstrated that focused firms, firms that focus on one product market, tend to do very, very well in the United States. Studies have also shown that increases in focus tend to be followed by stock price increases, and decreases in focus, efforts to diversify, often are followed by stock price decreases. Furthermore, research shows that spinoffs, when a company splits off one division and sets it out as an independent company in the market, those spin offs tend to outperform the overall stock market after separation from the parent company. In addition, the remaining parent company tends to outperform the market after the spinoff. This evidence has been accumulated over several decades in the U.S. and has proven to be a powerful rationale for companies slimming down and for less and less companies to pursue a strategy of unrelated diversification.

Now, we have to offer a few words of caution, though, before we draw wide-ranging conclusions from that academic research. Research does show that, on average, diversified firms trade at a discount. But about one third of diversified firms trade at a premium to their break-up value. Most of those are related diversifiers, like Disney.

There are some other issues with this research about the diversification discount. Some research suggests that firms that choose to diversify may be trading at a discount prior to diversifying. In other words, they're struggling; their core businesses isn't doing well, and therefore, they go diversify, sometimes into unrelated markets. So the poor performance actually comes first before the diversification.

Furthermore, the businesses that are acquired in diversifying acquisitions, they themselves sometimes tend to be poor performers. So companies buy a poor performer in hopes of driving improvements in the business. What this means is that we have to be really careful. When we analyze a particular company, we know the research. We know, in general, we should be skeptical in the U.S. of unrelated diversification. But, we have to look at each company in its own right and understand it strategy. And here's where things get a little fuzzy. Are companies related or unrelated diversifiers? Sometimes it's a little hard to tell. Management may be arguing that, in fact, the firm is pursuing a related diversification strategy, that synergies exist. Investors and analysts may be skeptical. They may look and say, no, we don't think this is actually a related strategy; it looks unrelated to us. We don't see powerful economies of scope. And therein lies the key question. Who is right, the investors or management? And you'll often see a back and forth going on on this.

In 2014, DuPont was facing this question. Investors and analysts were arguing that different parts of DuPont actually were not as related as management tended to believe, and those analysts wanted to see a break up of DuPont. On the other hand, executives at the company were arguing that it was a related diversification strategy.

Now, there are several invalid reasons for diversification, reasons that are sometimes used, well, often in the past were sometimes used, as justification for unrelated diversification. And these are invalid. And there are four of them. First, we're diversifying risk. We're going to have some businesses in the portfolio that tend to do well in a strong economy and other divisions that are counter cyclical, and therefore, when one is doing very well, it could offset others that aren't doing as well. And this is a less risky strategy, having different divisions that can balance each other out. This is invalid as a reason for diversification in the United States today.

There's a second invalid reason for diversification, and this is what we call cross-subsidization. This is when we have a portfolio of seemingly unrelated businesses at different stages of the business lifecycle. And what we're doing is taking the cash that's being generated by profitable, but mature, businesses and using it to fund growth in newer, high-growth industries. We could see this in a company called Allied Domecq several years ago. They were a European distilled spirits and wine company. They also tended to own some other companies that were cash cows, if you will. For example, they owned Dunkin' Donuts. What were they doing with the Dunkin' Donuts brand? Well, they were drawing cash out of that very profitable business and using it to expand further in the wine business, so they were cross-subsidizing from one unit to the other, though those units were really unrelated, no synergies at all between doughnuts and wine.

There's a third invalid reason that people pursue unrelated diversification, and that's that they sometimes are looking for revenue and profit growth because of problems in the core business. Fosters of Australia did this some years ago. They had a strong beer business, but one that had matured. There was no growth in the business. So they looked for other opportunities, wine in particular, where they might find new growth. But, in fact, we learned that beer and wine, well, they're not as related as you think. So we have to be careful when we define *related*. We don't mean just that the products themselves may be consumed together; we mean that there are truly powerful economies of scope between the businesses. And in Fosters case, they learned that beer and wine, well, there aren't such powerful synergies. So just looking for growth is not a valid reason to diversify.

And finally, we see sometimes where companies are trying to manipulate the stock markets. They're trying to take a business that maybe is very mature and not growing, and enhance its valuation in the eyes of investors by acquiring a newer, higher-growth business. The Washington Post did this some years ago with the ownership of Kaplan educational business. Kaplan was growing rapidly, and they were trying to use that to create a higher valuation in the market, though the newspaper business was lagging behind, all invalid reasons for diversification.

Now, what do we know about diversification of risk? Why is it not valid when a company says, we're pursuing this strategy because we want to make sure that we diversify risk. After all, we all know, as individuals, it makes good sense to diversify our investment portfolio. We don't want all our eggs in one basket. Well the key is this. You as an individual can diversify on your own much more effectively than the firm can do, and much more inexpensively. Why? Well, you could simply buy mutual funds, or index funds, and quickly diversify your investment portfolio. You don't need an extensive corporate office and bureaucracy at a large corporation to buy and sell whole businesses and amass a portfolio to achieve diversification. You can do it on your own.

Now, what's the premise here? The premise is that markets are relatively efficient. Now, this doesn't mean we have to believe markets are perfectly efficient. That doesn't mean we believe that every stock is perfectly and appropriately valued by investors. It simply means we believe the external capital market does a much better job of moving resources around and valuing opportunities than the so-called internal market. That is, that a manager at the top of the corporation is not as smart as the crowd, as the entire external market. And this is really important. And we have some evidence to back up that individuals are not as smart as the crowd.

What evidence is that? Well, we know, for example, that the typical portfolio manager at a mutual fund does not beat the market. On average, most mutual fund managers do not beat the market. That says that external capital markets are reasonably efficient. And therefore, if that's true, you as an individual investor, you can diversify on your own. You don't need a corporation, like Sarah Lee, to diversify for you by buying and selling unrelated business.

Now, what about cross-subsidization? Why is that invalid? Well, cross-subsidization, taking money from mature businesses and funding new opportunities, this came from a concept introduced by the Boston Consulting Group many years ago, the so-called BCG Matrix. They argued that an unrelated business, an unrelated corporation, could effectively classify its units in different ways. And they looked at two basic measures by which you could classify your businesses. One is, what kind of market share do you have, high or low, in a particular business? And how fast is that particular industry growing?

So suppose you have a unit that's in a slow-moving industry and you have low market share. They call that a dog. But if you're in a slow-moving industry and you have high market share, they call that a cash cow, a business that was generating a lot of cash and didn't have a lot of new investment opportunities in which to plow that cash back in. It was generating excess cash.

What about high-growth industries? Well, if you have low share in a high-growth industry, they called that a question mark, a possible, cool opportunity that could really turn out to be very profitable, but we don't know yet. We're in a high-growth industry, but we haven't yet established a prominent position. And finally, there are the stars, high-growth industry, high share, an excellent performer. What was the logic of this matrix? Well, the idea was to divest the dogs and milk the cash cows and take that excess cash from those slow-moving industries and plow it back in and invest in the question marks and help them grow, even if they were unrelated.

Now, what's wrong with this concept? Again, it presumes that managers inside the firm can allocate resources better than the external market, that they're smarter and that they know where the best new opportunity is and they can beat the market, very difficult to do. It even assumes that they know when and how new growth opportunities will emerge. It's difficult to figure that out.

What do we know? Well, we know individual investors have often said, wait. If there's excess cash in a business, why not give that back to the investor and let them go out and find the next new opportunity? Ask yourself this question. For these question marks, these promising new opportunities, where should they get their capital? Who is going to be better at funding them, venture capitalists, angel investors, private equity firms, or, the leaders of a large, bureaucratic, complex, mature corporation? Most today believe, in the United States, that we'd rather see those question marks depend directly on people who every day are looking at startups and figuring out which ones are promising and which ones aren't.

You know, Robert Kennedy was the chairman of Union Carbide, and he reflected on this BCG Matrix some years ago in a book by Bennett Stewart. And he said that when corporate management gets into the business of allocating resources between businesses crying for cash, it makes mistakes. The investment community, he says, is a better sorter outer. Bennett Stewart's work confirmed Kennedy's observation. It found that financial restructurings that severed the link between mature cash cows and promising growth opportunities increased market value. Bottom line, question marks should depend on the market for their capital, not on a large corporation cross-subsidizing from an unrelated business that happens to be a cash cow to a new opportunity. So both cross-subsidization and the diversification of risk are invalid reasons for unrelated diversification.

Well, then what might be a valid reason? Here we have to distinguish between something we call economies of scope, that we discussed with regard to Disney in a related diversification strategy, and something we call governance economies. Governance economies, potentially, can be a valid reason for unrelated diversification. What are governance economies? Well, unrelated diversification is when a corporate parent is not trying to add value to each of its businesses through the realization of synergies. Instead, the parent is operating each business fairly independently, and they're trying to realize this notion of governance economies, which is the idea of trying to add value by employing a comment-management system across all the units.

You're trying to use common management processes and best practices to drive performance. You're disciplining each management, overseeing and controlling the operations, transferring knowledge and best practice among them. You're managing the businesses better than they could be managed on their own. That's the premise here of governance economies. In short, the unrelated diversifier believes that these businesses are better off being managed by the corporate parent than independently. It's purely management skill that they're trying to leverage across their businesses, not tangible resources and capabilities, such as common distribution channels, common production facilities, common research and development.

Well, what's an example of a firm that has pursued governance economies, perhaps, successfully over the years? Most would point to General Electric as the classic example. Throughout the 20th century, GE was a high-performing stock, outperforming the stock market over that 100-year period. And they were clearly an unrelated diversifier, operating a broadcast network named NBC, a jet engine business, an appliance business, a lighting business, a wide range of businesses during the 20th century.

However, they had a management system, the GE way, a set of processes, a talent development machine, if you will, that spread across the businesses. They were instituting things like Six Sigma and spreading them across each unit. The GE workout process, the best practices transfer that Jack Welch introduced, each of these were efforts to instill a common management system across the units and enhance performance. And it appeared for years that GE did this quite successfully.

Now, this is easier to pull off when there's a clear dominant logic, or common theme, across many businesses. For many years, Emerson Electric was a successful unrelated diversifier, led by CEO Chuck Knight. But, each of the businesses was in manufacturing. Each was in a fairly mature sector. Each was pursuing a low-cost strategy. Each was with fairly mature technology. So there was a common thread, though the product markets were seemingly unrelated. It's much harder to pull off an unrelated business strategy when you have conflicting types of strategies, and different business models across the units, when you mix a differentiation strategy in one subsidiary with a low cost position and another.

So is GE still as powerful today in its exercise and execution of governance economies? Some have begun to question that, even calling for GE to be broken up as we've seen GE's stock underperform the market during the Jeff Immelt era as CEO. Why might it be that their governance economies today are not as powerful? Well, people have learned. People have learned about the GE way. The spread of knowledge is easy and costless in today's economy, so people have read about, and learned about Six Sigma. They've learned about GE's workout process, or transfer of best practices. And they've brought those practices to their corporation. In many cases, they've hired GE executives and brought them in to be able to do this. One thing I should note is, we have to worry about over confidence, or conceit, when someone says, they have a superior management skill or system they can apply across a broad range of businesses. It's pretty hard to apply the same system across really different markets.

Now, how do investors and analysts, and even managers, evaluate whether a company's whole is worth more than the sum of the parts? There are quantitative techniques we can use. One is a look at return on assets. And you could look at the return on assets of each unit within a company like Sara Lee or GE and compare that return on assets to what comparable focus competitors are doing. And you have to ask yourself the question: Are the units within a GE outperforming their direct rivals? If they are, then maybe there's some value being added by the GE corporate parent. If not, maybe they should be broken up. Similarly, we can actually do a comparison of the whole to the sum of the parts. We can evaluate what each of the units is worth if it was spun off, or try to estimate that. Add that all up, that's just sum of the parts; and compare it to what the current total market value of the firm is. And this is what's happening in 2014 with firms like HP, Symantec, eBay, and Gannett, where we've concluded that there's more value in breaking it up.

Now, what if we move around the world to different places? What does that tell us? Can we come to the same conclusions about unrelated diversification? Well, we cannot. Research by Tarun Khanna has shown that while unrelated diversification may no longer make sense in developed economies like the U.K. or the United States, when we go to emerging markets, like India, we may see something very different, where large, unrelated diversifiers may actually do quite well still today. Why is that?

Khanna pointed to the idea of Institutional voids. He argued that a capitalist economic system requires the effective functioning of certain institutions that enable parties to enter voluntarily into mutually beneficial transactions. Institutional voids occur when specialized intermediaries are absent.

Intermediaries are economic entities that insert themselves between a potential buyer and a seller in an attempt to bring them together and help them engage in a mutually beneficial transaction.

Consider, for instance, a firm pursuing a differentiation strategy trying to achieve high willingness to pay. Certain intermediaries may enable potential buyers to confirm the quality of the firm's products, say, Consumer Reports. Moreover, certain intermediaries may help the firm assess consumer tastes, like a market research firm. And, other intermediaries may certify high-quality, like government regulatory agencies. There are many intermediaries that help make transactions work in a developed economy, like the United States. In the capital markets, we have auditors who verify your financial statements so investors have confidence in giving you money. We have private equity providers, or venture capital firms, that help bring together savers with people who need capital.

In the labor markets, we have headhunting firms, and certification agencies, business schools, and relocation services that help match good candidates with great job opportunities. In the product markets we have certification agencies, we have regulatory agencies, and others, who help verify the quality of products. And through all markets, we have a judiciary that operates to enforce the rule of law and clear property rights. All of these intermediaries help make markets work in a developed economy.

But do those intermediaries exist in emerging markets? Not to the same extent. Therefore, what happens? Well, in this void, where these institutions don't exist, in steps the large corporation, the unrelated diversifier who can provide that value. So, if you're in India, a company like the House of Tata can create a lot of value as an unrelated diversifier, where we would question that strategy in the U.S.

Now, Khanna has actually looked at the evidence and shown that the diversification discount that we see in the U.S. is not existent in a place like India. Family business groups that are in unrelated businesses are ubiquitous, where we don't see many unrelated diversifiers anymore in the United States. And the percentage of conglomerates trading at discount, well, it's below 50% in India, while it's much higher than 50% in the U.S.

So let's take a look at the House of Tata for a moment. Consider the nature of inefficiencies in three markets in India: product markets, capital markets, and labor markets. And consider, too, the rule of law and property rights in that country. While India has come a long way, we still know that there are inefficiencies in these markets, and, we have a lot of corruption, meaning that the rule of law is not quite as clear and contracts not as enforceable. So what happens?

In steps the House of Tata. If there aren't clear ways to certify the quality of goods and services, Tata putting its name on a product gives the Indian people confidence that it's a high-quality good. If you're not sure where you can get talent for a new emerging business, well, you know if you're part of the Tata family, they can reallocate great talent from an established business and move it over, because they're really good at recruiting and developing talent.

And as for capital, well, they can move capital from successful businesses and push it into new emerging opportunities because the external capital market is not as effective or efficient at doing so in a place like India, so Tata steps into the breach.

And, if you're trying to launch a business, it can be difficult in a place like India. You have to navigate the politics to be able to do so. Well, how do you do that? You go to Ratan Tata, longtime head of the company, or its current management, and you ask for their help. And they use their connections with key political leaders to help you navigate the permitting and the regulatory process to be able to get the right things all lined up so you can launch your business. So Tata makes up for the inefficiencies in the market. And therefore, we see that they can add value to the businesses in their portfolio in a way an unrelated diversifier could not in a place like the United States.

Now, what's happened in the United States with regard to conglomerates or unrelated diversifiers since the 1960s and '70s? If we go back three or four decades, what we see is there were many of these unrelated diversifiers. They were high flyers, excellent performers—ITT, Textron, Sara Lee, Litton Industries, not just GE, but many of these kinds of firms. Today, many of these conglomerates have been dismantled.

As I noted, even in 2014 we're seeing more and more break ups of large corporations, even some that we thought were more related than unrelated. Well, what's changed in the United States since the '60s that would cause us to see this strategy shift from many successful, unrelated diversifiers to far fewer today, the dismantling of these large conglomerates? Well, think about the product, labor, and capital markets in the United States over the past four decades. They've become much more efficient.

If you were an entrepreneur in the '60s, did you have easy access to capital from angel investors and venture capital firms the way you do today? You did not. Were there customer reviews online to help you vouch for the quality of your product to build buzz and reputation? There were not. Were there as many opportunities to get access to the most talented people? Was it as easy to find the best people? It was harder to do so.

So with markets that were less efficient than they are today, conglomerates still made sense. In other words, the U.S. in the '60s looked a lot more like the emerging markets today, and so there was a valid rationale, with those Institutional voids, for unrelated diversifiers to fill that. Today, with far fewer Institutional voids in developed countries, we see far fewer unrelated diversifiers.

So we've seen a big shift in the kind of strategy that firms are pursuing, and we've seen pressure from investors and analysts who are calculating that break-up value, who are looking, and saying: Is the whole really worth more than the sum of the parts? Increasingly, we're seeing that happen with firms where management is claiming, no, no we're not unrelated. We're actually a related diversifier, and there are synergies. And investors are skeptical. Do we really see scope economies? Do we believe your governance economy argument? Do we really think you can use one management system to manage a wide array of unrelated businesses in different product markets?

So over time, more and more skepticism, because investors and analysts know that academic research that shows that focus wins over unrelated diversification. And so they've pressured firms, and more and more break ups have occurred. This is not to say that every break up make sense, but it does say that there's a lot of cynicism and skepticism about these strategies, and management must be ready to defend their diversification efforts.

So what are our overall lessons? The evidence says focus wins in the United States. We have to understand the difference between economies of scope in a firm like Disney, and governance economies in a firm like GE, and understand the potential limits of the governance economy argument in developed nations today. We have to understand that diversifying risk is not a valid reason to pursue an unrelated expansion. Investors in developed markets can diversify on their own quite easily and inexpensively. And we simply know that the manager of a company, much like the manager of a mutual fund, on average, is not going to beat the market. We can do better by investing in the market overall than trying to have a manager pick winners and losers by buying and selling companies in a portfolio. We can apply some quantitative tests to evaluate these companies. We can actually calculate the whole versus the sum of the parts and try to understand, do we believe that the whole is truly worth more than what these companies would be worth on their own? It's a difficult quantitative analysis with many assumptions. But it can be done.

And, finally, we understood that in emerging economies, it can still make sense to pursue a strategy of unrelated diversification the way the House of Tata has in India and other firms have done in many other emerging markets around the world. And Khanna's empirical research shows that these unrelated diversifiers are high performers.

So your assignment for this lecture, take a look at the corporate break ups that have occurred in recent years, eBay, and HP, Sara Lee, Fortune Brands, Tyco. What do you think of these? Do they make sense? And are there other companies headed for similar break ups moving forward? Try to identify at least one candidate, a firm where you think there are limited scope economies and where serious questions you should be raised about whether the whole is worth more than the sum of the parts. Can you predict the next great corporate break up?

Forward and Backward Integration
Lecture 10

Consider a firm that produces tractors, snow blowers, and other lawn and garden equipment. Traditionally, this company has distributed and sold its equipment through big-box stores, but now, management is pondering a shift in strategy: Should the company open its own chain of retail stores to exclusively sell its own products? The rationale behind this shift is that opening stores will allow the company to capture the profit margin currently being generated by outside retailers. But the firm can't capture the margin without spending a great deal of money to execute the new strategy. As we'll see in this lecture, a company must consider whether forward or backward integration makes economic sense.

Types of Vertical Integration
- Vertical integration comes in two forms: backward integration, which means that a firm produces its own raw materials or components, and forward integration, which means that a firm distributes its own products.

- Apple and its store network represent a classic example of forward integration. Other companies that use this strategy include Ducati, an Italian motorcycle company; Disney; and Fresenius, a company that makes dialysis equipment.

- Apple also engages in backward integration by designing, building, and selling its own operating system. Weyerhaeuser is another company pursuing a strategy of backward integration; the company manufactures paper products and owns its own forests.

Disney's Integration Decision

- The story of Disney's retail stores illustrates a situation in which a strategy of vertical integration may have made sense at one time but, perhaps, became more questionable as different players emerged in the toy retailing business.

- During the 1980s, Disney launched retail stores that initially prospered, but around the beginning of the 21st century, the chain began to struggle financially. Ultimately, Disney struck a deal with Children's Place, a children's apparel retailer, to take over the operation of Disney stores. After several years, however, Children's Place chose to terminate the agreement and turn the stores back over to Disney.

- Disney now faced an important choice: Should it try to operate and manage the stores or shut them down? Times had changed since Disney began its forward integration strategy. People now bought toys on the Internet or from large retailers, rather than independent toy stores. Disney decided to keep the stores, putting Jim Fielding in charge of the effort. He launched a redesign of the stores, with the goal of making them more of an experience that might raise willingness to pay.

- Disney's model here was the American Girl stores, which are deeply experiential. Girls go to the stores not only to buy dolls but also to get dolls fixed in the "hospital" if they're broken, to have lunch with their dolls, to get their dolls' hair done, and so on. Of course, such an experience requires a great deal of investment. A firm must consider whether it can generate enough new revenue to justify the expense.

- In Disney's case, the company also had to walk a fine line between creating too much of an experience, which might steer customers away from its theme parks, and too little of an experience, which might drive customers back to retailers where they could buy toys less expensively.

- One happy medium that some companies have chosen in terms of vertical integration is to operate flagship stores. With this approach, a company might open only a few stores in selected locations. The stores help build the brand and raise willingness to pay for the products, but the company does not retail its products exclusively in those stores or seek to operate a store in every mall in the country.

Rationale for Vertical Integration

- One reason for pursuing a strategy of vertical integration is to counter holdup. Recall the oil refinery and the pipeline. They might vertically integrate because each is so dependent on the other that they can't hold to a contractual agreement in an effective manner. Each is concerned about the opportunistic behavior of the other party.

- Another reason to pursue vertical integration is that there's some synergy between businesses at different points in the supply chain—perhaps economies of scale or scope.

- In addition, a company might backward integrate to secure access to a crucial input. Or a company might pursue vertical integration to foreclose access on the part of competitors—to stop them from having easy access to a scarce input.

- A firm may also backward or forward integrate to offset the bargaining power of suppliers or buyers or to elevate barriers to entry. The more vertically integrated a firm is, the more expensive it is for entrepreneurs to replicate that strategy.

- Yet another reason for pursuing vertical integration is to enhance the ability to differentiate products in the market.

- Finally, vertical integration allows firms to acquire important information that they might otherwise not have access to, such as customer feedback.

* There are real & obvious significant cost savings

Costs of Vertical Integration

- One of the major costs surrounding vertical integration is dulled incentives. With a built-in customer, a vertically integrated manufacturer may not have as great an incentive to perform well as an independent entrepreneur.

- In addition, conflicts of interest may arise. A company that has forward integrated may then compete with its own customers. This is the case, to some degree, with Apple. The firm competes with Best Buy, yet Best Buy is an important Apple customer.

- Vertical integration reduces a firm's flexibility to change suppliers. There are also higher fixed costs and management costs for vertically integrated businesses. Exit barriers rise significantly for vertically integrated businesses. Finally, a vertically integrated firm may experience internal conflicts, especially around the issue of prices charged by one component of the business to another.

Partial Integration

- As an alternative to full vertical integration, some firms have chosen *tapered* or *partial integration.* In this situation, a firm might use both outside retailers and its own stores, or it might use both outside suppliers and its own factories.

- One benefit of this approach is that it exposes in-house units to outside competition, increasing incentives to maximize performance. Partial integration also gives a firm more flexibility and enhances learning because knowledge can be transferred quickly from outside parties to internal units and vice versa.

- Strategic outsourcing might be considered one form of partial integration. In many cases, outsourcing arrangements allow firms to develop deep relationships, cultivating long-term partners but not pursuing full vertical integration.

Declining Trends in Integration

- In recent years, there has been a dramatic decline in vertical integration, particularly in developed nations in such industries as computers and automobiles. The reasons for this decline can be traced by to the transaction cost theory of Coase and Williamson.

- The transaction costs associated with using the market have decreased significantly. In other words, a firm can outsource much more easily today than it could 30 years ago. The web and easier travel and communication around the world have enabled firms to partner with others who may be quite distant.

Case Study: Zara

- A Spanish retailer named Zara has been wildly successful in recent years while pursuing an interesting vertical integration strategy. Zara produces a significant portion of its clothing in factories it owns in North Africa and Western Europe. This approach is different than Zara's competitors, such as H&M and Gap, which don't produce any of their own products. These retailers outsource all manufacturing to low-cost players in Asia or Latin America.

- Zara has pursued a strategy of following the great luxury apparel companies. After new fashions from these companies hit the runways, Zara produces its own similar designs quickly and in small batches for its stores.

- Interestingly, Zara has used a partial integration strategy. It outsources fashion basics, such as t-shirts, to low-cost manufacturers in Asia, while producing other fashions that it wants to be able to change quickly in house.

- Zara realizes a number of benefits from this vertical integration strategy. It doesn't end up with excess inventory if it makes a wrong bet on a particular fashion trend. The company is also able to change its product mix quickly. It doesn't have to commit to buying large quantities of clothing and, as a result, has fewer markdowns.

© kzenon/iStock/Thinkstock.

Capturing the margin is not a valid reason to pursue integration; a firm must be able to add value by owning different parts of the supply chain.

- Of course, Zara's labor costs are much higher than those of its rivals, but the firm's ability to have fewer and smaller markdowns offsets the labor cost disadvantage. There are also tremendous fixed costs associated with building and operating factories, as well as significant exit barriers. At times, Zara has had to take on debt in order to fund the building of its factories. Finally, the company has had to accept lower asset turnover. It does not generate the same use of assets and efficiency as a company that outsources completely.

- Zara has not pursued the same strategy everywhere around the globe. The company owns its own stores in Western Europe, but in some countries, it has set up joint ventures or franchises to operate stores.

- In writing about Zara, the journalist James Surowiecki articulates many of the philosophies of strategy we've discussed throughout these lectures on strategy. In particular, he notes that imitation of Zara would be difficult because it's an integrated system, not just a collection of parts.

Suggested Reading

Ghemawat and Nueno, "Zara."

Harrigan, *Vertical Integration, Outsourcing, and Corporate Strategy.*

Questions to Consider

1. What is an example of flawed logic used to justify vertical integration?

2. How do some firms achieve stronger competitive advantage through vertical integration?

3. What are some of the pros and cons of pursuing a vertical integration strategy?

Forward and Backward Integration
Lecture 10—Transcript

Suppose that a firm produces tractors, snow blowers, and other lawn and garden equipment. Traditionally, they've distributed and sold those tractors, snow blowers, and other pieces of equipment through big-box stores, such as Home Depot and Lowe's. Now, management is pondering a shift in strategy. They've decided that they'd like to open their own chain of retail stores where they will exclusively sell their own products, their own brand of equipment, and no other brands.

Management articulates the rationale for this strategic shift. They tell investors that they will improve the profitability of their business,, because they will capture the profit margin currently being generated by these outside retailers such as Lowe's and Home Depot. In other words, Lowe's and Home Depot mark up the product that they purchase from this manufacturer, and they then capture that markup when they make a sale. The company is arguing, why give that markup to Lowe's and Home Depot? We'll take it for ourselves by directly retailing our own products in our own chain of stores. Is this sound logic? I'm going to argue that, no, it is not at all sound, strategic logic.

We are going to capture the margin or the markup. What does that mean? Well, if we were to supply something in house, in other words, if we were to make our own components instead of buying them from an outside party, the argument is we won't have to pay the profit margin that the supplier of that component is generating. If such as this firm, which is selling snow blowers and the like, we retail it ourselves, the argument is we capture the profit margin that the retailer is generating when they make a sale. Why is this argument about capturing the margin a fallacy?

Well, think about retailing for a moment. This company is going to go out there and distribute and sell their own products in their own stores. Will they capture the profit margin? Well, yes, they will. But what will it take to capture that profit margin currently being generated by Lowe's and Home Depot? You have to invest in a lot of assets. There's no free lunch. You have to go out and build stores or lease them. You have to hire staff. You have to put fixtures in those stores. You have to train your staff and your sales people, and compensate them, create incentives for them to sell your products, train them in how to do so.

That means it's costly to go out and try to build that chain of stores and execute that strategy. There's no free lunch. You can't just capture the margin without having to spend a lot of money to do so. And the question is, are you spending it appropriately? The real issue, then, is who will conduct that retailing activity in the most efficient way possible? Who will generate the best return for investors by building out and operating retail stores? And the question then becomes not are you capturing the margin, but can you retail your products as effectively as outsiders can do so? Who's going to do it and generate a better return on assets for investors? And so you should only move to forward or backward integrate if it makes economic sense. You shouldn't do it simply because you're going to capture that markup or margin.

Vertical integration, that's the strategy we're talking about in this lecture. And there are two forms of vertical integration. Let's suppose we're a manufacturer of personal computers. We assemble personal computers, a firm like Dell, Hewlett Packard, or the like. Backward integration means that the manufacturer builds its own components, its own hard drives, it designs and builds its own operating system, or perhaps it's own microprocessors. Forward integration means it's choosing to distribute its own products through, perhaps, its own retail store network, like Apple does when it owns and operates its own retail stores in malls throughout the country.

What are some examples of vertical integration? For forward integration, an obvious example is Apple and its store network. But we have other companies that have embarked on forward-integration strategies, as well. Ducati, the Italian motorcycle company, owns a chain of stores that market its products. Disney stores in many malls around the country and around the world, we see Disney operating its own retail stores, selling exclusively Disney products.

To go outside of the consumer products business, we might look at a firm like Fresenius. Fresenius is a company that makes dialysis equipment, headquartered in Germany. In many countries, especially in the United

States, they've chosen to forward integrate. They also operate dialysis clinics, where patients come in for treatment. They're using the dialysis equipment made by Fresenius, but then you also have Fresenius medical staff performing the treatment on patients in these clinics, a strategy of forward integration.

What about backward integration? Do we have some examples of that? When Apple conducts the work to build, design, and sell its own operating system, that's backward integration. Many of its competitors, such as Dell and Hewlett Packard, do not make their own operating system. They're not backward integrated; they're buying an operating system from an outside party, namely Microsoft.

We also see that Weyerhaeuser is backward integrated. They sell paper products, cardboard, and other things, but they own their own forests. They cut the timber and then manufacture the products. So they're backward integrated. They're going back toward the earth, and they're owning the whole process from raw materials through finished paper products. These are examples of backward integration.

So let's dig deep on a story of vertical integration and see whether it makes economic sense. And here I want to look at the saga of Disney stores. An interesting one, because it's a strategy where vertical integration may have made sense at one time, and then, perhaps, became more questionable as a strategy as time evolved, as different players emerged in the toy retailing business, as new pressures emerged competitively that Disney had to face as it operated these stores in malls around the country.

So when did Disney launch this forward-integration strategy? It happened early in the tenure of Michael Eisner as CEO. During the 1980s, Disney launched retail stores. And initially, they prospered. And so Disney opened more stores, and they grew the business, and they achieved great financial success. Around the beginning of the 21st century, though, the chain began to embark on some difficult changes. It was struggling. Financial performance had lagged, and the company didn't know how to turn the business around.

Finally, they chose to strike a deal with Children's Place, another retailer known for being able to retail children's apparel quite successfully in its own chain of stores. Under this agreement, Children's Place would take over the operation of Disney stores in malls around the world. Now, this didn't mean they would rebrand the stores; the stores would continue to operate under the Disney brand, but Children's Place would bring its retailing expertise, its knowledge, its talent to these stores to try to improve their profitability.

It didn't work. After several years, Children's Place chose to terminate the agreement with Disney. It chose to turn the stores back over to the Walt Disney Corporation. Now Disney faced an important choice. What do we do? Do we take back control and start to operate and manage these stores for ourselves, or, do we shut down the stores? Do we admit that perhaps this strategy, which was once a prosperous one, no longer makes sense given a new competitive environment? After all, people are now buying their toys on the web, more and more we're buying toys from Walmart, from Toys "R" Us, and Target, not from independent toy stores in 2014.

Times have changed from the 1980s, when Eisner began this forward-integration strategy. Disney talked it over and decided to keep the stores. They put Jim Fielding in charge of the stores, and he began a strategy of redesigning the Disney stores. The goal was to make them more of an experience. What was going on there? Well, interestingly, at the time, Steve Jobs was on the board of directors of Disney. Having sold Pixar to Disney, he took a seat on the board, and he became a prominent shareholder of the Disney Corporation. And they consulted with Jobs. After all, he had forward integrated and opened Apple stores, and that had been very successful.

Jobs's argument was, you should only forward integrate if you're creating an experience in the stores that helps you raise willingness to pay, where you are truly enhancing the competitive advantage of this unit, creating something where people are willing to pay more for the product because your retailing it yourself, than if they were to buy the products at Walmart or Target. And are you selling enough unique products that aren't sold on the web or at Walmart, Target, and Toys "R" Us that draws people in as they see this exclusive offering in your own stores?

So Disney began to redesign, and they put a lot into it. In Manhattan, they shut down the store and actually moved to a new location with a more experiential design. They wanted to move more toward the kind of retailing experience that we see at a store like American Girl, where young girls go in to buy dolls, but not only do they buy a doll, they can take their old dolls to the hospital to get them fixed if they're broken. They can go to the cafe and have lunch with their doll. They can get the doll's hair done at the salon. In other words, American Girl made something that was deeply experiential, something that you couldn't outsource to a Walmart or a Target, something that you could only do in a store that exclusively sold your own products. Of course, this was expensive. You don't do this with little money. You've got to put a lot of money in, and the question is, can you generate enough new revenue to justify that?

There's an important point here, right? If you're going to operate your own stores, you've got to do something different that truly enables you to retail your product in a way that others could not do it for you. After all, Walmart and Target are much more efficient, much more effective; they have a lot more expertise in how to run a retail store. And they, therefore, have lower costs than you. The only reason, therefore, Disney should own its own stores is if they can raise willingness to pay for the products in the stores and for other Disney products that are sold in different places within the Disney portfolio.

Note the difference between Disney and Apple. The Apple stores are clearly experiential. After all, you go there, you receive training, counseling, questions. You go to the Genius Bar. There are things that happen in the store that aren't going to happen at a Best Buy. And so, therefore, you are adding value by owning your own store network. It's a little less clear if Disney has that same kind of value add by operating its own retail stores. So you see the conundrum Disney faces—create more of an experience.

But if it's too much of an experience, if you can easily meet the characters, such as Mickey Mouse and Donald Duck, at the stores, then why go to the park? If you have too little of an experience, then why not go to Target and buy the products less expensively? This is a real conundrum. You need the experience to give a reason or rationale for why should operate your own stores, but you don't want it to be too experiential, because you don't want to cannibalize your efforts to drive revenue at the parks and in other locations.

One happy medium that some companies have chosen, in terms of vertical integration, is operating flagship stores. Think American Girl or M&M World. Right? You can buy M&Ms in Manhattan at a store where they only sell the M&M family of products. Or you can buy American Girl toys at American Girl stores. But is there one of these stores in every mall in the country? There's not. They operate flagship stores. Just a few of these stores in certain locations, they draw people in, they're destinations. They help build the brand and raise willingness to pay for the products, but they're not trying to exclusively retail products only in their own stores, and they're not trying to operate one in every mall in the country.

So what, then, is the overall rationale for vertical integration now that we've looked at the story of a few companies trying this strategy? Well, first and foremost, you may do it because you have this holdup problem, you know, the oil refinery and the pipeline. Why might they come together and vertically integrate? Because each is so dependent on the other that they can't come to a contractual agreement and hold to that agreement in an effective manner. Each is worried about opportunistic behavior on the part of the other party.

You may do it because there's some synergy between businesses at different points in the supply chain. Economies of scale or scope, perhaps. You may vertically integrate, perhaps you might backward integrate, for example, if you want to secure access to a crucial input. Perhaps this component or raw material is scarce. You're worried about having enough of it to be able to produce enough of your finished product to meet customer demand, so you're going to backward integrate to make sure you've got access to key raw materials or key inputs. You may even do it to foreclose access on the part of your competitors, to stop them from having easy access to a scarce input.

You also may backward or forward integrate to offset the bargaining power of suppliers or buyers. What do I mean by that? Suppose you have some powerful suppliers who have negotiating leverage over you. Maybe you backward integrate so that you have a little more power at the bargaining table. You maybe know more about the cost structure of suppliers and what it takes to produce that good. And you have an alternative, you can get the product from your own factory and not have to rely on the outside party, and that gives you leverage at the negotiating table.

Similarly, you can do the same thing with offsetting the bargaining power of buyers. If you're worried about the fact that Walmart is such a tough negotiator at the table when you're looking to sell goods to them as a retailer, perhaps you want to retail the good yourself in certain stores, find a way around Walmart, so you're not as dependent on them.

Certainly you may do it to elevate barriers to entry. The more vertically integrated you are, the more expensive it is for an entrepreneur to come in and replicate that strategy. It's expensive for you, but it also raises the barriers for new players to come in. You may do it to enhance your ability to differentiate your product in the product markets. Can you raise willingness to pay through the kind of experience you create in your own distribution channel? Something Apple has tried to do and Ducati has, as well.

And finally, are you acquiring important information that you otherwise could not acquire. Now what do I mean by that? Well, if you leave retailing to outside parties, that means they're the ones touching your customer every day and talking to them. But maybe you want to be the one talking to your customer every day, because there's crucial data, information you could collect through that interaction. And therefore, you want to be forward integrated, because you want to be closer to that customer.

Well, that all sounds wonderful. There must be some risk or cost to vertical integration. There sure is. There's a real downside here we have to consider, and it starts with dulled incentives. Think about being backward integrated. If I'm not backward integrated, if I simply buy my components from outside parties, they, the independent entrepreneurs running those component manufacturing businesses, they have every incentive to work hard. They're playing with their own money, and they want to generate a good return.

If, on the other hand, I have my own factory, and I have a factory manager making a salary, they don't have the same incentive to really go after this business, because they know that, basically, the product they make has an automatic customer in the downstream manufacturing operation within the same corporation. So that's an issue.

There's also the issue of conflict of interest that emerges. So you now have forward integrated, but now, you're competing with your own customers. Apple is competing with Best Buy, yet Best Buy is a crucial Apple customer. And sometimes, that creates conflicts of interest, and that can be difficult.

Vertical integration also means it reduces your flexibility to change partners. If I'm outsourcing and I don't like what a component manufacturer is doing, I can switch. I can go find someone who's doing it better or someone who's got the next great technology. But if I'm doing it myself, it's harder to exit that business and to change, to change technology, to change processes, to do it differently.

There's also higher fixed costs in the business if you vertically integrate, and that can be difficult when times are tough. During a recession, if you've got high fixed costs and business starts to sag, can you cover those fixed costs? It's also harder to get out of the business; the exit barriers rise significantly. And there are internal conflicts that emerge as you try to get your different parts of the company to work together. One has to sell its parts effectively to a downstream business, and you have to use some artificial price to negotiate that internal sale for purposes of being able to record and track performance of each unit. And battles can emerge as people try to understand, well, what price should we use? What transfer price should we use to move a product from component manufacturing to final assembly?

And lastly, there are costs associated with managing very different businesses. There are really different managerial requirements to running a retail chain versus a manufacturing operation. Can the same executive team oversee such different businesses?

Now, one strategy that some have chosen as an alternative to full vertical integration is what we call tapered or partial integration. This is where you use some outside retailers, as well as your own stores. You use outside suppliers, as well as your own factories. You use a blend. Now, what are the benefits there? Well, you might expose your in-house units to outside competition, and that might be a way to make sure everyone has the incentive to maximize performance. It gives you more flexibility, and it allows you to learn quickly, because you can transfer knowledge from outside parties to internal units, and vice versa, by having a bit of both in the same firm.

You can embark on strategic outsourcing, choosing carefully about where you might do so. And you may have deep relationships in many cases, not just a transaction. So you have a long-term partner, as opposed to full vertical integration. The Japanese automakers really did this effectively in the '80s as they grew their business. And, in contrast, did General Motors. General Motors was highly vertically integrated, while the Japanese used long-term relationships and long-term partnerships to work with suppliers who were outside parties. But it wasn't just a hand off, dumping a product over the wall, from one factory the other. It was an intense relationship, where employees were in each other's factories working hard to coordinate their activity, much like they would be if they were employees of the same corporation. But in fact, they weren't. They were separate entities, but they were partnered closely to achieve optimal performance. And that kind of long-term relationship can be an alternative to full vertical integration.

What have we witnessed in recent years about vertical integration, particularly in developed nations in many industries, such as computers and automobiles? We've seen a dramatic decline in vertical integration. Well, why might that be? Well, let's go back to transaction cost theory, the theories produced by Coase and Williamson that we've talked about in prior lectures. The transaction costs associated with using the market have gone down dramatically. In other words, I can outsource much more easily today than I could 30 years ago. The web and easier travel and communication around the world has enabled me to partner with people in very different parts of the globe and to work with those who are much more efficient at doing something than I could be myself. That was much more difficult to do in the 1950s and '60s, and so vertical integration made more sense for a firm such as Ford or General Motors. But today we don't have to do that, necessarily, as the transaction costs of working with outside parties have fallen considerably.

So let's take a look at an example of a highly successful, vertically integrated strategy. One that's really counterintuitive, that has cut against the grain of what many in their own industry have been doing over the recent years, and that would be a Spanish retailer named Zara. Zara has been wildly successful in recent years, while pursuing an interesting vertical-integration strategy, in contrast to many of the rivals.

Zara produces a significant portion of their own clothes in their own factories in North Africa and in Western Europe, near their own home base in Spain. Why is that unique? Well, many of their competitors, such as H&M and The Gap, these apparel retailers don't produce any of their own products. They are purely marketing and retail machines. They outsource all manufacturing to low-cost players in Asia or Latin America.

Now, Zara has been very successful, and they've outperformed the average firm in the apparel industry. How have they done it and why has vertical integration helped them, when as we've said, many companies have moved away from vertical integration in recent years? Well, they pursue something called a fast-fashion strategy. They're not looking to be the company coming out with the bleeding-edge fashions before anyone else. They are looking to the great luxury apparel companies who are premiering new fashions on runways in Milan and Paris. And then what they're doing is pursuing a fast-follower strategy. They want to move quickly, nimbly, and flexibly to be able to see what's hot out there and bring it to market, and to do so at a price point that's much lower than what luxury apparel houses, like Gucci, might do.

How have they done that? Well, they produce their products in small batches, and they change their product mix very quickly and constantly. They're not producing huge batches of the same goods and putting them in all their stores for lengthy periods of time. If you go today, you'll see different clothes than you saw a month ago. And you may not see hot clothes that did very well stay in the stores for very long.

They don't produce all their clothes in house. Interestingly, they've used a tapered-integration or partial-integration strategy. They've outsourced some and kept others in house. What have they done? Well, those fashions, those fast fashions that they want to be able to change very quickly, they do those in their own factories. The basics, t-shirts, for example, things that don't change much year to year, they outsource those to low-cost manufacturers in Asia, capitalizing on the economies of scale and the efficiencies that those manufacturers have.

So what are the benefits of this vertical-integration strategy at Zara? Well, they don't end up with a ton of excess inventory if they make a wrong bet on a particular fashion. In other words, they're making fast, small bets. What's the result of that strategy? Being able to work very closely with their own factories, many of them in close proximity to their corporate headquarters in Spain, they're able to quickly change their product mix. They're not making a giant bet on a new fashion.

They don't have to sign a contract with someone in Asia with long lead times. And they don't have to commit to buying thousands and thousands of the same piece of new, fashionable clothing. As a result, by working with small, fast bets, they have far fewer markdowns. And when they mark down a product, it tends to be by a much smaller percentage, on average, than their rivals. They're not dumping excess inventory with sales all the time.

Now, that's pretty incredible. To be able to reduce markdowns is a huge boost to profitability in the retail business. Of course, there is a disadvantage to this vertical-integration strategy. Their labor costs are much higher than their rivals. Producing goods in Western Europe and in North Africa, well, that is much more expensive than doing so in Asia. But how do they make up for that? By being flexible. Being able to produce in small batches very quickly means fewer markdowns, means having to dump excess inventory much less frequently. The fewer markdowns, and the smaller markdowns, mean that they totally offset the labor cost disadvantage that they have and actually have better operating margins than their average retail rival.

Well, if this is such a great strategy, why aren't other apparel retailers following it? It's fundamentally risky. You have to be bold to be different, and you have to take some risk. Zara has been willing to do it. Most in their industry have not been willing to do it. What are the risks? There are tremendous fixed costs associated with backward integration at Zara. You have to build these factories, and that's expensive. And those costs are fixed. If you don't utilize the full capacity of those factories, then you've got a real cost problem.

There are also tremendous exit barriers. What happens if things don't work out at a particular factory? Can you shut it down? Well, if you're operating in Western Europe, given the law, and given the political context, it's very difficult to downsize or shut one of those factories. You cannot get out easily. You're tied down. And that's a risk. You also have to be able to fund these capital investments, and that means having to take out more debt, perhaps, which Zara has had to do at times in order to fund the building of these factories. And finally, you have to accept lower asset turnover. You're not going to generate the same utilization of assets and the same efficiency as a company that's completely outsourcing. And so you have to be able to make up for that with better profit margins, which they've done by having fewer markdowns. But if you don't get that, you run the risk of having much lower returns for your investors.

Now, interestingly, Zara has not pursued the same strategy everywhere around the globe. Do they have stores that they own in every country? They have not. In Western Europe, they own their own stores; they are forward integrated. But, in some countries, they set up joint ventures to operate stores. And in others, such as in the Middle East, they've actually worked with franchisees who own and operate the stores under a contractual agreement. So Zara exemplifies the idea that there's a spectrum of choices, from contracts and markets through full ownership, with franchising and alliances and joint ventures in between. And they've varied their corporate strategy, their vertical-integration strategy, to fit the conditions in certain countries.

In some countries, you have to joint venture; the governments will not allow you to have a wholly owned subsidiary. In others we have high political instability and really different cultures, so we want local franchisees with a stake in the business who know the local customs and who understand conditions. And, by working with franchisees, we put less capital at risk in a politically unstable environment.

Can Zara be easily copied? There was a great article about a decade ago by James Surowiecki in *The New Yorker*. Surowiecki is a regular columnist on business in that magazine, and he's the author of a great book called *The Wisdom of Crowds*. And writing about Zara, he articulates many of the philosophies of this course on strategy. He says, at one point, Zara is an integrated system, not just a collection of parts. You can't simply adopt elements of the system and expect similar results.

So think about what we've been preaching in this course, that a great strategy is not about a core competence, but an integrated system of capabilities, an integrated system that fits together really well to produce powerful competitive advantage. And what happens to rivals? They try to copy elements of the system, and not the whole thing, and cannot produce the same kind of results. And Surowiecki makes the argument that, with Zara, you have to be able to do everything they do, not just pieces of what they do, to make that vertical-integration strategy so successful.

So what are the lessons here? Well, don't just pursue vertical integration to capture the margin; that's not a valid reason to backward or forward integrate. You have to be able to add value by owning different parts of the supply chain. You have to be able to do things more efficiently or effectively than outside parties could do so. You have to understand the costs and benefits of that strategy, as well as the alternatives. Could you do it a different way through a long-term relationship, a joint venture, a franchising agreement? Some other way that you could achieve some of the benefits while not having to put all of the capital in yourself and try to manage it all yourself.

And finally, it's not an either/or issue. You don't have to say, are we going to vertically integrate or not, zero-one. You could choose a middle path we call tapered integration, where you do some forward or backward integration, but you still work with outside parties, and you achieve the learning that can happen when you mix the two together in the same corporation.

So now, for your assignment for this lecture. Take a look at some firms practicing vertical integration. Let's take two, for example; let's take Apple. Does vertical integration make sense at Apple? They make some of their own inputs, including their own operating system, and they run their own stores. Why might that make sense? And then, perhaps, contrast that with some retailers who are doing it where it looks like they're less successful. What's different at those retailers?

And then, look at a firm like Delta, in a very different industry. It's an airline that several years ago acquired an oil refinery. Why might they do that? Does it make sense or not given what we've discussed. And having reviewed that, hopefully we'll get a better understanding of the rationale and the risks of vertical integration strategies.

Mergers and Acquisitions—The Winner's Curse
Lecture 11

Mergers and acquisitions are part of daily life in the business world. It seems that almost every day we hear of a large company acquiring a small one with an exciting new product or two giant firms combining in a merger of equals. Unfortunately, there are many instances when these deals do not work out; in some instances, they even produce disastrous results. In this lecture, we'll look at the strategic logic behind mergers and acquisitions, the situations in which they make sense, and the situations in which they might actually decrease shareholder value.

Overview of Mergers and Acquisitions (M&A)

- A merger takes place when two firms come together to form a new, combined entity. An acquisition takes place when one company purchases another and takes charge. In some cases, two large companies come together in what they term a merger of equals, but in reality, there is no such thing as a merger of equals. In almost every case, one management team takes charge and asserts its authority over the managers in the other company.

- There is also an important distinction between friendly and unfriendly deals. Of course, a friendly deal takes place when one company acquires another and the selling party is accepting of the deal. In a hostile takeover, however, the target firm is not cooperative in the acquisition. The acquiring firm goes directly to the shareholders and tries to convince them to sell, even if management and the board of directors are against the sale.

- To understand how these deals work, suppose that the stock price of a target firm is $X per share. The acquiring firm tends to pay a significant premium over $X per share, sometimes 20% to 40% more than the shares are currently trading at in the market.

- Given that premium, the acquiring firm must believe that somehow the target firm will be more valuable as part of the corporation than it was as an independent entity.

- In other words, the acquiring firm must believe that economies of scope exist, and it has valued those synergies at the maximum premium that it is willing to pay for the target company.

- Acquisitions result in high returns for the target firm's shareholders, but in many cases, the share price of the acquiring firm declines slightly. This decline represents skepticism among investors that the firm can realize the synergies. Keep in mind that an acquiring firm must realize synergies in excess of the premium paid to get control of the target firm, and that is a difficult challenge.

- Many deals don't lead to long-run increases in shareholder value. The synergies that are produced do not exceed the premium that the acquiring firm had to pay. Part of the reason for this is that the target firm is also estimating the synergies. The target tries to understand the added value that will be created if it becomes part of a new entity, and it tries to capture most of the value of those synergies in the price it receives for selling the company. In many cases, the result is that the acquiring firm ends up overpaying.

Valuing Target Firms

- An acquiring firm can use a discounted cash flow technique to value a potential target—estimating the target's cash flows moving forward, then discounting those back to today's dollars. As part of that process, the acquiring firm is not only estimating the target's current financials but also trying to project the synergies into the cash flows going forward.

- There are also other methodologies for valuing a potential target, but the challenge with any of these techniques is that they often include many assumptions that can vary widely depending on who conduct the analysis. The conclusions of an analysis are also highly sensitive to just a few core assumptions, such as those about expected revenue growth, operating margins, and the challenges of realizing certain synergies.

- Another problem with these analyses is that not enough attention is paid to the costs involved in achieving the expected synergies. Polycom, a company that competes in the telecommunications and video-conferencing business, tries to estimate anti-synergies in its potential acquisitions—something most firms don't do. Polycom looks at the losses it might incur as it tries to bring two firms together.

The Winner's Curse

- Richard Thaler at the University of Chicago has tried to explain why bidders sometimes pay too much with an idea he calls the winner's curse.
  - At an auction, bidders have some value in mind for an object, but they don't know the value that others have placed on that object. The assumption at an auction is that the real value of the object is closest to the average bid.

The winner's curse is the idea that any winning bidder—at an auction or in the acquisition of a business—inevitably pays more than the underlying real value of the asset up for sale.

- o Of course, the highest bidder wins the auction, but if the underlying real value of the object is equal to the average bid, the winner has overpaid. That's the winner's curse.

- In the business world, the winner acquires a company, but it has paid more than the actual value for the company. The winner's curse is Thaler's explanation for the fact that many deals don't generate positive returns for shareholders.

Cost versus Revenue Synergies

- Executives considering an acquisition typically focus more on cost synergies than revenue synergies. In other words, they look at the ways in which expenses will be reduced, instead of thinking about opportunities to generate new sales if two firms are brought together.

- Of course, it's much easier to be explicit about cost synergies. Executives can point to specific layoffs, plant closings, or consolidations that will be executed. Revenue synergies tend to be more nebulous. How can you prove, for example, that a merger will open up new sales opportunities in a specific region?

The Principal-Agent Problem

- Typically, in a large, publicly traded corporation, ownership and control are separated. Ownership is divided up among many shareholders (principals), all of whom own tiny shares in the company. At the same time, control rests in the hands of a chief executive and his or her team (agents).

- Do the principals and agents have the same interests? The shareholders want optimal profits to maximize the value of their shares. The agent is also interested in profits, but he or she—like all individuals—also seeks to maximize personal utility and satisfaction. This might come in the form of monetary compensation, executive perks, power, publicity, and so on. Thus, executives are interested in a number of things that do not concern shareholders.

- The interests of the principals and agents can be aligned through incentives and monitoring.

  o For example, a company might give managers stock options to make them part owners of the company, or managers might be rewarded with bonuses for increasing profitability for shareholders. At the same time, shareholders usually institute a monitoring mechanism in the form of a board of directors.

  o But neither incentives nor the board as a control mechanism is perfect. Agency costs are the resulting misalignment that remains even after good incentive systems and monitoring devices are put in place.

- How do agency costs and the principal-agent problem explain inefficient M&A activity? Many executives may be interested in empire building, not just maximizing shareholder value. And the board may not be in a position to effectively question the CEO's judgment, or the CEO may have control of the board.

Herd Behavior
- Another explanation for M&As that go bad is herd behavior. In an effort to avoid being fired, a CEO might take a risk-averse approach to managing the company—an approach that entails copying other leading competitors. The thinking here is as follows: If others are vertically integrated, and you don't pursue that strategy, you run the risk of looking stupid if the strategy proves to be beneficial to shareholders at rival firms. But if following the herd doesn't work out, you can point to the fact that all of your rivals did the same.

- The late 1990s saw a wave of deals in the entertainment industry. But it seems unlikely that these deals occurred because each firm involved independently concluded that vertical integration made sense in the industry. It was probably the case that each executive team saw others in the industry pursuing vertical integration and decided to follow suit.

- In the early 2000s, the alcoholic beverage industry was also involved in a wave of acquisitions. Interestingly, in cases where two beer companies or two spirits companies came together, the deals worked out, with both companies benefiting from clear economies of scale and scope. But in deals that brought together beer, wine, and spirits, the economies of scope were not as clear and the deals didn't work. Herd behavior was a large part of the reason that the deals were launched in the first place.

Difficulties in Integration
- One of the challenges with any deal is that it's often difficult to integrate two or more companies. There may be obvious synergies with the firms, but realizing those synergies may be difficult. Two scholars, Philippe Haspeslagh and David Jemison, have done an interesting study of this phenomenon.

- Haspeslagh and Jemison concluded that how a firm goes about the acquisition decision-making process, how it does due diligence, and how it approaches the other firm all have a significant impact on the ability to integrate a company.

- Too often we see culture clashes and other friction that prevents the acquirer from realizing expected synergies. Sometimes, problems also arise when a firm that has had a great deal of experience buying small companies suddenly tries to acquire a large one.

Global Mega-Deals
- Scholar Pankaj Ghemawat, an expert in international strategies, has noted that a rule of three seems to have become conventional wisdom in many industries. Executives come to believe that ultimately, a certain industry may involve only three big players. If consolidation is inevitable, the executives seek to execute a merger or acquisition to secure a position for their firm as one of those three.

- According to Ghemawat, the assumption that the global economy is a winner-take-all economy has become common wisdom, but there's no evidence to support that premise. The theoretical links between the globalization of an industry and the concentration of that industry are weak.

- Executives, then, need to break free of the biases that lead them to pursue larger and larger deals. There are better, more profitable strategies for dealing with globalization than relentless expansion.

Suggested Reading

Bruner, *Deals from Hell*.

Ghemawat and Ghadar. "The Dubious Logic of Global Megamergers."

Gupta and Govindarajan, "Managing Global Expansion."

Thaler, *The Winner's Curse*.

Questions to Consider

1. Why do many M&As fail to deliver increased shareholder value?

2. Why do executives continue to pursue so many M&As despite the spotty record of past performance for such deals?

3. What alternatives to M&As might a firm pursue, and what are the pros and cons for these other options?

Mergers and Acquisitions—The Winner's Curse
Lecture 11—Transcript

Mergers and acquisitions are part of daily life in the business world. It seems that not a day passes without news of another new deal, a large company acquiring a small one with an exciting new product, or two giant firms combining in a merger of equals. Not all these mergers work out, though, some of them have disastrous results. Let's take three examples.

A while back, Daimler, the parent company of Mercedes, acquired Chrysler, one of America's three largest automakers. The purchase price? $36 billion. Some years later, Daimler sold Chrysler for $7.4 billion for an 80% stake. Though even that was actually not the real price, because much of that $7.4 billion was plowed back in to try to recharge Chrysler operations. In short, Daimler bought a company for $36 billion, and some years later, simply gave it away.

AOL-Time Warner, a $182 billion merger at the height of the dot-com boom, later split up after disappointing performance. And if we go back several decades, we can look at the New York Central and Pennsylvania Railroads coming together in a historic merger in the late 1960s. But that new firm went bankrupt after only a few years.

Unfortunately, there are too many instances where we've seen these mega deals go south and not produce results for shareholders. In this lecture, we'll take a look at why and how mergers and acquisitions happen, what's the strategic logic behind these deals, when do they make sense, and when might they actually decrease shareholder value.

What's a merger? A merger is when two firms come together to form a new, combined entity. An acquisition is when one company purchases another and takes charge. Now, sometimes we read about two large companies, like Daimler and Chrysler, and they articulate the notion that it's a merger of equals, two equal parties coming together to form a new, exciting company. In reality, there is no such thing as a merger of equals. In almost every case, one management team takes charge and begins to assert its authority over the managers in the other company. It's almost always the case that it's not, in fact, a merger of equals.

And then, of course, there's an important distinction between friendly deals and unfriendly deals. A friendly deal is when one company acquires another and the selling party is friendly; they are accepting of the deal. They're not fighting the acquisition. But sometimes, we have a company go in and try to execute a hostile takeover. That's when the target firm they're trying to acquire is not cooperative; they don't actually want to be sold. They want to stay independent. But a hostile takeover is when the acquiring firm goes directly to the shareholders and tries to convince them to sell, even if management and the board do not want to sell. And we'll look at why hostile takeovers may make sense in certain cases.

Now, how does one of these deals work? Well, let's suppose that the stock price of a target firm, a firm that's been acquired, trades at x dollars per share. The acquiring firm tends to pay a significant premium over x dollars per share when they do the deal, sometimes 20–40% more than the shares are currently trading at in the market. What happened? How could the value of the firm suddenly rise by 20–40%? The acquiring firm must believe that somehow this unit will now be more valuable as part of their corporation than it was as an independent entity. In other words, they must believe that economies of scope exist, and the acquiring firm has valued those synergies, and that value for the synergies becomes the maximum premium that they're willing to pay for this target company.

Now, who makes out? Who generates a wonderful return in these kinds of deals? Well, the target firm shareholders, they definitely do well; they get a premium for their shares. As I said, sometimes a very significant premium. The acquiring firm, well, in many cases their share price actually declines slightly. Why? Markets and investors are often skeptical that these firms can realize the synergies. Remember, not only do they have to realize synergies, but they have to realize synergies in excess of the premium they had to pay to get control of the target firm, and that is a really difficult challenge.

Many deals don't lead to long-run increases in shareholder value. The synergies that are produced do not exceed the premium that the acquiring firm had to pay. Now, there's a debate about how many deals work out and how many don't, and academics have studied this for some time. But all of them agree that a huge number of deals do not work out. Whether it's a majority or not, that's up for debate, but many deals do not produce long-run returns for the acquiring firm.

Remember, the target firm is estimating the synergies as well. They are trying to understand what added value will be created if we become part of this new entity, and they, therefore, are trying to capture most of the value of those synergies in the price that they take, that they get, for selling their company. So they're negotiating hard, and they're trying to get as many of those synergies embedded in the sale price. The acquiring firm may end up overpaying.

Now, you also see bidding wars emerge at times, where multiple firms are trying to acquire the very same company. And why might one firm be willing to pay much more than another firm for the same company? A valid reason would be that the acquirer feels that the target is more valuable to them than any other firm, that there are more synergies that will be produced if this target firm joins their company than if it joins any other company. That would be a valid reason, but sometimes that's not what actually drives the acquirer's behavior. They're simply bidding up the value and the price they're willing to pay because they want to win, and that can be dangerous. Getting in a bidding war and starting to irrationally value the target firm can cause long-term harm.

How do you value a deal? It can't be easy, right? How do understand the potential synergies of a company you haven't operated and managed, you've only understood from afar? Well, there are different methodologies. You're going to do what's called due diligence. You're going to study the firm and try to get to know it and understand it. And through that, you're going to try to project what it will be worth to you.

Now, what is a company worth? How do we understand that? That's a key question that investors and financial experts have looked at for many years. There are multiple methodologies for valuing a firm, but here's the quick way of thinking about it. When we buy a stock, what does that share price represent? Does it represent what the company has done in the past? Is it reflective of past earnings and performance? It's not, really. When you're buying a stock, you are becoming a part owner in a company, but you don't get the right to past earnings. You get the right to future earnings. So the value of a company today is equal to the net-present value of future cash flows. So using a discounted cash-flow technique can be a way that an acquiring firm values a company they're looking to buy. They're trying to estimate its cash flows moving forward, and then discounting them back to today's dollars. Why do they do that? Because a dollar today is worth more than a dollar tomorrow. Now, as part of that, they're not just estimating the current company's financials, but they're trying to project those synergies into those cash flows going forward as well.

But there are other methodologies. So for example, you may look at a price-earnings multiple methodology, or other financial techniques that you might use and compare the valuation from those techniques to a traditional discounted cash flow model. But here's the real challenge with any of these techniques or models, often they include many assumptions, assumptions that can vary wildly depending on who is conducting the analysis. And the analysis itself and its conclusions, we find that quite often the conclusions are highly sensitive to a few core assumptions.

What kind of assumptions? Assumptions about how much you expect revenue to grow in the future, assumptions about what you think will happen to operating margins or gross margins moving forward, assumptions about how challenging it will be to realize certain synergies, and as you tweak those assumptions, you often see dramatic changes in the estimated value of a firm you're looking to acquire. So what happens in many of these deals? Well, if executives really want to do the deal, they often keep working the assumptions till they get the valuation they want that will justify doing the deal. In other words, the analysis doesn't drive the conclusion, but instead, the conclusion—I want to buy this company—drives the analysis. And that can happen in many, many deals, and in fact, it happened to some extent in Daimler's acquisition of Chrysler.

Now, one problem in all of these analyses is that while a lot of attention is paid to valuing the synergies, not enough attention is paid to what investments will we have to make, what costs are there to achieving those synergies. At Polycom, a company that competes in the telecommunications and video conferencing business, when they would do deals, they often would talk about estimating the anti-synergies, something most firms don't do. In other words, what are the losses we might incur as we try to push two firms together? In other words, it's not all positive; sometimes there's some negatives of meshing two firms together.

Now, Richard Thaler at the University of Chicago has tried to give us an explanation for why sometimes bidders pay too much when they do deals. So he's articulated something he calls the winner's curse. Now suppose you have an auction, says Thaler, when the bidders do not know the actual value of an object that others have placed on that object. So, they think they have a value for the object, but they don't know what others value the object, and they're bidding in an auction.

Now, the bidders are each estimating the value and making a bid. And let's assume that the value is closest, the real value, is closest, to the average bid in the auction. So there are a lot of people bidding, people are putting different values on this thing that they're trying to buy, and the average bid is pretty close to the real underlying value. But who wins the auction? The highest bidder wins the auction. The highest bidder walks away with the thing that they've been trying to buy. But note, if the real underlying value of the asset is equal to the average bid, the winner, the highest bid, is overpaying for this asset. The winner's curse. The winner has achieved the thing that they've been striving to get, to acquire this company. But they've paid more than the actual value. And the winner's curse is Thaler's explanation for why we may see many deals that don't generate a positive return for shareholders.

Now, it's interesting to listen to executives. What do they say when they do a deal? They clearly are trying to convince investors, employees, and others that synergies exist. What kind of synergies do they talk about when they do a deal? Some studies have shown that they tend to talk much more about cost synergies than revenue synergies. In other words, they talk about ways that when you bring the two firms together, they can reduce expenses. They don't talk about how there are new opportunities to generate new sales of products by working together. Why do they spend more time talking about cost savings than revenue synergies? The argument is, it's much easier to be very explicit about cost synergies. You can point to specific layoffs, plant closings, consolidations that you are going to execute when you come together.

Revenue synergies? It's more pie in the sky. Will it really happen? We're going to work together to open new product sales opportunities in Latin America. How do you prove that you can do that? It's much easier to prove that we're going to consolidate two sales forces in Chicago and save money. So you see this emphasis on cost synergies and this tendency to not be able to be as explicit with revenue synergies. So if it's a revenue-synergy deal, investors often are very skeptical; they want to see the proof, but it's harder to prove revenue synergies.

Now let's look at some theoretical explanations for why some bad deals get done. We understand the winner's curse, and we understand that we may overpay. That's a practical reason why we may see some bad deals. But what's a conceptual explanation for some of the bad deals? Here we have to introduce something called agency theory and the principal-agent problem, an important branch of economics.

So one thing that the scholars in agency theory have noted is that we see the separation of ownership and control in the typical, large, publicly-traded corporation. Ownership, the shareholders, millions of them, many shareholders, and all of them tend to own a very tiny, tiny stake in this publicly traded corporation. So we have dispersed ownership, but control, that sits in the hands of a chief executive and his or her team. Control, the executives, well, they don't actually own the company. They run it day to day. There's a difference between the owners and the people running it. In this theory, we talk about the principal. The principal is the shareholder who owns the firm. The agent is the executive, the CEO and his or her team, that runs the firm.

Now, the question is, do the principals and the agents have the same interests? Well, think about if you're an entrepreneur and you run your own firm. You're a sole proprietor, you are both the principal and the agent.

So your interests are perfectly aligned. But in a large, publicly traded corporation, there's a separation between ownership and control. What are the shareholders interested in? They want to maximize the value of their shares. In other words, they want optimal profits.

What are the agents interested in? What are the CEO and the other executives interested in doing? Well, they want profits, but remember, ultimately, they're utility maximizers, as all individuals are. They want to maximize their own personal utility or satisfaction. What gives them satisfaction? Well, clearly, the firm's profitability makes them happier, but they care about other things. There are other issues that make them happy, how much they're compensated; what kinds of perks they have; how much power they have; the size of the firm, many people are happier running larger firms; they publicity that they receive, do they make the cover of Fortune magazine? Are they featured in Fast Company?

So the executives are interested in a number of things that are actually not the same as the shareholders. There's a gap here. There's a difference between the interests of executives, the agents, and the principals, the shareholders. Now, how do you align the interests of the principals and the agents? You do it through incentives and monitoring. Incentives, what do companies do? They make the managers part owners of the company. They give them stock options. They give them stock itself. They do other things to make them feel like owners, maybe a bonus plan so that they're rewarded for doing better by the shareholders.

But also, the shareholders institute a monitoring mechanism. We call it the board of directors. So we appoint a group of people who are there to oversee management. But neither incentives nor the board, as a control mechanism, are perfect. Agency costs are the resulting misalignment that remains even after good incentive systems and monitoring devices are put in place. Why is the board not perfect? Because it's difficult to come together on a quarterly basis, when you're not an expert in the business, and oversee management. And so it's not a perfect way to control management's activity. And incentive schemes, they're not perfect either.

So how do agency costs and the principal-agent problem explain inefficient merger and acquisition activity? Well, many executives, frankly, may be interested in empire building, not just maximizing shareholder value. They want to build a large organization; they want to make a big splash, be on the cover of Fortune for the great deal they've done. The board may not be in a position to effectively question the CEO's judgment. Moreover, the CEO may control the board in many ways. The CEO may be the chairman of the board, or the CEO may have had a big hand in selecting the board members, and so the board cannot make an independent judgment on whether this deal actually makes sense.

So if the principal-agent problem is one explanation for bad mergers and acquisitions that occur, another is herd behavior. What do we see in many corporations? We see the incentives for CEOs, well, they're heavily tilted toward not wanting to be fired. The CEO knows that, frankly, more and more executives are fired these days. The tenure of the average CEO has fallen. So how do you avoid being fired? Well, you might take a risk-averse approach to managing the company, and risk aversion, in part, might entail copying what other leading competitors do. If others are vertically integrated, and you don't, you run the risk of looking really stupid if the vertical integration strategy proves correct and really beneficial to shareholders at rival firms.

If you follow the herd, and do what others are doing that are leaders in the industry, and it doesn't work out, you can point to the fact that all of your rivals, including the leaders in the industry, did the same. So herd behavior is one behavior that explains why sometimes a lot of deals get done. Let's take a look at the entertainment industry, for example. In the late 1990s we saw a wave of big deals: AOL-Time Warner, NBC Universal, Viacom CBS, Disney acquiring ABC. Some of those deals worked out, others were disastrous, and some of them, well, those deals ended up getting undone. The companies later broke up.

Why did those deals happen in the first place? Was it because each firm independently was coming to the conclusion that vertical integration made sense in the entertainment and media business? Or, did each executive team look to others in the industry and see, well, Disney just bought ABC; vertical integration must be the wave of the future. And are they simply copying, for following, the herd. Too often, that's actually the underlying reason why deals get done, rather than truly independent examinations and analyses that look at the true value of bringing two firms together.

Let's take a look at another industry where we've seen huge herd behavior in the past, the alcoholic beverage industry. Now, I conducted a case study on the global wine business and on overall the global alcoholic beverage industry some years ago, focusing first on Robert Mondavi, a firm that I'd gotten to know and study with the cooperation of their management team, and then looking at many of their rivals. And I noticed something interesting happening about a decade ago, in the early 2000s, in the alcoholic beverage industry. Allied Domecq, they had acquired Dunkin' Brands; they owned Dunkin' Donuts and Baskin Robbins. They were doing that to draw cash from those businesses to fund new growth in their wine business.

Foster's, an Australian beer company, buying wine companies. Diageo, a company that made distilled spirits, and Guinness Beer entering the wine business through mergers and acquisitions. Southcorp, an Australian company, merging with another Australian wine company to provide and to create a huge behemoth in the Australian wine business. What's interesting about this is many of these deals did not work out. So everybody is off doing acquisitions in the alcoholic beverage business, and then many of the deals don't work out. Southcorp didn't work out at all. Foster's, it ended up splitting its beer and wine business.

Some deals did work out. Beer companies that came together, just two beer companies, no other alcoholic beverages, or two spirits companies coming together, many of those benefited from very clear economies of scale and scope, and they were good deals. But many deals that brought together beer, wine, and spirits, well, it turned out the economies of scope were not as clear. While those looked like related product markets, the synergies were not bountiful, and the deals came undone. Why did the deals happen in the first place? Herd behavior was a big part of the story.

Now, you might ask, what about hostile takeovers? Why do they happen? And are they all bad? Well, I would argue they're not all a bad thing. And here we have to talk about the market for corporate control. And what does that mean? Well, there are companies out there, whether we like to admit it or not, that are poorly managed. In some cases, the managers are not doing right by the shareholders. Maybe there's an agency problem; maybe managers are pursuing their own interests at the expense of shareholders. So why, then, might a hostile takeover be an important step toward improving performance?

Well, hostile takeovers can be a mechanism where someone comes in to take control of that corporation, to acquire it, and puts new management in place and empowers them to make key strategic changes to manage the company more effectively. Think of hostile takeovers as bringing governance economies to a firm that's been acquired that hasn't been governed or managed very effectively in recent years. Now, you'd like to be able to do this without having to do a hostile deal, right? There's some benefit from acquiring a company and having the cooperation of the people who work there. But if the people who work there are managing it poorly, you may have to execute a hostile deal to be able to take entrenched management and move them out.

So if we look at InBev, a large beer company that bought Anheuser-Busch, America's leading beer company, that began as a hostile takeover. They viewed Anheuser-Busch as poorly managed, as wasting shareholder resources. So what do they do? They launched a hostile deal, because they knew they could not get the cooperation of the Bush family, and one of the Bush family members who was CEO at the time. They put a lot of pressure on the board to sell.

Eventually, though, they came to a deal, and sometimes in these hostile deals we see what's called a bear hug, where the seller, the target firm, kind of hugs the firm looking to acquire them. They say, OK, we resisted for awhile, but we see the writing on the wall, and we'd rather do a friendly deal then be completely taken over in a hostile way. So not all hostile takeovers end as hostile. Some of them become a little more friendly during the course of the transaction. But ultimately it's about bringing new management to the table and improving the performance. And InBev clearly moved top management out at Anheuser-Busch and put their own top management in to try to drive better earnings, better performance, at a company with some historic brands, like Budweiser.

Now, one of the challenges with any deal, and why many deals don't work out, is that it's very difficult to actually integrate two or more companies together. You know, you look at this and you say, there's obvious synergies here. But making those synergies happen, that's no easy task. And two scholars, Haspeslagh and Jemison, have done an interesting study of this. They looked at a number of deals and came to the conclusion that how you go about the acquisition decision-making process, how you do the due diligence, how you approach the other firm, well, that has a great impact on the ability to then integrate that company.

And so they argued that, if you manage the process of deciding how to acquire a firm well, it enhances the probability that you can execute the integration effectively. But too often we see culture clashes, and we see other friction that emerges, and therefore, the acquirer is not able to realize the synergies that they expected. In the Daimler Chrysler merger, there were many flaws with the way Daimler went about making the decision to acquire Chrysler, and that had long-term negative repercussions on the ability to make the thing work.

Sometimes we also see problems of integration because a firm has had a lot of experience buying small companies, and now suddenly tries to do a very big deal. And the integration of a large firm is much more difficult. So Polycom, for instance, is a firm out in California who successfully acquired a number of small companies over the years. But then they acquired a very large East Coast competitor, and that turned out to be much more difficult from an integration perspective. The challenges associated with swallowing a large company are very different than buying a small start-up in Silicon Valley.

Now, finally we have to turn to the issue of these global mega deals. Why do they occur, and is there a good logic behind them? Well, in many cases what we hear from executives is, I think at the end of the day that this will be a situation where there will be three big players in our industry. And so consolidation is inevitable, and I need to be at the forefront of that, and we need to execute a merger or acquisition, because we want to be one of those three.

Scholar Pankaj Ghemawat, an expert in international strategies, noted that this rule of three has become conventional wisdom in many industries. Yeah, why three? And could three be the perfect number in every industry, from aluminum manufacturing to automobiles to retail? I mean, why three? And he's gathered a great deal of data on this issue, and here's what Ghemawat says.

He says the assumption that the global economy is a winner-take-all economy has become common wisdom, but there's no evidence to support that premise. The theoretical links between the globalization of an industry and the concentration of that industry are weak. Executives, then, need to break free of the biases that lead them to pursue larger and larger deals. There are better, more profitable strategies for dealing with globalization than relentless expansion.

And he's actually collected some data on this. He's seen that many industries have actually become more fragmented, not more concentrated or consolidated, as globalization has occurred. He's actually tracked this in a number of industries, like automobiles, and he's said this premise that, because of globalization, there will be three big winners at the end of the day, that the industry should become more consolidated, it hasn't held. We've actually seen the emergence of new players, particularly from emerging markets, and the industry become less consolidated over time. So he's questioned the validity of this conventional wisdom that underlies many deals.

Of course, there are alternatives to doing mergers and acquisitions. You may use a joint venture as an alternative to a merger. And there are a number of reasons why you might use joint ventures to enter foreign markets. Gupta and his colleagues have done interesting research on why, and they cite five reasons. Government regulations may require foreign firms to partner with local companies when entering a market. There may be high physical, cultural, and linguistic barriers and distance between a home country and host countries. And the local unit can operate relatively autonomously from the corporate parent in other countries, and so a joint venture may make sense in that kind of situation.

The partners have much to learn from each other in some cases, and that learning might be relatively balanced, and so a joint venture may be a great vehicle to learn from another company without fully merging with them. And lastly, a joint venture may make sense when a multinational doesn't have the capital, the financial resources, to expand into a foreign market on its own, and so a joint venture becomes a good vehicle for doing that.

Now, there are risks with these kinds of deals, just as there are risks with mergers and acquisitions. For the multinational firm, you may lose control over your intellectual property, and you may put your brand at risk by partnering with a firm in an emerging market. That young firm in an emerging market, they want your ideas, and they may take some of them and some of your property, your intellectual property, that's so valuable to you. And they may do things they damage your brand. But for the emerging market firm, they may grow too dependent on the multinational and not build their own capabilities and their own brand enough. So there's risk for them, too. So joint ventures are an alternative to mergers and acquisitions, but they're not a perfect solution either.

Why do so companies stick with deals that aren't making sense? Why do they not divest? Here comes the sunk-cost effective. Again, people throw good money after bad. They can't cut their losses, and they pour more money in trying to turn it around. Research, interestingly, shows that many divestitures occur when a new CEO takes charge. So the interesting research here shows that the previous CEO who made the deal typically doesn't want to divest, and so he keeps the business and throws more money in. But when a new CEO comes on board, they're not beholden to those sunk costs, and they're able to sell. Daimler sold Chrysler when a new CEO took over.

So what are the lessons here? Mergers and acquisitions are difficult to make work, and many firms overpay for various reasons. There are some good motives, but can you get the deal done at the right price? And the right motives aren't always in place. Integration, too, is a key challenge. In short, it pays to be skeptical about the possible benefits from any deal, given the history of failed deals that we know about.

So what's your assignment for this lecture? Find news of a recent merger or acquisition. Try to determine the premium that the acquirer has paid for that target firm, and then examine management's explanation of the synergies they expect from the deal. Do you think they can achieve those synergies? Can they justify the premium that they've paid? And then, what's happened to the stock of the acquiring firm? Do investors believe that the deal makes sense? And do you agree with them?

Launching a Lean Start-Up
Lecture 12

M any people have ideas for new products or services and would like to try entrepreneurship at some point in their careers. In this final lecture on competitive strategy, we'll take a look at the challenge of launching your own business. How can you apply the ideas from these lectures on strategy to building and running a successful venture? And how is entrepreneurship different than leading a large, complex organization?

The Marshmallow Challenge
- The marshmallow challenge is an exercise in which groups compete to build the tallest freestanding structure using only uncooked spaghetti, tape, string, and a single marshmallow. This exercise has been run with many groups of people from different fields and yields some interesting results.

- Recent graduates of business schools underperform the average on this challenge, as do lawyers and CEOs. Engineers, architects, and kindergarten students excel at the challenge.
  - In business school, students are taught to plan, then execute. They learn to set out goals and the means of achieving those goals in as much detail as possible. In the marshmallow challenge, that means coming up with the perfect design on paper before trying to build the structure. Many business school graduates don't even touch the marshmallow until near the end of the time allowed for the challenge.

  - In contrast, kindergarten students tend to pick up the marshmallow early on and start to play with it. In building their structures, they engage in trial and error. Instead of a linear plan-execute process, the kindergarten students do what great designers and entrepreneurs do: They test, experiment, and prototype.

- ○ Tom Wujec, a designer who frequently runs this challenge, has also found that CEOs do better when an administrative assistant joins their team. Wujec argues that because the assistants are good at facilitating work processes, they enable the team to work together more effectively; the assistants help other team members through a testing and prototyping process that leads to a taller structure.

- Peter Skillman, the creator of the marshmallow challenge, once said, "Enlightened trial and error succeeds over the planning of lone genius." This is true not just in building marshmallow structures but in launching new ventures, as well.

The Lean Start-Up
- In the past, the approach to launching an entrepreneurial venture was to conduct extensive market research, write a detailed business plan, and construct pro forma financial statements. In recent years, however, there has been a movement toward a new way of launching a venture, the lean start-up model. This approach is more iterative and less linear than the old one; it involves more learning and adaptation.

- Eric Ries is one of the pioneers of the lean start-up methodology. According to him, every start-up is a grand experiment that attempts to answer a question. But that question is not: Can this product be built? Instead, it's: Should this product be built, and can a sustainable business be built around it?

- This experiment, Ries says, is more than just theoretical inquiry; it's a first product. If it's successful, it allows the entrepreneur to get started with his or her campaign, enlisting early adopters, adding employees to each further experiment or iteration, and eventually, starting to build products.

- Notice that there's an important distinction between this approach and the experience of many entrepreneurs. An entrepreneur may have a great product in mind, but Ries points out that a great product concept is not a business. A business needs a business model, including an understanding of which customers actually need the product and what they need to get out of it. Meeting those needs involves adaptation, which can be difficult for many entrepreneurs if they fall in love with their own products.

- Ries articulates the notion of a minimum viable product (MVP). You start by figuring out what problem needs to be solved. What pain point is the customer experiencing? The starting point is not your great idea for a new technology but the customers' needs, based on the frustrations they're experiencing with current products and services.

- From there, you develop an MVP, which is that version of a new product or service that allows a team to collect the maximum amount of validated learning with the least effort. The idea here is begin to learn as soon as possible, then adapt, or "pivot," shifting your idea based on the learning that takes place.

- Here, it's crucial not to belabor the planning process but to get to that learning as soon as possible. In other words, pick up the marshmallow early. Get an initial concept, prototype, or product into customers' hands and collect feedback.

- The goal of the MVP is to test certain hypotheses or propositions related to what attributes customers care about, how they define quality, and whether or not they are willing to pay a certain amount for the product or service. These data allow you to determine, for example, whether you can command a price that is sufficient to cover your expenses.

- It's important for entrepreneurs to get comfortable with the idea of "good enough" in order to get the prototype into customers' hands as soon as possible and to listen to the feedback they receive. You must be willing to put out a product that may not be perfect and able to listen to people when they tell you what's not perfect about it.

The MVP Strategy in Large Firms

- It seems that many large organizations cannot pursue an MVP strategy because it's difficult for them to put a "good enough" product into the marketplace. People who work in large organizations are trained to have high quality standards, and the organizations themselves are intent on protecting their brands. Thus, to put out a product that's less than perfect runs the risk of harming the brand and damaging a firm's reputation for quality.

- David Kelley, founder of the leading product design firm IDEO, uses the idea of "failing often to succeed sooner" to drive the innovation process at his firm. This notion is also crucial in the context of entrepreneurship. Entrepreneurs must be willing to put something out in the market that is a "failure"; they must be able to listen to negative feedback and adapt.

  o Again, we can see why large companies have a problem with this. If you're a manager at a large company and your initial attempt at getting a new product into the marketplace is a failure, you run the risk of damaging your career. For this reason, managers in larger organizations tend to be risk averse.

  o Further, the culture of large organizations is such that they're not tolerant of early failures that are simply part of the creation process for new ventures.

- It's important to note, however, that not all failure is acceptable. Entrepreneurs and large companies should not spend inordinate sums to launch new ventures; instead, aim for small experiments and inexpensive prototypes that enable you to get feedback quickly and improve.

Lean Start-Ups in Today's Environment

- There's an argument to be made that it's easier to build and test an MVP today than might have been possible years ago. The cost of computer processing power has come down dramatically, and open-source software is now available that can help you launch your business. Further, access to capital and talent has generally become easier.

- The scholar Vivek Wadhwa has done some interesting research over the years on start-ups, looking at many of them in Silicon Valley, in particular.

© michaeljung/iStock/Thinkstock.

  o He has noted that today's laptops have the same processing power as many computers that cost millions of dollars in the

Yelp pivoted from its initial incarnation as a system for e-mailing recommendation requests to friends to an online review system of restaurants and local businesses.

1980s. For storage, you once needed server farms and racks of hard disks, but today, we have inexpensive cloud computing and cloud storage.

  o In short, it's easier to run an experiment today. You can launch a new venture without the need for a great deal of capital. As entrepreneurs like to say, you can rely on fools, friends, and family to get money and get a business off the ground.

- There has also been an explosion in the number of *start-up accelerators*; these are typically groups of experienced entrepreneurs or venture capitalists who coach entrepreneurs in launching new ventures.

  o Start-up accelerators take applications and accept new ventures into a cohort-based, residential program. The entrepreneurs live and work at the location of the start-up accelerator for about 12 weeks, where they get assistance, counseling, and some seed funding. In return, they typically give up a 6% equity stake to the owners of the start-up accelerator.

    o   The 12-week program culminates in a demo day, where potential investors are assembled, and the entrepreneurs get a chance to pitch their ideas to raise funding.

Gaining Investors

- Venture capitalists often say that they invest in the team, not just the product or the idea. Investors understand that most ventures will have to pivot multiple times in the early days—the idea won't be right at first. Thus, they try to find entrepreneurial teams that are open to new ideas, will listen to feedback, and are willing to adapt.

- In seeking investors, entrepreneurs must also have a business model, not just a product. As we've seen in these lectures, competitive advantage doesn't come from having the best technology or being the first mover in the marketplace. It comes from having an integrated system of activities that delivers value to the customer. That value must be enough to generate returns for investors and provide consumers with some surplus, some value beyond what they paid for the product.

- As an entrepreneur, you must ask yourself a number of questions about launching a new venture: What customer pain point are you trying to alleviate? What is your business model? Who is on your team? Are you willing to adapt and pivot? And perhaps the most important question is this: What makes you different, and can you sustain that position? With the ideas you've learned in these lectures, you should be ready to build on that advantage and defend it against potential rivals.

Suggested Reading

Bossidy and Charan, *Execution*.

Burgstone and Murphy Jr., *Breakthrough Entrepreneurship*.

Ries, *The Lean Startup*.

Wujec, "Build a Tower, Build a Team."

1. What questions should an entrepreneur consider before launching a new venture?

2. What advantages does a lean start-up approach have over traditional business planning for new ventures?

3. Where might entrepreneurs seek assistance as they try to launch a new venture?

Launching a Lean Start-Up
Lecture 12—Transcript

In this final lecture on competitive strategy, I would like to take a look at the challenge of launching your own business. Many of you would like to be an entrepreneur at some point in your career. You have an idea for a new product or service, and you'd love to run your own venture, to be your own boss. How can we apply the ideas from this course to helping you build and run a successful venture? And how is entrepreneurship different than leading a complex, large organization?

Let me start with an interesting and fun exercise that I run with many executives at many companies around the world. It's called the marshmallow challenge, designed by a man named Peter Skillman, who used to work for IDEO, one of the world's leading product-design firms, and executed by Tom Wujec, a designer, with many groups of people from different fields and domains around the world.

I'd like to tell you about this challenge, this exercise, and the results from Wujec running it in many different companies and organizations and different fields of expertise, and what he's found about how different people perform at very different levels on this exercise. It's called the marshmallow challenge.

What do you ask small groups of people to do in the marshmallow challenge? You give them some materials and ask them to build the tallest freestanding structure in 18 minutes. What materials do you give them? Well, you give them 20 strands of spaghetti, uncooked of course. You give them some masking tape, and some string, and you give them a single marshmallow, the kind you might roast with your kids over a campfire in the summer. Now there are few rules with regard to how they should go about building this freestanding structure. First and foremost, the entire marshmallow must be on top of the structure. You cannot split, break, or cut the marshmallow, and it cannot be anywhere but the top of the structure. You don't have to use all of the materials that have been given to your team, and you may break the spaghetti.

You also may cut the tape and the string for use in your structure however you like. There's a few other rules as well. You cannot move the table or other structure that you're building upon, and you cannot hang the structure in any way from the ceiling. It has to be free standing. The way I run it, I allow people to take materials to the top of the table but to no other surface, not the bottom of the table or any chairs nearby, or anything like that. And I don't allow anyone to use any outside materials during the challenge. Finally, the team has to let go of the structure when the buzzer goes off when time runs out.

Typically I find that even senior leaders of large corporations have a blast running this challenge. I've done it in many different settings from large Fortune 500 companies to small start-ups. I've done it with 800 students in the gymnasium at Bryant University, where I teach. It's a fascinating and fun exercise, but it has some deep lessons about entrepreneurship that are important for anyone choosing to launch their own venture.

So what do the results show? There's a great Ted Talk by Tom Wujec, the designer who has run this challenge many times with different groups of people. And what has he found? Well, who performs really poorly on this marshmallow challenge? It turns out recent graduates of business school underperform the average. It's pretty interesting. Lawyers don't do very well on it either. CEOs, they do a little better than average, but not spectacularly. Who excels? Well it turns out kindergarten students do great on this challenge. So the engineers and architects, now Wujec points out, thankfully, engineers and architects do well on this challenge. After all, they're designing buildings every day.

But why do kindergarten students do so well and business school graduates do so poorly? And that's something that he explains by looking at how business school students, graduates, and executives, how do they think? How do they go about their work versus a kindergarten student? Well, you're taught in business school to plan and then execute. You develop a clear concept of what you're trying to achieve. You set out your goals and your means of achieving those goals. And you detail that out as much as possible.

In the case of the marshmallow challenge, that means coming up on paper with the perfect design and talking through its strengths and weaknesses and debating them with other team members. And then, you move to execution. Once you've got your perfect design, you start to build your tower. That's the simple plan-execute model, the very linear model that many people pursue when they're trying to achieve this challenge.

But what does the kindergarten student do? The kindergarten student tends to pick up the marshmallow very early on. And they start to play with it and try different things. You see a lot of trial and error with the kindergarten student groups, the kind of trial and error that adults don't engage in. Now why is trial and error so important? Well, if you look at what happens with executives when they do this, or business school graduates, I've watched and noticed that many of them don't even touch the marshmallow until the 16- or 17-minute mark. So they design, they argue over the design, they sketch it out, they build, and then they pick up the marshmallow. And it turns out, they've assumed a marshmallow is very light. But with the tower of spaghetti, tape, and string, a marshmallow is quite heavy, and their tower tips over.

Now, the kindergarten students don't run into that problem. Why? They've been experimenting with the marshmallow all along. They've been doing what great designers and great entrepreneurs do. They've been testing, experimenting, and prototyping. So instead of a linear process of planning and executing, they're coming up with a very rough concept, and they're trying it out. They're building a crude prototype or test. They're playing with the marshmallow. They're getting a sense for how heavy it is and what kind of a structure might hold it up.

And then, they're adapting and they're changing their structure, they're changing their prototype. Maybe they're scrapping it entirely if their initial structure doesn't work at all. So the kindergarten students are engaging in the kind of rapid prototyping that great entrepreneurs and great designers do.

Now it's interesting, in his results, Wujec finds that CEOs do better when an executive admin, an administrative assistant, joins their team. Why is that? And he argues, his hypothesis is, that those administrative assistants, they are particularly attuned to watch carefully the work process. And they're very good at facilitating the work process. So they get the team to work together more effectively, and they help them through a testing and prototyping type process that leads to a higher structure.

So we see this interesting disparity between those who go about planning, then executing, versus those that test and prototype. What does that have to do with entrepreneurship and business strategy? Well, as Peter Skillman, who founded this challenge, who created it, once said, he said, "Enlightened trial and error succeeds over the planning of lone genius." And this is true not just in the marshmallow challenge, but in launching a new venture.

So if we think about how we typically launched entrepreneurial ventures in the past, well, the old way was to conduct extensive market research, to build a detailed business plan, perhaps more than 100 pages, and within that, to clearly build detailed, pro forma financial statements, forecasts of exactly the revenues and the expenses you expected in the outgoing years. Is there a different way to launch a new venture? Well, in recent years there's been a movement called the lean start-up. It's a new way to launch a venture. It's different than the old sort of planning and executing model. It's more iterative. It's less linear. And it involves more adaptation and learning so as to get the strategy right, not the first time, but as quickly as possible so you can succeed in the marketplace.

Eric Ries is one of the pioneers of this lean start-up methodology, and he articulates it as follows. He says the lean start-up methodology has, as a premise, that every start-up is a grand experiment that attempts to answer a question. The question is not, can this product be built? Instead, the questions are, should this product be built, and can we build a sustainable business around this set of products and services? This experiment, he says, is more than just theoretical inquiry. It's a first product. If it's successful, it allows the manager to get started with his or her campaign, in listing early adopters, adding employees to each further experiment or iteration, and eventually, starting to build a product. That's the lean start-up philosophy.

Now notice, there's an important distinction between that approach and what happens to many entrepreneurs. Many entrepreneurs have a great technological solution. They have a product in mind. But Ries points out that a great technology or a great product concept does not a business make. You need a business model. You need to know what customers actually need this and what does the customer actually need out of that product? You can't fall in love with your own idea. And so you have to adapt, and that adaptation can be difficult for many entrepreneurs.

So, he articulates this notion of an MVP, a minimum viable product. So you start by figuring out, what problem needs to be solved? What pain point is there that the customer is experiencing? Not what's your idea for a great new technology, but what does the customer need based on the frustrations they're experiencing with current products and services? And then, Ries is arguing that we develop a minimum viable product, his MVP. What is that? He says the minimum viable product is that version of a new product or service which allows a team to collect the maximum amount of validated learning with the least effort. The notion here is begin to learn as soon as possible, and then, adapt. Entrepreneurs now talk about the pivot. You pivot or adapt, you shift your idea based on the learning that takes place.

Now what's crucial here is that you get to that learning as soon as possible, that you not belabor the planning process. You don't spend years writing the 100-page business plan before you execute. In other words, you've got to pick up the marshmallow quickly, early. And picking up the marshmallow means getting an initial concept, prototype, product out into customers' hands and collecting feedback, and not spending all your time building spreadsheets that project revenues and expenses for something, frankly, that it's going to be very hard to estimate and to understand in advance. So let's get it out there, and let's collect real user feedback, and let's build upon that. Let's get our MVP into the customers' hands as soon as possible.

Now, what are you trying to accomplish with this MVP? Ries argues you're trying to test certain hypotheses. This scientific method that he's advocating, what does that mean, to test hypotheses? Well, he says, there are certain kinds of propositions that you want to collect information about, certain hypotheses that you could articulate before you put that prototype in the hands of customers. What kinds of hypotheses? You might say, the customer cares about XYZ. The customer defines quality as such. The customer is willing or not willing to pay this certain amount for this product or service.

Those are hypotheses. You have hypotheses about what the customer needs, what they define as quality, and what they're willing to pay for. And now what do you do? You test those hypotheses. You begin to collect data to see, OK, this may be a great product, but can we command a price sufficient to cover our expenses? That's a very different question. You may have a great technology, but no one's willing to pay enough for you to be able to sell it at a profit.

Now getting this prototype into people's hands means getting comfortable with good enough. What do I mean by that, good enough? Well, you can't hold the prototype forever trying to perfect it. You have to be able to get it into people's hands early, even if it's imperfect. It's got to be good enough, not perfect. How do you know what's good enough? That's a really difficult test for an entrepreneur. And many entrepreneurs, they don't want to release their baby before it's perfect.

The way I like to describe this is that, if you're a parent, and you have your firstborn child, and you're going to go to church for the first time with this baby, you're going to do a lot to prepare for that first venture out of the house. You're going to bathe the baby, you're going to pick out a beautiful outfit, and if they have hair, you're going to comb that little bit of hair they have. And then you put some baby lotion on them and you put their nice new patent-leather shoes on, and you take them out in a beautiful blanket so they stay warm.

What's the fear for every couple who has a new baby for the first time? Having three children, I know the fear; you don't want anyone to call your baby ugly. But what do great entrepreneurs do? They're willing to allow others to call their baby ugly. In other words, they're willing to put out a product that isn't perfect, and they're willing to let people say what's not perfect about it and quickly adapt, not fall in love with their idea. And the problem with many entrepreneurs is they're not listening. Even if they put out that prototype, they're hell bent on getting their idea to market. And they've worked on it so hard, they're so passionate about their idea, they don't want to listen to feedback. So it's not enough to just get the prototype out there. You also have to be willing to listen and understand that it's not perfect, and take the criticism, as harsh as it may be. It's difficult to do.

Now, contrast this with strategy making in large firms. If the right strategy for building a new venture is to get good enough out in the marketplace, to build prototypes, collect feedback, to use an MVP strategy, can large organizations do that? I would argue that many large organizations cannot. It's difficult for them to put a good enough product out in the marketplace. Why? Well, they've been trained to work to get something that's precise out there, to have high quality standards. They've been intent on protecting their brand throughout their existence.

So to put a product out there that's imperfect, it runs the risk of harming the brand, of damaging their reputation for quality. They run the risk of being criticized by fellow managers or by their boss for having something that's getting negative feedback from customers. So typically, when we work in a large organization, it's difficult to follow a lean start-up methodology. But entrepreneurs can do it. They have less to lose. They're not worried about an existing brand. They're not worried about what their boss may think of them. So they can build that prototype, and they can be OK with failure. But it takes an open mind. It takes an entrepreneur who's willing to not fall in love with their idea and who's willing to take feedback. And not every entrepreneur is willing to do that.

David Kelley is the founder of the leading product design firm, IDEO. And he has a wonderful phrase that he's instilled at his firm to drive the innovation process. And he talks about the notion of failing often to succeed sooner. And this is really crucial in the context of entrepreneurship. You have to be willing to put something out there that is "a failure," that will, perhaps, be trashed by customers, that will receive a lot of negative feedback. You have to be OK with that, and you have to pick yourself up, take the feedback, and adapt.

Again, you see why large companies have a difficult problem with this. Large companies are averse to failure. If you're a manager at a large company, and you're trying to get a new product out into the marketplace, and your initial attempt is a failure, you run the risk of really harming your career, of not getting promoted, or worse, and so, there's great risk aversion on the part of managers in larger organizations. They're not ready to accept failure. And the culture of large organizations is such that they're not tolerant of those early failures that are simply part of the new-venture creation process.

So larger companies, if they're going to plot innovative strategies for the future and bring new products and services to market, they have to become a little more tolerant of failure, not all failures; we don't want the billion dollar bet. That's a terrible bet, and that leads to huge losses. What we'd like to see is small bets, experiments, tests, prototypes. Those kinds of efforts, if they fail, are not very expensive, and allow us to learn effectively. So there's a difference between the entrepreneur who raises a ton of capital and puts out a product and spends a ton of money, versus the entrepreneur, or the person in a big firm try to launch a new venture, who runs small experiments, cheap, inexpensive, fast prototypes to get feedback and to improve. Not all failure is acceptable.

Do we have some examples of successful pivots of companies that started out with one direction and one strategy and adapted based on customer feedback, that got their MVP out there in the market, and that saw what users wanted, how they reacted, what they liked and disliked, and generated improvements? Well, it's interesting to look at three firms that really moved pretty significantly from their roots in the early stages of the strategy-creation and adaptation process.

Let's take Yelp. Yelp started out as an automated system for e-mailing recommendation requests to friends. What has it become? It's an online review system for restaurants and local businesses. Many people have a Yelp app on their phone, and if they're in a city they're not familiar with, they quickly turn to Yelp to find nearby restaurants or other local businesses, and they look to what others are saying about those businesses before they go give them their dollars.

How about Twitter? Twitter, of course, is a very successful social media platform today. But did they start out that way? They did not. They were a podcasting start-up in their initial incarnation, but they adapted. And how about a firm that we all know, and many people love, some maybe not, but Starbucks is a very successful company. But did they start out with the strategy that we see today? They did not. They started off selling coffee beans and espresso machines. They've become a cafe that sells brewed coffee and coffee drinks of various kinds. They evolved.

Howard Schultz and the team that led them in the early days, they watched what users wanted; they listened to the customer; they interacted with them; they tried things in some of those early stores. And from that initial feedback, they adapted. They still sell coffee beans, after all. But they realize that people wanted brewed coffee and drinks of various kinds. They didn't just want to buy beans that they could then grind and brew at home. They pivoted, and that's what great entrepreneurs do.

So there's an interesting question. Are lean start-ups more possible today than in the past? In other words, could it be that it's easier to build an MVP, to test and prototype today than it was years ago? Well, there's an argument to be made that, in fact, it is easier, more feasible today. The cost of computer-processing power has come down dramatically. There's open-source software available that you can get to help launch your business. Cloud computing has changed the entire nature of computing in many companies. And, access to capital and talent has fundamentally shifted.

When I went to Harvard Business School as an MBA student in the early 1990s, most graduates went off to investment banking or management consulting. Very few people went directly from business school to the start-up community. Today, you see many, many people going to business school and looking to directly launch a new venture. They don't want to work for a large corporation. They want to be their own boss. They have a great idea, and they'd like to try it. So the ability of start-ups to recruit talent, well, there's a lot of young talent that wants to work in a new company. So it's more feasible in many ways to launch a lean start-up today than in the past.

Vivek Wadhwa has done some interesting research over the years on start-ups, in particular, looking at many of them in Silicon Valley. He's noted that today's laptops have the same processing power as the many computers that cost millions of dollars in the 1980s. For storage, you once needed server farms and racks of hard disks. Today, you have cloud computing and cloud storage, and they're cheap.

In short, you can run an experiment. You can get an MVP off the ground. You could launch a new venture, and you don't need tons of capital. As entrepreneurs like to say, you can rely on fools, friends, and family to get your money, and you can get a business off the ground. You don't necessarily need venture capital or angel investors at the beginning for many businesses. That's how inexpensive it's become.

Now, there are organizations that help entrepreneurs, and there's a lot of controversy that has emerged as to whether or not these organizations are helpful or not. We call these start-up accelerators. And there's been an explosion of the number of start-up accelerators around the world. They help entrepreneurs get their new ventures off the ground. Here's how it works. They take applications. Typically, a start-up accelerator is a group of experienced entrepreneurs or venture capitalists who are there to help coach and help work with entrepreneurs who want to get their new venture off the ground. They recruit them. They take applications from people who have a new venture idea, and maybe have a team that's started to come together, and who want some help. And, they screen the applications.

And what they do is accept certain new ventures into a cohort-based, residential program. A venture team, a couple of partners who have an idea, would go to the location of that start-up accelerator, and they would reside there for 12 weeks, and they would get some office space. They would get assistance, counseling, and a little bit of seed funding. In return, they typically would give up a 6% equity stake to the owners of this start-up accelerator.

And then, they would work. They would work on their deal every day, on their venture, and they would get help, not just from the people running the start-up accelerator, but from a wide range of experienced capital providers and entrepreneurs in the local community, people that we call mentors in these start-up accelerators, who are willing to donate their time and effort, in part because they want to help young entrepreneurs, and in part because they want early access to great new ideas that they might invest in. And so there's an opportunity at these accelerators to learn from other entrepreneurs. And ultimately, the 12 weeks culminates in what's called the demo day, where potential investors are assembled and each entrepreneur gets a chance to pitch their idea, potentially raise funding.

Now this sounds like a great way to foster new ventures and to help sharpen the strategy for someone who may not have a lot of experience, but has a great idea. But the question has emerged, is there a start-up accelerator bubble? They've emerged in every city around the globe, it seems like. Can they all really have enough experience to mentor appropriately? Are they all giving good advice and counsel? Can they do the coaching that's necessary? Or are they taking equity stakes and not giving enough in return?

Some of these are very successful. I did a case study recently on Betaspring, who's been rated by academics who study start-up accelerators as one of the best start-up accelerators in the country. They're based in Providence, Rhode Island. Of course, we've also heard of some very famous ones, like Y Combinator and Techstars, and they've had some very successful exits, i.e., companies that have gone on to achieve great valuations and raise great capital. But not all of them have succeeded.

So this is one way to get help if you're an entrepreneur. But there are others as well. Increasingly, there are more and more resources out there, some of them free, to help you if you want to launch a new venture. But what's going to compel people to invest in your new venture? Well, venture capitalists often say that they invest in the team, not just the product or the idea. What does that mean? It means they're evaluating the capabilities of that top team, the backgrounds, the expertise, the way they think those people are working together. Why are they focused on the team and not just the idea? Because those investors, they know that most ventures will have to pivot multiple times in the early days. In short, the idea won't be right the first time. Like Twitter, like Starbucks, like Yelp, there'll be real adaptation that has to take place.

So let's not bet on the idea in and of itself; let's bet on the team. Is that team open enough to new ideas? Will they listen to feedback? Are they willing to put an MVP out there and then adapt? And so venture capitalists are becoming better at being able to understand whether or not this initial approach will work, whether the team is capable of adapting and pivoting as necessary. And remember, investors are more than funds providers. They can be great mentors too. As an entrepreneur, you're not just looking for capital. You're looking for advice and counsel, and that's important as you're searching for money, to think about who can help you, not just who can provide you the funds to get your venture off the ground.

Now, there's been some interesting work by Burgstone and Murphy on what they call breakthrough entrepreneurship. And they argue, at the basic level, people typically spend money on two things. First, they readily spend money to combat pain. Second, they spend money to pursue pleasure. So they argue, can you describe the pain your company solves and why anyone should care, in just a few words? Can you then persuade a prospective customer to spend money to purchase your product using your simple explanation? This is really important, that you not just think about the technology of the product, but you articulate what pain you're alleviating. How are you helping the customer? And even more than that, do you have a business model, not just a product?

What do I mean by having a business model? Well, what have we learned in this course? We've learned that competitive advantage doesn't come from just having the best technology or being the first mover in the marketplace. It comes from having an integrated system of activities that delivers value to the customer, enough value that you can generate returns for investors, as well as provide that consumer some surplus, some value beyond what they paid for the product.

So having a great business model is really important. Take the iPod; it wasn't the first MP3 player out there in the market, but it was the first to put together the right business model. The iPod-plus-iTunes business model made for a successful new business. So in short, you have to ask yourself the question, how will you make money? Not just, do I have a great idea? Or do I have a product that I think is cool? Do users need it? Does it alleviate their pain? And do I have a business model that allows me to generate enough revenue to cover my expenses?

So here a few questions, then, in summary about launching a new venture. Number one, what customer pain point are you trying to alleviate? Number two, what is the business model that enables you to turn customer demand into profitability? Who is on your team? And what value does each person bring to your team? Number four, am I willing to adapt and pivot, or am I falling in love with my initial idea, such that I'm not listening? And finally, where am I going to get assistance, mentorship, connections, funding? Am I going to use an accelerator? Am I going to reach out to an angel investor? Am I going to go to a school and get help of professors? Where am I going to get help to get my venture off the ground?

So finally, the key question, of course, as we've learned throughout this lecture series is, what makes you different? Ultimately, strategy comes down to being different. You have to ask the question, what makes you different or unique? Can you sustain that positioning? Can you build a moat around your castle such that new players cannot imitate you and even surpass you? And are you making the tough choices?

Are you trying to be all things to all people, or are you making trade offs? Are you very clear about who your target market is and who it isn't? And are you willing to say no to certain things that all your competitors are doing, because you're going to take a different path? Are you willing to stand firm on that, even when others, including your customers, ask you to do those things? Are you all things to all people? Or are you tailoring what you do to deliver excellence to a certain segment of customers that you're trying to please the most?

In closing, I'd like to give you one final assignment. Do you have a business idea that you'd like to pursue, a new venture you'd like to get off the ground? What customer need or pain point does it address? How would you test that idea in an inexpensive way, very quickly? What experiment would you run? And what might the MVP look like for your idea?

In closing, I'd like to thank you for listening to this lecture series. I hope you found it helpful. I hope you can apply these ideas in your own businesses, whether it's a large organization or a new venture. You've learned, I hope, that great firms make trade offs, that they make those tough choices, and they build an integrated system of activities and try to sustain that advantage by scanning constantly for new threats, whether from imitators or substitutes.

But most of all, we have to remember, it's really difficult to stay on top. It's hard to sustain advantage. Many firms we've seen have stumbled badly, and many of the leaders today, as I deliver these lectures, they won't be leaders tomorrow. So we have to be constantly attuned to where new rivals will come from and entrants may come in to challenge our position. But hopefully, with the ideas in this course, you'll be ready to take on those battles, to build advantage, and defend that advantage in your business. Thank you.

Critical Business Skills:
Operations

Thomas J. Goldsby, Ph.D.

Critical Business Skills: Operations

Scope:

The world is full of great business ideas—products and service concepts that hold immense promise for businesses and the customers they serve. Yet what is the value of a great idea? It amounts to little if a business cannot execute—that is, produce the product or service in conformance with customer expectations in such a way that customers feel great about buying it. In the best case, customers even take pride in their association with products and services they buy. And that's the goal of any company: to develop a band of loyal patrons—or even fans—who not only buy the products but convince others to buy them, too! You know the companies that enjoy this kind of following: Amazon, Apple, Costco, Nike, Southwest Airlines, and Starbucks, among others.

These are some of the companies we'll examine in this section of the course, exploring the ways in which these firms take great ideas from concept to reality by way of operational excellence. Operations is the business activity that enables companies to keep the promises they make to their customers. It includes the sourcing of materials and goods, the conversion of those inputs into something that someone wants to buy, and the delivery of those goods. Quite simply, it's how great ideas get turned into great products and services that a customer can purchase. And operations management is the discipline of getting the most out of a company's people, processes, and technologies.

We'll explore the fundamental aspects of operations that organizations use to translate good ideas into winning businesses, covering such essential topics as inventory management, supply management, distribution and logistics, and performance measurement. We'll take a close look at how companies are competing through supply chain management and examine the latest trends and research on business strategies that enhance agility, resilience, and sustainability. Among the most strategic of all operations decisions is the determination of whether to make or buy—to insource or outsource business activities. This determination is a multifaceted one, subject to the organization's proclivity for control and its appetite for flexibility. We'll consider how companies can leverage both internal and external resources to extend their reach in the market and ensure profitability.

In light of today's hypercompetitive market environment, organizations of all kinds are seeking to implement processes that create the greatest value for the business and the customers it serves. Companies are emulating the success of legendary operations companies, such as Toyota and its famed production system, in order to maximize value and rid themselves of activities that waste resources and distract the business from its customers. We'll explore how organizations of all kinds can achieve optimal outcomes through implementation of management methods based on Lean Thinking. We will also consider the Six Sigma method for continuous improvement, devised by Motorola in that company's pursuit of variation reduction in its operations. These continuous improvement methods can be applied anywhere that work is performed.

We'll also explore the latest technological developments that promise to revolutionize both operations and business itself. Can you imagine having the ability to pick out a product online, download the blueprint, and have it manifest before your eyes? That's the promise of three-dimensional printing, and companies are putting this technology to work today! General Electric's aviation business is producing critical parts for aircraft turbines through this new-to-the-world additive manufacturing method. Minds in the business world are racing with the potential of such technologies.

Through these lectures, we'll see that operations are instrumental as a value generator and competitive differentiator in every business, ensuring that the right products and services are available in the right form and quantity at the right place and time—and at a competitive price. We'll come to realize that operations management touches virtually every facet of our everyday existence and ensures our quality of life. ■

The Power of Superior Operations
Lecture 13

O perations is the business activity that enables companies to keep the promises they make to customers. It includes sourcing materials and goods, converting those inputs into products that customers want to buy, and delivering the products. Operations management is the discipline of getting the most out of a company's people, processes, and technologies. In these lectures, we'll explore the fundamental aspects of both these activities. We'll cover such essential topics as inventory management, supply management, distribution, and performance measurement. We'll look at how companies compete through supply chain management and examine the latest research on business strategies that enhance agility, resilience, and sustainability. Finally, we'll consider how companies can leverage internal and external resources to survive and thrive.

Vision and Market Strategy

- To understand the role of operations in an organization, we need to know where it fits into the big picture of business decision making. Most companies begin with an overall vision that drives all their functional strategies, including operations. The vision is the statement of how the company wants to be known and sought in the marketplace. Functional strategies establish how the company intends to live up to the promise of its vision.

- The first thing companies typically do after establishing a vision is to devise a market strategy, consisting of the image to be portrayed in the market. In turn, operations strategy is usually regarded as a supporter of the marketing strategy. Depending on how a company wants to be viewed in the marketplace, it will formulate operations to support that vision.

- Harvard professor Michael Porter has identified three competitive market strategies from which a business might choose: low cost, valued differentiation, and a combination of these two.

○ Companies using a low-cost strategy seek to win business by having products and services that reflect a price advantage. These products and services are considered of sufficient quality to warrant consideration but are ultimately chosen because they represent good value in the eyes of customers.

○ With a differentiation strategy, companies seek to distinguish themselves on merits other than low price. In fact, they try to garner premium prices in light of the uniqueness of their products and services. Differentiation is usually preferred over a low-cost strategy because it tends to result in healthier and more sustainable margins and yields customers who are less likely to be swayed by competitors that offer a lower price.

○ The third market strategy identified is a combination of the first two. This approach is rare, though it could be argued that Southwest Airlines implements it quite well. Southwest offers low prices on air travel yet performs high on key operational measures, such as on-time service and customer care.

Some high-end carmakers employ a differentiation strategy, seeking to distance themselves from competitors based on higher levels of comfort, performance, and aesthetics.

Operations Strategy

- Once a company chooses one of the three competitive market strategies, it must then decide how to execute, devising an operations strategy that supports the vision and market strategy. Again, it's important for the operations strategy to match the competitive market strategy. Buying premium supplies or investing heavily in operations geared toward unique customer outcomes while trying to compete on price won't work, nor will using low-cost, standard-commodity materials while trying to persuade customers to pay for a customized experience.

- Another consideration in the selection of operations strategy is the age of the business. Businesses in their infancy usually start with a single or a limited number of products and services. The size and geography of the market is usually small at the outset of the business, as well. For companies at this stage, a single operations strategy usually suffices. But once the business grows in size and complexity, multiple strategies may be used at once, and they may need to change over time.

- What are the operational differences between a company using a low-cost strategy and one that competes on differentiated products? Let's first consider the low-cost scenario.
  - In competitive markets, low cost usually translates into low prices, and low-cost competitors often find themselves in a "race to the bottom." The combination of global competition and the Internet has sped up this race by providing a greater array of competing options and transparency on prices for goods and services in different markets. This makes price advantages fleeting.

  - When competing based on price alone, Charles Darwin's theories of population ecology come to mind: Only the strong and adaptable survive. If you lay down the challenge of price competitiveness, you essentially try to kill off everyone else in the market, and you become the target that other low-cost providers seek to kill.

- As mentioned earlier, one alternative is to pursue a hybrid strategy, competing on a combination of valued differentiation and low cost. One factor that allows Southwest Airlines to do this is that the company doesn't provide service everywhere in the United States. Instead, Southwest is selective; cities actually market themselves to Southwest in hopes of landing its services.
  - Southwest also keeps costs in check through strategic operations. For instance, it uses a single model of aircraft for all its flights, allowing for standardization in spare parts and maintenance. Further, no first-class service is offered.

  - The picture of differentiation here is not achieved through fanciful offerings or unique approaches. It comes by way of limiting the company's focus and executing well.

Operational Capability: Processes
- Operational capability is the composite of processes, people, and technology used to execute an operations strategy. Processes define "what you do." All work is conducted in processes, and today, we spend a great deal of time studying processes with techniques offered by improvement methods, such as Lean Thinking and Six Sigma.

- Lean Thinking is dedicated to mapping and eliminating waste from processes. Mapping processes enables companies to capture the steps involved in doing work. Some steps are value added, meaning that the customer cares about these activities and is willing to pay for these aspects of the work. Value-added steps usually change the appearance of a product or its performance in some way that's noticeable to the customer. All other steps are considered non–value added and should be reduced or even eliminated from the process.

- Six Sigma is dedicated to reducing variation in processes. When variation in inputs or in work performance exists, you can expect variation in the outputs of the process. Unwelcome variations are called *defects*, which are the enemy of consistent quality and lead to adverse customer experiences.

o   In statistics, sigma ($\sum$) is the Greek notation for standard deviation, the mathematical measure of variation. To calculate the capability for a process in terms of variation, it's first necessary to calculate the defects per million opportunities. A *defect opportunity* is any action that strays from the accepted standard for delivery of a perfect product or service.

o   This defect calculation then converts into a level of sigma performance. The more sigmas, the narrower the variation band for the process, meaning that the process is operating within very narrow tolerances with less observed variation— and that's the goal.

Operational Capability: People

- Obviously, the people component of capability speaks to who does the work. This so-called soft side of operations is often the "hard stuff" to figure out. Humans are complex creatures, and understanding what might motivate one person, let alone large groups of people, is extremely difficult.

- One consideration that factors into the critical role of people in operations is automation, which continues to be on the rise in many settings. But not all work lends itself to automation. Specifically, automation struggles with nonstandard tasks or situations. Further, in some circumstances, customers prefer interacting with another person, as opposed to a computer screen.

- It seems that at least for the foreseeable future, we will continue to rely on people to perform many critical tasks. But a fundamental question that companies must ask when executing an operational strategy is whether they will do the work themselves (*insourcing*) or whether they will hire others to do the work on their behalf (*outsourcing*).

Operational Capability: Technology

- The final component of operational capability is technology, specifically, the assistance received from both equipment and information technology to enable higher-performing processes. Technology lends great convenience and enhanced capabilities to work and everyday life, but it should not drive strategy. Business strategies that rely first on technology can be too easily duplicated by competitors—and leapfrogged when a better technology comes along. Competitive advantage achieved through the other aspects of capability—processes and people—can be more difficult to copy.

- The idea of technology as an enabler of process refers to the use of technology to help make sense of complex situations or those laden with data and information. Decision support tools, such as statistical software and business analytics, can help with these problems. In addition, data capture and communicative technologies can help when a company is unable to "see" a process and its performance. GPS, for instance, is wonderful technology for illuminating an otherwise hard-to-see process from afar.

- Finally, any physical equipment that might be used to lighten the load or speed up the work also represents technology. Companies should embrace equipment technology when it advances processes and allows them to avoid sending people into hazardous situations.

- The challenge of operations management is to use operational strategy to guide the processes, people, and technology that constitute operational capability to achieve business success. This isn't a quick or easy task, and once you think you've got it figured out, it's probably time to revisit the decisions. All organizations—from start-ups to multinational corporations—must adapt to stay relevant to customers, and adapting the company's operations is a critical part of that process.

Suggested Reading

Browning and Sanders, "Can Innovation Be Lean?"

Davenport, Mule, and Lucker. "Know What Your Customers Want Before They Do."

Schroeder, Goldstein, and Rungtusanatham, *Operations Management in the Supply Chain.*

Simchi-Levi, *Operations Rules.*

Questions to Consider

1. Why is it important to link a company's operations strategy to the overall business strategy?

2. How can an operations strategy provide identity for a company?

3. Can you think of examples of companies that win in the marketplace through distinctive operations strategies or well-executed operations?

The Power of Superior Operations
Lecture 13—Transcript

Apple CEO Tim Cook takes the stage to the roar of an adoring mob of fans and media, as the pop of a thousand flashbulbs adds glitter to the dreamlike scene. Cook teases the crowd with a story just to build a little anticipation, and when he finally unveils the latest Apple gadget, the crowd erupts with raucous excitement. The market reaction is enthusiastic, too: People line up for days to get their hands on the new device, and it quickly becomes the sales leader in its product category because it defines the category.

How does Apple do it? What goes on behind the scenes to make such wild success possible? A big part of the answer is smart operations.

Operations is the business activity that enables companies to keep the promises they make to their customers. It includes the sourcing of materials and goods, the conversion of those inputs into something that someone else wants to buy, and the delivery of those goods. Quite simply, it's how great ideas get turned into great products and services that a customer can purchase. *Operations Management* is the discipline of getting the most out of a company's people, processes, and technologies. Time and again, at least as of this lecture, Apple has proven itself better and faster at taking ideas from the mind to the market than its competition.

But organizations of all kinds and sizes have achieved excellence in operations; and operations isn't just for manufacturers. Amazon.com, Southwest Airlines, Disney theme parks, FedEx, Starbucks, Mayo Clinic, and Meals on Wheels all owe a significant part of their fame and fortunes to superior operations. What they all know is that to build and keep loyal customers, you need operations that are strategically designed and soundly executed.

In this course, we'll explore the fundamental aspects of operations and operations management that organizations use to translate cool ideas into winning businesses. We'll cover essential topics like inventory management, supply management, distribution, and performance measurement. We'll also take a close look at how companies are competing through supply chain management and examine the latest trends and research on business strategies that enhance agility, resilience, and sustainability. We'll consider how companies can leverage internal as well as external resources in order to survive and thrive.

To understand the true role of operations in an organization, you need to know where it fits into the big picture of business decision making. Even great operations companies don't ordinarily lead with an operations strategy; rather, they begin with an overall vision or mission that drives all their functional strategies including operations. Succinctly, the vision is the statement of who we want to be; how we want to be known and sought in the marketplace. Functional strategies, then, establish how we intend to get there; to live up to the promise of the vision.

The first thing companies typically do after establishing a vision is to create a market strategy consisting of the image they want to portray in the market. The image requires supporting messaging to the target markets they want to serve. Operations strategy usually is regarded as a supporting strategy for the marketing strategy. Depending on how you want to be viewed in the marketplace, you'll formulate operations to support that vision.

Harvard professor Michael Porter has identified three competitive market strategies from which a business might choose. The first is a low-cost strategy. Companies employing a low-cost strategy seek to win business by having products and services that reflect a price advantage. These products and services are considered of sufficient quality to warrant consideration, but are ultimately chosen because they represent good value in the eyes of customers. Walmart is known for employing an everyday low-price strategy that reflects this orientation. Little Caesars's "Pizza Pizza" motto suggests that you can buy two Little Caesars pizzas for the same price as one pizza at a competitor. I think we'll agree that Walmart and Little Caesars don't represent prestige, but that's not what they're going after. In both cases, they're selling value, and narrow margins can be overcome by high sales volume, moving a lot of merchandise.

A second market strategy involves differentiation. Here, companies seek to distinguish themselves on merits other than low price. In fact, they try to garner premium prices in light of the uniqueness of their products and services. German carmakers like BMW, Mercedes, and Porsche seek to distance themselves from competitors based on higher levels of comfort, performance, and aesthetics, such that a premium price is justified in the market. Here, prestige is an important part of the value proposition.

Differentiation is usually the preferred strategy to low cost. Why? Because differentiation tends to result in healthier and more sustainable margins. If you can gain recognition as offering something unique, you're more likely to enjoy a following of customers willing to pay a little more to enjoy those distinct benefits, and those customers are less likely to be swayed by competitors that offer a lower price. Given global competition for products, maintaining a price advantage can be fleeting today.

The third market strategy identified by Professor Porter is a combination of the first two. It suggests that perhaps it's possible to compete on valued differentiation and low cost. This combination is quite rare, though. Some even describe it as a "unicorn" strategy; something talked about but never seen. I'd argue, though, that Southwest Airlines implements this strategy really well. They offer low prices on air travel, yet perform very high on key operational aspects like on-time service and customer care. They also have flight crews with good senses of humor, which doesn't hurt.

Once one of these three competitive market strategies is chosen, you must think about how to execute, devising an operations strategy that supports the vision and market strategy. Again, it's really important for your operations strategy to match the competitive market strategy. Buying premium supplies or investing heavily in operations geared toward unique customer outcomes while trying to compete on price just won't work. You'll spend your way right of business.

Another consideration in the selection of operations strategy is the age of the business; where it finds itself in the business life cycle. Businesses in their infancy usually start with a singular or limited number of products and services. The size and geography of the market is usually small at the outset of the business, too. It's rare for an upstart company to truly take on the world. Rather, we try to take on our little corner of the world in hopes that we can grow with the expanding range of the market. Then, neighboring markets hear about the great things we're doing and ask us to move on in. Or, we think the product or service format would work elsewhere and we take the initiative to another market to expand our footprint. A resounding example of this kind of growth is Starbucks. Starting from a single coffee shop in Seattle in 1971, the company today operates more than 18,000 stores in 62 different countries. That didn't happen overnight, though it might seem that way to the casual observer.

The point here is that when the business is focused on a few products or services in a small geographic market, a single operations strategy usually suffices. But as the business grows in size and complexity, multiple strategies might be employed at once, and they may need to change from time to time. While Starbucks is known for its premium coffee served expertly by skilled baristas, the company also now sells prepared juices, food products, and music CDs that are complements to the focal product, the coffee. The operational strategy employed on these complementary items can be different than with coffee. Coffee is what sets the company apart, so a differentiated strategy is used here. But the items under the glass counter are more commodity—you can find them in several other shops and stores— forcing Starbucks to be somewhat more sensitive to price on these goods.

Another example of how operations strategies can expand and change over time is found in the auto industry. Toyota, among the world's largest automakers, is known for producing high-quality, reliable cars at very competitive prices. Yet in 1989, they decided to also compete in the high-end luxury market by introducing the Lexus brand. The operations employed to produce Lexus cars were different from those used to make the mainline Toyota products. For instance, it wasn't until recently that the company produced Lexus vehicles in locations outside of Japan. For nearly two decades, the company maintained such tight controls on the assembly of the premium cars and SUVs that they wouldn't build them anywhere else, despite the fact that cars sporting the Toyota badge were produced in more than a dozen different countries. Over time, production capabilities in the U.S. and Canada have risen to the point where not only does Toyota produce Lexus cars there for the North American markets, but they export them to locations around the world. This reflects a change in operations strategy tied to growing markets and rising capabilities.

What are the operational differences between a company employing a low-cost strategy and one that competes on differentiated products? Let's start with the low-cost scenario. In competitive markets, low cost usually translates into low prices. Low-cost competitors often find themselves in a "race to the bottom." The combination of global competition and the Internet has sped up this race by providing a greater array of competing options and transparency on prices for goods and services in different markets. That makes price advantages fleeting.

When competing based on price alone, Charles Darwin's theories of population ecology come to mind: Only the strong and adaptable parties survive. It's not a place for the faint of heart. If you lay down the challenge of price competitiveness, you essentially try to kill off everyone else, and you become the target that other low-cost providers seek to kill off. At least with differentiation strategies, you usually have multiple ways to set yourself apart. With low cost, it comes down to this one criterion: price. Commodities like those found in agricultural and construction trades commonly compete like this.

As I mentioned earlier, one alternative is to pursue a "hybrid" strategy, competing on a combination of valued differentiation and low cost. It's a tough thing to pull off, but one thing that allows Southwest Airlines to do it is that they don't provide service everywhere in the United States. They're not trying to serve every little town and city through the hub-and-spoke systems employed by most of their competitors; instead, they're selective. Cities actually market themselves to Southwest in hopes of landing their services.

Back in the late 1990s, the city leaders of Des Moines, Iowa attempted to recruit Southwest Airlines to the Midwestern city. Southwest saw the proposal and passed. They did enter the market some years later, but they do business where they choose, and they keep their costs in check through strategic operations. For instance, they use a single model of aircraft, the Boeing 737, for all of their services. This allows for standardization in spare parts and in their maintenance operation. Also, their pilots must only be certified to fly this one aircraft, making their pilots more interchangeable, too. And, no first-class service is offered. The picture of differentiation here isn't achieved through fanciful offerings or doing things vastly differently from the competition; it comes by way of limiting the company's focus and executing very well.

The same might be said of boutique grocery retailer Trader Joe's. Rather than stocking 120,000 different items like a typical Walmart store, a Trader Joe's store stocks about 4,000 different items, 80% of which are private brands sold exclusively there. In total, Trader Joe's offers a unique yet limited assortment of products that helps to keep prices affordable, right down to the extremely affordable Charles Shaw wines, known affectionately as "Two Buck Chuck," which as of this taping retails for $2.49.

The examples of Southwest Airlines and Trader Joe's show a collaboration between each company's business and operations strategies. While you can choose an operations strategy that suits your overall business strategy, at some point you have to execute. Let's turn our attention to operational capabilities, which is the composite of processes, people, and technology employed to execute your operations strategy.

Processes define what you do. All work is conducted in processes, and today we spend a great deal of time studying processes with techniques offered by improvement methods like Lean Thinking and Six Sigma. Let me give you a brief synopsis of each of these methods.

Lean thinking is dedicated to eliminating waste from processes. By mapping processes, we capture the steps involved in doing our work. Some steps are what we call value added, meaning that the customer cares about these activities and is willing to pay for these aspects of the work. Value-added steps usually change the appearance of a product or its performance in some way that's noticeable to the customer. All other steps are considered non-value-added and should be reduced or even eliminated from the process. A "leaned-out" process is one that's wrung out the waste, leaving only the value-added work and essential supporting steps, like keeping the accounting books and observing rules and regulations. Lean processes provide the value that customers seek and do it in less time with fewer resources.

A company that we've already discussed in this lecture, Toyota, serves as the inspiration for Lean Thinking. A major research study conducted at MIT in the 1980s uncovered something special about Toyota. By virtue of its Toyota Production System, the company was able to deliver more product of higher quality with fewer plants, fewer people, and less material in less time than the competition, all amounting to lower costs. One of the research team members remarked that, when you think about it, Toyota was lean, and the label stuck.

The other process improvement method, Six Sigma, applies the rigor of the scientific method to work processes and is dedicated to reducing variation in those processes. When we have variation in inputs or variation in how work is performed, we can expect variation in the outputs of a process. Unwelcome variations are called defects, and defects are the enemy of consistent quality, leading to adverse customer experiences with our products and services. It was an engineer at Motorola Company, Mr. Bill Smith, who devised the Six Sigma methodology in the 1980s.

What does the term *Six Sigma* itself refer to? Those of you who've studied statistics know that $\sum$ is the Greek notation for standard deviation, the mathematical measure of variation. To calculate the capability for a process in terms of variation, we determine the defects per million opportunities. A defect opportunity is any action that strays from the accepted standard for delivery of a perfect product or service. This defect calculation then converts into a level of sigma performance. The more sigmas, the narrower the variation band for the process, meaning that the process is operating within very narrow tolerances with less observed variation, and that's the goal. Bill Smith wanted Motorola to perform at a Six Sigma level, which translates to no more than 3.4 defects per million opportunities in the production of the company's electronic products. If that sounds like a really high standard of quality, it is. The Six Sigma method comes equipped with an array of statistical tools that help to identify the root causes of variation and guide corrective actions.

Can Lean and Six Sigma be applied together, you ask? Sure, we call this Lean Six Sigma, or Lean Sigma for short. What you'll find is where there's variation in work processes, we usually find waste, too. The two methods attack the same business challenge of eliminating quality deficiencies in the pursuit of perfection.

Now let's consider the people aspect of operational capabilities. Obviously, this component of capability speaks to who does the work. The so-called soft side of operations is often the hard stuff to figure out. Humans are complex creatures, and understanding what might motivate one person can be difficult enough. Figuring out how to motivate large armies of people in an operation can overwhelm even the best business leader.

Allow me to offer a few considerations that factor into the critical role of people in operations. Automation and the use of robots continue to be on the rise in many operational settings, especially for highly repetitive tasks or those involving hazards. But not all work lends itself to automation. This is for two reasons: For one, automation struggles with non-standard tasks, or to recognize circumstances beyond the range that a computer program can anticipate. Artificial intelligence is closing this gap, but robots aren't yet smart enough to recognize non-standard situations or to accommodate them fully. The other reason for limiting automation is simply one of preference. There are some interfaces where people simply prefer a smiling face as opposed to a screen. I have a colleague who refuses to use the automated check in at airports, preferring instead to check in with a charming agent at the guest counter. It's nice when it works out that way, right? That the agent is charming and helpful? It seems that for the foreseeable future anyway we'll continue to rely on people to perform many critical tasks, both behind the scenes and in interfacing with our customers.

But as for who to rely on: A fundamental question that we must ask when executing an operational strategy is whether we as a company must do the work ourselves or whether we'll hire others. This is referred to as *insourcing* (when we do it ourselves) or *outsourcing* (when we hire others to act on our behalf). Outsourcing has been all the rage over the past three decades, as companies elect to focus on things that they do really well. These are called the core competencies of the company. Many companies that once manufactured products now hire outside companies to produce products on their behalf. This is true of most fashion brands and electronics companies. While they still may develop product designs and product prototypes, they don't make any of the products that bear their brand names. Some companies have pursued outsourcing with suppliers in countries with low-cost labor. This practice of offshoring was particularly common in the early 2000s.

Some who offshored have since brought work back into the company when control of operations was lost or inflation drove up the cost in what was once a low-cost country. Others have continued to outsource but have elected to reshore, or bring the work back to domestic suppliers. Regardless of who employs the workforce, it's essential that employees know what's expected of them, that they're trained, prepared, and motivated to do the work, and that their safety is assured.

The final component of operational capability that I'll address in this lecture is technology; specifically, the assistance we receive from both equipment and information technology to enable higher-performing processes. Technology lends great convenience and enhanced capabilities to work and everyday life, but I caution people not to let it drive strategy. Rather, seek technology as an enabler of the work processes. Business strategies that rely first on technology can be too easily duplicated by competitors and leapfrogged when a better technology comes along. Competitive advantage achieved through the other aspects of capability—process and people—can be more difficult to copy.

What do I mean by recommending that you use technology as an enabler of a process? I'm referring to the use of technology to help us make sense of complex situations or those laden with data and information. Decision support tools like statistical software and business analytics can help us with these problems.

Technology can also help us when we're unable to see a process and its performance. Data capture and communicative technologies help in these situations. GPS, for instance, is a wonderful technology for illuminating an otherwise hard-to-see process from afar. When we marry GPS with expected checkpoints, we can be notified if a shipment is late, for instance. Shipping companies like UPS and FedEx use this technology effectively to let us know where a package is in transit, offering insight as to when we can expect delivery.

Finally, any physical equipment that we might use to lighten the load or speed up the work represents technology, too. We need to embrace equipment technology when it advances our processes, and especially when it prevents us from sending people into hazardous situations where they're at risk of injury.

The challenge of Operations Management is to use operational strategy to guide the processes, people, and technology that constitute operational capability in order to achieve business success. It isn't a quick or easy task. Further, once you think you've got it figured out, it's probably time to start all over again and revisit these decisions. The decisions are anything but static. As opportunities and threats present themselves, the operations of the company must adapt. In the fortunate situation of growth, maintaining quality when the business expands can be a real predicament.

Let's look at a case study that sheds light on how to use Operations Management to bring a company vision into reality. Note that this example features operations in two ways: one, in the production of the product, and two, in the provision of service, bringing both production operations and service operations into scope.

In Columbus, Ohio, Jeni's Splendid Ice Cream is a treasured institution. In a product category market that's seemingly oversaturated with options, Jeni's stands out for its unique flavors, product quality, and first-rate service. Like most businesses, though, Jeni's started from humble beginnings. Founder Jeni Britton Bauer had the idea of producing artisanal ice creams using the freshest ingredients from nearby dairy, fruit, and vegetable farms. With the pledge to make "the best ice creams we could imagine," she opened her first shop in downtown Columbus in 2002.

The ice creams are produced in small batches from the freshest ingredients. The milk, for instance, is all sourced from grass-grazed cows on dairy farms located within 200 miles of Columbus. The flavor ingredients are all -natural and free from stabilizers, with most fruits and vegetables sourced from nearby farms. The product has received countless accolades, and a *New York Times* review once indicated that Jeni's had—and I quote here—"surpassed the creativity of all other ice cream makers with its versions like goat cheese and Cognac fig sauce." But my personal favorite is Salty Caramel; it's really good, trust me. In the shop, you'll find friendly faces who know all about the ice creams and yogurt products on the menu. These "Ice Cream Ambassadors," as they're called, are asked, according to a recent job posting, to "provide consistent, world-class service to every single customer; exhibit passion for the community, an eye for detail, a willingness to clean (a lot), stamina (to serve people in long lines), and the ability to work in an exciting, fast-paced environment."

In total, what we have here is an example of a differentiated product and service experience, for which Jeni's is able to charge a premium price. Jeni's isn't the destination if you're looking for just any old ice cream. Jeni's is where you'll find Jeni's ice cream and knowledgeable service around the product, and those differences justify the premium.

But success brings its own challenges. When demand exceeded the capacity of the single shop downtown in Columbus, Jeni's opened up new locations around town, to the current count of 10 shops. The question became one of scale: Could Jeni's continue to provide the same high quality in the product and service experience at multiple locations throughout the city? So far, the small company—and more importantly, the market—have answered with a resounding "Yes." But to do so, Jeni's had to find a way to scale up its operations formula, much like a cook who usually makes meals for 4 suddenly has to prepare a banquet for 100. Then came the next challenge: grocery retailers. They started clamoring to stock Jeni's product throughout the region. This required a new set of operations to package the ice cream for grocery sales. We also now see vending machines around the city also stocking the ice creams. You can guess the next chapter: opening shops outside the region, which the company has done with new shops in Cleveland, Atlanta, Nashville, Charleston, South Carolina, Chicago, and New York City.

Only time will tell if Jeni's will be able to achieve the same success in these other locations, replicating its business model. Taking a so-called winning formula on the road has worked for some companies in the past, but not for others. It could be that Jeni's will still need to make more changes to the operations part of its formula to accommodate the growth. But adaptation is what good operations management is all about.

All organizations, from startups to huge multinational corporations, must adapt to stay relevant to customers, and adapting the company's operations is a critical part of that process. Adaptation is the only timeless secret of success, and Charles Darwin let the secret out. The only difference between life in the natural world that he examined and life in the business world is that innovative companies can actually force the evolution. They can create needs that customers themselves didn't realize they had.

This brings us back to Apple. Before it was invented, did it ever occur to you that you needed an app that simulates bubble wrap that you can pop on your iPhone or iPad at your leisure? It relieves stress almost as well as the real bubble wrap. Apple has created not only the hardware to make these things possible but also the App Store, which makes available more than 1.2 million different apps and counting that allow you to use your mobile device in almost any way you wish. Apple doesn't even create most of the apps that the App Store sells; it simply makes it possible for others to invent and sell them and takes a cut of the proceeds, which amounted to more than $10 billion in 2013. That's another smart move: A great operations company is one that takes advantage of change. It doesn't view new preferences, tastes, or ideas as problems, but as opportunities to seize.

Operations is the capability behind innovation. It delivers on the promise, and that's what makes it one of the most exciting, vital, and dynamic aspects of business in the 21st century.

Leaner, Meaner Production
Lecture 14

A s we saw in the last lecture, operations is the business activity that fulfills the promises that companies make to their customers. It includes sourcing materials and goods, converting those inputs into something that customers want to buy, and delivering the goods. Production operations are those that involve the provision of actual goods as opposed to services. Production operations for physical goods are also referred to as manufacturing operations and have the primary function of converting inputs into desired outputs for customers. They represent the greatest value-adding activity in all of business, transforming the useless into the useful.

The "Make-vs.-Buy" Decision

- One of the most fundamental decisions that any company interested in selling products must make is whether to produce the product in-house or to hire an outside company to manufacture the product on its behalf. This determination of insourcing versus outsourcing is often called the "make-vs.-buy" decision. Both options are considered part of production operations, but they involve different organizational arrangements.

- In making this decision, the place to start is with simple economics: determining what it would cost your company to produce the product—taking into account fixed capital costs and the costs of running the operation—versus what a contract manufacturer would charge for its services.
  - Complicating this analysis is the expectation of future sales. If the product is a big hit, you could cover your fixed-cost investments with the increasing sales volume, but you might also have to expand operations in a hurry.

  - Another complication can arise when customers ask for different items or unique packaging. Just as we consumers seek unique, differentiated products, so, too, do business customers.

Large retailers and distributors want to be able to offer product assortments that can't be found anywhere else. That can create a problem if you sell to and through many different retailers.

- Contract manufacturers excel at making adaptations because manufacturing is their core competency. They tend to have skills in developing proper tooling and quick changeovers from one product to another. They can also offer economic advantages because the production facility is shared with multiple clients, and costs are spread across these clients.

- For these reasons, many young companies that are bringing products to market for the first time choose outsourcing over insourcing. They can get into business without having to build a factory and invest in manufacturing equipment and a trained workforce.

- However, there are also disadvantages to outsourcing, the most significant of which is control. You take the risk that the contract manufacturer won't have your best interests at heart when producing your goods. There's even the risk that a company that learns how to make your product could steal it.

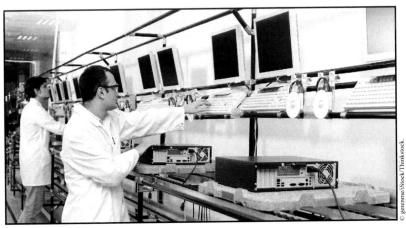

It's estimated that the global market for contract manufacturing in electronics is more than $450 billion.

- For that reason, you need to analyze the transaction costs associated with hiring an outside party. Transaction cost analysis (TCA) is a distinct branch of economics that examines the costs of monitoring another party to act on your behalf.

Outsourcing Considerations

- Companies that outsource often opt for suppliers in countries where wages for labor are lower than in developed economies—a practice known as *offshoring*. However, some companies have later retracted this decision when they find that they've underestimated the transaction costs and the amount of oversight required with offshore manufacturing. This is particularly true when manufacturing problems make product recalls necessary.

- Another circumstance that would warrant reconsideration of outsourcing is the discovery of labor abuses at contract manufacturing locations. Public pressures and, increasingly, government regulations are forcing companies to be more transparent about who they hire, where suppliers are located, and the standards in place to ensure that work practices are consistent with Western norms.

- If you still elect to hire an outside manufacturer—despite these cautions—work with an attorney who is seasoned in negotiating such deals. This is especially important when doing business across national boundaries.

Manufacturing Strategies

- If you decide that you're better off making your product yourself, you first need to decide what manufacturing strategy you will use. There are five primary strategies to consider.

- The first strategy is called *ship-to-stock*, or a *full anticipatory strategy*. Under this strategy, companies put complete faith in their sales forecasts, using those numbers to drive purchasing, production, and distribution. In other words, a company builds and distributes products in advance of demand and hopes that it has estimated correctly.

- Companies use this strategy in situations where customers expect to find the product on the shelf, buy it, and make use of it immediately. Thus, this strategy is used for virtually everything sold in, for example, grocery stores.

- Of course, with this strategy, when you underestimate demand, you are left with disappointed customers. And when you overestimate demand, you're left with extra inventory that you may need to mark down or even write off.

- One step away from ship-to-stock is the *make-to-stock strategy*. In this case, companies buy materials in advance and manufacture products in accordance with sales forecasts, but they do not allocate the goods to distribution locations until they receive customer orders and know exactly where to ship.
  - This delaying of the delivery step allows companies to hold inventory centrally for all distribution locations and, thus, get by with lower inventories.

  - But holding inventory centrally and postponing delivery until orders are in hand means that customers have to wait for delivery.

- The next strategy is called *assemble-to-order*, *configure-to-order*, or *mass customization*. With this strategy, materials are procured in advance of demand and products are made only to a semi-finished state. The finished product doesn't take shape until the company learns exactly what the customer wants. This strategy is ideal for basic products that can be sold with small differences.
  - This strategy allows a pool of common inventory to cover the needs of customers who are looking for something slightly different, again, reducing inventory requirements but requiring additional time to perform the final touches on the goods and deliver them.

  - Toyota provides an excellent example of mass customization with its Scion brand of cars. The cars are manufactured to a generic state in Japan but held in large supplies by major

U.S. distributors. Customers select options from the company website, and when an order is confirmed, the closest distributor alters the base model according to the customer's requests.

o Through this assemble-to-order strategy, Toyota is able to provide customers with seemingly limitless choices yet with much less inventory than if the company pre-built cars to cater to customer demands. However, under this system, customers have to wait a few days or a few weeks to take possession of their cars.

- The fourth manufacturing strategy is the *make-to-order strategy*. In this scenario, the manufacturer has the raw materials on hand but does not commit to assembling them until receiving a customer order. In delaying the assembly process, the manufacturer has even more flexibility to accommodate diverse customer preferences related to product form and function. Such a strategy might be used for a highly customized luxury vehicle.

- The fifth strategy is the least speculative of all for the producer: the *buy-to-order strategy*. Here, the producer awaits the customer order before even purchasing the raw materials. This allows for products to be truly custom-built, but customers must expect longer wait times under this system. Such arrangements are sometimes used in the provision of large industrial products, such as aircraft or satellites, or in homebuilding.

- Large manufacturers often use multiple strategies to accommodate their varieties of products. Smaller companies generally start off with one of the less risky and less speculative strategies, such as buy-to-order or make-to-order, so that they can conserve cash for investments other than inventory.

- Lean Thinking has had a significant influence on the management of inventory as it relates to production strategies.

o Traditionally, companies relied on inventory to deal with a variety of problems. For example, the problem of inaccurate sales forecasts or unreliable suppliers can be solved just by having more than enough inventory to cover any shortfalls or late shipments.

o Lean Thinking, however, encourages companies not to rely on inventory. Instead, companies should improve their forecasts or design flexible operations that make them less dependent on forecasts and more responsive to actual demand. Companies are also encouraged to work only with reliable suppliers or to help existing suppliers deliver better materials more reliably.

Developments in Production Operations

- Advanced technologies are making significant changes in the world of production operations. In fact, one major development is threatening the entire system of factory-based mass production that we have known over the past century. This revolution is the advent of three-dimensional printing, creating what's known as *form-on-the-spot*.

  o This technology has found use in the production of models and prototypes in recent years, but the prospects for using form-on-the-spot production have set minds racing in the operations field. Just as we now download music and books from the Internet, imagine downloading three-dimensional blueprints, hitting the print button, and watching physical goods take shape right before your eyes!

  o To date, three-dimensional printing is limited to simple products with simple materials. That situation is changing quickly though; such companies as General Electric are making significant investments in advancing the manufacturing capabilities of the printing equipment.

- Another development to watch is the rise of *nearshoring* and *reshoring*. Although some companies continue to favor outsourcing of manufacturing operations to suppliers in low-cost countries, there is also a trend in the opposite direction.
  - Companies have learned that it's difficult to anticipate all the things that can go wrong with offshoring, such as frequent power outages, high labor turnover, and so on. In reaction to this reality, many companies that once offshored to low-cost countries are regionalizing their supply chains, meaning that they are seeking to produce closer to the markets they're trying to serve.

  - *Nearshoring* refers to the practice of producing close to the focal market, probably in a location that still offers some cost advantage but with less uncertainty than far-off locations. *Reshoring* refers to bringing once-offshored manufacturing back home.

- Finally, the next significant wave of innovation in production operations may come with the focus on sustainability. Our ability to serve a growing population in a more sustainable fashion will be at the forefront of corporate decisions and national policy in the coming years. This could mean choosing different materials and creating products using manufacturing processes and energy sources that don't pollute the air, land, or water.

- Production operations is a key factor in all these developments. Whether it drives them or simply incorporates and adapts to them, it will be central in the years ahead to some of the most dramatic changes in how we live, how we create, and how we interact with our planet.

Suggested Reading

Kazmer, "Manufacturing Outsourcing, Onshoring, and Global Equilibrium."

Shih, "What It Takes to Reshore Manufacturing Successfully."

Simchi-Levi, Peruvankal, Mulani, Read, and Ferreira, "Is It Time to Rethink Your Manufacturing Strategy?"

Williamson, "Outsourcing."

Questions to Consider

1. Why would a company elect to outsource the production of products bearing the company's brand name? What are the risks inherent in outsourcing?

2. How do you select the right manufacturing strategy for a product? What makes it the "right strategy"?

3. How does the pursuit of sustainability affect decision making in production operations?

Leaner, Meaner Production
Lecture 14—Transcript

Do you remember buying shoes when you were a kid? Not those dull dress shoes, but shoes for school or play? Nike was just making its way to the national market when I was a kid, and it was a big deal to pick among the shoes with either the red, blue, or black swoosh. Oh, the choices.

It's a different story today, right? Shoes come in every color you can imagine, but now you can select the mix of colors for a wholly customized shoe. Through the NIKEiD website, you can take a base model and customize it to your heart's content. Or download the NIKEiD app, take a photo of something that you want the shoes to match, and let the app design the shoe for you. How cool is that? Nike offers a prime example of how production operations are changing the way we live today. Thanks in part to new technologies, production operations are leveraging the preferences of consumers to provide us with not only variety but customization, and delivering our customized products in a short amount of time at a reasonable cost.

Operations, you'll recall, is the business activity that fulfills the promises that companies make to their customers. It includes the sourcing of materials and goods, the conversion of those inputs into something that someone else wants to buy, and the delivery of those goods. Production operations are operations that involve the provision of actual goods. Production operations for tangible, physical goods are also referred to as manufacturing operations and have the primary function of converting inputs into desired outputs for customers. They represent the greatest value-adding activity in all of business. They transform the useless into the useful; something that someone's willing to pay for. Let's look at how production operations work.

Why might you find yourself needing to make a product in the first place? Few businesses set out wanting to manufacture something, anything. No, instead, they recognize some unmet need out there; a market opportunity for a product that no one else provides or a way to build an existing product better or cheaper. The making of the product is simply a response to the need; the opportunity to create value and sell it.

New products may come in one of two kinds: product extensions or new-to-the-world products. The most common new product is the extension variety, which is usually an adaptation of an already successful product; a way of making that product better in some way. We see these in the grocery business all the time, like Coca-Cola adding lime flavor to the Diet Coke, or Frito-Lay introducing a new flavor of Doritos chip. These products don't tend to require the same level of research and development or prototyping when compared to really new products that have a longer path from the picture in the inventor's mind to tangible form. New-to-the-world products require added demonstration and testing.

Once the product concept proves functionally viable, it must prove its viability from a market and economic standpoint. The question becomes: "I wonder if I could sell this?" With the firm belief that enough people just might want to buy your product and that no one else is serving that need, you can turn your attention to how to make it. Can you make it at such a cost that you could sell it for something more to earn a profit? With affirmative responses to these questions and some financial backing, congratulations: You're a budding entrepreneur.

To be a successful entrepreneur, though, you need to make your vision a reality and become an actual provider of a new product. That's where production operations comes in. Notice that I didn't say you need to become the manufacturer of a new product, but the provider. A fundamental decision that any company interested in selling products must make is whether to produce the product in-house or to hire an outside company to manufacture the product on its behalf. This determination of insourcing or outsourcing is often called the "make versus buy" decision. Both options are considered part of production operations, but they involve very different organizational arrangements. The choice between the two can be pretty complicated, so let me break it down for you.

We'll start off with some simple economics: What would it cost you to produce the product? Here, you'll need to take into account the property, plant, equipment, and associated taxes and depreciation. Once fixed capital expense investments are tabulated, you need to turn your attention to the costs of running the operations, including the buying of materials, securing labor, and paying utilities. A simple cost-per-unit can be calculated by dividing the sum of the annual costs by the volume you expect to produce. This simple average can then give you a basis to shop against the prices that outside companies would charge you for their services. With a web search and some homework, you can locate a contract manufacturer, or many, willing to produce your product for a price. The trick is to compare the anticipated quality and price that the outside vendor offers with the quality you'd achieve and the costs you'd incur in-house.

Complicating the analysis is the expectation of future sales. If the product's a big hit, you could cover your fixed-cost investments with the increasing sales volume, but it might also require you to expand the operations in a hurry. Also, life as a do-it-yourself manufacturer can get complicated quickly when customers start asking for different items or unique packaging. Remember our NIKEiD example? Just as we consumers seek unique, differentiated products, so, too, do business customers. Big retailers and distributors want to be able to say that they offer product varieties and assortments that can't be found anywhere else. That might be fine, but what if you sell to and through many different retailers, all demanding unique products? OK, now you've got a problem. But contract manufacturers excel at making adaptations because manufacturing is their core competency; it's what they do. They tend to have skills in developing proper tooling and quick changeovers from one product to another since they typically serve a multitude of customers. They also can offer economic advantages as the production facility is shared with multiple clients. The costs get spread across all of these clients.

Sounds good, eh? That's why many young companies that are bringing products to market for the first time choose to buy over make. They can get into business without having to build a whole factory and invest in manufacturing equipment and a trained workforce first. But there are also disadvantages to going to the outside, and the biggest one is control. You find yourself at the mercy of an outside party to do the job for you. The risk is that the contract manufacturer won't have your best interests at heart when producing your goods. There's even the risk that the company learns how to make your product and they could steal it, maybe by making a small alteration to it, or in countries with poor oversight of intellectual property rights, stealing your product design outright.

For that reason, you need to analyze the transaction costs associated with hiring an outside party. Transaction cost analysis (or TCA) is a distinct branch of economics that examines the cost of monitoring another party to act on your behalf. Professor Oliver Williamson of UC-Berkeley received the Nobel Prize in Economics in 2009 for advancing the theory of Transaction Cost Economics. Transaction costs include the cost of being taken advantage of and monitoring the outside party to ensure that they act in accordance with your expectations. This may seem like a long ways from production operations, but it's all part of getting a product to market successfully.

The make versus buy decision isn't unique to new or small firms; it's something that even the giant purveyors of brands entertain. This is certainly the case with most fashion apparel companies. They hand over their design sketches and sometimes the materials to a contract manufacturer that fulfills every step, from fabrication through distribution to retailers. Many other industries do the same thing. It's estimated that the global market for contract manufacturing in medical devices is approximately $50 billion and the electronics market is over $450 billion, with both expecting robust growth for the foreseeable future.

Many companies looking to outsource opt for suppliers in low-cost countries, where wages for labor are far lower than in developed countries. This practice of offshoring has gained widespread adoption in many industries. It's been said that the three scariest words in U.S. business in the early 2000s were "the China price," the term that powerful customers like Walmart used to demand rock-bottom prices from their suppliers. It often occurred that when one company elected to offshore operations to a low-cost country, all competing companies suddenly found themselves at a cost disadvantage and had to follow suit.

Some who've elected to outsource end up retracting that decision when they find out that they've underestimated the transaction costs involved and the amount of oversight required to ensure supply of good-quality products proves too taxing. This is particularly true when manufacturing problems make product recalls necessary. Recalls can be a nightmare for companies. They're very costly to manage and can cause irreparable damage to a brand image.

Another circumstance that would warrant reconsideration of outsourcing is the discovery of labor abuses at contract manufacturing locations. Such were the concerns with electronics manufacturing in China and apparel manufacturing in Bangladesh. Public pressures and, increasingly, government regulations are forcing companies to be more transparent about who they hire, where the supplier's located, and the standards in place to ensure that work practices are consistent with Western norms. Nike, which was once the focus of great criticism, now discloses the street address and worker profile of the more than 700 factories that produce its branded products around the world, and anyone can access this information right there on the company's website. Some companies go even further: They go so far as to reward whistleblowers at contract manufacturers who report valid labor safety concerns.

In cases of quality defects, recalls, and labor abuses, companies are learning that they can't simply blame the independent manufacturer that may be located several thousand miles away. If it's your brand on the product, you'll be held fully accountable in most courts and also in the court of public opinion, and public opinion can be far more damning. Just ask Kathie Lee Gifford. Way back in 1996, a clothing line sold at Walmart bearing her name was tied to sweatshop labor conditions in Honduras. She went on to become a champion for human rights and child protection legislation, but the association of her name with immoral labor practices lingered for many years.

If, despite these cautions, you still elect to hire an outside manufacturer to produce your product, work with an attorney seasoned in negotiating such deals who knows the ins and outs of doing business in the sourcing and distribution markets. Don't just rely on an independent broker to set up the deal. This is especially important when doing business across national boundaries. Put simply, it's no place for an amateur to tread. There's too much at risk.

Let's say you decide that you're better off making your product yourself. What are the key production operations decisions and best practices that you need to be aware of? The first big decision is to determine the manufacturing strategy to employ, and there are five primary strategies to consider. What sets them apart is the timing of the work that's done.

The first strategy is what's called ship-to-stock. This is what we call a full anticipatory strategy. Under ship-to-stock, we put complete faith in our sales forecast, using those numbers to drive the buying of materials, the production of goods, and the distribution of those goods. In other words, we build and distribute the products in advance of demand and we hope that we guess right, building enough of the product and positioning it in the market. That's a pretty tough thing to pull off, and inevitably we'll either come up short or long on the numbers. Why would we subject ourselves to such torment? Because our customers expect to find the product on the shelf, buy it, and make use of it immediately. This is the scenario that virtually everything sold in conventional stores uses, like a grocery item. We expect the grocery item to be on the shelf, so companies have to work in advance of us going to the store to acquire the item. Consumers walk into a store expecting to find shelves stocked with the stuff they want to buy. They don't walk in and examine samples and place an order for later delivery. Of course, when you underestimate demand, you're left with disappointed customers. When you overestimate demand, you're left with extra inventory that you need to mark down or even write off. These are the perils of a full anticipatory strategy.

One step away from ship-to-stock is the make-to-stock strategy. This strategy also puts a lot of faith in the sales forecast to drive actions. In this case, you buy materials in advance and produce the product in accordance with the forecast, but you don't allocate the goods to your distribution locations until you receive the customer order and know exactly where to ship it. This delaying of the delivery step allows you to hold inventory centrally for all distribution locations. Holding inventory in one location allows you to get by with less inventory as you pool or gather all the uncertainty of the market at one location. But holding inventory centrally and postponing delivery until you have the order in hand does mean that the customer will have to wait for the delivery.

As we progress along this continuum of manufacturing strategies, this is what you can expect to see: With each new strategy, you'll notice that we hold less inventory, which saves money, but we require customers to wait longer to receive the goods they want, which can put us at risk of losing sales.

The next strategy in the lineup goes by different names. It's sometimes called assemble-to-order, configure-to-order, or mass customization. With this strategy, materials are procured in advance of demand and products are made only to a semi-finished state. The finished product only takes shape when you learn exactly what the customer wants. This strategy is ideal when you have the same basic product that can be sold with small differences or mass customized. The customization, then, occurs only after you have the order in hand. This allows a pool of common inventory to cover the needs of customers looking for something slightly different, again reducing the inventory required but requiring additional time to perform the final touches on the goods and to deliver them.

Toyota provides a great example of mass customization with their Scion brand of cars. At scion.com, prospective buyers can select from an array of options to equip their FR-S or xB model car. These are two of the five basic models Scion produces. Even though the cars are manufactured to a generic state in Japan, Scion usually promises customers delivery in less than two weeks. How can they do this when it can take up to four weeks for the cars to travel across the Pacific to U.S. shores? Major U.S. distributors hold large supplies of the cars in their generic state. One distributor is on the east coast and the other on the west coast. When a customer hits "confirm" on a custom-build order, the distributor closest to the customer gets to work on that base model, adding the sport shocks and struts, changing out the interior, or altering the base model in any way the customer requests.

Through this postponed assemble-to-order strategy, Toyota is able to provide customers with seemingly limitless assortment, yet with much less inventory than if they pre-built the cars to cater to demand. The truth is there's no way that a carmaker could accurately anticipate the precise specifications of customers anyway. However, customers do have to wait anywhere from a few days to a few weeks to take possession of their new wheels under this system. We'll see if this kind of manufacturing arrangement spreads to more product categories, but it appears very promising.

The fourth manufacturing strategy on our continuum is the make-to-order strategy. In this scenario, the manufacturer has the raw materials on hand, but doesn't commit to assembling them until receiving the customer order.

In delaying the assembly process altogether, the manufacturer has even more flexibility to accommodate diverse customer preferences as to the product form and function. This might be the case of a highly customized luxury vehicle. If you want to take possession of a new Ferrari 458 Italia, be prepared to wait up to two years. Savor the anticipation of that delivery day.

An example that I use in class that's a little more approachable from a student's perspective doesn't happen in a factory at all, it happens at the Chipotle Mexican Grill, the fast-casual restaurant chain that boasts nearly 2,000 locations. When you arrive at a Chipotle, you enter what amounts to a product assembly line with an array of ingredients that can fill your made-to-order burrito. You choose the ingredients you want and the staff customizes your food item right there in the line. Make-to-order production allows for even greater variation to be accommodated with less inventory on hand. Yes, this is the strategy employed by Nike with the NIKEiD example I shared at the outset of the lecture.

The fifth and final manufacturing strategy we'll cover is the least speculative of all for the producer: it's the buy-to-order strategy. Under buy-to-order, the producer awaits the customer order before even committing to the raw materials. This allows for products to be truly custom from the ground up since the producer isn't committed to anything at first. But expect a longer wait if you're the customer of such a system, since everything is delayed until a firm order lands in the hands of the producer.

Where do we see such arrangements? These are a little less common than the other strategies, but you might see buy-to-order production in the provision of really big industrial purchases, like aircraft, satellites, and missile defense systems. Manufacturers of these multi-million dollar machines don't usually sell these items out of a warehouse. They collaborate with customers to develop designs and then commit to building them. This process can sometimes take several years. You might also see buy-to-order in the manufacturing of houses, buildings, or commissioned works of art. Here, again, lengthy discussions are usually conducted between a producer and buyer in order to understand exactly what the customer wants in the form and function of the product. But it should ensure that only the required materials are purchased, and it can be the least wasteful of inventory. You just need a customer who's willing to wait.

Those are the five basic manufacturing strategies that a producer of goods can employ. Large manufacturers often employ multiple strategies to accommodate their different customers with the variety of products that the customers seek. Smaller companies start off with a single strategy, and they're advised to go with the less risky and less speculative strategies like buy-to-order or make-to-order so that they can conserve cash for investments other than inventory.

Eventually, though, customers' tolerance for waiting can give way and rising competition can influence producers to move toward the other end of the spectrum: being more speculative and taking on more inventory of different kinds. Lean thinking has had significant influence on the management of inventory as it relates to production strategies. Traditionally, companies relied on inventory to deal with problems that you might encounter in the course of serving customers. You have inaccurate sales forecasts? Just be sure to make more than enough inventory and don't worry about the forecast. You have unreliable suppliers? That's OK. Buy so much inventory to ensure that you're covered when suppliers ship late or have quality problems. You have your own problems with product quality? Just make enough good stuff along with the bad so that you can tap into the good stuff when you need it. In other words, inventory is often counted on to cover up problems elsewhere in a company's operations.

Lean thinking, though, encourages you not to rely on inventory. Instead, you should address the problems. Figure out how to improve the forecast or design flexible operations that can make you less dependent on the forecast and more responsive to actual demand when it happens. Only work with reliable suppliers or help existing suppliers to deliver better materials more reliably. Instead of accepting quality problems in your own operations, expect perfection and continuously improve your processes toward that goal. Deal with your problems and address them at the root cause so that once they're solved, they don't reappear. That's the philosophy that took Toyota from the small automaker they were to the world's largest automaker of high-quality cars and trucks. Their success has motivated countless other companies to emulate them. It's estimated that more than 90% of all U.S. manufacturers make use of the Lean principles that Toyota developed.

With the advent of advanced technologies, production operations has embarked on a new and exciting journey. Developments in this area have been of an incremental nature over the past several decades, but one major development is threatening the entire system of factory-based mass production that we've known over the past century.

The revolution we are watching closely is the advent of 3-D printing, or layered printing. Imagine a printer that, rather than creating an image in two dimensions on a flat surface of paper like a conventional document printer, instead prints in layers, in three dimensions, creating so-called form-on-the-spot. 3-D printing technology has found use in the production of models and prototypes in recent years, but the prospects for entering into form-on-the-spot production have set our minds racing in the operations field. Just as we download music and books over the Internet today, allowing us to consume these media without leaving the comfort of our homes, might it be possible to download 3-D blueprints, simply hit "print," and watch physical goods take shape right before our eyes?

To date, 3-D printing is limited to simple products with simple materials. That's changing quickly, though, as companies like General Electric are making huge investments in advancing the manufacturing capabilities of the printing equipment. Companies are also investing in material sciences so that advanced alloys can be developed for use in 3-D printing's additive manufacturing processes. GE currently has more than 300 3-D printers at work, and its aviation business expects to produce more than 100,000 different parts via 3-D printing by 2020.

Keep an eye on this technology as it progresses along the lines of so many other game-changing technologies, like the cell phone or the videocassette recorder before it. Capabilities of the technology will improve and prices will drop as the product gains popularity, justifying investment in R&D and expansion in production lines. Especially promising in the near term is the opportunity to customize products through form-on-the-spot at retail locations.

Another development to watch is the rise of nearshoring and reshoring. While some companies continue to favor outsourcing of their manufacturing operations to suppliers in low-cost countries, there's a trend in the opposite direction, too. As it turns out, it's hard to anticipate all the things that can go wrong with offshoring until they occur. Frequent power outages, extraordinarily high labor turnover, traffic jams that last for days or even weeks, and cargo containers that simply never show up because they got washed overboard in transit. These things really happen, and the costs incurred to remedy these problems can be monumental. In the case of a quality grievance that results in a product recall, it's conceivable that a company might never salvage a tarnished brand. Even in less severe circumstances, many companies today are realizing that the toll of producing in far-off locations may just be too high.

In reaction to this reality, many companies that once offshored to low-cost countries are regionalizing their supply chains, meaning that they're seeking to produce closer to the markets they're trying to serve. Nearshoring refers to the practice of producing close to the focal market, probably in a location that still offers some cost advantage but with less uncertainty than far-off locations. For many U.S. companies, this might mean serving the U.S. market from Mexico instead of China.

Reshoring refers to bringing once-offshored manufacturing back to home shores. It's a strategy that carries a lot of political momentum, but it can also make good business sense. GE, Motorola, Whirlpool, and Caterpillar are some of the U.S.-based companies to have adopted reshoring in recent years, to much fanfare and reportedly with favorable results.

While much excitement surrounds developments like 3-D printing, nearshoring, and reshoring, I believe that the next big wave of innovation in production operations will be in yet another important area of change: the focus on sustainability. Our ability to serve a growing population in a more sustainable fashion will be at the forefront of corporate decisions and national policy in the coming years. With rising wealth and a budding middle class in developing countries around the world, it'll be imperative to find creative means to support teeming demand with our finite natural resources and without irreparably harming the environment. That could mean choosing different materials and creating products using manufacturing processes and energy sources that don't pollute the air, land, and water. I can envision the day when the world gathers with anticipation to see the latest custom-built fuel cell sports car, and my bet is that it's not far off.

Production operations is a key factor in all of these developments. Whether it drives them or simply incorporates and adapts to them, it'll be central in the years ahead to some of the most dramatic changes in how we live, how we create, and how we interact with our planet.

Refining Service Operations
Lecture 15

O ver the past several decades, the United States has seen a major shift in its economy—from being dominated by manufacturing to focusing more on services. This shift is reflected in the fact that today's services sector represents nearly 70% of the nation's gross domestic product. In addition, six out of seven people in the workforce are employed in services. In this lecture, we will examine the essentials of managing successful service operations, taking into account the complex psychology involved in winning over customers through great experiences. As we'll see, there are significant differences between service operations and product-oriented operations, yet service operations can still borrow some important concepts from the science of the production world.

Defining *Services*

- The term *services* refers to a wide variety of activities, from consumer services, such as health care, restaurants, retail, and banking; to industrial and professional services, such as advertising, transportation, and legal services; to government and civil services, including schools, emergency services, and postal delivery.

- Perhaps the most fundamental difference between production operations and service operations is the intangibility of services as a deliverable.
    - Although service operations may sometimes have some of the attributes of physical products, the deliverable in services is an outcome or experience for the customer.

    - In some ways, this can make the management of services more complicated and challenging than making a physical product, where the specifications and requirements tend to be more concrete.

Assessing Services

- One of the most significant developments in modern service operations has been the establishment of the service quality scale (SERVQUAL). Devised by academics, SERVQUAL is a measurement system dedicated to assessing customer satisfaction with services. It has revolutionized how we think about and assess service delivery.

- SERVQUAL's basic premise for discerning customer satisfaction is simple: It compares the customer's perception of the service as it was actually rendered against the expectations the customer had going into the service arrangement. If the perceived performance exceeds expectations, then the customer is satisfied. If expectations are not met, the customer is said to be dissatisfied.

- SERVQUAL assesses service quality by comparing expectations and perceptions of performance across five important dimensions. These dimensions, listed below, form the acronym RATER.
  - Responsiveness: how promptly the service provider responds to the needs of the customer.

  - Assurance: the level of the customer's ease that the service will be conducted in accordance with his or her wishes.

  - Tangibles: the physical aspects of the service provision, including the facilities, equipment, and personnel that will shape the customer's experience.

  - Empathy: the sense of caring and understanding extended by the service provider to the customer.

  - Reliability: the ability to perform the service on a dependable and accurate basis compared to what is promised.

Arguably, building relationships is of much greater importance in service industries than in production businesses because service comes down to trust—trusting that the outcome will be what the customer is seeking.

- In addition to providing a scale of service quality, SERVQUAL also identifies several *service gaps* that can irritate or repel customers. These include an inability to match performance with expectations, differences in expectations between the provider and the customer, and the perception of performance.

Process Improvement: Lean Thinking

- Because effective service is so important to meeting customer demands, a field of study known as *process improvement* has developed for refining service operations. This discipline comes from production operations.

- All work—whether it's manufacturing widgets or making espressos—is completed in processes, and each process involves a series of steps in which inputs are converted into outputs for a customer. The two most influential methods for process improvement are already familiar to us from the production operations context: Lean Thinking and Six Sigma. The premise of both these methods is that all processes can be improved. This reasoning is particularly true in services because they rely on people, who are prone to errors.

- One principle of process improvement that can help achieve high-performing services is the concept of *standard work*. This involves finding the best way to complete a work task, documenting it, and teaching it to others. This is a simple idea, but it's hard to achieve in service environments, where operators tend to develop individual patterns of behavior. And when no standards exist for work, you can expect different qualities in the outcome. The challenge for services is to provide consistently good outcomes for customers.
  - In 2009, Starbucks set out to address this problem by setting up its Lean Innovation Lab. The goal was to develop and test different ways to perform store routines in search of the best way to perform all varieties of work, including cleaning up, restocking displays, and preparing coffee.

  - The initiative had numerous benefits. By finding and standardizing its best practices, Starbucks ensured a cleaner and more appealing sitting area and reduced the amount of time and wasted motion involved in brewing and serving coffee. Creating standard work routines resulted in achieving positive customer experiences more consistently, which has fueled top-line growth and reduced costs.

- Another valuable way to apply lean principles in service settings is to compare process time with *takt time*. *Takt* is a German term that refers to the targeted or goal time for an activity—the amount of time in which an activity must be completed in order to keep pace with demand. In contrast, *process time* refers to the amount of time required to actually complete the activity.
  - Consider, for example, a men's grooming salon. The owner of the salon would like to achieve as much throughput as possible in the shop. Many of the costs associated with the shop are fixed; thus, the more customers served, the more revenue and profit can be achieved.

o Let's say that on average, it takes 20 minutes for a stylist to give a simple haircut. This is the process time for the work. Over the course of an 8-hour day, a stylist could serve 24 customers, or 3 per hour. But what if the shop has demand for 80 haircuts a day? Clearly, that demand cannot be met with one stylist because it translates to 26 ⅔ hours of work.

o The takt time to keep pace with this demand is determined by dividing 8 hours (480 minutes) by 80 customers; the result is 6 minutes. But the process time is more than three times that! Clearly, the owner will need more resources to serve 80 customers in 8 hours.

o This comparison of process time and takt time can be helpful in determining the amount of resources needed to get a job done in an allotted amount of time. But the real lesson here is not to simply take these numbers as a given. By finding the best way to perform the work, companies can reduce the process time required to serve their customers, making them better able to meet greater demand.

• Another variable that companies sometimes overlook when managing the supply-demand equation is their ability to alter demand through pricing. That's not a service operations decision per se, but it can have a significant impact on the provision of services. For example, Dell has long used a "sell-what-you-have" strategy that drives customers to the products the company has high in inventory and away from items that are at risk of going into backorder. This is accomplished by simply changing the price for these items in a dynamic manner.

• Related to the pace of demand, something that anyone working in services knows is that if you have to staff a business at all times to handle unexpected peaks in demand, you'll have significant downtime. To address this problem, Lean Thinking sets forth the concept of *heijunka*, a Japanese term that refers to the smoothing out of demand. Such smoothing out can be accomplished by offering discounts or other promotions to drive business to off-peak times and avoid the problem of paying staff to sit idle.

Process Improvement: Six Sigma

- The Six Sigma approach can also be applied to service environments. As mentioned earlier, the term relates to the standard deviation in a process. Standard deviation is a measure of variation. When there is variation in inputs or variation in how work is performed, the result will be variation in outcomes.

- Six Sigma encourages businesses to root out the sources of variation and establish greater precision in how work is conducted. This approach refuses to accept the idea that to "err is human" and seeks to eliminate the sources of error—not the people but the actions they perform that lead to error and defects.

- By definition, Six-Sigma performance is achieved when defects number fewer than 3.4 per 1 million opportunities for defect. Achieving that level of defect-free performance is probably not attainable in human-driven processes, such as those found in most services. But whether an organization achieves 6 sigma, 4 sigma, or 2.5 sigma is not what really matters. What matters is whether the company and its processes are improving. And if the firm is improving faster than its competition, that bodes well for the future.

Service-Dominant Logic (SDL)

- One business theory that has drawn a good deal of attention recently is *service-dominant logic* (SDL), which to some degree unites the principles of service operations and production operations. SDL suggests that businesses move away from marketing goods to a notion of co-creation of value. The idea is that in a purchase situation, customers are buying more than just a product; they're buying the ability to use the product in the pursuit of enjoyment. There is an ongoing relationship between the customer and the product, and that creates new business opportunities for the provider.

- This is a fundamentally different way to view a product and, in turn, to sell the product. It is not an end in its own right but part of a solution. We see similar transitions to a solution orientation occurring in many industries. Xerox, for example, has moved away from selling copiers to business customers. Instead, it installs a multifunction copier in an office, and the customer is charged for its use based on pages copied and documents scanned, printed, and mailed. This shift in orientation has turned what might have been one-time sales into lucrative, ongoing revenue streams.

- Notice that there is a physical product at the center of the services that Xerox provides. The new focus, however, is on a creative solution that doesn't involve dumping the product in the lap of the customer, then walking away. Rather, it involves establishing and maintaining a relationship with the customer. It becomes much more difficult for competitors to sway customers with grandiose promises when customers trust your company to deliver desired outcomes reliably.

Suggested Reading

George and George, *Lean Six Sigma for Service.*

Hsieh, "Zappos's CEO on Going to Extremes for Customers."

Kastalli, Van Looy, and Neely, "Steering Manufacturing Firms towards Service Business Model Innovation."

Ramdas, Teisberg, and Tucker, "Four Ways to Reinvent Service Delivery."

Rawson, Duncan, and Jones, "The Truth about Customer Experience."

Zeithaml, Parasuraman, and Berry, *Delivering Quality Service.*

1. What makes the provision of services different from production operations? Is it easier in some ways and harder in others?

2. Name a service company that you would consider great. What makes this company great?

3. How do the principles of operational excellence found in Lean Thinking and Six Sigma help a service business to compete more effectively?

Refining Service Operations
Lecture 15—Transcript

Over the past several decades, the United States has seen a major shift in its economy: from being manufacturing-dominant to focusing more on services. This shift is reflected in the contribution to gross domestic product, where today's services sector represents nearly 70% of the nation's GDP. More pronounced, though, is the shift in employment. In 1960, the nation's largest employer was manufacturer General Motors. Today, it's Walmart, which employs over 1.4 million Americans. Services, in total, employ six out of seven people in our workforce. Retail and food services alone represent 18% of the national employment, and the trend doesn't look to be slowing down.

In this lecture, we'll examine the essentials of managing successful service operations, taking into account the complex psychology involved in winning over customers through great experiences. We'll see that there are significant differences between service operations and product-oriented operations, yet service operations still borrow some important concepts from the science of the production world. In some situations, the two worlds merge in interesting ways. When we say "services," we refer to a wide variety of activities, from consumer services like healthcare, restaurants, retail, and banking; to industrial and professional services like advertising, transportation, and legal services; to government and civil services, including schools, emergency services, and postal delivery.

Perhaps the most fundamental difference between production operations and service operations is the intangibility of services as a deliverable. While service operations may sometimes have some of the attributes of physical products, the deliverable in services is an outcome or experience for the customer. In some ways, this can make the management of services more complicated and challenging than making a physical product, where the specs and requirements tend to be more concrete.

One of the most significant developments in modern service operations was the establishment of the service quality scale, or SERVQUAL for short. SERVQUAL is a measurement system dedicated to assessing customer satisfaction with services. Devised by professors "Parsu" Parasuraman of the

University of Miami, Valerie Zeithaml of the University of North Carolina, and Len Berry, Texas A&M University, in the late 1980s, SERVQUAL has revolutionized how we think about and assess service delivery.

SERVQUAL's basic premise for discerning customer satisfaction is simple: It compares the customer's perception of the service rendering against the expectations the customer had going into the service arrangement. If the perceived service exceeds expectations, then the customer is satisfied. Should expectations not be met, the customer's said to be dissatisfied. The bigger the gap between expectations and perceived performance, the more extreme the emotion, either satisfaction or dissatisfaction.

The SERVQUAL scale assesses service quality by comparing expectations and perceptions of performance across five important dimensions. The first is responsiveness: how promptly the service provider responds to the needs of the customer. The second dimension is assurance: the level of the customer's ease that the service will be conducted in accordance with his or her wishes. Next are the tangibles: the physical aspects of the service provision, including the facilities, equipment, and the personnel that will shape the customer's experience in the service arrangement. The next dimension is empathy: the sense of caring and understanding that a service provider extends to the customer. The final dimension is reliability: the ability to perform the service on a dependable and accurate basis compared to what's promised. The SERVQUAL scale is sometimes referred by the acronym RATER, for responsiveness, assurance, tangibles, empathy and reliability.

Allow me to share a recent example that will illustrate these five dimensions of service quality. My son, Aiden, and I share a common passion for athletic shoes. I'm an avid runner and he's a basketball and football player, but we have a penchant for the latest athletic shoes. For his most recent birthday, he insisted on a pair of Nike shoes that had just hit the market. Being the shoe nut, too, I understood and began out hunt for the shoes. A web search quickly uncovered Zappos as a possible vendor. I'd never purchased from the company before, but had heard many great things about their customer service so I decided to take a closer look. Of course, what I wanted to buy was a tangible product, shoes, but it was Zappos's service operations that made those shoes available and it's their service performance that generates raves for the company.

Instead of ordering the shoes online, I decided to call the company. Promptly on the second ring, a young man by the name of Daniel introduced himself and asked how he could help. I explained the situation and Daniel indicated he'd be happy to help make my son's birthday wish come true. He even explained that by calling in to the customer service line, I'd receive a complimentary upgrade to free second-day delivery. That really appealed to me because Aiden's birthday was just a few days away. I enjoyed a pleasant chat with Daniel and he assured me that the shoes would arrive in plenty of time. Sure enough, the shoes arrived in pristine condition two days later, as promised. Later that same day, I received a handwritten card from Daniel, thanking me for my business and inviting me to visit the company's headquarters the next time I was in Las Vegas. Who sends written thank you cards today? Daniel did, and it floored me.

Let's run through the RATER criteria quickly. Was the service responsive? Yes, the customer service representative answered the phone promptly and promised speedy delivery, which was realized. Assurance? Yes, I was assured that the right product would arrive in plenty of time for the birthday occasion. Oh, and the price was very competitive, too, which provided me with a sense of assurance that I was getting a good deal. Daniel also indicated that if we weren't satisfied for any reason, we could return the shoes at no charge, which made me feel better about buying the product without the benefit of actually seeing it. Tangibles? The Zappos website was easy to use, the shoes themselves were of the quality my son and I expected, and card from Daniel was a nice touch. Empathy? Again, I was impressed with Daniel's sense of concern for my situation. Would the world end if the shoes arrived late? No, but I felt like Daniel was invested in solving my problem and he was committed to seeing it through. Reliability? After all was said and done, the correct shoes arrived, as promised, and I was billed the right amount.

In sum, Zappos went five-for-five on the SERVQUAL dimensions. I came away from the shopping experience not merely satisfied, but delighted. Satisfied customers might come back and buy from the provider again, but delighted customers are more likely to tell others about their great experience, which can be priceless. Daniel's actions set me up for a great experience, and then the operations personnel behind the scene at the Zappos's fulfillment center did their job and got the right shoes to us in a timely manner. What's not to like?

This helps to explain why Zappos has become the juggernaut in shoes, handbags, and other fashion merchandise. In 2009, Jeff Bezos of Amazon. com took an attitude of "If we can't beat 'em, join 'em" and acquired Zappos for $1.2 billion. Since the acquisition, Amazon and Zappos continue to march toward domination of Internet retailing through a combination of immense product assortment and industry-leading service. Zappos's long-time CEO Tony Hsieh encourages customer service reps to not just take orders, but to have open and honest dialogue with customers rather than rely on scripts, which has become the industry norm. Also, there's no limit on the duration of calls, which violates every rule of call center efficiency. It's reported that one call lasted more than 10 hours. That's clearly an outlier, but it underscores the emphasis on relationship-building that so many other Internet retailers simply discount.

Arguably, relationships are of much greater importance in service industries than in production businesses because service all comes down to trust; trusting that the outcome will be what you're seeking. In product systems, there's usually a disconnect between the people who do the work and the people who experience the product in use. There's a lesson here for those working in production businesses: There's a very strong service component to what you do, too, in providing a product, such as making sure that the product is available when and where a customer wants to acquire it, and being available should the customer have any questions about the product and its use, or concerns associated with the invoice for the order as well as standing behind the product when it fails to live up to the customer's expectations. These are the intangible aspects of the product-service bundle that product-oriented companies need to have well in place.

In addition to providing a scale of service quality, SERVQUAL identifies several so-called "service gaps" that can turn customers off. An inability to match performance with expectations is but one of them. Another is found when the service provider and customer have different expectations of the service that will be rendered. If there's a gap here, you can reasonably expect a gap in the post-service evaluation, too. For this reason, it's important for the expectations to be ironed out at the outset of the engagement.

Another gap of note is grounded in a term I mentioned earlier in the assessment of satisfaction and dissatisfaction: the perception of performance. Since services incorporate a host of intangibles in their rendering, they leave much open to interpretation, and perceptions are important. I once experienced a service situation where I was working for a company and an important customer complained about our deliveries consistently arriving late to a retail distribution center. We thought our truck deliveries were consistently on time. Eventually, we decided to go to the customer's site and watch a truck actually arrive. When the truck passed through the gate of the receiving yard, we pointed at it saying "There! See, the truck's here! Not only on time, but early!" It was then that the customer's representative said that the truck doesn't actually arrive until it's backed up at a receiving dock at the facility. We were seeing the same metric—a very basic one, on-time delivery—in two different ways based on where the endpoint was in the process. It was a small but very important distinction that severely strained the relationship with our biggest customer. Clearly, we had to iron out the confusion.

Handling customer expectations presents a slightly different challenge. I often ask my students if it's more important to manage expectations or perceptions of performance in delivering services to customers. We debate it for a while and inevitably conclude that it's critically important to manage both expectations and perceptions. The funny thing about expectations, though, is that they're always evolving. Even if you enter into a contract that's several inches thick, you can expect that customers' expectations will change over the contract's lifetime, and customers will usually come to expect higher levels of service or more services than the agreement specified. You have to continually manage those expectations.

Managing expectations can become especially important when you bail a customer out of a bad situation. Say a customer finds herself in a bind and you move mountains and make the impossible happen. Rather than delivering service in the typical time, you shift your priorities and resources to help the customer out. Guess what? You've just proven that you can perform a miracle, and that miracle can very easily become the new norm if you're not careful.

How do you handle that, especially if you can't provide the same level of service day in and day out? I recommend that you pick up the phone, call the customer, and say something like "I'm pleased that we were able to help you out of this tough situation. We put everything else on hold to get this project done for you. Please realize that this was a special situation and we'd like to work with you to figure out how to avoid this kind of crisis in the future." You get the idea: We're managing the expectation. Of course, if the whole experience teaches you that you can deliver at a heightened level, then you have a new service offering and you can charge accordingly for it.

Because effective service is so important to meeting customer demands, a whole field of study has developed on how to refine service operations. It comes from production operations, and it's called process improvement. All work, whether it's manufacturing widgets or making espressos, is completed in processes. Each process involves a series of steps where inputs are converted into outputs for a customer, and the two most influential methods for process improvement are already familiar to you from the production operations context: Lean and Six Sigma. Let's take a look now at how they can be applied to achieving excellent service operations.

The premise of both Lean and Six Sigma is that no process is perfect and that all processes can stand to improve. This reasoning is particularly true in services because they rely on people, even more so than manufacturing operations, which have become increasingly automated over time. "To err is human" goes the old adage, and that's a simple fact in services: We rely on people to do much of the work, and people are prone to errors. The lessons for managing human resources in service environments are too complex and too many in number to address in this one lecture, but let's turn to what we know about processes that can help to achieve reliable, high-performing services.

One principle of process improvement is the concept of standard work. This means finding the best way to complete a work task, documenting it, and teaching it to others. This is a pretty simple idea, but it's hard to achieve in service environments where operators tend to develop individual patterns of behavior. When no standards exist for the work, you can expect different qualities in the outcome. Different procedures by different workers result in different experiences for customers; some good, some bad. How do we provide a consistently good experience for customers?

That was the problem that Starbucks set out to address in 2009 when the company set up its Lean Innovation Lab. The goal was to develop and test different ways to perform store routines in search of the best way to perform all varieties of work in the coffee shops, including cleanup, restocking the displays, and preparing the coffee. As it turned out, the benefits of the initiative were many. By finding and standardizing its best practices, Starbucks ensured a cleaner and more appealing sitting area and reduced the amount of time and wasted motion involved in brewing and serving the coffee. Creating standard work routines resulted in positive customer experiences more consistently, and this fueled top-line growth and reduced cost.

Wendy's has implemented standard work to achieve the fastest drive-through experience in the quick-service restaurant industry. (They prefer that we not call it fast food.) Whereas competing restaurants talk about adding extra drive-through lanes to deal with demand surges, Wendy's has reduced the lead time—the amount of time it takes to fill the order—which enables the store to handle more volume in a given period. As of this taping, Wendy's takes, on average, 134 seconds to fill an order compared to McDonald's 189 seconds and Burger King's 198 seconds. That may not sound like much, but by saving about a minute with each order over the course of a day, Wendy's is able to serve many more customers and to do so with fewer staff.

This points us to another valuable way to apply Lean principles in service settings: by comparing process time with something called *takt time*. *Takt* is a German term that refers to the targeted or goal time for an activity; the amount of time in which you must complete an activity in order to keep pace with demand. In contrast, process time refers to the amount of time required to actually complete the activity. Let's look at an example to show how these two measures relate to one another.

We'll focus on a service that I use from time to time: a men's grooming salon. The owner of the salon would like to achieve as much throughput as possible in his shop. Many of the costs associated with the shop are fixed, meaning that they don't change with the number of customers that pass through the shop. The more customers, the more revenue, and the more profit. Let's say that on average it takes 20 minutes for a simple haircut. This is the process time for the work. Over the course of an 8 hour day, a stylist could tend to 3 customers an hour, or 24 customers for the day. What if the shop has demand for 80 haircuts in a day? Can we take care of all 80 customers in the one 8-hour shift? Clearly not with only one stylist, because we have 80 × 20 minutes, or 1,600 minutes of work to do. That's 26 2/3 hours of work, and that's a long work day.

No, we'll need to turn customers around much quicker. In eight hours, we have 480 minutes. Divide the 480 by 80 and we determine a *takt* time, the pace of demand, to be one customer every 6 minutes. But our process time is more than three times that, at 20 minutes. What this means is that we'll need 20/6, or 3 1/3 times more resource to get the job done in the allotted eight hours. That means 3 people full-time and a 4th person for another two to three hours to get all 80 customers in and out the door in eight hours. We'll also need more chairs, sinks, and grooming supplies in the same proportion to allow each stylist to keep pace.

This comparison of process time and *takt* time can be helpful in determining the amount of resources that we need to employ to get the job done in an allotted amount of time. But the real lesson here is not simply to take these numbers as given. Think back to the Starbucks and Wendy's examples of a few minutes ago. By finding the best way to perform the work, both companies reduced the process time required to serve their customers, making them better able to meet greater demand.

Are there work steps in our grooming salon that could be removed or done faster, or are there mistakes that could be eliminated, requiring less rework? Perhaps one employee could do the job of sweeping the salon floor so the stylists could focus exclusively on cutting hair and getting more haircuts done per hour. By thinking through the work and devising best-practice standard work, we can reduce the amount of time it takes to do the job. Also, ensuring that we do the job right the first time ensures that we don't have to spend time going back and fixing problems.

Another variable that companies sometimes overlook when managing the supply-demand equation is their ability to alter demand through pricing. That's not a service operations decision per se, but it has a big impact on the provision of services. Consider Dell's direct-to-consumer model of selling computers online. They've long employed a "sell-what-you-have" strategy that helps to drive customers to the products they have in high inventory and away from items that are at risk of going into backorder. How? By changing the menu price for these items in a dynamic manner. When they run short on something, the price goes up. When an item's in oversupply or at risk of becoming obsolete, it gets featured or marked down in price. In this way, they influence demand on items; not just how much demand and how many customers, but when demand happens.

Related to the pace of demand, something that anyone working in services knows is that if you have to staff a business at all times to handle unexpected peaks in demand, you'll have immense amounts of slack. To address this problem, Lean also provides us with the concept of *Heijunka*, a Japanese term that means "smoothing out of demand." (Remember that it was Japanese carmaker Toyota that gave us the concept of Lean in the first place.) In a manufacturing environment, it's not uncommon to have one shift that works feverishly and another that doesn't. Manufacturers also run out of capacity on some days and have idle capacity on others. Something similar happens in service operations, and the problem can be especially challenging at the retail level.

Consider a bricks-and-mortar store where customers walk in off the street at unpredictable times. The thing about a physical shop is that it doesn't expand or contract with the volume of business; it's a fixed size. You're paying rent on the full space, regardless of the number of customers. If you own the space, then you're paying taxes on the footprint of the property regardless of how it gets used day in and day out, and paying staff to sit idle can get very expensive. There are plenty of reasons why it would be beneficial if you could smooth out customer demand.

Let's say customers have a habit of showing up in a big rush on Fridays, just before the weekend. Is there a way that you can possibly influence them to come in on a Wednesday or Thursday instead? There is, and that's why you might see other stores offering aggressive pricing, discounts, or other promotions to drive business to those off-peak days. Doing the same would allow you to serve more customers over the course of the week, and reduce the frustration and disappointment faced by customers who are left waiting or turned away during the peak times. In spite of the price reductions, you might realize higher profits, too. Some companies are turning to social media like Facebook and Twitter to bolster demand during off-peak times, offering "flash" discounts or special deals to their followers. The risk of this strategy is that you might get people addicted to the lower prices and they might refuse to pay full price in the future, but some companies seem willing to take that risk.

Six Sigma, too, can be applied in service environments. The term, you may recall, relates to the standard deviation in a process. Standard deviation is a measure of variation. When we have variation in inputs or variation in how work is performed, we'll have variation in outcomes. Six Sigma implores us to root out the sources of variation and establish greater precision in how work is conducted. Six Sigma refuses to accept the idea that to "err is human" and seeks to eliminate the sources of error; not the people, mind you, but the actions they perform that lead to error and defects. By definition, Six Sigma performance is achieved when defects number fewer than 3.4 per one million opportunities for defect. Achieving that level of defect-free performance isn't very attainable in human-driven processes such as those found in most services, but whether an organization achieves Six Sigma, Four Sigma, or Two-Point-Five Sigma isn't what really matters. What matters is whether the company and its processes are improving. That's the name of the game, and if you're improving faster than your competition, that bodes very well for your future.

Keep in mind that the enemy of Lean and Six Sigma is complacency. As soon as you feel like your service is good, maybe better than anyone else's, and that's enough, brace yourself for the fall. If there were such a thing as business obituaries, they'd be littered with companies that were on top of the world only to vanish when they thought they had it all figured out. Consider giant retailers Montgomery Ward, Blockbuster, and Circuit City. There are many more such examples.

One business theory that's been drawing a lot of attention lately is service-dominant logic, which to some degree unites the principles of service operations and production operations. Service-dominant logic, or SDL as it's known, suggests that businesses move away from the marketing of goods to a notion of co-creation of value. The idea is that when I buy running shoes, what I'm actually buying is something more. It's my ability to employ the shoes in the pursuit of everything that I enjoy about running: the fitness, the experience of the great outdoors, and the ability to run as fast and free from injury as possible. There's an ongoing relationship between me and the footwear. Together, we create the outcomes that I seek, and that creates new business opportunities for the running shoe company.

This is a fundamentally different way to view a product, and in turn to sell the product. It's not an end in its own right, but part of a solution. We see similar transitions to a solution orientation occurring in many different industries. Xerox, for example, has moved away from selling copiers to business customers. Instead, it installs a multifunction copier in an office and the customer is charged for its use based on pages copied and documents scanned, printed, and mailed. Apple has me hooked with apps. It allows me to constantly refresh my iPhone with information and entertainment content that I seek, even as my interests evolve. For both Xerox and Apple, this shift in orientation has turned what might have been one-time sales into lucrative, ongoing revenue streams.

Notice that there's a physical product at the center of the services that Xerox and Apple provide. The new focus, however, is on a creative solution that doesn't involve dumping the product in the lap of the customer and then walking away. Rather, it involves establishing and maintaining a relationship with the customer. It becomes much more difficult for competitors to sway customers with grandiose promises when customers trust that you'll deliver desired outcomes reliably.

Effective service operations are the key to managing high-performing relationships successfully, and that's one big reason why they're growing in importance. Think about how your business can seize this moment where services increasingly dominate the business landscape.

Matching Supply and Demand
Lecture 16

S ales and operations planning (S&OP) is a proven method for finding the balance between promise making and promise keeping. The process consists of the integration of a company's sales forecasts with the operations plans from the purchasing, production, and logistics departments. In this lecture, we'll examine the specific inputs and organizational requirements needed to achieve this balance.

Background on Sales and Operations Planning (S&OP)

- Most businesses are composed of different departments, such as sales, marketing, accounting, purchasing, production, logistics, R&D, and HR. The reason for this is that humans deal with complexity by becoming specialized, developing knowledge and skill sets that allow us to perform specific functions.

- A functional orientation helps us ensure that we "cover all the bases" in an organization, but it's sometimes difficult to establish balance and coordination across the departments. This is particularly true when the departments are in conflict with one another. There is a natural tendency in times of conflict to defend our turf, rather than to give in and pursue outcomes that might benefit the collective good. Further, companies often have measurement systems in place that reinforce "functional silos" and turf wars.

- Perhaps the greatest divide found in organizations is the one between the demand and supply sides of the business. The customer-facing departments responsible for generating demand—namely, sales and marketing—are held accountable for top-line revenue. Meanwhile, the supply-side operations departments, such as purchasing, production, and logistics, have the responsibility of delivering on that demand but doing so at the lowest possible cost to ensure that the company nets margins and profits.

- These two forces often find themselves at odds. The promise makers in sales and marketing blame operations for an inability to satisfy the demand they've worked to create. At the same time, the operations personnel take offense at what they see as sales and marketing's casual approach to making promises that probably shouldn't have been made in the first place.

- It's important to get promise makers and promise keepers on the same page because failing to deliver on customer orders or being forced to temper demand affects the company's credibility in the marketplace and creates opportunities for competitors. Undersupply opens the door for the competition, and oversupply leaves excess inventory that must either be marked down or written off. Sales and operations planning (S&OP) was designed to address these problems.

- Fundamentally, S&OP is about gathering and sharing information. Thus, the first step is to form an S&OP team of senior departmental representatives from within your company and gain the buy-in of the parties involved. As the term *S&OP* suggests, the key function of this team is planning.

© Jacob Wackerhausen/iStock/Thinkstock.

The goal of the monthly S&OP team meeting is for all parties to arrive at a common vision of what's expected in the coming month and to share a commitment to doing their part to fulfill that vision.

- The sales and marketing representatives should work together to bring forward the sales picture for the coming months.

- The purchasing, production, and logistics reps prepare capacity plans, with ready explanations for any anticipated changes in operating capacity.

- Finance and HR play consultative roles related to the deployment of financial and human resources.

- New product development speaks to the readiness and timing of product launches that can be expected to siphon resources from existing products.

Sales Forecasting
- Considerable work takes place within each department leading up to the monthly meeting of the S&OP team. Sales and marketing should collaborate to coordinate promotions and other strategies that might be in place to bolster sales. These team members also generate short-term sales forecasts, typically covering a period of one to three months. Sales forecasts come in one of two varieties: qualitative or quantitative.

- Qualitative forecasts are essentially best guesses—forecasts made without necessary data; however, these forecasts are not shots in the dark. They rely on the opinions of experts who are closest to the market—field sales representatives and headquarters marketing managers. These experts base their judgments on market intelligence, including trends for sales of related items, demographic changes, and responses to market inquiries and field testing of products or services. In the absence of sales history—as with completely new products—qualitative estimates are often the best options available.

- Quantitative forecasting methods come in many different forms. Ideally, they rely on data from past sales of the same item. In the absence of this information, they might use historical sales of similar or complementary items.

  o The easiest but least informed quantitative forecast is a *simple average*. Here, a company divides the average sales over an entire year by 12 months and makes its plans with the expectation of selling approximately the same volume each month.

  o The *moving average* technique looks at recent history only—perhaps the last 3 months—to gauge the anticipated sales for the month ahead.

  o *Exponential smoothing* looks at the previous month's sales forecast and the actual sales from that same month. An *alpha value*, or *smoothing factor*, is then applied that governs how much emphasis is placed on each factor. The sum of actual sales multiplied by alpha and forecasted sales multiplied by −1 alpha yields the forecasted value for the coming month. This approach is intended to take some of the emotion out of the forecast while still relying on recent data.

  o The *regression analysis* method offers a predictive model that allows many factors to be considered at once, including the unique influence of trends, seasons, and cyclical influences. This method is used for products that have been in existence for some time and for which extensive sales data are available.

- Most companies use a combination of quantitative and qualitative forecasting methods. The ideal approach is to generate a quantitative forecast as a baseline, then have experts weigh in on those numbers. Were there unusual occurrences in recent months that affected the historical data? Are there any expected occurrences in the near future that could affect the forecast? Blending historical data with expert opinion brings together the best of both worlds.

Capacity Planning

- The other side of the S&OP equation is capacity planning, specifically, planning for supply, production, and the combination of logistics and distribution. Limits in any of these can impair the company's ability to accommodate the expected demand found in the sales forecast.

- Supply capacity probably rests beyond the direct control of your firm. It's dependent on the capacity of your suppliers and your ability to extract supplies from them. Typically, companies have some suppliers that seem to be able to offer limitless supplies and others that present constraints. The constraints may be absolute, meaning that there are limits to these suppliers' ability to serve you, or the added volume may simply come at a price. Companies need to understand both of these because they can influence the volume and price of supplies that can be acquired.

- Supply and production capacity come together in the materials requirements plan (MRP), which expresses the quantity and timing of supplies required to feed production. The MRP is usually driven by the production forecast, or the master production schedule (MPS). This schedule illustrates what the company expects to produce over a period of time, often a month, and can be broken down into weekly or even daily plans for production. Clearly, the sales forecast should influence this production forecast.

- The third capacity plan necessary for S&OP is one for logistics and distribution. Here, there may be capacity constraints on how much product can be stored and moved over a period of time. That capacity may be limited by warehouse space available, the size of storerooms, or the number of transportation vehicles available. Your company may own these capacities, or it may hire outside companies to provide the required space and transport.

Flexibility in S&OP

- With the compilation of the sales forecast and capacity plans for supply, production, and logistics and distribution, you have what you need to make decisions at the S&OP planning meeting. The goal of the meeting is to come up with a single set of numbers that everyone will work toward in the coming period.

- However, the S&OP process doesn't end with agreement on a common set of numbers. Once the month begins and sales start to trickle in, everyone needs to communicate about potential problems with the forecast. The same is true for operations plans. Countless forces could be at work, threatening to alter your best-laid plans for meeting demand.

- The often-forgotten component of S&OP is flexibility, which must be built into operations to accommodate the unexpected. The more flexible your operations, the more variation your system can accommodate and the less likely your customers are to experience any negative consequence as a result of fallible planning. Should you not be able to accommodate customer needs, you must devise priorities to determine which customers to serve with your limited supplies.

Integrated S&OP

- These same principles for managing supply and demand within a company can also be applied across companies in the *supply chain*, meaning the entire system of inputs, outputs, and distribution. That is, companies can collaborate with suppliers and customers to realize a common vision of the business they will conduct together.

- To understand this idea, imagine a see-saw. On one end is a large box labeled *Demand*. On the other end are two smaller boxes labeled *Capacity* and *Inventory*. Positioned in the middle of the see-saw is the fulcrum on which it rests, labeled *Plan*.

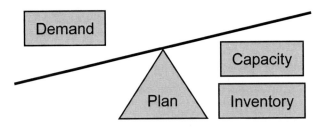

The see-saw analogy captures the benefits of integrated business planning; in the event of increases in Demand, moving the Plan closer to the Demand side allows companies to get more leverage from existing Capacity and Inventory.

- The see-saw is in balance when the weight of the Capacity and Inventory together counter the weight of Demand. If Demand were to grow, more weight would be needed in Capacity and/ or Inventory to bring the see-saw back into balance. Yet there is another possibility—the fulcrum. What if you were to move the Plan closer to the Demand side of the see-saw? With that action, you get increased leverage from existing Capacity and Inventory.

- The lesson here is that if you can plan closer to demand—that is, forecast demand more accurately—then you need less capacity and inventory to fulfill demand. The answer is sharing information and collaborating within companies to find the balance between demand and supply.

- Now, imagine lining up multiple see-saws side by side and working with people at each one to find the right balance for each of the see-saws in tandem. That would represent the notion of *integrated business planning* across companies in the supply chain. No doubt, it's a challenge, but it's one that yields significant benefits for the players.

Suggested Reading

Box, Jenkins, and Reinsel, *Time Series Analysis*.

Kahn, "Solving the Problems of New Product Forecasting."

Muzumdar and Fontanella, "The Secrets to S&OP Success."

Stahl and Wallace, "S&OP Principles."

Wallace and Stahl, *Sales and Operations Planning*.

Questions to Consider

1. How does the struggle between promise making and promise keeping shortchange or challenge the performance of a company? Why is it important to keep these two in balance?

2. We know that forecasts will not be perfectly accurate. What are the implications of this fact for our capacity plans? Is it wise to build in extra capacity to deal with peak demand?

Matching Supply and Demand
Lecture 16—Transcript

A few years back, I was conducting a workshop with a group of production and distribution managers from a large consumer goods company. We were talking about the challenge of sales and operations planning, when one by one their smartphones started buzzing, directing their attention away from the class. One by one, the managers excused themselves to attend to something urgent. When we reconvened for lunch a few hours later, I took the opportunity to ask what had happened. They explained that their sales organization had cut a deal with a major customer on one of their company's products, and these production and distribution managers were the last people to hear about it. When they got the word, they had to scramble to see if they could actually deliver on the sales team's promises. The managers were struggling with the very problem that I'd been trying to show them how to avoid.

This lecture is devoted to that same subject: sales and operations planning, or S&OP. It's a proven method for finding the balance between promise making and promise keeping. The process itself consists of the integration of a company's sales forecasts with the operations plans from the purchasing, production, and logistics departments. We'll examine the specific inputs and organizational requirements needed to achieve this balance. Let's get started!

First, a little context: Why is it that there's a chasm between sales and operations in the first place? Why do we need a formal process to bring these parts of a business together? To say that businesses are complex organizations is an understatement. Most businesses are composed of different departments; departments like sales, marketing, accounting, purchasing, production, logistics, R&D, and human resources. Why? Because this is the way that we deal with complexity. We divide and conquer. We become specialized, developing knowledge and skill sets that allow us to perform specific functions. This makes more sense to us than building an organization full of generalists; people that might have mile-wide but inch-deep knowledge about how to run the business.

While a functional orientation helps us to make sure that we cover all the bases in our organization, it's sometimes difficult to establish balance and coordination across the departments. This is particularly true when we find the departments in conflict with one another. There's the natural tendency in times of conflict to retrench and to defend turf rather than to give in and pursue outcomes that might benefit the collective good. Companies often have measurement systems in place that reinforce functional silos and turf wars.

Perhaps the greatest divide found in an organization is the one between the demand and supply sides of the business. The customer-facing departments responsible for generating demand, namely sales and marketing, are held accountable for top-line revenue, sometimes at any cost. Meanwhile, the supply-side operations departments found in the business, like purchasing, production, and logistics, have the responsibility of delivering on that demand, but doing so at the lowest possible cost so that at the end of the day the company nets margins and profits.

These two forces find themselves at odds with one another. The promise makers in sales and marketing blame the operations spokesman for an inability to satisfy the demand that they've so tirelessly tried to create. Meanwhile, the operations personnel take offense with what they see as sales' and marketing's very casual approach to making promises that probably shouldn't have been made in the first place, putting them in an impossible spot from time to time.

Why is it important to address this gap; to get promise makers and promise keepers on the same page? When we fail to deliver on customer orders or have to temper demand that impacts our credibility in the marketplace and creates opportunities for our competitors. Undersupply opens the door for the competition. Yet, when we oversupply the market, we're left with excess inventory that must either be marked down or written off. When we fall into the trap of marking down inventory time and again, customers get conditioned to expect the markdowns. They learn to wait and refuse to pay full price. My wife knows that Macy's will mark down Christmas cards by 75% every December 26, and she's always poised to pounce on these predictable clearance sales.

With undersupply, we can expect blows to customer confidence, potentially losing sales in the immediate- and long-term, and with oversupply we incur the costs of holding excess inventory or aggressive discounting that runs the risk of watering down the brand.

Sales and operations planning was designed to address this problem. The concept was developed by management consultants at the consulting firm of Oliver Wight in the 1980s. The 1980s were a time in which personal computer technology was just being harnessed to address complex everyday problems. With a proven method, technology to support it, and successful case studies at major companies, word of S&OP spread very fast. Soon, businesses everywhere were pursuing the improvements in forecast accuracy, productivity, sales, on-time delivery, and inventory savings that they'd been hearing about.

Where do we sign up? What are the inputs to S&OP? How is it done? Fundamentally, S&OP is about gathering and sharing information. The first step is to form an S&OP team of departmental representatives from within your company and gain the buy-in of the parties involved. If the process fails to fully involve the sales and operations departments, the effort is without hope. But the process really should also involve other key stakeholders in the discussion of the company's key resources, including departments like finance, HR, and new product development. It's important to have these areas well-represented in planning discussions. Being well-represented means having senior leaders from these departments on the S&OP team. Sending a junior member to participate in this process won't help to advance it. For one, the junior member lacks the authority to make critical decisions for the department. Two, it signals a marginal commitment from the senior leaders. Either could stop the process in its tracks.

Just getting to the stage of the organization agreeing to resolve conflict that's brewed over a long period can be a major hurdle for some companies. In one extreme example, I heard of a CEO sacking a marketing executive because the executive refused to participate to the level necessary for success. The CEO, intent on making S&OP a reality at his company, put the executive who was in charge of distribution in charge of marketing, too, to concentrate the responsibility with one person, ensuring that no one would get in the way. Again, that's an unusual example, but it sent a clear message of the CEO's intent.

It helps if someone known and respected in the organization is tabbed with a leadership role for the S&OP process. It should be a primary responsibility for this person, and not just one of many side jobs. As the term *S&OP* suggests, the key function of the S&OP team is planning. The sales and marketing representatives should work together to bring forward the sales picture for the coming months. The purchasing, production, and logistics reps prepare capacity plans with ready explanations for any anticipated changes in operating capacity.

Finance and HR are present in consultative roles related to how financial and human resources might be deployed in the business. New product development can speak to the readiness and timing of new product launches that can be expected to siphon resources from existing products.

Not many among us enjoy meetings, but a well-managed monthly meeting proves more effective than merely distributing spreadsheets around the organization. The face-to-face meeting is important for quickly resolving discrepancies and conflicts. The idea is that all parties leave the meeting with a common vision of what's expected in the coming month and committed to doing their part to fulfill the vision. There's something about making commitments eye-to-eye that helps make them stick.

Considerable work takes place within each department leading up to the monthly summit. Sales and marketing should collaborate to coordinate promotions and any strategies that might be in place to bolster sales. The generation of a sales forecast can be one of the trickiest propositions in all of business. It represents the department's best guess of the future. But it can be disheartening to realize that the only absolute about a forecast is that it'll be wrong. The only question is whether it'll be an over-forecast, overshooting the actual sales, or an under-forecast, shooting too low, and how large the forecast error will be. The further out the forecast, the greater the propensity for error. It's like throwing a dart at a dartboard in many ways. The further back you stand, the less likely for a bull's-eye strike and the more likely you'll miss the board entirely. Step up a little and your accuracy improves. For that reason, we put more faith in short-term forecasts than the longer-term variety. The forecast for the upcoming one-to-three-month period is pretty typical in the S&OP process.

Another tricky component to sales forecasting is the value-laden nature of it. What I mean is that a sales organization that shoots too low can be regarded as overly cautious, lax, or sandbagging, setting low expectations. This can happen when salespeople are rewarded for sales exceeding the forecast. Yet, a sales organization that routinely overestimates their forecasted sales soon gets figured out, too, and their numbers lose credibility.

Allow me to provide a short review of the most common forecasting methods. Forecasts come in one of two different varieties: qualitative or quantitative. Qualitative forecasts are essentially best guesses; they're forecasts made without the necessary data. That said, they shouldn't be shots in the dark. No, they're expert-based opinions. The experts are those people who are closest to the market: the field sales representatives who can comment on what's going on in their respective markets. Marketing experts back at the headquarters will usually weigh in, too. They base their judgments on market intelligence, including trends for the sales of related items, demographic changes occurring in the markets, and the responses to market inquiries and field testing of the products or services in question.

In the absence of any sales history, qualitative estimations will be the best options available. This is especially true for those new-to-the-world items that have never been introduced before. Such was the case with the Segway personal scooters some years back. Do you know the ones I'm talking about; those two-wheeled devices that you drive by leaning to and fro? You're likely to see them in major airports or at tourist destinations like Miami's South Beach or San Francisco's Pier 39. The world had never seen such a thing before. Would people give up driving, walking, or riding bicycles to use a Segway scooter? These were the questions that the inventors had to ask themselves. At the end of the day, their initial sales forecasts were best guesses pulled out of the air with some backing from data grounded in related activities and products.

Quantitative forecasting methods come in many different forms. They rely on numbers; data from past sales of the same item, ideally. In the absence of this information, you might use historical sales of similar items or complementary items. An example of similar items might be replacement doors and windows for a house; the two may be replaced at a similar rate. Complementary items might be PCs and monitors, as they're often sold together. If you have data for the sales of one item, you can deduce the demand for a similar or complementary item. When we use figures for such past sales, we call it a time-series forecast because we're projecting from the past into the future.

The easiest but least informed quantitative forecast is that of the Simple average. In a Simple average, you might look at the average sales over an entire year and divide by 12 months. If you sell 1,200 units in a year, the average is 100 units per month. You'd simply expect to sell that same volume month over month.

The Moving average technique looks at recent history only. You might look at just the past three months, for instance, to gauge the anticipated sales for the month ahead. If we were to see sales of 100, 200, and 300 for the previous three months, our average over that time is 200 units.

Exponential smoothing is a forecasting method that acts a little differently, and it involves a simple formula. It looks at the previous month's sales forecast as well as the actual sales from that same month. We then apply what's called an alpha value; that governs how much weight or emphasis we'd on each factor in the calculation. The alpha value is a subjective value that's based on expert opinion. It's also known as the smoothing factor. Alpha will range from zero to one. A large alpha above 0.5 places more emphasis on actual sales from last month, and then the balance of one minus alpha is applied to the forecasted value from last month. We multiply actual sales times alpha and the forecasted sales by one minus alpha. When we add the two composites, you get the forecasted value for the coming month.

Smoothing is intended to take some of the emotion out of the forecast while still relying on recent data. By including the forecasted value from the previous month, you're carrying a smoothing influence forward month to month. When an item's been in existence for quite some time, you can rely on sales data to track trends, seasonality, or cyclical influences. All of these factors, and many more, can be integrated into a regression analysis forecast.

The regression method offers a predictive model that allows many factors to be considered at once. The unique influence of trends, seasons, and cycles can be determined from the regression, as can the influence of many other factors for which data exist. In the case of the sale of football tickets, other factors might include the average temperature or number of rainy days in the month. I'll admit that I'm a fair-weather fan. This level of detail makes regression a very powerful forecasting method.

Most companies employ a combination of quantitative and qualitative forecasting methods. The ideal approach is to generate a quantitative forecast as a baseline using whichever quantitative method you prefer. Experts can then weigh in on those numbers. Was there anything unusual in recent months that affected the historical data? Is there anything expected in the road ahead that could also affect the forecast? Blending historical data with expert opinion brings together the best of both worlds. Letting the data speak and providing a forward view, plus an occasional voice of reason, allows us to employ objective and subjective inputs in bringing forward our best guess of the future.

Like any process, forecasts can always be improved. Leading companies devise multiple forecasts using different methods and learn over time which methods prove most effective. They then continue to challenge and revise those models.

Now for the other side of the sales and operations planning equation: the capacity to accommodate this demand. There are three capacities that we generally concern ourselves with. These include the capacities of supply, production, and the combination of logistics and distribution. Limits in any of these can impair our ability to accommodate the expected demand found in the sales forecast. This is the check to ensure we only make promises we're confident of keeping.

Supply capacity is something that likely rests beyond the direct control of your firm. It's dependent on the capacity of your suppliers and your ability to extract supplies from them. The typical experience is that you have a wide range of suppliers. Some seem able to offer limitless supplies and others present constraints. The constraints may be absolute, meaning there are limits to their ability to serve you, or the added volume may simply come at a higher price. You need to understand both of these, as they can influence the volume of supplies you can acquire, in total and at what price.

Supply and production capacity come together in the materials requirements plan, or MRP, which expresses the quantity and timing of supplies required to feed production. The materials requirements plan is usually driven by the production forecast, which is often expressed in yet another three-letter acronym: the master production schedule, or MPS. This schedule illustrates what the company expects to produce over a period of time, often a month, and can be broken down into weekly or even daily plans for production.

Clearly, the sales forecast should influence this production forecast. The difference in the two forecasts can be capacity constraints in production, or a preference by production to make something different. Why would production elect to make something different? It could be that the production planners have learned over time that the sales forecast isn't so accurate and they make their own adjustments. Or it could be that the production department has incentives in place that might influence its preferences. It's common, for instance, for a company's executives to evaluate production performance based on cost per unit produced. When that's the case, production management is inclined to pursue economies of scale, producing the items that they can build at the lowest cost and running them in very large batches. It's a gaming of the system, for sure, but it's extremely common. This kind of gamesmanship should be put to rest with an effective S&OP process because the process puts sales and production in direct communication with each other so they can understand each other's goals and constraints.

The third capacity plan that we bring to the S&OP table is the one for logistics and distribution. Here, we may have capacity constraints on how much product we can store and move over a period of time. That capacity may be limited to the space in our warehouses, the size of our storerooms, or the number of transportation vehicles that we have at our disposal. You may own these capacities or you might have to hire outside companies to provide you with the space and transport you require. Similar to hiring outside suppliers, you might run into a spike in prices when you demand more than your fair share of these outside capacities. Again, this is knowledge that needs to be brought to the table.

With the compilation of the sales forecast and capacity plans for supply, production, and logistics and distribution, you have what you need to make decisions at your S&OP planning meeting. The goal of the meeting is to come up with a single set of numbers that everyone will work toward in the coming period. The S&OP process doesn't end with agreement on the common set of numbers, however. Once you're into the month and sales start to trickle in, everyone needs to communicate when the forecast looks to be falling apart (and we know that it will). Also, the same could be said of our operations plans. Countless forces could be at work, threatening to alter our best-laid plans for meeting the demand.

When a crisis or new constraint presents itself that, too, should be communicated so that the sales team can direct demand away from the affected products or offer adjusted delivery dates to navigate the situation. The often-forgotten component of S&OP is flexibility: flexibility that you need to build into your operations to accommodate the unexpected. The more flexible your operations, the more variation that your system can accommodate and the less likely that your customers will experience any negative consequence due to fallible planning.

However, should you not be able to accommodate customer needs, there comes a time to make tough choices. You must devise priorities when the constraints prove too much and supply can't meet demand. Among the hard decisions is figuring out which products to supply or produce when capacities are limited. Also, when distribution capacity is constrained or the inventory of goods faces shortage, we must decide who to serve with our limited supplies. Do we serve customers on a first-come/first-serve basis, or do we reserve the short supply for our most valuable customers? It doesn't make everyone happy, but you can see why companies want to make sure that their best customers don't get shorted. Customers with high status membership in their airline's frequent flyer programs rarely get bumped from oversold flights, right? The airlines are practicing good demand management there.

I hope that you're seeing the benefit of achieving balance between supply and demand through S&OP. What we've talked about thus far is actually called enterprise S&OP—that is, S&OP for a single company—but S&OP can be applied more broadly than that. What if we apply these same principles in managing the supply and demand across companies in the supply chain, meaning our entire system of inputs, outputs and distribution? That is, what if we collaborate with our suppliers and customers to see a common vision of the business we'll conduct together?

A classic example points to why we should try to iron out the kinks in our supply and demand plans across company boundaries in the supply chain. Way back in 1958, an article appeared in the *Harvard Business Review* by Professor Jay Forrester of MIT. Professor Forrester documented something called demand amplification. Let me set the scenario for you.

Picture a supply chain with multiple levels. A manufacturer distributes product to a distribution center. Distributors buy product from the manufacturer's distribution center, and the distributor sells product to retailers, who sell to consumers like you and me. Inventory flows from the manufacturer toward retailers, and demand then flows in the reverse direction. Professor Forrester examined what happens when demand for an item suddenly increases by a mere 10% at the retail level. In his research, he found that retailers usually require a little time before they detect the small rise in demand. Once recognized, they don't know exactly where that demand will level off, so they increase their orders on the distributor by 16%.

Imagine that you're the distributor: You suddenly receive an order that's 16% higher than normal. Like the retailer, you don't know where this demand will tail off, so you try to get ahead of it and increase your order on the manufacturer's distribution center by 28%. You see where this is going, right? The distribution center sees a spike of 28% and extrapolates this surge to try to get ahead it, placing an order on the factory that is 40% larger than normal. The factory then must react to this surge and increases production by 40%.

This is all in reaction to an actual change in demand at retail of 10%. We may not have the inventory when we need it, but when the supply chain catches up, it catches up in spades. We're left with tons of excess inventory that may over time have to be flushed or sold at a deep discount just to clear it out.

Today, the phenomenon is known as the bullwhip effect. Despite advanced technologies and an air of cooperation among businesses, the bullwhip effect phenomenon remains alive and well, more than a half century after Professor Forrester first documented it. The solution to this problem requires planning across company lines with select customers and suppliers. We refer to this as integrated S&OP or integrated business planning. Closely related is the concept of collaborative planning, forecasting, and replenishment, which goes by the acronym CPFR. As of this taping, grocery retailers and their vendors have been using CPFR for about 20 years.

While it takes considerable time to coordinate plans and actions across the companies, integrated S&OP and CPFR dramatically reduce the surprises that had become an unfortunate but common experience in doing business. Also, case studies show that more customers find what they want in-stock with less inventory in the system. That's a win-win. We ordinarily expect to add inventory to improve in-stock performance. Instead, companies are replacing inventory with the ready exchange of information.

As you can imagine, one key factor in all of this information sharing and coordination is the use of advanced information technologies. One popular technology is enterprise resource planning, or ERP. Many large companies are using ERP systems effectively to gather and share essential data within the company, but increasingly with trusted suppliers and customers, too. Also, ERP is becoming more accessible for small and medium enterprises thanks to the rise of cloud computing and companies that offer software as a service. Yet, more important than the technology is a willingness to share critical data, whether by electronic means or otherwise. Many companies find that the telephone still works just fine for this purpose.

Let me summarize with an analogy: Imagine a seesaw. On one end is a big box labeled "demand." On the other end are two smaller boxes labeled "capacity" and "inventory." Positioned in the middle of the seesaw board is the fulcrum upon which the board rests and the fulcrum is labeled "plan." Our seesaw is in balance when the weight of the capacity and inventory together counter the weight of demand. If demand were to grow in size, we'd need more weight in capacity and/or inventory to bring the seesaw back into balance. Yet, there's another possibility: the fulcrum. What if we were to move the fulcrum, the plan, closer to the demand side of the seesaw? With that action, we get more leverage from the capacity and inventory that we already have.

The lesson here is that if we can plan closer to demand—that is, if we forecast more accurately in the short term—then we need less capacity and inventory to fulfill the demand. The answer is sharing information and collaborating within our companies to find that balance between demand and supply.

Imagine lining up multiple seesaws side by side and working with people at each one to find the right balance for each of the seesaws in tandem. That would represent the notion of integrated business planning across companies in the supply chain. No doubt, it's a challenge, but it's one that yields huge benefits for its players.

Rightsizing Inventory
Lecture 17

Inventory can be among the most valuable assets for a company—and it certainly seems that way when you don't have enough to feed your business or serve your customers! But having too much inventory can be a bad thing, too. Even if it's just in storage, inventory can consume many resources in your business—resources that could be put to more productive use elsewhere. In this lecture, we'll explore the fundamentals of rightsizing inventory through inventory management. The primary goal of inventory management is to determine what to inventory and in what quantities to maintain just the right amount of inventory—no more and no less!

Inventory Management Metrics

- Companies hold inventory in the hopes of generating more sales and in fear of facing a *stockout*—a lack of inventory—resulting in the inability to serve customers. But holding inventory is expensive. The financial impact of holding inventory is measured in the form of *inventory carrying costs*, or *holding costs*. The more inventory a business holds, the higher these carrying costs are.

- The primary component of inventory carrying cost is the opportunity cost of capital, that is, the cost of having money tied up in inventory that could be put to use elsewhere in the business, perhaps in new technology or staff training. In addition to the opportunity cost of capital, the inventory carrying cost calculation also includes insurance and taxes associated with holding inventory. And there are risks to holding inventory, including the risks of the inventory becoming damaged, stolen, obsolete, spoiled, or out of date.

- Aside from inventory carrying cost, a key metric of inventory management performance is *inventory turns*. This measure can be calculated on an item-by-item basis or across a company for all its items. The aggregate calculation provides an overall measure of inventory efficiency. It's calculated by dividing the cost of goods sold by the dollar value of average inventory. A company that can generate more sales on lower inventory has a higher number of turns, suggesting a more efficient operation.

○ The item-specific measure of inventory turns provides a good read on the company's efficiency with respect to an individual item.

○ For instance, an item that generates 20 turns a year compared to another that generates only 5 is four times as efficient from an inventory standpoint. The 20-turn item might be labeled a "fast mover," and the 5-turn item might be a "slow mover." Fast- and slow-moving items can be managed differently in light of the different burdens they impose on the business.

- Increasingly, companies are using inventory turnover not only as a means of self-evaluation but also as a way to evaluate their suppliers. Many large retailers, for instance, use a measure known as *gross margin return on inventory* (GMROI) to evaluate the attractiveness of a supplier's goods. This is a hybrid measure that combines gross margin and inventory turns in a single metric.

○ Let's say that an item enjoys a 20% margin for the retail store but turns only three times per year. The GMROI would be $0.2 \times 3 = 0.6$. Some sources claim that an item must achieve a 3.2 GMROI to break even, but that's a broad guideline.

○ GMROI offers a good way to compare different items within a product category and can help retailers decide which items to stock and where to stock them.

Product Proliferation
- Product proliferation, or the growth in the number of items a company stocks, is among the greatest challenges facing businesses today. Companies are eager to introduce new items, believing that doing so drives sales growth, and that's often true. But companies are also reluctant to eliminate items. The result is an ever-growing assortment of items that add cost and complexity.

- Small businesses are especially prone to this problem. When a business is small and trying to grow, it wants to promise the world to its customers, but the weight of inventory to fulfill that promise is simply too heavy. Believe it or not, poor cash flow resulting from holding too much inventory can be blamed for more failures among small businesses than almost any other culprit.

- Having only one or a few brands within a product category is the driving strategy of such grocery retailers as Save a Lot, ALDI, and Trader Joe's. By carrying only one item in most product categories, these stores manage their inventory much more efficiently and, in turn, offer more competitive prices for their products.

Inventory Management Strategies

- There are four basic inventory management strategies. These strategies can be distinguished based on how a business interacts with its suppliers in choosing how much and how often to order.

With today's inventory-tracking technologies, many companies monitor inventory at all times and manage accordingly.

- The simplest option is a *fixed quantity–fixed frequency strategy*. With this strategy, a business orders the same quantity every time an item needs to be replenished, and the order is placed on a scheduled basis.

- The next strategy is the *periodic review method*, or *P-system*, where *P* stands for a fixed *period* of review. This strategy is also sometimes referred to as a *min-max approach*.

  ○ Once an inventory count is taken (perhaps every 10 days) and it's realized that a reorder point has passed, managers order up to a maximum level for that item—a predetermined quantity that the company is willing to hold. The periodic method of inventory management is variable in terms of quantity ordered but fixed in terms of timing.

  ○ Companies using this method establish reorder points that are a little higher than those used by companies that monitor inventory constantly. As a result, under the P-system, companies tend to carry a little more inventory. They also run the risk, however, of incurring prolonged stockouts when they're not on top of runs on inventory.

- Of the other two as-needed inventory strategies, one involves ordering in fixed quantities and the other allows for variable quantities. Using the fixed-quantity strategy, known as a *Q-system*, a company might order as needed in minimum order quantities imposed by the supplier, or the company might determine the quantities needed for itself. One common fixed-quantity approach is known as the *economic order quantity* (EOQ). This approach balances the annual cost of holding inventory and the annual administrative cost of processing orders.

- Ordering in fixed quantities, though, does not take advantage of the flexibility that companies seek today. That's why many have advanced to the fourth strategy, where neither the order quantity nor the timing of orders is fixed. This is a *just-in-time* (JIT) *strategy*.

○ Rather than counting on large lots and infrequent ordering, JIT companies resort to small order sizes and high frequency. When demand is brisk, they increase either the batch size or the frequency, depending on costs. However, the focus is on keeping inventories low and replenishing only what's depleted when it's depleted.

○ Companies often employ a *kanban* ("signboard") system to signal demand and the need for replenishment. The electronic versions of these systems are known as *e-kanbans*.

Choosing the Best Strategy

- As noted previously, most companies don't manage a single product but several different ones. The largest companies might have more than a million items to track and manage, and even a simple business can have an inventory of several hundred items. Clearly, this adds to the complexity of managing inventory and, often, the need to implement multiple inventory strategies.

- To address this complexity, most companies use some form of grouping for their inventory, such as an ABC classification scheme.
  ○ Under such a scheme, A items are those that sell in high volume, earn high margins, or are sold to the company's best customers; new products might also be labeled A items. These items are the ones for which the company tries to ensure ready availability. The company may be willing to take on a greater supply of A items to be certain that they're available; a stockout on these items could be detrimental to the company.

  ○ B items are of a somewhat lower priority and generally require a closer look to determine exactly how to manage them. If they're relatively new, "on the rise," or not expensive from a holding-cost standpoint, then a company might be willing to take on a greater supply. However, if these items are fading in popularity, easily substituted, or ordered by less important customers, then having a lower supply in inventory would be optimal.

○ Finally, C items are those that are on their way out. They may be unprofitable items, costly to keep, or on their way to becoming *dead stock*.

- Clearly, companies can create more complex classification schemes by simply adding letters to provide greater granularity. Also, a multi-letter scheme might be used to capture different dimensions. For example, a CBC item might be slow moving, marginally profitable, and sold to less valuable customers than a triple-A item.

Innovations in Inventory Management
- In light of the intense focus on inventory management in recent years, innovations present themselves frequently. One such innovation is the use of radio frequency identification (RFID) to track inventory as it flows through the supply chain. RFID technology comes in two basic types.
  ○ Active RFID involves attaching a small device to each product. The device has its own power source and emits a signal to indicate its location, enabling the product to be tracked. This technology is used in the transport of very large items, such as military armaments and shipping containers.

  ○ With passive RFID, the RFID tag can hold much more data than the traditional barcode, providing a unique identifier for that specific item and unit. With the added memory capacity, companies can track not only the unique identifier for that unit but also the production date, lot number, and special data, such as whether the good is hazardous or recyclable.

  ○ Electronic readers positioned at the inbound and outbound doors of facilities send energy to the passive RFID tag. This energy activates the tag, which sends a signal back to the reader with all of the data encoded in the tag. Because the whole process is automated, hundreds of items can be read at once. This compares favorably to traditional barcodes, which can be read only one at a time and often rely on people with handheld scanners to correctly scan each unit in and out of inventory.

- Another technological innovation that could affect inventory management dramatically is three-dimensional printing. Being able to create form-on-the-spot has tremendous implications for what companies stock in inventory and where they stock it. Among the more exciting developments is the prospective use of this technology in the production of on-demand medical devices and artificial body parts. Three-dimensional printing could alter our businesses, create new opportunities, and change the way we think about inventory.

Suggested Reading

Callioni, de Montgros, Slagmulder, Van Wassenhove, and Wright, "Inventory-Driven Costs."

Gruen and Corsten, "Stock-Outs Cause Walkouts."

Shepard, *RFID*.

Spear and Bowen, "Decoding the DNA of the Toyota Production System."

Waller and Esper, *The Definitive Guide to Inventory Management*.

Questions to Consider

1. What influences whether the holding of inventory is a blessing or a curse?

2. What are the problems raised by a stockout?

3. How do you rightsize inventory—that is, determine the right amount of inventory to hold? Is the rightsized inventory a moving target? Are there times and circumstances when you might be willing to hold more inventory?

4. Why do companies try to lighten their balance sheets of inventory toward the end of reporting periods (e.g., quarters, fiscal years)?

Rightsizing Inventory
Lecture 17—Transcript

Inventory can be among the most valuable assets for a company. It certainly feels that way when you don't have enough to feed your business or to serve your customers. But having too much inventory can be a bad thing, too. Even though it just sits there, inventory can consume a lot of resources in your business, resources that could be put to more productive use elsewhere.

How big a factor is inventory in a company's business? At any point in time, U.S. businesses are holding more than two trillion dollars in inventory. The Department of Commerce generates a measure each month called the inventory-sales ratio, or IS ratio, which compares inventory levels to sales. That number usually runs in the range of 1.30. That means that U.S. businesses typically hold about 30% more inventory at any point in time than what they're selling.

In this lecture, we'll explore the fundamentals of right-sizing inventory through inventory management. The main goal of inventory management is to determine what to inventory and in what quantities in order to maintain just the right amount of inventory, no more and no less.

Why do companies hold inventory in the first place? In hopes of generating sales. It's hard to sell what you don't have, and we fear disappointing a customer. A stockout is when we fail to serve a customer because we lack the inventory, and customers can react in any number of ways to a stockout. They might be courteous and accept a backorder, a raincheck if you will; a promise to provide the goods once we have the inventory available. Increasingly, though, they're not so understanding. Instead, they're likely to look for a substitute item. If they're brand loyal customers, they might look for the item at another location or seek out a different supplier. But they're also prone to getting frustrated and giving up on the product altogether. What if they like the substitute just as well, or they tell their friends about the stockout and suggest that they try a different store? Clearly, the residual effects of a single stockout can be substantial in today's highly competitive markets.

But holding inventory is expensive. How expensive? Businesses measure the financial impact of holding inventory in the form of something called inventory carrying costs or holding costs. The more inventory you hold, the higher the carrying costs. The primary component of inventory carrying cost is the opportunity cost of capital: having money tied up inventory that could be put to use somewhere else in the business. In other words, if you have $10,000 of inventory, what else could you be doing with it? Maybe you could invest in new products or new technology. You could invest in training and education of your staff, or maybe upgrading facilities. The point is, there are other uses for that capital than having it tied up in a not-so-liquid asset. This is especially true for cash-strapped companies. In addition to the opportunity cost of capital, other factors that might go into the inventory carrying cost calculation include insurance and taxes associated with holding inventory. There are also aspects of risk to holding inventory, including the risks of inventory becoming damaged, stolen, obsolete, spoiled, or out of date.

Inventory carrying cost aside, what are the other key metrics for inventory management performance? The most talked about one is inventory turns. The measure of inventory turns offers us a picture of inventory velocity. Of course, high velocity means that you're selling the merchandise quickly. Inventory turns can be calculated on an item by item basis or across a company for all of its items. The aggregate calculation provides an overall measure of inventory efficiency. It's calculated by dividing cost of goods sold by the dollar value of average inventory. If a company can generate more sales on less inventory, the higher its turns, the more velocity, suggesting a more efficient operation. Wall Street analysts use this measure as a way to assess the overall operational efficiency of a company.

The item-specific measure of inventory turns, though, provides a good read on the company's efficiency with respect to an individual item. When it comes down to managing inventory, you really want to have this specific level of knowledge. Fortunately, computerized recordkeeping of inventory makes this analysis much easier, allowing us to compare the performance of one item against another. For instance, an item that generates 20 turns a year compared to another that generates only 5 turns a year is four as efficient from an inventory standpoint. We might label the 20-turn item as a fast mover and the 5-turn item as a slow mover. Fast- and slow-moving items can be managed differently in light of the different burdens they impose on the business.

But increasingly, companies are using inventory turnover not only as a measure of self-evaluation, but also as a way to evaluate their suppliers. Many large retailers, for instance, are using a measure called gross margin return on inventory, or GMROI as it's often called, to evaluate the attractiveness of a supplier's goods. GMROI is a hybrid measure that combines gross margin and inventory turns into a single metric. Let's say that an item enjoys a 20% margin for the retail store but only turns three times per year. $0.2 \times 3 = 0.6$. Some sources claim that an item must achieve a 3.2 GMROI score to break even, but that's a very broad guideline. GMROI offers a good way to compare different items within a category. Retailers, for instance, only have so much space in their stores. They have to decide which items to stock and where to stock them. Only select items will get the primo space in the store: the eye-level shelves or the end-of-aisle displays.

Let's examine how a retailer might use this comparative metric: One item provides low margins of 6% but turns weekly, or 52 times per year, for a GMROI of 3.12. The other item has margins of 15% but turns only monthly, 12 times, for a GMROI of 1.8. The retailer would be wise to put more emphasis on the first item than the second and might elect to only stock the first item. This would likely drive sales up for that item, though some customers might be upset by the discontinuation of the second item. It's a difficult decision, for sure.

Product proliferation, or the growth in the number of items that a company stocks, is among the greatest challenges facing businesses today. Companies are always eager to introduce new items, believing that it drives sales growth, and that's often true. But companies are very reluctant to get rid of items. That results in an ever-growing assortment of items that add cost and complexity. Product proliferation has been described as a cinder block around the neck of the company and its profitability. This is especially true for small businesses. When you're small and trying to grow, you want to promise the world to your customers, but you can't afford to stock the world.

The weight of inventory is simply too heavy. Believe it or not, poor cash flow resulting from holding too much inventory can be blamed for more failures among small businesses than almost any other culprit.

My daughter Emma loves to cook and to watch television programs about cooking. One show that we enjoy watching together features a business expert who helps out troubled restaurants. I'm always amazed at how diverse a menu these restaurant operators present. I mean, a Mexican restaurant that offers chicken wings and spaghetti? No joke. But if an item's on the menu, you'd better have it, and that means you need to keep the ingredients and supplies on hand to cook all those foods. That's inventory. The smarter decision would be to keep those items off the menu. Limit the assortment and focus your efforts.

Having only one or a few brands within a product category is the driving strategy of grocery retailers like Save-A-Lot, Aldi, and Trader Joe's with their limited assortment approach. By carrying only one item in most product categories, they can manage their inventory much more efficiently, and in turn offer more competitive prices for the products they sell.

What are the different strategies that companies can use to manage inventory? There are four basic strategies. We can distinguish them based on how a business interacts with its suppliers in choosing how much to order and how often to order. The most simple option is a fixed quantity-fixed frequency strategy. This is where you order the same quantity every time you need replenishment, and you place this order on a schedule basis. This is the arrangement that I have with my local newspaper. They deliver precisely one newspaper to me every day. That's a fixed quantity on a fixed frequency. When I head out of town on vacation, I have to contact the newspaper and tell them to stop delivery. When my Buckeyes win a national championship, I might want an extra copy, so I'd need to contact the company and say, "Hey, send me an extra one." (Sadly, that doesn't happen often enough for my liking.)

With this strategy, you need to figure out how much you want and how often. I read a newspaper each and every day, so that seems about right. But if you're buying something more complex, it requires more thought. Also, some suppliers might impose a minimum order quantity that requires us to buy more than we might prefer. Whether it's of our own choice or imposed on us, the larger the order quantity, the less frequently we'll need to order supplies.

Why would a supplier impose a minimum order quantity on us? Because although it doesn't usually get registered as a ledger item, there's such a thing as order processing cost. That's an administrative cost measured in time, effort, and technology used to place an order. Each time that our supplier receives an order from us, they also incur a cost to process the order as well. That's one reason that suppliers impose minimum order policies on small orders: to ensure that they at least cover their cost of doing business, and that's understandable. You've probably seen such a policy when small retailers require a minimum dollar amount for customers making purchases with credit cards, as credit card companies sometimes charge transaction fees to these small businesses.

The other three inventory strategies employ what's called reorder point logic. That's fancy language for saying that we track the inventory and reorder when we reach a certain level of on-hand inventory. When we reach the reorder point, it triggers an order.

One strategy doesn't require us to keep close tabs on inventory. Instead, we might check inventory, say, every 5 or 10 days. That would be a periodic review method, or P system, where the letter "P" stands for a fixed period of review. This strategy is also sometimes referred to as a min-max approach. Once an inventory count is taken and it's realized that a reorder point has passed, managers will order up to a maximum level for that item; a predetermined quantity that you're willing to hold. The periodic method of inventory management is variable in terms of quantity ordered but fixed in terms of timing.

Companies using this method establish reorder points that are a little higher than when you monitor inventory constantly. As a result of only occasionally checking inventory and having a higher reorder point, they tend to carry a little more inventory. They also run the risk, though, of incurring prolonged stockouts when they're not on top of runs on inventory. Reorder points and maximum levels can be adjusted at different times of the year to better accommodate peak and low seasons, but they shouldn't change often.

The periodic review method has given way to strategies that emphasize managing inventory in real time. With today's inventory tracking technologies like barcodes and radio frequency identification, many companies keep an eye on the inventory at all times and manage accordingly. This allows them to be alerted to items that are running dangerously low and to keep less inventory on average by way of this alertness. These advanced technologies can often pay for themselves pretty quickly.

Of the as-needed inventory strategies, one involves ordering in fixed quantities and the other allows for variable quantities. Using the fixed-quantity strategy, known as a Q system, a company might order as needed in minimum order quantities imposed by the supplier, or the company might determine the quantities that it feels are best. One fixed-quantity approach that has been a mainstay for over a century now is something called economic order quantity, or EOQ. The EOQ balances the annual cost of holding inventory and the annual administrative cost of processing orders. Many people continue to be drawn to it based on its simple logic.

Ordering in fixed quantities, though, doesn't take advantage of the flexibility that companies are seeking today. That's why many have advanced to the fourth strategy, where neither the order quantity nor the timing of orders is fixed. This is a just-in-time strategy, which has gained much fame and attention in recent decades. People often associate it with automotive manufacturers like Toyota and Honda. However, just-in-time or JIT systems are found in all varieties of industries.

The primary difference between JIT and the other three approaches is that we must exert generous diligence on our inventory. It takes a lot of focus and discipline to operate on this basis, when inventory is kept to an absolute minimum yet running out of it can literally shut down the business. For that reason, it's unwise to consider such a system when supplier lead times are long or unreliable. Rather than counting on large lots and infrequent ordering, JIT companies resort to very small order batch sizes and high frequency. When demand is brisk, they increase either the batch size or the order frequency depending on the costs of doing each. However, the focus is on keeping inventories low and replenishing only what's depleted when it's depleted.

Companies often employ a *Kanban* system to signal demand and the need for replenishment. *Kanban* is a Japanese term that means "signboard." Traditional *Kanban* systems use paper cards to serve as visual signals of inventory consumption and the need for replenishment. Today, the systems have converted to electronic means, using what's called e-Kanbans.

Despite their challenges, we see JIT systems in place in many different businesses today. Perhaps foremost in their adoption are hospitals that rely on available stores of medical supplies, devices, and pharmaceuticals, yet they don't want to buy any more of these extremely expensive, often perishable items than they need. Many believe that better management of our inventories in healthcare supply chains can dramatically reduce our cost of care while also improving the quality of care.

As you might expect, inventory is a focal point for companies that embrace Lean thinking. Lean thinking, remember, suggests that we eliminate all forms of waste in our businesses so that we're focused on performing value-added work that satisfies customers; work that they're willing to pay for. Inventory is regarded as one of those wastes to eliminate. Rather than viewing inventory as an asset in the business, as its position on the balance sheet would suggest, Lean thinkers regard it as a liability.

In fact, a gentleman by the name of Taiichi Ohno, who is often credited with devising the famed Toyota production system, once said: "The more inventory a company has, the less likely they will have what they need." What did Mr. Ohno mean by this counterintuitive observation? He seemed to suggest that just because you have a lot of inventory doesn't mean that you have the stuff that customers actually want. In fact, the more inventory you have, the less likely you'll have the right stuff. The suggestion is that the inventory can make us very complacent; to feel as if we have everything that we need. It also allows for a sense of disconnection between us, our customers, and suppliers. All of those conditions are bad; it's bad business and it doesn't encourage us to get better. The obvious challenge to being

Lean, though, is the risk of disappointing customers when demand surges or when supply is disrupted. These are risks, for sure. How Lean companies deal with these risks is the subject of another lecture.

Now that we've reviewed the four inventory strategies, which one's best? It doesn't always come down to selecting a single strategy. As noted previously, most companies don't manage a single product, but several different ones. The largest companies like 3M and General Electric might have more than a million items that they must track and manage. A large retail store with a modern multi-department format might house 120,000 different items under one roof. Even the simplest of businesses can have an inventory of several hundred items. Clearly, this adds to the complexity of managing inventory and often the need to implement multiple inventory strategies.

In order to address this complexity, most companies employ some form of grouping their items across their inventory. The most common is an ABC classification scheme. Under such a scheme, A items are those that sell in high volume, earn high margins, or are sold to the company's best customers. These are the items for which the company tries to ensure ready availability. New products that are in the throes of a major launch might also be labeled as A items. The company may be willing to take on a little more supply of these A's to be certain that they're available, as a stockout on them could be really detrimental to the company.

B items are of a somewhat lower priority. We might not need to stock as great a supply, for a stockout here wouldn't have the same implications as for A items. B items generally require a closer look to determine exactly how to manage them. If they're relatively new or on the rise, then you might be willing to take on a little more. If they're not expensive from a holding cost standpoint, there again you might be willing to take on a little more. However, if these items are fading in popularity, easily substituted, or ordered by less important customers, then having lower supply of inventory would be optimal.

Finally, C items are those that are on their way out. They may be unprofitable items, costly to keep, or they're on their way to becoming what we call dead stock, having lost their resell value. Given the short lifecycle of electronic products today in light of the quick advances, they can quickly transition from an exciting new A item, to a mature B item, to a C item in the declining stage. C items should be cleared out to make room for the next new thing. This can happen in less than a year with today's smartphones, for instance.

Clearly, you can create a more complex classification scheme by simply adding letters—D, E, F, and so on—to provide greater granularity. Also, you can create a multi-letter scheme to capture different dimensions with the designation. For example, let's say that we want to manage inventory according to how brisk the sales are for an item, the profitability of the item, and who's buying it. An AAA item is one that is high volume, very profitable, and purchased by our preferred customers. We'd manage such an item very differently from, say, a C BC item that would be slow moving, marginally profitable, and sold to less valuable customers. While we make every effort to ensure availability of the AAA item, the CBC item might be on the chopping block. Or we might choose not to stock it, but rather order it from suppliers only when we receive a request for it.

Allow me to share a short case study that illustrates how one small company manages a large array of inventory in multiple locations. Cole Hardware is a family-run business in the San Francisco Bay Area. They operate four store locations in the Bay Area, each one stocking a wide array of items that any handy do-it-yourselfer might need for those household jobs. They stock fasteners, tools, fixtures, and much, much more, about 45,000 items at each store location. Everything received by the store gets scanned and it's added to the computerized inventory management system. Also, items get scanned at the checkout to indicate that they're leaving the inventory. Some items are likely to be high-volume, critical A items and others are slower moving, less critical B and C items. Really expensive A items might be managed on a just-in-time basis, an effort to try to ensure availability without taking on expensive inventory. In other instances, one of Cole Hardware's big vendors might require minimum order sizes on such a relatively small customer, requiring a Q system with the same order quantity applied each time the stores need something. Should the store sell bulk construction materials like lumber, gravel or sand, those materials might be managed on a periodic basis, where the inventory is checked from time to time and ordered up to the level deemed a maximum for the season. Some items, like nuts and bolts, might be sold on such a steady basis that they're delivered on a fixed schedule, fixed quantity basis.

In other words, it's possible for a single business to employ a multitude of strategies to accommodate different items and their respective demands. Further, it's possible that some items will shift from one strategy to another as they transition from one sales season to another, going from an anticipatory strategy like a Q system in peak season to a response-based JIT system when the peak demand subsides.

In light of the intense focus directed to inventory management in recent years, innovations are always presenting themselves. One innovation I mentioned earlier is the use of radio frequency identification, or RFID, to track inventory as it flows through the supply chain. RFID technology comes in two basic types. One type is what's called active RFID. Active RFID involves attaching a small device to each product. The device has its own battery power source and is capable of emitting a signal to indicate its location so the product can be tracked. This is the technology used in the transport of very large items like military armaments and shipping containers.

The second type of RFID is the one gaining greater attention in recent years, and that's the passive RFID. This technology has been called "barcodes on steroids," as it's regarded as a much improved method over traditional barcode technology found on virtually every carton and package sold today. The passive RFID tag can hold much more data than the traditional barcode, providing a unique identifier for that specific item and unit. With the added memory capacity, one can track not only the unique ID for that unit, but also indicate the production date, lot number, as well as any other special data like whether the good has hazardous or recyclable content. Electronic readers are positioned at the inbound and outbound doors of facilities, and these readers send energy to the passive RFID tag. This energy activates the tag, which sends a signal back to the reader with all of the data encoded in the tag. Since the whole process is automated, requiring no human involvement, hundreds of items can be read at once. This compares favorably to traditional barcodes, which can only be read one at a time and often rely on people with handheld scanners to correctly scan each unit in and out of inventory.

I'm sure you've seen the person running the checkout counter at your grocery store who from time to time will casually scan one item several times instead of scanning each item, even though you might have somewhat different items in your cart, like different colors or flavors. Guess what? This really messes up the inventory counts on that stuff. RFID promises to take care of these types of data entry problems.

Clearly, the potential for RFID technology is immense. Not long ago, it was believed that virtually everything we buy would use this technology by now. Aggressive mandates were initiated by major companies like Walmart, Target, and even the U.S. Department of Defense back in the mid-2000s, but the use of RFID has yet to achieve its expected results. Some claim that the economics aren't yet in place; that it remains too expensive for use. Others claim that the technology isn't yet ready; that the readers are unable to capture all of the data for large volumes of items at once, thereby suggesting that the technology doesn't justify the investment. But keep a close eye on RFID. New applications seemingly crop up every day where it's used effectively.

Another technological innovation that could affect inventory management dramatically is three-dimensional printing. Being able to create form-on-the-spot has tremendous implications for what we stock in inventory and where we stock it. Among the more exciting developments is its prospective use in the production of on-demand medical devices, and even artificial body parts. We're only starting to get our heads around how this technology could alter our businesses, create new opportunities, and, yes, change the way we think about inventory. Rather than stocking products in their final form and positioning that inventory in many locations, it's conceivable to position 3-D printers at these locations instead to create the final form of products only when customers demand them. Instead of stocking expensive finished goods on a speculative basis, guessing how much to build in advance of the need and where to keep it, companies could stock raw materials. Raw materials are cheaper than finished goods and they're less likely to become obsolete since they can be made into different types of products. This would dramatically reduce risks and lower holding costs.

Change is the only constant, so they say. That certainly seems to apply to the notion of managing inventory. The effort to "right size" inventory is constantly in flux, with changes in business and new technologies seeming to come online all the time. But that's what makes it so fun and challenging. As soon as you think you have it figured out, the variables change and you have to find a new solution.

Managing Supply and Suppliers
Lecture 18

When most people think of purchasing, procurement, or supply management, they think of the department responsible for buying the "stuff"—raw materials, spare parts, and so on—that feeds the business. This function doesn't sound especially interesting until we consider the fact that supply management can render the company profitable or unprofitable based on the terms negotiated with suppliers; it also serves as the gatekeeper of quality. In this lecture, we'll explore how effective supply management practices can be leveraged not only to keep the business running but also to set it apart from others. We'll examine fundamental questions surrounding what to buy, how to select suppliers, and how to make good suppliers excited to get your company's business.

The Evolution of Supply Management

- The traditional role of the purchasing department in an organization was to acquire the necessary materials, goods, and services to feed the operation and to do so at the lowest possible prices. Over time, purchasing evolved into procurement, which expanded the set of purchasing activities and elevated the strategic focus of the tasks. Beyond merely "buying stuff," procurement professionals assessed the quality of competing suppliers and established supplier qualifications and material specifications.

- Over the past two decades, procurement has given way to modern supply management, which is even more strategic for the business and collaborative with suppliers. Supply management seeks to achieve competitive advantage by working effectively with choice suppliers, even engaging suppliers early in the development of new products and services. These days, supply management not only controls a considerable share of the company's budget, but it influences the competitiveness of the company through its connection with other business strategies and departments.

- One industry phenomenon that has accelerated the influence of supply management is the rampant adoption of outsourcing over the past three decades. As we've seen, companies are electing to outsource activities that they no longer view as their strengths, and with this decision, the role of supply management expands. Supply management usually assumes responsibility for selecting the outside suppliers, negotiating the arrangements, and monitoring the provision of services.

Centralized and Decentralized Supply Management
- Once a company determines what it will buy, the supply management organization can take shape. Critical to forming the organization is understanding the scope of the work required. If the company operates from multiple locations, how much responsibility will rest with a central purchasing organization and how much will rest with buyers at each location? Organizations opting for centralized control decide what to buy, select the suppliers, and initiate the orders, all from headquarters. Field personnel verify that the quantity and quality of supplies meet expectations but do not make strategic decisions.
  - The benefits of such a system include consolidating the spend and ensuring that the company achieves volume discounts from suppliers and high-priority service by virtue of putting large chunks of the business in the hands of fewer suppliers. Centralized control can also support greater standardization of supply across various field locations. The disadvantage of a centralized system is that it doesn't allow field operations to exert their influence on suppliers or to address their specific needs.

  - In contrast, decentralized control allows the field locations to act autonomously, to freely choose suppliers and to negotiate directly with them. Although the individual needs of the locations can be addressed in these arrangements, the volume of the spend may not be sufficiently large to warrant the most competitive price or highest-priority service from suppliers.

- Most good-sized companies pursue a blended strategy, which involves headquarters centralizing the planning of supply and field locations controlling the buying actions. Such arrangements try to achieve balance between the control of centralization and the flexibility of decentralization, though strategic decisions are left with headquarters.

Supplier Relationship Strategies

- A company's strategy for engaging suppliers is based in large part on what is purchased. Most companies must acquire "mission-critical" supplies—items that influence the quality of the products and services the company provides or that are visible to customers. The opposite of these visible and mission-critical items are the invisible, commodity items. Whereas a firm might emphasize quality with mission-critical items, price might be the highest priority with commodity items.

- The amount of attention directed toward supplier relationships also depends on how critical the supplies are to a company's products and services. A supplier of maintenance, repair, and operating supplies that don't go directly into a product typically doesn't warrant the same attention as a supplier that can help a company win or lose in the marketplace.

- How many suppliers of a given input is ideal? Competing theories weigh in on this question.
   o Some believe that fewer suppliers is better, even going so far as to recommend sole sourcing. The benefit of this approach is that the spend is concentrated in one place, which should elevate the volume discount. It's also easier to manage one supplier than several.

   o However, the dependency inherent in sole-sourcing arrangements drives many supply professionals away from pursuing them. Placing all of a company's business for a given input in the hands of a single supplier may eliminate the positive influences of competition on price and quality.

- Another school of thought on the ideal number of suppliers seeks to incite a feeding frenzy among multiple suppliers. The belief is that this situation intensifies competition and encourages suppliers to cut prices to the bone. This is usually a short-term proposition, however, because suppliers are interested in large chunks of business that are repetitive, allowing them to smooth their own operations and reduce transaction costs.

- Often a "middle-ground" strategy is preferred. Most progressive companies avoid sole sourcing where possible, yet they're not constantly on the prowl for new suppliers. Rather, they examine the portfolio of items and services they buy and look for opportunities to consolidate the spend, which will provide leverage in negotiations. They also look for opportunities to collaborate with suppliers of critical parts.

Selecting Suppliers

- It has become common for large supply management organizations to spend a preponderance of their time qualifying suppliers, that is, establishing standards for doing business with the company. In light of the vast interest in serving large companies, corporations use qualification as a way to filter the interest, requiring prospective suppliers to meet standards in quality, capacity, safety, and ethical performance.

- Once the qualifications are in place, a company can approach the supply market. Of course, the method of approach depends on both the company's situation and what it is buying. Seasoned buyers often know who to contact first—which suppliers have the capabilities, capacity, and pricing to be competitive. In some cases, a company might set up a reverse auction, inviting select players to compete in real time for the business and choosing the supplier that brings forward the lowest price.

- If simply putting the business out to bid and shopping for low price is not the answer, then companies may have to take an intermediate step to see what prospective suppliers have to offer.

This process involves "interviewing" suppliers through a request for information (RFI), a request for quote (RFQ), or a request for proposal (RFP).

Total Cost of Ownership

- In making supplier selections, most companies today are looking beyond purchase price. Instead, they're considering what's known as the *total cost of ownership* (TCO) associated with the purchase. This is a way of bringing a life-cycle perspective into the procurement of goods and services.

- The life-cycle perspective makes sense because TCO considers not only the purchase price but all the costs associated with acquisition, such as the costs of financing the purchase and preparing the business to use the materials or products. To that end, TCO also factors in the costs of use, including the cost of carrying inventory.

- But it's in the determination of a product's post-use factors that the life-cycle perspective of TCO can alter the landscape of the purchasing decision. These post-use factors include the costs of dissatisfied customers, such as warranty, recall, or liability costs, as well as the environmental impacts of products and packaging material in the post-use phase.

- In sum, the life-cycle perspective espoused in TCO revolutionizes the act of buying. It's a 180-degee turn from traditional purchasing practice and requires much deeper thought than simply shopping for prices and specs ever accommodated.

Keeping Suppliers Engaged

- One tip for keeping suppliers engaged and working hard for your firm is to maintain open communications, especially with suppliers that are critical to your business. Invite suppliers to tour your facilities and request a tour of theirs. Seeing the products and services in use can inspire discussion and illuminate opportunities for improvement.

- You should also provide regular feedback to all strategic suppliers. Issue a monthly supplier scorecard, for instance, to rate performance on a few metrics that are important to your business and explain, in general, how the supplier is doing. The basic dimensions of performance usually include quality, cost, and delivery.

- Progressive companies also turn the mirror around and ask suppliers how satisfied they are with the focal firm as a customer. Such assessments usually examine the ease of doing business with the customer and are generally conducted by third parties.

© Katarzyna Białasiewicz/iStock/Thinkstock.

Providing a scorecard for supplier performance should serve as a conversation starter, enabling both parties to see the potential for improvement and to develop a mutually beneficial relationship.

- Leading-edge companies are also moving toward *supply chain competition*. Companies no longer compete merely head to head but also supply chain to supply chain, pitting their entire input-to-delivered-output systems against those of their rivals. With that in mind, there's a race to win the best, most innovative suppliers. These are the suppliers that possess unique intellectual property, processing capabilities, and branding to bolster your products and services.

- Beyond working with suppliers, you want to enlist them to help you compete. This can take the form of early supplier involvement, where suppliers help to devise the next generation of products and services. It may result in joint-venture opportunities or licensing arrangements when the market proves promising. At a minimum, the involvement of suppliers early in the new product development process can highlight the limitations or challenges that you'll encounter should you elect to proceed with a bold new technology.

Suggested Reading

Ellram and Krause, "Robust Supplier Relationships."

Ellram and Siferd, "Purchasing: The Cornerstone of the Total Cost of Ownership Concept."

Monczka, Handfield, Giunipero, and Patterson, *Purchasing and Supply Chain Management*.

Tate, *The Definitive Guide to Supply Management and Procurement*.

Questions to Consider

1. How has supply management progressed beyond the tactical activity of buying?

2. Why is it important to engage other business functions in strategic conversations with suppliers?

3. What are the risks of having too few and too many suppliers of a critical input?

4. How does the lifecycle perspective of TCO change the orientation of a buying organization?

Managing Supply and Suppliers
Lecture 18—Transcript

When most people think of purchasing, procurement, or supply management, they ordinarily think of the business department responsible for buying stuff that feeds the business. It could be the raw materials, produced goods, spare parts, services, or even office supplies. But whatever it involves, the action of buying stuff doesn't sound especially glamorous or sophisticated. That might be the case if the department's sole responsibility were negotiating price with suppliers, shaking hands, and moving on.

But modern supply management is anything but mundane. Let's consider, for instance, that this one department can account for well over half of the company's total spend. Let's also consider that this one department can itself render a company profitable or unprofitable based on the prices and terms negotiated with suppliers. Supply management also serves as the gatekeeper of quality for the company. Procuring shoddy supplies is a surefire way to incur defects in your products that can get passed along to customers. Along with considerations of quality, the company's position on sustainability will rest in large measure with the greenness of the inputs procured through supply management. Finally, let's also consider that this function sets the tone for suppliers' eagerness to collaborate and innovate with your company. Clearly, we're talking about a series of decisions that involve the long-term profitability and lasting reputation of the company; a set of strategic considerations essential for any organization to manage effectively.

In this lecture, we'll explore how you can leverage effective supply management practices to not only keep the machine running in your business, but also to set it apart from others. We'll examine fundamental questions around what to buy, how to select suppliers, and how to make the really good suppliers excited about doing business with you.

There was a time when supply management was, in fact, a lot less exciting than it is today. The traditional role of the purchasing organization was to acquire the necessary materials, goods, and services essential to feeding the operation and to do so at the lowest possible price. The purchasing group might from time to time be called out for purchasing supplies in the wrong quantities, either too little or too much, or of inferior quality, but buyers were generally responsible for finding that lowest price. The work itself was rather transactional in nature. Once suppliers were selected and negotiations closed, buyers kept their eyes on inventory levels and purchased replenishments as needed.

Over time, purchasing evolved into procurement, which expanded the set of activities and elevated the strategic focus of the tasks. Beyond merely buying stuff, procurement professionals assessed the quality of competing suppliers and established supplier qualifications; requirements that suppliers must meet in order to compete for the business. They went beyond auditing supplies to establishing material specifications. They also got out of the office and inspected suppliers' processes and tried to understand the suppliers' costs, not just the prices they charged. They developed an understanding of supplier operations and opportunities for quality improvements by engaging in a more immersive experience with suppliers, one of value engineering, where buyers and suppliers figure out ways to reduce costs together.

The evolution continued to a point where over the past two decades what I just described for procurement has given way to supply management, which is even more strategic for the business and collaborative with suppliers. As you'll see, supply management seeks to achieve competitive advantage by way of working most effectively with choice suppliers. This might mean engaging suppliers early in the development of new products and services, or soliciting ideas for new products and services from suppliers. Strategic supply management means engaging in continuous improvement of processes with suppliers, lending resources to one another to problem solve, reduce waste, and make it better and easier to do business. It may also mean forming strategic alliances with select suppliers and, on occasion, forming joint-venture activities or cobranding products.

This brings us to modern times, where supply management controls not only a considerable share of the company's budget, but influences the very competitiveness of the company through its connection with other business strategies and departments. One industry phenomenon that has accelerated the influence of supply management is the rampant adoption of outsourcing over the past three decades. As we've seen, companies are electing to outsource activities that they no longer view as strengths of the company, choosing instead to focus on a limited number of core competencies. As companies decide to buy services through outsourcing provisions rather than make or perform activities themselves, the role of supply management expands. Supply management usually assumes responsibility for selecting the outside suppliers, negotiating the arrangement, and monitoring the provision of services.

The decision to make or buy, which we've explored previously, involves a series of complicated questions that have become vital for supply management personnel. As you'll recall, however, the ultimate question focuses on control. If we sense that there's much to be gained or much at risk with particular business activities, then control seems essential and companies will usually elect to internalize these activities and responsibilities. Where control is less essential, we entertain outsourcing. Business process outsourcing continues to be adopted at unprecedented rates, whether it's production, information technology, customer service, logistics, legal services, or other functions.

Once it's determined what the company will buy, the supply management organization can take shape. Critical to forming the organization is understanding the scope of the work required. If the company operates from multiple locations, how much responsibility will rest with a central purchasing organization and how much will rest with each location? Organizations opting for centralized control decide what to buy, select the suppliers, and initiate the orders, all from headquarters. Field personnel will verify that the quality and quantity of supplies meets expectations, but will make no strategic decisions.

The benefits of such a system include the consolidation of the spend, ensuring that the company achieves volume discounts from suppliers and high-priority service by virtue of putting large chunks of the business in the hands of fewer suppliers. Centralized control can also support greater standardization of supply across the various field locations. Imagine, for instance, if every McDonald's restaurant could order supplies from any vendors the location chose. Would the experience for the customer be uniform from location to location? In pursuit of that uniform experience, McDonald's corporate office tightly controls the supply arrangements for the store locations.

The disadvantage of such a system, though, is that it doesn't allow the field operations to exert their influence on suppliers, or to address any of their specific needs. When operations differ considerably across locations, it can be difficult for the central organization to understand the diverse needs of the field operations. Decentralized control allows the field locations to act autonomously, to freely choose suppliers and to negotiate directly with them. While the individual needs of the locations can be addressed in these arrangements, the volume of spend may not be sufficiently large for suppliers to warrant the most competitive price or highest priority service.

Most good-sized companies pursue a blended strategy, which involves headquarters centralizing the planning of supply and the field locations controlling the buying actions. Central planning includes the selection of suppliers and negotiations on volumes, quality, and pricing. Such arrangements try to achieve balance between the control of centralization and the flexibility of decentralization, though strategic decisions are left with headquarters.

With the organization in place, companies then set forward a strategy for engaging suppliers. The strategy will be based in large part on what's purchased. Most companies must acquire what I call mission critical supplies. These are the items that influence the quality of the products and services your company provides. These items may also be visible to customers. The counter to these visible and mission-critical items are the invisible, commodity items. Whereas you might emphasize quality with the mission critical stuff, price might be the highest priority with the commodity items. Also, the amount of time you spend worrying about supplier relationships will largely depend on how critical the supplies are to your products and services. A supplier of maintenance, repair, and operating supplies that don't go directly into your product won't warrant extensive preparation and negotiation, compared to a supplier that can help you win or cause you to lose in the marketplace. Given the complexities associated with working the suppliers of mission critical inputs, let's focus on these dealings.

You might ask: How many suppliers of a given input are ideal? There are competing theories weighing in on this question. Some believe that fewer suppliers is better, even going so far as to recommend sole sourcing; having one supplier responsible for a given item. The benefit of sole sourcing is that you concentrate the spend in one place, which should elevate the volume discount. It's also easier to manage one supplier than several. Through a close working relationship, sole sourcing might foster a high level of collaboration between a company and its supplier.

The dependency inherent in sole sourcing arrangements drives many supply professionals away from them, however. By virtue of placing all of one's business for a given input in the hands of a single supplier, you may be cutting out the positive influences on competition for price and quality. In other words, the supplier could act opportunistically, taking advantage of the dependent arrangement to raise prices and not offer the priority you might be justified in enjoying. Quite simply, you could be held captive to the supplier.

This isn't an enviable position to be in, and you may not even have a choice in the matter: There may be only one supplier for a given input, forcing you to go with a sole source arrangement. When that's the case, companies sometimes revisit the make versus buy decision and consider creating what they were going to purchase instead. This can require a lot of capital and can distract you from your primary business. A company would have to feel very vulnerable and disadvantaged to insource something that had previously been outsourced, but it happens. Boeing resorted to this strategy to support production of the 787 Dreamliner aircraft. When the closely watched launch of the project fell behind schedule, Boeing acquired major airframe and parts suppliers to ensure that the job got done.

A well-heeled business might also buy its supplier and take control of the supply of input in order to limit access to competitors or to make its competitors dependent on it for that input. Amazon.com acquired a company called Kiva Systems in 2012. Kiva is a market-leading developer of material handling equipment—things like high-speed conveyer systems and robotic devices—used in the storing and sorting of products in high-volume distribution centers. Through the acquisition, Amazon acquired an in-house provider of technology that's dedicated to supporting the company's aggressive growth plans. It also took a venerable supplier away from its competitors. The acquisition carried a price tag of $775 million, but many analysts believe that it was a smart move in light of what it does for Amazon and how it impacts the competition.

Another school of thought on the number of suppliers to work with is to hire many suppliers and to incite a feeding frenzy mentality among them. The belief is that by not allowing the company to be dependent on any one or few suppliers, competition will intensify and suppliers will cut prices to the bone to get the company's business. This is usually a short-term proposition, however, as suppliers usually look for large chunks of business that are repetitive, allowing them to smooth their own operations and reduce transaction costs.

In fact, the feeding frenzy usually consists of a group of desperate suppliers vying for the business and fails to induce the stronger players to compete, since the stronger players are able to more freely pick and choose among the business opportunities. Further, you're less likely to pursue continuous improvement with suppliers under the bargain shopping arrangement since suppliers aren't plugged into your business. They never get a chance to really know your business, and the cost of managing a diverse array of suppliers can be taxing.

Here, too, we tend to see a middle ground strategy that's usually preferred. Most progressive companies will avoid sole sourcing , and yet they're not constantly on the prowl for new suppliers. Rather, they look at the portfolio of items and services they buy. They look for opportunities for consolidating the spend, which will provide leverage in negotiations. They look for opportunities for collaboration with suppliers of critical parts and try not to only get the best price for these inputs, but to win over the interest of these suppliers.

Where over-dependencies present vulnerability, companies will seek some redundancy; additional suppliers that can reduce the dependency and incite a level of honesty and competition in the business. Many companies elect to dual- or tri-source the supply of critical items to provide an element of competition, while still providing each supplier a sufficient piece of the action to bring forward the best of what they have to offer. The allocation won't always be, say, a 50-50 split between the two vendors of an item and instead might float from year to year to reward a supplier for exemplary performance or to incite competition.

With the right number of suppliers determined, how do companies go about selecting their suppliers? Again, I'll focus on the supply of critical parts here, as the procurement of commodity items is largely based on availability and price. The selection of suppliers for critical inputs is more involved, as you can imagine. It's become common for large supply management organizations to spend a preponderance of their time qualifying suppliers. Supplier qualification is the practice of establishing standards for doing business with the company. In light of the vast interest in serving large companies, corporations employ qualification as a way to filter the interest, requiring prospective suppliers to meet standards established in areas of quality, capacity, safety, and ethical performance. It's the way that supply managers demonstrate to their higher-ups that they've done their homework on selecting suppliers.

Once the qualifications for competing for business are in place, you can finally approach the supply market. But how do you go about this? Do you pick up the phone and start calling suppliers, or do you post your business to an industry bulletin board and wait to field calls? Your approach will depend both on your situation and, again, what you're buying.

If you're a seasoned buyer of an item, then you'll likely know who to contact; who has the capabilities, capacity, and pricing to be competitive. You might even set up something called a reverse auction, where you invite select players to compete in real time for the business, choosing the supplier that brings forward the lowest price. What makes a reverse auction reverse from a conventional auction? Two things: One, it's the buyer that initiates the sale as opposed to the seller, who'd do so in a conventional auction; and two, the lowest bid wins the auction, not the highest bid as you'd find with a seller-initiated auction. I equate reverse auctions to online dating: Don't be surprised if everything isn't as it appears once the goods are delivered. If you base a supply decision entirely on price, you may find that what you order falls short of your standards.

If simply putting your business out to bid and shopping for low price isn't the answer, then you'll likely have to take an intermediate step to see what prospective suppliers might have to offer. This is usually the case when buying something new. It also applies when you want to renew the competition for the business. In either case, you'll engage in a formal interviewing process; and here I'm talking about interviewing a company that, at the outset, typically happens on paper. There are three basic forms of such interviews: the request for information (known as an RFI); a request for quote (RFQ); and a request for proposal (RFP). I'll explain each briefly.

The RFI is where you solicit basic information from prospective vendors, trying to figure out who they are and what they have to offer. It's usually the precursor to a request for quotes or proposals. The request for quotes is where you spell out what you're looking for in a product or service and seek the vendors' best provision and price. Finally, the request for proposals is more open-ended. You present a problem to the prospective vendors and ask for solutions. As you can imagine, RFPs are the most complex responses to evaluate and judge, but can lead to breakthrough thinking when you're open to ideas.

When it's time to make supplier selections, most companies today are looking beyond the purchase price of the products and services they buy. Instead, they're considering what's known as the total cost of ownership, or TCO, associated with the purchase. This is a way of bringing a so-called lifecycle perspective into the procurement of goods and services. That term makes sense because TCO considers not only the purchase price, but all of the costs associated with acquisition, like the cost of financing the purchase and preparing the business to use the materials or products, incorporating the full lifecycle of the input over the course of its use. To that end, total cost of ownership also factors in the cost of use, including the cost of carrying inventory.

But it's in the determination of a product's post-use factors that the lifecycle perspective of TCO can really alter the landscape of the purchasing decision. In post-use, we might concern ourselves with the costs of dissatisfied customers. These customers might find defects in the goods or services attributed to the inputs that we purchased. There may be warranty costs associated with addressing these unhappy customers. The issue might escalate into a recall, which can be exorbitantly expensive for a company. If the item poses hazards of any kind, product liability might factor in.

Finally, companies are taking greater interest in and responsibility for the environmental impacts of products and packaging material in the post-use phase. Can the product be reused, remanufactured, or recycled? If the product doesn't contain reusable content and must be discarded, is there any special handling required? In sum, the lifecycle perspective espoused in Total Cost of Ownership revolutionizes the act of buying stuff. It's a 180-degee turn from traditional purchasing practice and requires much deeper thought than simply shopping for prices and specs ever did accommodate.

I'm going to skip over the negotiation and legal aspects of supply management, as those topics justify courses all to themselves. Rather, I'd like to offer some tips for keeping your suppliers engaged and working hard for you. The first tip relates to maintaining open communications with your suppliers, especially the ones that are most critical to your business. No one likes to be kept in the dark about how things are going, and the best suppliers are the ones that are ready to make adjustments when needed.

A bad scenario that I hear about from time to time involves suppliers losing business without having the opportunity to remedy a problem. In fact, they often don't even know there's a problem, or at least they're not aware of its severity in the eyes of the customer. The best way to keep this from happening is to talk, but even better meet on a regular basis. In what I call high-touch relationships, this involves meeting not only in public or at headquarter locations, but going to where the work is performed. See the products and services in action and talk about what you see. This can inspire great discussion and also illuminates opportunities for improvement.

At a minimum, you should provide regular feedback to all suppliers that are considered strategic for your business. A supplier scorecard might be issued monthly, for instance, to indicate performance on a wide array of performance dimensions and metrics. Be careful, though, not to overload the scorecard with too much data. It should serve as a mechanism for general evaluation, a conversation starter. Focus on the vital few measures that are most important to your business and explain in general how the supplier's doing. The basic dimensions of performance usually include quality, cost, and delivery. Other aspects, like invoice accuracy, responsiveness to problems, and ease of doing business can be added, too. Again, the purpose of a supplier scorecard is to provide a means of regular feedback and to point to improvement opportunities.

Progressive companies are turning the mirror around, though, and asking suppliers how satisfied they are with the focal firm as a customer. Did you follow that? Companies are asking their suppliers how satisfied they are in serving the companies, their customers. Assessing supplier satisfaction is a fairly new phenomenon. It can be critically important when companies are chasing the interests of a common group of suppliers and trying to gain stature as a preferred customer to the best suppliers. Such assessments usually examine the ease of doing business. Does the customer company throw surprises at the supplier? Does the supplier regard the customer company as fair in its dealings? Are the benefits achieved through collaboration divided in an equitable fashion? Such assessments are rarely conducted by the customer companies themselves, as there would be too much fear on the part of suppliers in openly complaining about their customers. Instead, these surveys are conducted on behalf of companies by independent consultants or academics. They may also be conducted on an industry-wide basis, providing a very rich database of benchmarks to use in future decision making.

Beyond merely evaluating suppliers, progressive companies also take the time to recognize excellence. It's not uncommon for customer companies to host annual banquets or quarterly gatherings where they assemble their suppliers for a celebration of past successes and offer a look toward the future. You may also have heard horror stories of these meetings turning into browbeating sessions or demands for pricing concessions, but I'd warn strongly against using public forums for this purpose. Who'd bother to show up the next year? No, use it as a time to engender camaraderie and bolster the team spirit that's essential to winning in today's competitive business environment.

What are the latest supply management practices that today's leading-edge companies are employing? They're moving toward what's known as supply chain competition. Companies no longer merely compete head to head, but also supply chain to supply chain, pitting their entire input to delivered output systems against those of their rivals. With that in mind, there's a race to win the hearts, minds, and attention of the best, most innovative companies, your suppliers. These are the suppliers that possess unique intellectual property, processing capabilities, and in some cases, branding to bolster your products and services.

Beyond merely gaining the attention of these suppliers, though, you want to enlist them to help you to compete. This can take the form of early supplier involvement, where suppliers help to devise the next generation of products and services. Early supplier involvement will marry up the technical personnel across the companies to devise a common picture for the future. It may also result in joint-venture opportunities or licensing arrangements when the market proves promising. At a minimum, the involvement of suppliers early in the new product development process can highlight the limitations or challenges that you'll run into should you elect to proceed with a bold new technology.

The PC industry is laden with intense collaborations between hardware manufacturers and software providers. For instance, how did Intel ever make it important to us consumers to have Intel inside our computers? They worked closely with PC manufacturers to devise leading technologies and worked out deals to have their logo placed on the outside of the hardware itself. That's pretty good for a supplier of what would otherwise be an invisible part of the computer. It then became important for the PC makers to show that an Intel processor chip was inside the machine, working its magic. Computers lacking the Intel logo, then, were at something of a disadvantage. This speaks to supply chain competition: two or more companies working together to set themselves apart in the market.

Clearly, if collaboration is to endure between companies, it's essential that both parties benefit from the collaboration, so it also becomes important to figure out how to divvy the financial and non-financial rewards that come from the relationship. I mention non-financial rewards here, for dollars, cents, and long-term contracts aren't the only way to compensate a supplier for a good idea. Being easier to do business with, providing access to markets, intelligence, or other resources can be very helpful to suppliers, not to mention devising case studies or facilitating introductions to other prospective customers. These can be some of the non-financial ways to reward a supplier. There's clearly room for creativity in figuring out how to engage and reward suppliers for bringing forward innovations in products and processes.

Of all the strategic supply management initiatives gaining adoption today, supply risk management is perhaps getting the most buzz. In fact, it's such a big and pressing topic that I'll devote an entire lecture to the subject of running an agile and resilient business at the end of this course. For now, suffice it to say that in a world where things are moving so fast and complexity's increasing, companies must make every effort to stay on top of the supply base in order to mitigate risk. This means understanding where any possible hiccup in supply operations can impede or possibly shut down your business. The situation in which no supply manager wants to find him or herself is explaining how and why a supplier problem prevented the company from serving its customers or why a supplier produced poor quality or violated ethical standards. These instances shed a negative light on the company by virtue of the business relationship that the supply manager oversaw.

As the complexity of business increases, companies are increasingly being held accountable for the social and environmental actions they take. The accountability isn't limited to the operations performed directly by a company, but also by those parties with which it does business in the supply chain. This has forced companies to shine a light into the dark corners of their supply chains to understand who's doing what throughout the full scope of operations from material extraction through assembly, distribution, and consumption. Sometimes companies are being held accountable for the post-use phase as well, as the lifecycle perspective of total cost ownership reminds us.

These are some of the things that keep supply managers up at night. They don't have easy jobs, but that's the price of working in an area that's become so important to business success.

The Long Reach of Logistics
Lecture 19

L ogistics is the business function responsible for ensuring that the right products are available in the right quantities at the right place and time to meet customer expectations. The field of logistics embraces the transportation and distribution of products, but it's something more: It's the overarching planning, timing, optimization, and coordination involved in getting products where they need to be, when they need to be there. In this lecture, we'll examine three key aspects of logistics: the role of logistics in providing the company's "reach" in the market through its chosen distribution strategy, the logistics network required to support the distribution strategy, and the operational aspects of logistics—the movement, storage, and technology used to meet customer requirements.

Distribution Strategies

- *Distribution* refers to the spreading of product throughout the marketplace so that a large number of people can buy it. It encompasses the warehousing, transportation, and tracking of goods into the marketplace, all of which requires strategy. We'll begin by considering three distribution strategies: intensive, exclusive, and selective.

The business of logistics is substantial: About $1.4 trillion is spent each year in the United States alone to support the storage and transportation of goods.

- Some businesses, such as Coca-Cola or General Mills, aspire to have their products in the hands of every customer in a region or market. This is called *intensive distribution*. In order for these companies to earn sizeable profits on their narrow margins, they must sell tremendous volumes of their products. In essence, they use intensive distribution to "blanket the market" with their products.

- At the opposite extreme from intensive distribution is *exclusive distribution*. This strategy involves getting products in the hands of a limited number of people but offering a "high-touch" or customized buying experience. This approach is often associated with high-priced luxury goods, such as jewelry, fashion merchandise, and sports cars. Manufacturers that use exclusive distribution tightly control production and distribution. They either distribute the goods themselves or align with a limited number of distributors and retailers.

- The third strategy, *selective distribution*, fits somewhere between the intensive and exclusive distribution approaches. Companies pursuing selective distribution have more customers than exclusive providers and fewer than intensive competitors. Distribution might be selective in terms of the number and types of customers reached or in terms of the locations served.

- Depending on the desired intensity of the market coverage, any one of these three alternatives might support a company's competitive basis—how it intends to "win" in the market. And many companies employ multiple distribution strategies, using different approaches for different brands under the company's umbrella.

Logistics Networks
- The term *logistics networks* refers to the locations from which a business operates and the functions or purposes of those locations. Every business must consider the network over which it wants to conduct business such that it: (1) reaches customers with its products and (2) can access key sources of product supply. It's here we realize that logistics is involved in both the inbound and outbound sides of the business.

- Finding the right number and placement of locations involves not just science but art.
    - The art comes in the sense of importance that is imparted to customers by establishing a store or warehouse location near them or by setting up a convenient catalog or website ordering system.

    - Yet it's impossible to be located close to all customers when they're scattered about a large geographic area. This is where companies rely on science to figure out how to achieve the greatest reach with the fewest facilities. The goal here is the optimal blend of market access and cost containment.

- The science of logistics has its origins in military science, and commercial enterprises have borrowed the idea of the *center of gravity* from military strategists.
    - In the military, the center of gravity of an enemy is its concentration of forces in a conflict; it represents a source of vulnerability.

    - In business, the center of gravity represents the best place to locate a distribution point given the inbound supply and outbound distribution locations. It's the optimal point at which the total distance that must be covered in from supply locations and out to demand locations is minimized. To serve large markets, most businesses elect to operate from several locations.

- Competition can also fuel the need to increase the number of distribution and store locations. When a rival establishes a presence in a market, it creates a need to match the competitor's strategic move. Restaurant chains and retailers routinely demonstrate this behavior.

- Of course, there are a few checks on the logic of adding more locations to a logistics network. For instance, more facilities means a higher warehouse and real estate investment, and a company can expect to invest more in inventory as it adds distribution points in its network.

○ It has been proven that a company will need more *safety stock* inventory when it adds locations to its network. Safety stock is the inventory held just in case there's an increase in demand or a delay in supply. This is opposed to *cycle stock*, which is inventory a company maintains to cover itself for forecasted sales and normal supply lead times. The greater the uncertainty a company faces, the more safety stock it requires.

○ The *square root rule* predicts that the amount of safety stock a company holds will double when the number of locations quadruples. In other words, if a retailer increases its store count from one location to four, the safety stock inventory held across the four stores will be twice as much as when the company had a single location. This expected increase in inventory discourages companies from adding too many facilities to their networks.

○ Transportation costs can also make adding too many distribution points unattractive. Adding locations means that a company also has to ship to those locations. Even though the company gets closer to customers on the outbound side of the business, inbound transportation costs can be prohibitive.

○ The final check on the logic of adding locations to better serve a market is *cannibalization*. When sales flatten and saturation is achieved in the market, any sales gain for one location is accomplished at a loss to another location. Obviously, when the gain comes at the expense of a competitor, that's good. But when it comes at the expense of a company's partner locations, there may be little or no benefit.

• Determining the "right" number of locations is something of a moving target for many companies because markets are dynamic and logistics networks are fairly permanent or, at least, costly to change. To help accommodate the need to expand and contract logistics networks, some businesses seek the help of third-party logistics providers (3PLs), which own warehouse and transportation assets to help their clients expand and contract as needed.

- In lieu of outsourcing, some companies work with distributors and wholesalers to achieve broader coverage in a larger market than they could attain on their own. This practice is known as using indirect channels of distribution.
    - The obvious disadvantage to such arrangements is that the company loses direct touch with the end customer, who now buys from the intermediary.

    - In addition, the intermediary is likely to also sell products offered by competitors. Consequently, the manufacturer must try to appeal not only to the end customers but also to the intermediaries in the hopes that they'll stock and actively sell the firm's products.

Operational Factors
- Once a company has its distribution strategy and logistics network in place, it must turn to the operational side of logistics: delivering to customers or store locations. Here, the focus is on the *order cycle*, or *lead time*, which is the amount of time from order receipt to delivery. Much of the execution in this stage of the logistics process rests with transportation, which represents what is often called the "last mile" segment of the order cycle: the physical delivery of goods on time and safely to customers.

- Choosing the right means of transporting goods can have major cost and service implications for a company. Naturally, speed and dependability usually come at a higher price. It may cost 70% more to ship a product the next day to a customer than to use two-day delivery. There are five basic modes of transportation, each with its own cost and service implications: truck, rail, air, water, and pipeline.
    - Truck transportation is the most common means used today, given that it is so readily available and is generally regarded as fast and reliable.

○ Air transportation tends to be preferred for time-critical deliveries that must cover long distances, such as urgent cross-country or international shipments. High-value goods, such as consumer electronics and pharmaceuticals, often move by plane, as do highly perishable items (e.g., fresh-cut flowers) or products with short market life-cycles (e.g., fashion apparel).

○ Transportation by railroad is popular for shipments that allow for longer transit times over longer distances, such as hauling grains from Iowa to New York or coal from West Virginia to Arizona.

○ Transportation by water, including rivers, great lakes, and oceans, is preferred for the transport of massive quantities of goods when time is not critical and navigable waterways connect the origin and destination points.

○ Finally, pipeline transportation is currently limited to commodities that are fluid in nature, such as oil and gas.

• Sometimes, the best transportation solution involves combining modes for shipment in what's known as *intermodal transportation*. Although most items will move by truck at some point in their distribution, this mode of transportation can be expensive, energy intensive, and environmentally unsound. For these reasons, rail may be used more often in the future.

• The future could also be marked by new modes of transportation, such as the unmanned aerial drones—small programmable helicopters—that Amazon is experimenting with for home deliveries from order fulfillment centers. Experiments are also in place to test underground pipelines for shipping nonliquid cargo and blimps for moving large cargo over oceans.

- Advanced technologies in information systems are also influencing logistics activities. These technologies include transportation and warehouse management systems, as well as communicative technologies, such as the Internet, GPS, and RFID, used to link companies, enhance information exchange, and improve visibility of supply and demand across companies. In sum, there is immense change altering the logistics landscape and the means by which companies achieve "reach" in the market.

Suggested Reading

Arvis, Saslavsky, Ojala, Shepherd, Busch, and Raj, *Connecting to Compete 2014*.

Goldsby, Iyengar, and Rao, *The Definitive Guide to Transportation*.

McGoldrick and Barton, "High-Tech Ways to Keep Cupboards Full."

Murphy and Knemeyer, *Contemporary Logistics*.

Questions to Consider

1. How does effective logistics management affect a company's ability to compete?

2. Is logistics becoming more or less important in today's marketplace? Why?

3. Can you think of an example where poor logistics execution ruined your day?

The Long Reach of Logistics
Lecture 19—Transcript

Have you ever gone shopping expressly to buy something that a store advertised, only to find that the item wasn't available when you showed up? How'd that make you feel? Probably frustrated that you bothered to make the trip only to come away empty-handed.

What would you guess is the percentage of time that items are out of stock? One percent of the time, five percent, more? In a grocery setting, the number can be as high as 20%. It doesn't seem that high, though, does it? Why is that? Because the grocery store's literally full of products, and we can usually check everything off our shopping list by making substitutions right there in the grocery aisle. The size you're looking for isn't on the shelf? Just buy a larger or smaller size. The flavor you're looking for isn't available? It's a good time to try a new flavor, don't you think? Your favorite brand is missing? Try a different brand.

But substitutions aren't always possible. Research shows that retailers lose about 4% of sales due to stockouts. That may not sound like much, but in an industry that operates on razor thin margins of 2–3%, that can make the difference between profit and loss. Stockouts became such a big problem at Walmart in 2013 that the company started tying executive compensation to in-stock performance at the store shelf.

The topic for this lecture is the discipline that, among other things, seeks to keep stockouts from happening: logistics. While we often talk about the logistics of a meeting or the logistics of a trip, the logistics we're exploring here's the business function responsible for ensuring that the right products are available in the right quantities and condition at the right place at the right time to meet customers' expectations. The field of logistics embraces the transportation and distribution of products, but it's something more: It's the overarching planning, timing, optimization, and coordination involved in getting products where they need to be, when they need to be there.

Wherever there's a physical separation between a source of supply and points of demand, it's the job of logistics to find a way to close the gap by delivering goods to customers in an effective and efficient manner. When logistics works well, it largely goes without notice, for we expect that the stuff we want will be available when and where we want it. But there's a lot of thought, even science, which goes into assuring that products reach customers.

The business of logistics is substantial. About $1.4 trillion is spent each year in the United States alone to support the storage and transportation of goods. That's about 8% of the nation's gross domestic product. Let me put it another way: Nearly a dime out of every dollar spent in the U.S. goes toward logistics activity.

In this lecture, we'll examine three key aspects of logistics. The first is logistics' role in providing the company's reach in the market through its chosen distribution strategy. From there, we'll discuss the logistics network required to support the distribution strategy. Finally, we'll look at the operational aspects of logistics: the movement, storage, and technology used to meet customer requirements.

First, let's look at distribution strategy. *Distribution* is the spreading of product throughout the marketplace so a large number of people can buy the product. It's how customers access our products. It encompasses the warehousing, transportation, and tracking of our goods into the marketplace, and this requires strategy. We'll consider three distinct distribution strategies for accessing the market: intensive, exclusive, and selective distribution.

Some businesses aspire to have their products in the hands of every customer in a region or market. This is called intensive distribution. Consumer goods companies like Coca-Cola, General Mills, and Unilever seek to have their products in every household. In order for these companies to earn sizeable profits on their narrow margins, they must sell tremendous volumes of their products, engaging in contentious battles for market share. General Mills sells about 180 million boxes each year of America's favorite breakfast cereal. Yep, Cheerios; Honey Nut Cheerios is actually the most popular flavor. In essence, companies like General Mills employ intensive distribution to blanket the market with their products.

At the opposite extreme to intensive distribution is exclusive distribution. Exclusive distribution involves getting products in the hands of a limited number of people, but offering a high-touch or customized buying experience for customers. This approach is often associated with high-priced luxury goods like jewelry, fashion merchandise, and sports cars. Manufacturers employing exclusive distribution tightly control production and distribution. They either distribute the goods themselves or align with a limited number of distributors and retailers who must often be licensed to carry their merchandise. Unsanctioned channels, or so-called black markets, sometimes manifest around these brands.

A third strategy, selective distribution, fits somewhere between the intensive and exclusive distribution approaches. Companies pursuing selective distribution have more customers than exclusive providers and fewer than intensive providers. Distribution might be selective in terms of the number and types of customers reached or in terms of the locations served. Depending on the desired intensity of the market coverage, any one of these three alternatives might support a company's competitive basis; how it intends to win in the marketplace. Many companies will employ multiple distribution strategies, using a different approach for different brands under the company's umbrella.

In the auto industry, many manufacturers possess multiple brands in their portfolio. General Motors has Chevrolet, Buick, Cadillac and GMC, as well as brands that they sell outside the U.S. market like Opel, Vauxhall, and others in Europe. Honda has its flagship brand and the Acura line. These companies employ intensive distribution for their mainstay brands and selective distribution for their premium brands. For instance, there are more than 1,400 Toyota dealerships in the U.S., but only 230 dealers for the company's Lexus brand. Small cities with a population of 30,000 or more are likely to have a Toyota dealership, yet it requires a city to have four to five times that population to have a Lexus dealership.

There's a strong correlation between the distribution strategy employed by a company and the number and placement of locations required to support that strategy. The second aspect of logistics we'll examine, the logistics network, involves the locations from which a business operates and the function or purpose of those locations. Every business must consider the network over which it wants to conduct business such that it, first, reaches customers with its products, and second, can access key sources of product supply. It's here that we realize that logistics is involved in both the inbound and outbound sides of the business.

Finding the right number and placement of locations involves not just science, but art. The art comes in the sense of importance that you impart to customers. If you establish a store or warehouse location near customers, what message does that convey to them? It conveys that they're important. If, on the other hand, you welcome customers to order from your catalogue or website and then tell them that they can expect delivery in a week, what does that convey to them? Yet, it's impossible to be located close to all customers when they're scattered about a large geographic area. Stores and warehouses are expensive. That's where you rely on science to figure out how you can achieve the best reach with the fewest facilities. You want the optimal blend of market access and cost containment.

The science of logistics is nothing new; in fact, it has its origins in military science, ensuring that warfighters are sufficiently armed, fed, and clothed for battle. That's been recognized for centuries as a key to winning military conflicts. In fact, historians argue that logistics factored significantly in the empire-building campaigns of every great leader, dating back to Thutmose III of Egypt, who invaded Lebanon by sea in the 15th century B.C. It's believed that logistical failures by British forces helped to secure American independence nearly 240 years ago. The same could be said of every battle since. Today, logisticians are among the first forces on the ground at the outset of any effective military campaign.

One term that military strategists use routinely is center of gravity. The center of gravity of an enemy is its concentration of forces in a conflict. It represents a source of vulnerability. If one can knock out a key enemy base or supply depot, then the opposing force is hamstrung and unable to support its warfighters on various fronts.

Commercial enterprises put logistical lessons from the battlefield to use in everyday business. In business, the center of gravity represents the best place to locate a distribution point, given the inbound supply and outbound distribution locations. It's the optimal point at which the total distance that must be covered in from supply locations and out to demand locations is minimized.

Let's look at an example to help illustrate the center of gravity concept. Imagine, for instance, that your company wants to serve customers throughout the United States on an intensive basis. You might elect to hold all of your inventory in a single location; say, Topeka, Kansas. This seems like a good choice, since Topeka is a geographically central location for your market. But what if 80% of your sales come from the Eastern United States? That would pull your center of gravity toward the east. A location like Columbus, Ohio might make more sense, assuming that you can supply the distribution location efficiently. This helps to explain why my hometown, Columbus, Ohio, is known as a distribution city. It serves as a center of gravity in the logistics networks of many companies.

Customers located close to Columbus are pretty happy about this, for their orders get filled and delivered quickly. However, customers in Seattle, Washington might not be, because it takes longer for deliveries to reach that more distant location. The most direct driving route from Columbus to Seattle is just over 2,400 miles; that's about 35 hours of driving time. For this reason, most businesses elect to operate from several disparate locations to serve a large market like the United States, and the number of locations to operate tends to grow as the business grows.

Competition can also fuel the need to increase the number of distribution and store locations. When a rival establishes a presence in a market, it creates a need to match the competitor's strategic move with one of your own. Restaurant chains and retailers routinely demonstrate this behavior. Have you ever noticed that when a Target store opens in a locality, Walmart is soon to follow, or vice versa?

But there are a few checks on the logic of adding more locations to a logistics network. Of course, more facilities means a higher warehouse and real estate investment, but you can also expect to invest more in inventory as you add distribution points to your network. Why is that? It's been proven that a company will need more safety stock inventory when it adds locations to its network. Safety stock is the inventory that a company holds just in case there's an increase in demand or a delay in supply. This is opposed to the inventory called cycle stock that a company maintains to cover itself for forecasted sales and normal supply lead times. The greater the uncertainty a company faces, the more safety stock that's required.

Mathematicians have devised something called the square root rule, which predicts that the amount of safety stock that a company holds will double when the number of locations quadruples. In other words, if a retailer increases its store count from one location to four, the safety stock inventory held across the four locations will be twice as much as when the company had a single location. The expected increase in inventory will discourage a company from adding too many facilities to its network.

Transportation costs can also make adding too many distribution points unattractive. When you add locations, you have to keep in mind that you have to ship to these locations. Even though you're getting closer to customers on the outbound side of the business, it's on the inbound side to these locations that transportation costs can consume you.

The final check on the logic of adding locations to better serve a market is that of cannibalization. When sales flatten and saturation is achieved in the market, any sales gain for one location is accomplished at a loss to another location. When the gain comes at the expense of a competitor, that's good, marking an advance in market share. When the gain comes from the retailer's own partner stores, though, there may be little or no benefit at all. Have you ever driven down a street only to pass a steady stream of McDonald's restaurants, seemingly on every block? The same might be said of Subway or Starbucks. These companies seek intensive coverage of the markets they serve, especially in densely populated areas. McDonald's operates about 14,000 stores throughout the U.S. This means that the average U.S. consumer is never more than 20 miles from a McDonald's restaurant. Subway boasts 26,000 U.S. stores, making them nearly omnipresent around the United States. When the restaurants are clustered closely together, like in most metropolitan areas, the competition can be intense, with individual stores fighting for business. Cannibalization occurs when the consumer buys from one Subway store instead of another.

Determining the right number of locations is something of a moving target for many companies because markets are dynamic and logistics networks are fairly permanent, or at least very costly to change. That's why companies often progress on a growth path, adding facilities along the way, only to stop at some point and realize that they've become oversaturated in coverage. They then remove a large number of facilities, but soon start to grow again. It's like a pendulum swinging.

To help accommodate companies' need to expand and contract their networks, some businesses seek the help of third-party logistics services. Third-party logistics providers, or 3PLs as they're known, own the warehouse and transportation assets to help their clients expand and contract as needed. Outsourcing, as you'll recall, involves hiring an outside company to perform one or more activities on your behalf. Companies of all kinds rely on 3PLs today to provide dynamic network solutions. Internet retailers who lack conventional brick-and-mortar stores often outsource the entirety of their distribution needs to capable third-party logistics companies. For these reasons, the U.S. third-party logistics industry totaled $146 billion in 2013. The global market for these services was estimated at nearly $800 billion. Both the U.S. and global markets continue to grow.

In lieu of outsourcing, some companies work with distributors and wholesalers to achieve broader coverage to a larger market than they could attain on their own. When manufacturers rely on intermediaries like distributors and wholesalers, we say they're using indirect channels of distribution. The obvious disadvantage to such arrangements is that you lose direct touch with the end-customer, who now buys from the intermediary. Some of the intensity that you're seeking with intensive distribution is lost here. Also, the intermediary is likely to sell products offered by your competitors, too. Consequently, you must now try to appeal not only to the end customers in the market but also the intermediaries, in hopes that they'll stock and actively sell your products.

Exclusive distribution—and to a lesser extent, selective distribution—tends to work through fewer intermediaries. It employs direct channels, selling direct to the end customers as a way to ensure high-touch service and build customer affinity for the brand and its products.

Once a company has its distribution and logistics network in place, it needs to focus on the operational side of logistics: delivering to customers or store locations where customers will obtain its products. Here, we focus on what's known as the order cycle or lead time, which is the amount of time from order receipt until delivery. The faster and more reliable our lead time, the happier customers will be. Research has shown that better availability and lead time reductions are important ways to gain business.

Actor-writer Woody Allen once quipped that "Eighty percent of success is showing up." Logisticians would largely agree with that assertion. But showing up promptly can be just as important.

Procter & Gamble, the world's largest consumer goods company, is well aware of this reality. P&G has long managed its business on the basis of successfully meeting what it calls the "Two Moments of Truth." The first moment of truth is associated with ensuring that the P&G product is available when and where the consumer wants to buy it. The second moment of truth, then, is when the product performs as the consumer expects. What P&G realized is that the second moment of truth doesn't happen with failure in the first moment. You can't enjoy the benefits of fresh breath and white teeth if the Crest toothpaste isn't on the store shelf. The company took this idea so seriously that it created a senior position it called Director of First Moment of Truth to help ensure that it received its due attention.

It takes great planning and execution to deliver on that first moment of truth. Much of the execution in this stage of the logistics rests with transportation. Transportation represents what we often call the last mile segment of the order cycle: the physical delivery of goods on time and safely to customers. Transportation also represents the biggest share of logistics cost for most companies. Of the $1.4 trillion spent for all logistics activity in the United States in 2013, transportation accounted for $852 billion of this sum, or 62% of logistics cost. Transportation alone accounts for just over 5% of U.S. Gross Domestic Product. Choosing the right means of transporting goods can have major cost and service implications for a company. Naturally, speed and dependability usually come at a higher price. It may cost 70% more to ship a product next day to a customer than to use two-day delivery.

There are five basic modes of transportation, each with its own cost and service implications. You no doubt are of them, but you may have never given them much thought. Companies can move product by air, truck, rail, water, or pipeline.

Let's start with truck transportation. It's the most common means today, given that it's so readily available and is generally regarded as fast and reliable. Most products will move by truck at some point in their distribution. Air transportation tends to be preferred with time-critical deliveries that must cover long distances, like urgent cross-country or international shipments. High value goods like consumer electronics and pharmaceuticals often move by plane. Items thought to be highly perishable, like fresh-cut flowers, or products with short market lifecycles, like the latest fashion apparel, often move by plane, too. Transportation by railroad is popular for shipments that allow for longer transit times over longer distances, like hauling grains from Iowa to New York or coal from West Virginia to Arizona. Transportation by water—including rivers, Great Lakes, and oceans—is preferred for the transport of massive quantities of goods when time is not so important and navigable waterways connect the origin and destination points. Finally, pipeline transportation is currently limited to commodities that are fluid in nature, like oil and gas. Big energy companies often rely on pipelines to transport immense volumes of oil and natural gas.

Sometimes, the best transportation solution involves combining the modes for a shipment. This is called intermodal transportation. Consider the path for a container full of toys going from Hong Kong to Dallas, Texas. The container might move by truck from the Chinese factory to the port in Hong Kong. It might then travel on a huge ship, along with thousands of other containers, to Los Angeles. From LA, the container would move by train to Dallas, and then finally by truck to the customer location on the north side of the city. This whole sequence might take three weeks compared to an overnight flight by plane, but the cost of shipping by plane is almost 20 times greater than by ship, making the intermodal option attractive despite the big difference in transit time.

The five modes of transportation offer different levels of service in terms of speed, reliability, and capacity. While most items will move by truck at some point in their distribution, moving things by truck can be expensive, energy intensive, and generate too much greenhouse gas emissions. Transportation, in total, consumes 13 million barrels of oil each day in the U.S., and tops all other commercial activities in terms of greenhouse gas emissions. This strikes many as an unsustainable solution.

For these reasons, I expect that we'll use railroads to move freight and people much more in the years ahead. Rail is a much more fuel efficient and lower emission form of transport, but it also would help to take a lot of trucks off the roadways. I don't know about you, but I get a little nervous sharing the roads with all those trucks. Trucking companies are also having a hard time finding enough drivers to operate those trucks, and this is leading to an unprecedented level of cooperation between trucking companies and railroads, in which trucking companies have started selling intermodal services for truck-rail-truck combinations. Trucks provide the local pickup and delivery services, while railroads handle the long distance between the two localities, the origin and the destination.

Iconic investor Warren Buffett made a major investment in the railroads in 2010 when his firm, Berkshire Hathaway, purchased the Burlington Northern Santa Fe Railroad. At $34 billion, it's Berkshire Hathaway's largest acquisition to date. Mr. Buffett is clearly very bullish on the future of the railroads, and I'd have to agree.

The future could also be marked by modes of transportation that we've never seen before, like the use of aerial drones for short-distance home deliveries. Amazon made headlines in 2014 by announcing that the company is experimenting with unmanned aerial drones, small programmable helicopters, for making home deliveries from nearby order fulfillment centers. Other companies like FedEx have since announced their intentions to use drones, too. The Federal Aviation Administration will have to clear the way, though, as regulations currently oppose the use of drones for commercial purposes, despite their common usage for military and recreational purposes.

Experiments are also in place to test other new modes of transportation, like underground pipelines for shipping non-liquid cargo, or using lighter-than-air vehicles—blimps—for moving really big cargo.

Advanced technologies in information systems are also influencing how we fulfill logistics activity. Technologies like transportation management systems and warehouse management systems are helping companies manage the complexities of these operations and make smarter decisions. I recently toured a large automated distribution center operated by giant retailer Target, where a warehouse management system directed robotic equipment on which items to pick, pack, and ship to Target's store locations, designing each load for optimal storage efficiency in the store. The system actually knew where each item belonged in each of the 280 stores that the distribution center served, and it did everything with item-level shipping accuracy greater than 99.8%. That's pretty hard for us humans to pull off without the aid of automation.

Communicative technologies, like the Internet, GPS, and radio frequency identification link companies, enhance information exchange, and improve visibility of supply and demand across companies. Improved visibility is yielding innovations in how companies work together. One such advent is the development of vendor-managed inventory, or VMI. As its name implies, VMI is where a vendor or supplier of a product assumes responsibility for managing inventory that resides at a buyer's location. Under these arrangements, the vendor is held accountable for any stockouts the buyer experiences.

Some companies have gone a step further than VMI, with vendor-owned-and-managed inventory, or VOMI. Here, the vendor not only manages the inventory residing at a customer location, but retains ownership of it until the product's sold. This sounds like consignment, doesn't it? Consignment often carries a negative connotation, so it goes by other terms like VOMI or scan-based trading. But whenever possible, I recommend that small business owners seek these arrangements with their vendors, as they free up cash for the business yet allow for a wider assortment of goods to be available. These kinds of terms can often be established with vendors who are looking to gain a foothold in a market. Be on the lookout for these opportunities.

Radio frequency identification, or RFID, which has become important in inventory management, offers a new level of inventory visibility at the individual item level on the shelf. It can be programmed to help companies like P&G ensure that the first moment of truth is fulfilled by actively pinging store managers when a product is down to its last few units on the shelf. This can prevent stockouts that often occur because of failures to replenish store shelves.

In sum, there's immense change altering the logistics landscape and the means by which companies are achieving reach in the market. Some products no longer even need to move by physical means. This lecture, for instance, was once delivered exclusively on CD or DVD format. Today, I suspect that many of you are streaming it over the Internet. Media products that can be broken down into data bits move in a virtual sense today. With the advent of 3-D printing, which we've considered previously, physical products may move in a similar manner on a large scale soon.

Clearly, much has changed in logistics, but even greater change could still be upon us. I'm excited about how these technologies can transform the ways we live and do business.

Rethinking Your Business Processes
Lecture 20

Virtually everything we do involves a process, whether it's filing a legal brief, performing a surgical procedure, or making a product. But even though they go on all around us, we tend not to think deeply about processes or even notice them. In business, however, finding ways to improve processes has become indispensable to success. Companies use *process thinking* to determine what work really needs to get done and how to get the most of their available time and resources. This perspective focuses company efforts on the outcomes that create *defensible value*. In this lecture, we'll explore this concept and look at some simple tools for improving the processes that matter to your organization.

The Voice of the Customer and the Voice of Business

- It's often said that there are two voices we should listen to when making any business decision: the voice of the customer and the voice of the business. The voice of the customer tells us what customers are seeking in the way of product or service attributes and, more importantly, the outcomes they want to have fulfilled through the products and services they buy. Those outcomes, given a price the customers pay for them, render an assessment of value; therefore, *value* is defined as "quality given the price paid."

- Outcomes speak to the question: Does the product use or service experience satisfy—or better yet—delight the customer? To address outcomes, it's useful to take the time to listen to customers and understand their needs before engaging in a series of hit-and-miss "improvements" that might miss the mark!

- The voice-of-the-customer concept reminds us that the "right things" for a business to do should be in line with providing outcomes that customers want and are willing to pay for. This last piece—the "paying for"—brings in the voice of the business.

- This voice directs our attention to such needs as revenue, profitability, growth, image and stature, meaningful jobs for employees, and so on. In order for a business to survive and thrive, it must look after these needs.

- Thus, the "right things" for the business to pursue are those that generate value in the eyes of customers and generate the business outcomes the organization needs.

Process Mapping

- Once you've figured out what outcomes to pursue—the "right things"—the next logical question is how to do these things "right," that is, how to achieve efficiency and effectiveness in the work processes performed. The first step here is to understand the current state of your processes, starting with those that are in clear need of help.

- The next step is to make the chosen process visual by capturing it in a *process map*. You can make this diagram using software or draw it out on a large sheet of paper or poster board. It's helpful to get the various people involved in the process to help you devise the map. The example on the following page is a process map for taking a trip by commercial airline.
  - The experience of taking an airline flight is captured here in eight steps: (1) researching the ticket, (2) buying the ticket, (3) getting the boarding pass, (4) clearing security, (5) walking to the gate, (6) boarding the plane, (7) riding out the flight, and (8) and collecting luggage. Limiting the process map to between 8 and 12 steps is usually good enough for a first pass; you can always add more detail later if you find a trouble spot requiring deeper analysis.

  - Note that step 4, acquiring the boarding pass and checking luggage, involves another party, the airline ticket agent. The involvement of other actors or locations in the process is delineated in a *swim lane*, an additional line of actions that

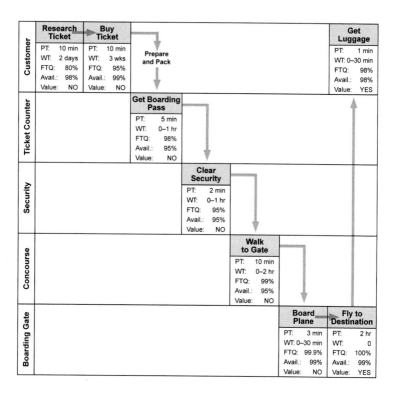

runs parallel to the main line. Each actor in the process has his or her own swim lane, as does each physical location. When the process moves from one actor to another, the transition is shown by drawing a line from one swim lane to another.

- The first pass at the process map does not mark the end of the review but, rather, the beginning. To the extent that others are involved in the process, you should confer with them to see if their version of the process jibes with yours and to discuss and resolve discrepancies. This discussion may reveal important misunderstandings or conflicts that stand in the way of process improvement.

Process Time, Wait Time, and Cycle Time

- Once agreement is reached on the first-pass map, it's a good time to reflect on the process as a whole, asking whether any steps or even the whole process could be eliminated. If you determine that the process remains essential, it's time to do a deeper analysis by populating the basic work steps with additional data, such as the amount of time required to complete each step (*process time*). You can also estimate the amount of time spent waiting within each step and between the various steps.

- In our air travel example, the sum of the process times across the eight steps is 161 minutes. Remember, this is the actual amount of time in which the actors in the process are engaged in work associated with booking the flight, reaching the plane, taking the flight, and collecting luggage. Of these 161 minutes, 120 are associated with the flight itself. The total wait time across the process is 23 days and 5 hours.

- The sum of the process and wait times is the *cycle time* for the process—the total time elapsed from process initiation to conclusion. In our example, the cycle time is 33,581 minutes. Note that the vast majority of cycle time is associated with the three-week period that elapsed between buying the ticket and taking the trip. Of the more than 33,000 minutes, only 161 involve actual work performed by the key actors in the process. This amounts to just under 0.5% of the total cycle time!

- The wait time for a flight might strike you as normal, but you might be surprised to learn that such a low level of time efficiency is common in both personal and business work processes. In fact, it's rare to find a measure of time efficiency greater than 10%. This speaks to the considerable slack time found in most processes. A process map helps to illuminate such wasted time.

First-Time Quality and Resource Availability

- Two other important factors to consider when analyzing processes are first-time quality (FTQ) and resource availability. *FTQ* refers to the percentage of time that a given work step is completed successfully on the first try. *Resource availability* refers to the percentage of time that the various resources required to perform a work step are available.

- The FTQ and availability levels for the whole process are calculated by multiplying together all the percentages for each factor.
  - In our scenario, the FTQ for the process is 68.6%. In other words, about 70% of the time everything about the flight process goes according to plan. The other 30% of the time, something goes wrong somewhere in the process.

  - Multiplying the availability percentages across the eight steps yields a total availability for the process of 79.9%.

- With the calculated totals for FTQ and availability in hand, look for the culprits that could affect these two outcomes to the greatest extent. In the case of FTQ in our scenario, researching the ticket (80% FTQ) is a major contributor to quality failure. Meanwhile, availability suffers somewhat at the ticket counter, the security checkpoint, and the departure gate—all locations where lines form and travelers must wait.

- Bear in mind that yields for FTQ and availability will only decline or, at best, sustain overall performance when more work steps are identified in a process. This is not only a mathematical reality of multiplying their values but also an operational reality. The more complicated a process becomes, the more opportunities for error, delay, and disruption are introduced. With that in mind, it's wise to try to simplify processes by reducing the number of steps involved. This, in fact, is a principle of Lean Thinking.

Labeling Work Steps

- To help in identifying which steps to eliminate from a process, Lean Thinking recommends assigning a subjective label to each work step. That subjective label is whether or not the step is a value-added one. In other words, does the step contribute defensible value to the process?

- If the elimination of a step would diminish the value of the process outcome in any way, it should be labeled "value added" and should remain intact in the process. In fact, you might explore ways in which you can add even more value through such a step. But if you can eliminate a step without interfering with the process, it should be labeled "non–value added."

- Note that some steps in the process may be non–value added but still necessary, such as observing laws and safety measures. These steps should be labeled "essential (or necessary) non–value added." Still, you should look for ways to reduce the time invested in these work steps.

- In our example, we might identify only two steps as value added: the air travel itself and collecting the luggage at the destination. In other words, travelers want to reach their destinations safely and find their suitcases on the baggage carousel; everything else in the process merely assists in making those outcomes possible.
  - These two value-added steps account for only 121 of the more than 33,000 minutes of the process; thus, the value-added time accounts for only 0.36% of the total cycle time. This low value is not out of the norm for such an analysis.

  - Unfortunately, the six non–value-added steps are essential to taking the trip, but ample opportunities for improved efficiency might still be found. For example, a traveler could use a smartphone to check in for the flight, streamlining the collection of the boarding pass. The point here is that all the steps in the process should be scrutinized for potential improvements.

- Adding the "value-added" and "non–value-added" labels converts the process map to a *value stream map*. This in-depth assessment of the current state of the process allows you to identify trouble spots or unnecessary steps in the process. You might also go a step further and create a *future state map* that adjusts the process to fit your vision. If the outcomes are commensurate with or exceed the value of the time, effort, and resources invested, then you can redefine how the work should be conducted in the future.

Suggested Reading

Dennis, *Lean Production Simplified.*

Garvin, "The Processes of Organization and Management."

Martichenko, *Everything I Know about Lean I Learned in First Grade.*

Rother and Shook, *Learning to See.*

Staats and Upton, "Lean Knowledge Work."

Questions to Consider

1. What is the value of visualizing a process by mapping it?

2. What should you take away from a process map that reveals that a process is performing at a throughput efficiency (ratio of value-added time to total cycle time) of less than 1%?

3. How should management address a situation where most of a person's work time is devoted to non–value-added work?

Rethinking Your Business Processes
Lecture 20—Transcript

Processes fill our lives. Virtually everything we do involves a process, whether it's making a product, filing a legal brief, performing a surgical procedure, completing a tax return, delivering a lecture, or digging a ditch. But even though they go on all around us, we tend not to notice processes or really think deeply about them very often. Hopefully, after this lecture you will, because finding ways to improve processes has become indispensable to business success. I'm going to provide you with some simple tools and methods for figuring out how to improve the processes that matter to your organization.

Every process can be improved. This is a principal belief of the world's highest performing and most admired organizations. Companies like Apple, Google, Amazon, and Toyota are always pressing for better products, services, and ways to bring more value to market. By constantly challenging themselves, they believe that they can stay ahead of competitors who are less inclined to adapt and change. In this way, they have an intrinsic motivation that supersedes anything that the competition might throw at them as they relentlessly pursue improvement.

At Toyota, every team member is not only encouraged but expected to call out problems, or so-called defects, in the processes in which they participate. Imagine a work environment in which everyone is focused on doing things better and solving problems; an environment focused on adding value through work that truly matters. These are the organizations that frustrate the competition because they never stand still. Learning the basics of process thinking will enable you to bring that same kind of focus on improvement to your business.

What is process thinking? In a nutshell, it's a method for figuring out what work really needs to get done and how to get the most out of our time and resources. Process thinking embraces the mantra of "Doing the right things right." Let's break that down. Doing the right things means focusing your efforts on outcomes that create what I call defensible value. Defensible value means that you can rationalize the efforts involved in pursuing some desirable outcome; that the effort is worth it. You need to be able to defend its value in your eyes, the eyes of your organization, and the eyes of the customers you serve. This can often be achieved by simply talking out the work. By rising above the work to explain what we do and why, we often realize that we find ourselves consumed with activities that perhaps don't need to be performed, or at least not by us. Why? Because the work doesn't yield defensible value; we're not focusing on the right things.

The other half of the "Doing the right things right" mantra, "doing things right," refers to performing work in the most efficient manner possible. Once we figure out what needs to get done, we concern ourselves with "How?"

Let's start, though, by talking a little more about the right things. In business, we often speak of two voices that we should listen to when making any business decision. These are the voice of the customer and the voice of the business. The voice of the customer, as its name implies, means hearing what customers have to say; what they're seeking in the way of product or service attributes, but more importantly the outcomes that customers are looking to have fulfilled through the products and services they buy. Those outcomes, given a price the customers pay for them, render an assessment of value. Value is therefore defined as quality, given the price paid.

In keeping with our discussion so far, let's focus on outcomes rather than quality; for outcomes are really what customers want, not just something that looks and performs as expected. Does the product in use or the service experience satisfy, or better yet delight, the customer? Those are outcomes, and they apply equally to products or services. In order to address those outcomes, it certainly helps if we take the time to listen to customers and understand their needs before engaging in a series of hit and miss efforts that will result in frustration for the customer and for us. Let's try to get it right the first time.

The voice of the customer concept reminds us that the right things for us to do should be in line with providing outcomes that customers want and are willing to pay for. This last piece, the "willing to pay for," brings in the voice of the business. The voice of the business directs our attention to the needs of the business; the needs for revenue, profitability, growth, image, stature, meaningful jobs for employees, all of that. In order for the business to survive and thrive, it must look after these needs. Suffice it to say that the right things for the business to pursue are those things that generate value in the eyes of customers and generate the business outcomes that your organization needs.

Once you've figured out what outcomes to pursue, the next logical question becomes how to do these things right; that is, how to achieve efficiency and effectiveness in the work processes performed. The first step is to understand the current state of your processes, or how work is currently performed. Only then can you seek to makes things better through what's called continuous improvement.

What process or processes should you consider first? I recommend starting with one that's in clear need of help. Is there a part of your life or business that's causing a lot of stress for you? Maybe customers are complaining, or your own colleagues are pressing you about something? Is this a stress that others feel, too? This might be a good place to start. Don't be discouraged by having to change the minds of others or by perceived resistance that you might encounter when talking about change or the need for improvement, for change is difficult for all of us.

What process thinking does better than any other method is help others to feel the pain that you experience in your work processes and to see the pain that customers experience in the process. How is this done? By making processes visual. Process thinking brings processes to life by capturing them in simple diagrams called process maps. A process map takes us through a process step by step. You can make one using PowerPoint or other software, but you don't have to. All you really need to get started are some Post-it notes, a large sheet of paper or poster board, and a good understanding of the work steps involved. It helps if you can get the various people involved in the process to help you devise the map.

Let's walk through an example. Any kind of process will do, so let's pick one that just about everyone's familiar with: taking a trip by commercial airline. I'd like to encourage you to think about this process and your own experiences as I describe my experience in eight distinct steps, which I'll lay out in the process map in a line from left to right.

Upon learning that I must take a trip by plane, I start by researching the ticket. This research usually involves going to the website of my preferred airline and checking the flight availability and prices. Occasionally, I search additional airlines, but most times I can find an acceptable set of flight options and prices at my preferred carrier. I'll bundle all of the research activities into one step here and put it at the beginning of the process map. There's no need at this point to complicate the map with all the intricacies of what researching flight options entails. I find that limiting the process map to between 8 and 12 steps is good enough for a first pass. We can always dive deeper and add more detail in a second pass if we find a trouble spot requiring deeper analysis.

OK, back to our map. Once I've completed my research on the flight options, I perform the next step of buying the ticket, so I'll add that to the map. If the first step doesn't happen, I can't move to the second step. Notice also that we're focused on the way the process is typically performed. There are always exceptions, and sometimes we want to focus on how we address these exceptions, but we usually stand to improve most by examining how we deal with normal circumstances. In this case, we transition from researching to buying the ticket.

The third step in the process doesn't happen until some time much later, usually weeks later when I'm ready to take my trip. In the meantime, I plan the trip activities and pack my bags, but the next action captured on our map occurs once I arrive at the airport. That's step four: the acquisition of the boarding pass and dropping off my luggage at the airline ticket counter. Here, we should indicate on the map that another party, the airline ticket agent, is involved in this step. The involvement of other actors or locations in the process is delineated in a swim lane; an additional line of actions that runs parallel to the main line. Each actor in the process has his or her own swim lane, as does each physical location. When the process moves from one actor to another, we show that transition by drawing a line from one swim lane to another.

A similar transition occurs in step five: clearing security, where we need to add another swim lane to illustrate the handoff in the process to another location and actor. In the next step, step six, I walk to the gate and submit my boarding pass. Finally, in step seven, I board the plane, take my seat, and ride out the flight until we reach the destination, at which point I disembark the plane and collect my luggage—that's step eight—to close out the process.

This first pass in the process map doesn't mark the end of the review, but rather the beginning. To the extent that others are involved in the process, you should confer with them to see if their version of the process jives with yours. Is the sequence correct? Are there any glaring omissions? Discrepancies should be discussed and mutually resolved. They may reveal important misunderstandings or conflicts that stand in the way of process improvement.

Once agreement is reached on the first-pass map, it's a good time to step back and reflect on the process drawn out before you. Ask yourself: Does anything seem unnecessary? In fact, is the whole process necessary at all? If you determine that the process remains essential, it's time to do a deeper analysis by populating the basic work steps with additional data, such as the amount of time it takes to complete each step. We call this the process time. We can also estimate the amount of time that's spent waiting within each step as well as between the various steps. These time data can be observed and measured on what's called a time-and-motion basis, with an independent observer, equipped with a stopwatch, monitoring repeated performance of the work steps to derive average values for the process and wait times. Or you can simply ask the people who do the work: "What's the typical amount of time it takes you to complete your work?" and "How much time do you spend waiting and not actually performing your work?" The people who do this work regularly are usually good judges of the time involved. Again, it's helpful if the actors in the process are involved in the process, too, since we'll be seeking their ideas for improvement and relying on them should we, after the process, change their work in some way.

In our air travel example, let's say that it takes me about 10 minutes to complete step one, the research of the various flight options. However, let's assume that I don't ordinarily buy the ticket right away, which is the second step; let's say I wait two days. That's just my personal preference: to shop first, then ponder the trip and not make any rash purchasing decisions. With some reflection and additional trip planning, I may elect to drive or travel by some other means, or I may elect not to take the trip at all. However, most times, I'll return to the airline website a few days later and complete the purchase of the ticket. The intervening two days represent wait time in the process.

Purchasing the ticket, step two, requires 10 minutes of process time. But then I wait three weeks before performing step three, which is the initiation of the trip itself. Why the long wait here? If you travel often by plane, you probably know the answer. The airlines usually charge very high prices for flights in the few weeks preceding travel. This is a simple method of profit maximization for the airlines. They charge higher prices to desperate last-minute travelers and garner the most revenue they can for the last remaining seats on the plane. As a result, I typically buy my airline tickets about three weeks ahead of the actual travel.

Once we've got time estimates for each step in the process, we can tally the times. The sum of the process times across our eight steps is 161 minutes. This is the actual amount of time in which I and my fellow process actors are engaged in work associated with booking the flight, reaching my plane, taking the flight, and collecting my luggage. 120 of these 161 minutes are associated with the flight itself. Likewise, we can tally the wait time across the process, which sums to a considerable 23 days, five hours. Adding the sum for the process times and the sum for the wait times together, we arrive at what is called the cycle time for the process. This is the total amount of time that elapses from initiation of the process until it's concluded. In our example, the cycle time is 23.32 days, or 33,581 minutes.

Note that the vast majority of cycle time is associated with the three-week wait that elapsed between buying the ticket and taking the trip. Of the more than 33,000 minutes, only 161 involve actual work performed by the key actors in the process. This amounts to just under one-half of 1% of the total cycle time. The wait time for a flight might strike you as normal, but what you might find surprising is that such a low level of time efficiency is very common in both personal and business work processes. In fact, it's rare to find a measure of time efficiency greater than 10%. This speaks to the considerable slack, or idle time, found in most processes. A process map helps to illuminate such slack or wasted time.

In addition to analyzing time data, it can also be worthwhile to assess two more important aspects of the process. These are the first-time quality and resource availability. First-time quality refers to the percentage of time that a given work step is completed successfully on the first try. In our example, I noted that the vast majority of the time, I'm successful in finding a flight option at an acceptable price, such that I elect to travel by plane instead of using another means of travel or simply not taking the trip. Through simple approximation, I estimate that my first-time quality (or FTQ for short) for researching flight options is about 80%. Then, about 95% of the time, I'm successful in actually buying the ticket that I sought to purchase. The other 5% of the time I lose out on flights that are already booked up or no longer affordable. This could be because of my two day delay in booking the flight while I ponder the options. Let's say I enter the first-time quality for the remaining six steps on a similar basis.

Resource availability refers to the percentage of time that the various resources required to perform a work step are available. I estimate that about 98% of the time, I have a working computer and Internet connection to conduct my ticket research. On the other end of the transaction, the computer server at the airline needs to be functioning so flight options are available for me to peruse and consider. Like with estimates of FTQ, approximate percentages are good enough. Where ready data exist on aspects of your process map, go ahead and use that data. But for most purposes, the on the spot insights of the key actors will suffice.

On a related note, where times and percentages vary greatly from instance to instance in a process, some people prefer to capture worst case scenarios, running with the longer times and lower percentages. This is a fine approach when your greatest concern is dealing with these worst case scenarios. But, more often, we concern ourselves with typical scenarios, and therefore it makes sense to use data that represent normal conditions in the process.

Just as we tabulated the summed process time, the summed wait time, and total cycle time for the process, we can now calculate the first-time quality and availability levels for the whole process. These values are calculated by multiplying all the first-time quality percentages by one another, and all the availability percentages by one another for the eight process steps. The FTQ, expressed as a percentage for each step in order, is 80, 95, 98, 95, 99, 99.9, 100, and 98.

Roughly, what do you think the final FTQ percentage will be for the whole process? If all eight steps were conducted at 100% precision, the FTQ would be 100%. But there was only one such activity in our example, getting me to my destination safely, which fortunately is a good one; that's the one that I want to have a very high percentage on. But for each activity that falls short of 100% quality, the total FTQ for the process will head south. Our first activity, researching the ticket, was rated at 80%, so right out of the gate our FTQ will come in no higher than 80%.

After multiplying all eight FTQ values together, we find that the first-time quality yield for the process is 68.6%. In other words, about 70% of the time, everything goes according to plan, from the researching of the airline ticket to taking the trip and collecting my luggage at the destination. The other 30 or so percent of the time, something goes wrong somewhere in the process. Does that sound about right for your travel experiences?

In a similar fashion, we multiply the availability percentages across the eight steps, with the steps estimated individually at 98, 99, 95, 95, 95, 99, 99, and 98%, all values in the mid- to high-90s but nothing at 100%. We expect availability of resources to ratchet downward a little with each step. When we multiply those eight values, we find that the total availability of the process is 79.9%. About 80% of the time, the actors and resources are available to do the work when the work is ready. When resource availability is less than 100%, there will be waiting in the process that can be attributed to lacking resources of some kind.

With the calculated totals for first-time quality and availability in hand, look for the biggest culprits that could affect these two outcomes. In the case of first-time quality in our scenario, researching the ticket is the major contributor to quality failure with that 80% value. Meanwhile, availability looks to suffer somewhat at the ticket counter, security checkpoint, and the departure gate, all locations for which lines form and waiting occurs.

Bear in mind that yields for first-time quality and availability will only decline, or at best sustain overall performance, when more work steps are identified in a process. This isn't only a mathematical reality of multiplying their values but also an operational reality. The more complicated a process becomes, the more opportunities for error, delay, and disruption are introduced. With that in mind, we should seek to simplify our processes by reducing the number of steps involved. This, in fact, is a principle of Lean thinking, the popular process improvement methodology I've discussed before.

To help in identifying which steps we can eliminate from a process, Lean thinking recommends that we take one more pass through our process map. This time we assign a subjective label to each work step. That subjective label is whether or not the step is a value added one; in other words, does the step contribute defensible value to the process? Would the elimination of that step diminish the value of the process outcome in any way? If so, we can label the step as value added, and it should remain intact in the process. In fact, we might explore ways in which we can add even more value through such a step. But if we can eliminate a step without interfering with the process, it should be labeled non-value added.

Some non-value added steps may be necessary in our process, however. Observing laws and safety measures might be regarded as non-value added in the eyes of customers, but we can all agree that they remain essential in our process. These steps are labeled as essential non-value added or necessary non-value added. Still, we should look for ways in which we might reduce the time invested in these work steps.

Returning to our example, let's assume that I, the customer of the air travel process, take a hardline approach to assessing the value in each work step. Of the eight steps, I label just two as value added: the air travel itself and collecting my luggage at the destination. What this says is that as the customer and primary actor of the process, I don't especially enjoy or find value in the other steps. If you find joy in shopping for air travel or in one of the procedural steps, then you might consider these as value added. But in my case, I simply want to reach my destination safely and find my bags on the baggage carousel. Everything else merely assists in making that outcome possible. The two value added steps account for only 121 of the more the

33,000 minutes of the process. The value added time accounts for a very small proportion of the total cycle time, just 0.36%. Again, this really low value isn't out of the norm for such an analysis.

Unfortunately, the six so-called non-value added steps are essential to taking the trip, so that I can travel in a safe and secure manner, abiding by established rules and regulations. That said, ample opportunities for improvement in efficiency can be found. For instance, I could compress the whole process by delaying the search and the purchase of the ticket, though I risk not finding a seat or paying a higher price at the last minute. Also, I could use my smartphone to check in for my flight, streamlining the collection of my boarding pass. I might also join a frequent flier program that provides privileges like expedited security clearance. And I suppose I could run to my gate rather than walking casually, gaining exercise along the way. The point is that we might scrutinize the process and not simply accept it as a fact of life.

This final pass of labeling work steps as value added or non-value added converts our process map into what's called a value stream map. This in-depth assessment of the current state of our process allows for the identification of trouble spots in the process: items that cause pain, take too much time, or simply aren't needed.

What would you like your process to look like in the future, assuming that you deem the process and its outcomes worth pursuing? To help yourself reach that goal, create a future-state map, adjusting the process to fit your vision. If the outcomes are commensurate with or exceed the value of the time, effort, and resources invested, then you can redefine how the work should be conducted in the future.

If the outcomes fall short of expectations, don't give up just yet. Determine if there's a way to enhance the value or reduce the inputs poured into the process. The cost-benefit ratio of an altered process might make the process attractive in the end. Keep in mind also that people often don't realize a good thing until it's gone, so be careful when deciding to discontinue a process altogether.

When improving a process, it's sometimes a good idea to devise two future state maps, one for the near term and another for the long term. A near-term future-state map embodies the improvements that can be made, say, within three months with existing resources. This map typically reflects an evolution of the current process, eliminating non-value added steps, reducing essential non-value added steps, and looking for ways to enhance the value added.

However, when greater change or revolution is sought in a process, then a longer-term future-state map is necessary. Revolution calling for dramatic changes in a process might require a change in skill sets, new technologies, or changes in business terms with outside parties, like customers and suppliers. These changes can't happen overnight, so save them for the long-term future-state.

Process thinking and the mapping procedure that I've described offer an effective way to bring together the actors in any process and to find better ways to do the right things right. Don't allow your processes to operate invisibly. Shine a light on them; challenge them. Figure out what work really needs to get done and how to do it best. Then perform that work with purpose and passion.

Bibliography

Strategy

Ager, David, and Michael Roberto. "Trader Joe's." Harvard Business School Case Study #714419, 2013.

Anderson, Chris. *Free: The Future of a Radical Price*. New York: Hyperion, 2009.

———. *The Long Tail: Why the Future of Business Is Selling Less of More*. New York: Hyperion, 2005.

Arbesman, Samuel. "Fortune 500 Turnover and Its Meaning." *Wired*, June 5, 2012. http://www.wired.com/2012/06/fortune-500-turnover-and-its-meaning.

Bossidy, Larry, and Ram Charan. *Execution: The Discipline of Getting Things Done*. New York: Crown Business, 2002.

Brandenburger, Adam, and Barry Nalebuff. *Co-opetition.* New York: Currency Doubleday, 1997.

Bruner, Robert. *Deals from Hell: M&A Lessons That Rise above the Ashes*. New York: Wiley, 2005.

Burgstone, Jon, and Bill Murphy, Jr. *Breakthrough Entrepreneurship: The Proven Framework for Building Brilliant New Ventures*. San Francisco: Farallon Publishing, 2012.

Christensen, Clayton. *The Innovator's Dilemma: When New Technologies Cause Great Firms to Fail*. Boston: Harvard Business Review Press, 1997.

Coase, Ronald. "The Nature of the Firm." *Economica* 4, 16 (November 1937): 386–405.

Collis, David, and Cynthia Montgomery. *Corporate Strategy: A Resource-Based Approach*. New York: McGraw-Hill, 2004.

Coughlan, Peter. "Leader's (Dis)Advantage." Harvard Business School Note #701084, 2001.

Coughlan, Peter, Debbie Freier, and Patrick Lee Kaiho. "Competitor Analysis: Anticipating Competitive Actions." Harvard Business School Note #701120, 2001.

Dixit, Avinash, and Barry Nalebuff. *The Art of Strategy: A Game Theorist's Guide to Success in Business and Life.* New York: W.W. Norton, 2008.

Ghemawat, Pankaj, and Fariborz Ghadar. "The Dubious Logic of Global Megamergers." *Harvard Business Review* 78, 4 (July-August 2000): 65–72.

Ghemawat, Pankaj, and Jose Luis Nueno. "Zara: Fast Fashion." Harvard Business School Case Study #703497, 2003.

Ghemawat, Pankaj, and Jan Rivkin. "Creating Competitive Advantage." Harvard Business School Note #798062, 1998.

Gupta, Anil, and Vijay Govindarajan. "Managing Global Expansion: A Conceptual Framework." *Business Horizons* 43, 2 (2000): 45–54.

Harrigan, Kathryn. *Vertical Integration, Outsourcing, and Corporate Strategy.* Washington, DC: Beard Books, 2003.

Hitt, Michael, Robert Hoskisson, and Duane Ireland. *Competing for Advantage.* Cincinnati, OH: ITP Southwestern, 2004.

Khanna, Tarun, and Krishna Palepu. *Winning in Emerging Markets: A Roadmap for Strategy and Execution.* Boston: Harvard Business Review Press, 2010.

Kim, W. Chan, and Renée Mauborgne. *Blue Ocean Strategy: How to Create Uncontested Market Space and Make Competition Irrelevant.* Boston: Harvard Business Review Press, 2005.

Lafley, A. G., and Roger Martin. *Playing to Win: How Strategy Really Works*. Boston: Harvard Business Review Press, 2013.

Lepore, Jill. "The Disruption Machine: What the Gospel of Innovation Gets Wrong." *The New Yorker*, June 23, 2014. http://www.newyorker.com/magazine/2014/06/23/the-disruption-machine?currentPage=all.

McGrath, Rita. *The End of Competitive Advantage: How to Keep Your Strategy Moving as Fast as Your Business*. Boston: Harvard Business Review Press, 2013.

Montgomery, Cynthia. *The Strategist: Be the Leader Your Business Needs*. New York: Harper Business. 2012.

Moon, Youngme. *Different: Escaping the Competitive Herd*. New York: Crown Business, 2010.

Porter, Michael E. *Competitive Advantage: Creating and Sustaining Superior Performance*. New York: Free Press. 1985.

———. *Competitive Strategy: Techniques for Analyzing Industries and Competitors*. New York: Free Press, 1980.

———. "What Is Strategy?" *Harvard Business Review* 74, 6 (November-December 1996): 61–78.

Ries, Eric. *The Lean Startup: How Today's Entrepreneurs Use Continuous Innovation to Create Radically Successful Businesses*. New York: Crown Business, 2011.

Rivkin, Jan W. "Dogfight over Europe: Ryanair (A)." Harvard Business School Case Study #700115, 2000.

Shankar, Venkatesh, and Gregory Carpenter. "Late Mover Strategy." In *Handbook of Marketing Strategy*. Edited by V. Shankar and G. Carpenter, pp. 362–375. Gloucestershire, UK: Edward Elgar Publishing Ltd., 2012.

Shapiro, Carl, and Hal Varian. *Information Rules: A Strategic Guide to the Network Economy.* Boston: Harvard Business Review Press, 1998.

Stewart, G. Bennett. *The Quest for Value.* New York: Harper Collins, 1999.

Suarez, Fernando, and Gianvito Lanzolla. "The Half-Truth of First Mover Advantage." *Harvard Business Review* 83, 4 (April 2005): 121–127.

Thaler, Richard. *Winner's Curse: Paradoxes and Anomalies of Economic Life.* New York: Free Press, 1991.

Williamson, Oliver. *Markets and Hierarchies: Analysis and Antitrust Implications, A Study in the Economics of Internal Organization.* New York: Free Press, 1975.

Wujec, Tom. "Build a Tower, Build a Team." TED Talk. February 2010. http://www.ted.com/talks/tom_wujec_build_a_tower?language=en.

Yoffie, David, and Mary Kwak. *Judo Strategy: Turning Your Competitors' Strength to Your Advantage.* Boston: Harvard Business Review Press, 2001.

Operations

Andraski, Joseph C., and Jack Haedicke. "CPFR: Time for the Breakthrough?" *Supply Chain Management Review* 7, no. 3 (2003): 54–60.

Arvis, Jean-François, Daniel Saslavsky, Lauri Ojala, Ben Shepherd, Christina Busch, and Anasuya Raj. *Connecting to Compete 2014: Trade Logistics in the Global Economy.* Washington, DC: The World Bank, 2014.

Box, George E. P., Gwilym M. Jenkins, and Gregory C. Reinsel. *Time Series Analysis: Forecasting and Control.* New York: John Wiley & Sons, 2013.

Browning, Tyson R., and Nada R. Sanders. "Can Innovation Be Lean?" *California Management Review* 54, no. 4 (Summer 2012): 5–19.

Callioni, Gianpaolo, Xavier de Montgros, Regine Slagmulder, Luk N. Van Wassenhove, and Linda Wright. "Inventory-Driven Costs." *Harvard Business Review* 83, no. 3 (2005): 135–141.

Cespedes, Frank V., James P. Dougherty, and Ben S. Skinner III. "How to Identify the Best Customers for Your Business." *MIT Sloan Management Review* 54, no. 2 (2013): 53–59.

Compdatasurveys. "Lean Practices Aid Manufacturers in Doing More with Less." August 7, 2012. http://www.compdatasurveys.com/2012/08/07/lean-practices-aid-manufacturers-in-doing-more-with-less/.

Cooper, Robin, and Robert S. Kaplan. "Measure Costs Right: Make the Right Decisions." *Harvard Business Review* 66, no. 5 (1988): 96–103.

———. "Profit Priorities from Activity-Based Costing." *Harvard Business Review* 69, no. 3 (1991): 130–135.

Davenport, Thomas H., Leandro D. Mule, and John Lucker. "Know What Your Customers Want before They Do." *Harvard Business Review* 89, no. 12 (2011): 84–92.

Dennis, Pascal. *Lean Production Simplified.* 2nd ed. New York: Productivity Press, 2007.

Dinges, Thomas. "What Will Drive Growth in Contract Manufacturing?" *EBN Online.* October 26, 2010. http://www.ebnonline.com/author.asp?section_id=1096&doc_id=199047.

Driscoll, Mary. "Why Companies Keep Getting Blind-Sided by Risk." *Harvard Business Review* (July 2013).

Elkington, John. *Cannibals with Forks: The Triple Bottom Line of Twenty-First Century Business.* Mankato, MN: Capstone, 1997.

Ellram, Lisa M., and Daniel Krause. "Robust Supplier Relationships: Key Lessons from the Economic Downturn." *Business Horizons* 57, no. 2 (2014): 203–213.

Ellram, Lisa M., and Sue Perrott Siferd. "Purchasing: The Cornerstone of the Total Cost of Ownership Concept." *Journal of Business Logistics* 14 (1993): 163.

Emerson, Richard M. "Power-Dependence Relations." *American Sociological Review* (1962): 31–41.

Epstein, Marc J., and Adriana Rejc Buhovac. *Making Sustainability Work: Best Practices in Managing and Measuring Corporate Social, Environmental, and Economic Impacts.* San Francisco: Berrett-Koehler Publishers, 2014.

Fisher, Marshall L. "What Is the Right Supply Chain for Your Product?" *Harvard Business Review* 75 (1997): 105–117.

Forrester, Jay W. "Industrial Dynamics: A Major Breakthrough for Decision Makers." *Harvard Business Review* 36, no. 4 (1958): 37–66.

Friedman, Thomas. *The World Is Flat: A Brief History of the Twenty-First Century.* New York: Farrar, Straus and Giroux, 2005.

Gardner, John T., and Martha C. Cooper. "Strategic Supply Chain Mapping Approaches." *Journal of Business Logistics* 24, no. 2 (2003): 37–64.

Garrison, Ray, Eric Noreen, and Peter Brewer. *Managerial Accounting.* 14th ed. Chicago: McGraw-Hill/Irwin, 2011.

Garvin, David A. "The Processes of Organization and Management." *MIT Sloan Management Review* 39 (2012).

General Electric. "Additive Manufacturing Is Reinventing the Way We Work." http://www.ge.com/stories/advanced-manufacturing.

George, Michael L., and Mike George. *Lean Six Sigma for Service*. New York: McGraw-Hill, 2003.

Goldsby, Thomas J., Deepak Iyengar, and Shashank Rao. *The Definitive Guide to Transportation: Principles, Strategies, and Decisions for the Effective Flow of Goods and Services*. New York: Pearson Education, 2014.

Gruen, Thomas, and Daniel Corsten. "Stock-Outs Cause Walkouts." *Harvard Business Review* 82, no. 5 (2004): 26–27.

Hoske, Mark T. "Use Total Cost to Justify Automation for Reshoring." *Plant Engineering*. February 19, 2014. http://www.plantengineering.com/single-article/use-total-cost-to-justify-automation-for-reshoring/50772139fd9a659707ee4ca39996fcdb.html.

Hsieh, Tony. "Zappos's CEO on Going to Extremes for Customers." *Harvard Business Review* 88, no. 7 (2010): 41–45.

Huston, Larry, and Nabil Sakkab. "Connect and Develop: Inside Procter & Gamble's New Model for Innovation." *Harvard Business Review* 84, no. 3 (2006): 58–66.

Kahn, Kenneth B. "Solving the Problems of New Product Forecasting." *Business Horizons* 57, no. 5 (2014): 607–615.

Kaplan, Robert, and Steven R. Anderson. *Time-Driven Activity-Based Costing: A Simpler and More Powerful Path to Higher Profits*. Boston: Harvard Business Review Press, 2013.

Kaplan, Robert S., and David P. Norton. *The Balanced Scorecard: Translating Strategy into Action*. Boston: Harvard Business Review Press, 1996.

Kaplan, Robert S., David P. Norton, and Bjarne Rugelsjoen. "Managing Alliances with the Balanced Scorecard." *Harvard Business Review* 88, no. 1–2 (2010): 114–120.

Kastalli, Ivanka Visnjic, Bart Van Looy, and Andy Neely. "Steering Manufacturing Firms towards Service Business Model Innovation." *California Management Review* 56, no. 1 (Fall 2013): 100–123.

Kazmer, David Owen. "Manufacturing Outsourcing, Onshoring, and Global Equilibrium." *Business Horizons* (2014).

Kiron, David, Nina Kruschwitz, Knut Haanaes, and Ingrid von Streng Velken. "Sustainability Nears a Tipping Point." *MIT Sloan Management Review* 53, no. 2 (2012): 69–74.

Lambert, Douglas M. *Supply Chain Management: Processes, Partnerships, Performance.* Sarasota, FL: Supply Chain Management Institute, 2012.

Lambert, Douglas M., and A. Michael Knemeyer. "We're in This Together." *Harvard Business Review* 82, no. 12 (2004): 114–124.

Lee, Hau L. "The Triple-A Supply Chain." *Harvard Business Review* 82, no. 10 (2004): 102–113.

Malone, Thomas W. *The Future of Work: How the New Order of Business Will Shape Your Organization, Your Management Style, and Your Life.* Cambridge, MA: Harvard Business School Press, 2004.

Martichenko, Robert. *Everything I Know about Lean I Learned in First Grade.* Cambridge, MA: Lean Enterprise Institute, 2008.

McGoldrick, Peter J., and Peter M. Barton. "High-Tech Ways to Keep Cupboards Full." *Harvard Business Review* 85, no. 3 (2007): 21–22.

Monczka, Robert, Robert Handfield, Larry Giunipero, and James Patterson. *Purchasing and Supply Chain Management.* Independence, KY: Cengage Learning, 2008.

Mukherjee, Amit S. *The Spider's Strategy: Creating Networks to Avert Crisis, Create Change, and Really Get Ahead.* New York: FT Press, 2008.

Murphy, P. L., and A. M. Knemeyer. *Contemporary Logistics*. 11th ed. Upper Saddle River, NJ: Prentice Hall, 2014.

Muzumdar, Maha, and John Fontanella. "The Secrets to S&OP Success." *Supply Chain Management Review* 10, no. 3 (2006): 34–41.

Parasuraman, A., Valarie A. Zeithaml, and Leonard L. Berry. "Servqual." *Journal of Retailing* 64, no. 1 (1988): 12–40.

Peloza, John, Moritz Loock, James Cerruti, and Michael Muyot. "Sustainability: How Stakeholder Perceptions Differ from Corporate Reality." *California Management Review* 55, no. 1 (Fall 2012): 74–97.

Porter, Michael E. *Competitive Advantage: Creating and Sustaining Superior Performance*. New York: Simon and Schuster, 2008.

Ramdas, K., E. Teisberg, and A. L. Tucker. "Four Ways to Reinvent Service Delivery." *Harvard Business Review* 90, no. 12 (2012): 99–106.

Rawson, Alex, Ewan Duncan, and Conor Jones. "The Truth about Customer Experience." *Harvard Business Review* 91, no. 9 (2013): 90–98.

Reeves, Martin, and Mike Deimler. "Adaptability: The New Competitive Advantage." *Harvard Business Review* (2011).

Reichheld, Fred. "The Microeconomics of Customer Relationships." *MIT Sloan Management Review* 47, no. 2 (2006): 73.

Rother, Mike, and John Shook. *Learning to See: Value-Stream Mapping to Create Value and Eliminate Muda*. Cambridge, MA: Lean Enterprise Institute, 2007.

Sáenz, María Jesús, and Elena Revilla. "Creating More Resilient Supply Chains." *MIT Sloan Management Review* 56, no. 3 (2014).

Bibliography

Schroeder, Roger G., Susan Meyer Goldstein, and M. Johnny Rungtusanatham. *Operations Management in the Supply Chain: Decisions and Cases*. New York: McGraw-Hill/Irwin, 2013.

Sheffi, Yossi, and James B. Rice Jr. "A Supply Chain View of the Resilient Enterprise." *MIT Sloan Management Review* 47, no. 1 (2005).

Shepard, Steven. *RFID: Radio Frequency Identification*. New York: McGraw-Hill Professional, 2005.

Shih, Willy C. "What It Takes to Reshore Manufacturing Successfully." *MIT Sloan Management Review* 56, no. 1 (2014): 55–62.

Simchi-Levi, David. *Operations Rules: Delivering Customer Value through Flexible Operations*. Cambridge, MA: MIT Press, 2010.

Simchi-Levi, D., A. Clayton, and B. Raven. "When One Size Does Not Fit All." *MIT Sloan Management Review* 54, no. 2 (2013): 15–17.

Simchi-Levi, David, James Paul Peruvankal, Narendra Mulani, Bill Read, and John Ferreira. "Is It Time to Rethink Your Manufacturing Strategy?" *MIT Sloan Management Review* 23, no. 2 (2012): 20–22.

Simchi-Levi, David, William Schmidt, and Yehua Wei. "From Superstorms to Factory Fires: Managing Unpredictable Supply-Chain Disruptions." *Harvard Business Review* 92, no. 1–2 (2014).

Smith, Larry, Joseph C. Andraski, and Stanley E. Fawcett. "Integrated Business Planning: A Roadmap to Linking S&OP and CPFR." *Journal of Business Forecasting* 29, no. 4 (2010).

Spear, Steven, and H. Kent Bowen. "Decoding the DNA of the Toyota Production System." *Harvard Business Review* 77 (1999): 96–108.

Staats, Bradley R., and David M. Upton. "Lean Knowledge Work." *Harvard Business Review* 89, no. 10 (2011): 100–110.

Stahl, Robert A., and Thomas F. Wallace. "S&OP Principles: The Foundation for Success." *Foresight: The International Journal of Applied Forecasting* 27 (2012): 29–34.

Tate, Wendy. *The Definitive Guide to Supply Management and Procurement: Principles and Strategies for Establishing Efficient, Effective, and Sustainable Supply Management Operations*. New York: Pearson Education, 2013.

Vargo, Stephen L., and Robert F. Lusch. "Evolving to a New Dominant Logic for Marketing." *Journal of Marketing* 68, no. 1 (2004): 1–17.

Wallace, Thomas F., and Robert A. Stahl. *Sales and Operations Planning: The "How-To" Handbook: How It Works; How To Implement It with Low Risk and Low Cost; How To Make It Better and Better*. Montgomery, OH: T. F. Wallace, 2010.

Waller, Matthew A., and Terry L. Esper. *The Definitive Guide to Inventory Management: Principles and Strategies for the Efficient Flow of Inventory across the Supply Chain*. New York: Pearson Education, 2014.

Wight, Oliver. "Transition from S&OP." http://www.oliverwight-eame.com/en-GB/integrated-business-planning/transition-from-sop.

Williamson, Oliver E. "Outsourcing: Transaction Cost Economics and Supply Chain Management." *Journal of Supply Chain Management* 44 (April 2008): 5–16.

Wilson, Rosalyn. *25th Annual State of Logistics Report: Ready for a New Route*. Lombard, IL: Council of Supply Chain Management Professionals, 2014.

Womack, James P., Daniel T. Jones, and Daniel Roos. *The Machine That Changed the World*. New York: Simon and Schuster, 2008.

Zeithaml, Valarie A., Anathanarayanan Parasuraman, and Leonard L. Berry. *Delivering Quality Service: Balancing Customer Perceptions and Expectations*. New York: Simon and Schuster, 1990.

Bibliography

Finance and Accounting

Alvarez, F., and M. Fridson. *Financial Statement Analysis.* 3rd ed. New York: John Wiley & Sons, 2002.

Beasley, Mark S., Joseph V. Carcello, Dana R. Hermanson, and Terry L. Neal. "Fraudulent Financial Reporting, 1998–2007: An Analysis of U.S. Public Companies." http://www.coso.org/documents/cosofraudstudy2010_001.pdf.

Berk, Jonathan, and Peter DeMarzo. "The Time Value of Money." In *Corporate Finance,* 2nd ed., chapter 4. New York: Pearson Education, 2011.

Brealey, Richard A., Stewart C. Myers, and Franklin Allen. *Principles of Corporate Finance.* 10th ed. New York: McGraw Hill/Irwin, 2011.

Cafferky, M., and J. Wentworth. *Breakeven Analysis: The Definitive Guide to Cost-Volume-Profit Analysis.* New York: Business Expert Press, 2010.

Collins, Daniel W., W. Bruce Johnson, L. Mittelstaedt, Lawrence Revsine, and Leonard C. Soffer. *Financial Reporting and Analysis.* 3rd ed. New York: McGraw Hill/Irwin, 2015.

Comiskey, Eugene E., and Charles W. Mulford. *The Financial Numbers Game: Detecting Creative Accounting Practices.* New York: John Wiley & Sons, 2002.

Damadoran, Aswath. *The Little Book of Valuation: How to Value a Company, Pick a Stock, and Profit.* Hoboken, NJ: John Wiley & Sons, 2011.

Easton, Peter D., Mary Lea McAnally, Gregory A. Sommers, and Xiao-Jun Zhang. *Financial Statement Analysis and Valuation.* 3rd ed. Chicago: Cambridge Business Publishing, 2013.

Eldenburg L., and S. Wolcott. *Cost Management: Measuring, Monitoring, and Motivating Performance.* 2nd ed. Hoboken, NJ: John Wiley & Sons, 2011. See particularly chapter 3: Wiley.com/college/sc/eldenburg/ch03.pdf.

English, James. *Applied Equity Analysis.* New York: McGraw-Hill, 2001.

Ittelson, Thomas R. *Financial Statements*. Rev. ed. New Jersey: Career Press, 2009.

Kieso, D., J. Weygandt, and T. Warfield. *Intermediate Accounting*. 15th ed. New York: John Wiley & Sons, 2013.

Mayo, Herbert, B. *Basic Finance: An Introduction to Financial Institutions, Investments, and Management*. 10th ed. New York: Cengage Learning, 2012.

Merrill Lynch. "How to Read a Financial Statement." http://ospflor63. stanford.edu/upload/handouts/Merrill_Lynch.pdf.

Modigliani, F., and M. Miller. "Corporate Income Taxes and the Cost of Capital: A Correction." *American Economic Review* 53 (3, 1963): 433–443.

———. "The Cost of Capital, Corporation Finance and the Theory of Investment." *American Economic Review* 48 (3, 1958): 261–297.

Mullins, David W. "Does the Capital Asset Pricing Model Work?" *Harvard Business Review*, January–February 1982: 105–113.

U.S. Securities and Exchange Commission. "Beginner's Guide to Financial Statements." http://www.sec.gov/investor/pubs/begfinstmtguide.htm.

Organizational Behavior

Bazerman, M., and M. H. Neile. *Negotiating Rationally*. New York: Free Press, 1991.

Blanchard, K. *Leading at a Higher Level: Blanchard on Leadership and Creating High Performing Organizations*. Upper Saddle River, NJ: Prentice Hall, 2007.

Blauner, A. *Coach*. New York: Warner Books, 2005.

Carnegie, D. *How to Win Friends and Influence People*. New York: Simon and Schuster, 1998.

Chandler, A. D. *Strategy and Structure*. Boston: Harvard Press, 1963.

Colquitt, J. A., J. A. LePine, and M. J. Wesson. *Organizational Behavior*. New York: McGraw Hill, 2015.

Cross, R., and A. Parker. *The Hidden Power of Social Networks*. Boston: Harvard Business School Press, 2004.

Deutschman, A. *Change or Die: The Three Keys to Change at Work or in Life*. New York: HarperBusiness, 2007.

Drucker, P. *Managing for Results*. New York: Harper & Row, 1964.

French, J. R. P., Jr., and B. H. Raven. "The Bases of Social Power." In *Studies in Social Power*. Edited by D. Cartright. Ann Arbor, MI: University of Michigan, Institute for Social Research, 1959.

Goleman, D., R. Boyatzis, and A. McKee. *Primal Leadership: Realizing the Power of Emotional Intelligence*. Boston: Harvard Business School Press, 2002.

Goodwin, D. K. *Team of Rivals: The Political Genius of Abraham Lincoln*, New York: Simon and Schuster, 2005.

Gordon, J. *Training Camp*. Hoboken, NJ: John Wiley and Sons, 2009.

Greenberg, J., and R. A. Baron. *Behavior in Organizations*. Upper Saddle River, NJ: Pearson Education, 2008.

Haudan, J. *The Art of Engagement*. New York: McGraw-Hill, 2008.

Kotter, J. P. *Leading Change*. Boston: Harvard Business School Press, 1996.

Lencioni, P. *The Advantage: Why Organizational Health Trumps Everything Else in Business*. San Francisco: Jossey-Bass, 2012.

————. *The Five Dysfunctions of a Team*. San Francisco: Jossey-Bass, 2002.

Longenecker, C. O. "The Best Practices of Great Leaders." *Industrial Management* (July/August 2014): 20–25.

———. "Career Survival and Success in the 21st Century." *Drake Business Review* (Fall 2011).

———. "The Characteristics of Really Bad Bosses." *Industrial Management* (September/October 2011): 10–15.

———. "Coaching for Better Results: Key Practices of High Performance Leaders." *Industrial and Commercial Training* 42, no.1 (2010): 32–40.

———. "The Consequences and Causes of Ineffective Organizational Training Practices." *The HR Advisor* (November-December 1997): 5–13.

———. "Getting Better Results: Ten Leadership Imperatives." *Drake Business Review* (Winter 2010).

———. "How the Best Leaders Motivate Workers," *Industrial Management* (January/February 2011): 8–13.

———. "Key Practices for Closing the Management Skills Gap." *HRM Review* (May 2010): 19–25.

———. "Maximizing the Transfer of Learning from Managerial Education Programs." *Organizational Development and Learning: An International Journal* 18, no. 4 (2004): 3–6.

Longenecker, C. O., and S. S. Ariss. "Creating Competitive Advantage through Effective Management Education." *Journal of Management Development* 21, no. 9 (2002): 640–654.

———. "Leading in Trying Economic Times: Imperatives for Handling the Heat." *Industrial Management* (September/October 2009): 8–12.

Bibliography

Longenecker, C. O., D. J. Dwyer, and T. C. Stansfield. "Barriers and Gateways to Workforce Productivity: Lessons to Be Learned." *Industrial Management* (April-March 1998): 21–28.

―――. "The Human Side of Manufacturing Improvement: A Study of Productivity through People." Business Horizons (March-April 1997): 7–17.

Longenecker, C. O., and L. S. Fink. "Closing the Management Skills Gap: A Call for Action." *Development and Learning in Organizations: An International Journal* 20, no. 1 (2006): 16–20.

―――. "Developing a Learning Organization: The Top Management Leadership Factor." *Effective Executive* (June 2008): 46–51.

―――. "Fixing Management's Fatal Flaws." *Industrial Management* (July/August 2012): 12–17.

―――. "How Top Managers Develop: A Field Study." *Organizational Development and Learning: An International Journal* 20, no. 5 (2006): 18–20.

―――. "Improving Management Performance in Rapidly Changing Organizations." *Journal of Management Development* 20, no. 1 (2001): 336–346.

―――. "Key Criteria in 21st Century Management Promotional Decisions." *Career Development International* 13, no. 3 (2008): 241–251.

Longenecker, C. O., and D. Gatins. "Gateways to Management Development in Rapidly Changing Organizations." *Development and Learning in Organizations: An International Journal* 25, no. 3 (2011): 3–6.

Longenecker, C. O., and A. M. Leffakis. "Serious about White Collar Productivity." *Industrial Management* (November/ December 2002): 27–33.

Longenecker, C. O., and M. J. Neubert. "Barriers and Gateways to Management Cooperation and Teamwork." *Business Horizons* (September-October 2000): 37–44.

———. "The Management Development Needs of Front-Line Managers: Voices from the Field." *Career Development International* 8, issue 4 (2003): 210–218.

———. "The Practices of Effective Managerial Coaches: Voices from the Field." *Business Horizons* 48 (2005): 493–500.

Longenecker, C. O., M. J. Neubert, and L. S. Fink. "Causes and Consequences of Managerial Failure in Rapidly Changing Organizations." *Business Horizons* 50, no. 2 (March/April 2007): 145–155.

Longenecker, C. O., G. R. Papp, and T. S. Stansfield. "Quarterbacking Real and Rapid Organizational Improvement." *Leader-to-Leader* no. 51(Winter 2009): 17–23.

Longenecker, C. O., and P. Pinkel. "Coaching to Win at Work." *Manage* (January-February 1997): 19–21.

Longenecker, C. O., and J. L. Simonetti. *Getting Results: Five Absolutes for High Performance.* San Francisco: Jossey-Bass, 2001.

Longenecker, C. O., J. L. Simonetti, N. Nykodym, and J. A. Scazzero. "Thinning the Herd: Twelve Factors Affecting Downsizing Decisions." *The H.R. Advisor Journal* (March-April 1997): 16–22.

Longenecker, C. O., and T. C. Stansfield. "Why Plant Managers Fail: Causes and Consequences." *Industrial Management* (January-February 2000): 24–32.

Longenecker, C. O., T. C. Stansfield, and D. J. Dwyer. "The Human Side of Manufacturing Improvement." *Business Horizons* (March-April 1997): 7–17.

Longenecker, C. O., T. C. Stansfield, and G. R. Papp. *The Two-Minute Drill: Lessons for Rapid Organizational Improvement from America's Greatest Game.* San Francisco: Jossey-Bass, 2007.

Longenecker, C. O., and R. Yonker. "Leadership Deficiencies in Rapidly Changing Organizations: Multisource Feedback as a Needs Assessment Tool—Part I." *Industrial and Commercial Training* 45, no. 3 (2013): 159–165.

———. "Leadership Deficiencies in Rapidly Changing Organizations: Multisource Feedback as a Needs Assessment Tool—Part II." *Industrial and Commercial Training* 45, no. 4 (2013): 202–208.

Ludwig, Dean C., and Clinton O. Longenecker. "The Bathsheba Syndrome: The Ethical Failure of Successful Leaders." *Journal of Business Ethics* 12, no. 4 (1993): 265–273.

Nahavandi, A. *The Art and Science of Leadership.* 5th ed. Upper Saddle River, NJ: Prentice Hall, 2009.

Nelson, B. *1001 Ways to Reward Employees.* New York: Workman Publishing, 1994.

Neubert, M. J., and C. O. Longenecker. "Creating Job Clarity: HR's Role in Creating Organizational Focus." *The HR Advisor Journal* (June/July 2003):17–24.

Phillips, D. T. *Run to Win: Vince Lombardi on Coaching and Leadership.* New York: St. Martin's Press, 2001.

Rosenbach, W. E., R. L. Taylor, and M. A. Youndt. *Contemporary Issues in Leadership.* 7th ed. Boulder, CO: Westview Press, 2012.

Ulrich, D., J. Zenger, and N. Smallwood. *Results-Based Leadership.* Boston: Harvard Business School Press, 1999.

Yourdon, E. *Death March.* Upper Saddle River, NJ: Prentice Hall, 2004.

Marketing

Agarwal, Pankaj, and Richard P. Larrick. "When Consumers Care about Being Treated Fairly: The Interaction of Relationship Norms and Fairness Norms." *Journal of Consumer Psychology* 22, 1 (2012): 114–127. A research article investigating the different types of relationships consumers form with companies and how those relationship types affect perceptions of fairness.

Ansoff, Igor. "Strategies for Diversification." *Harvard Business Review* 35, 5 (September–October 1957): 113–124. The article that introduced the Ansoff matrix, a framework accounting for the different ways companies can increase sales.

Chernev, Alexander. *Strategic Marketing Management*, 7th ed. Chicago: Cerebellum Press, 2012. An introductory marketing textbook.

Chernev, Alexander, Ryan Hamilton, and David Gal. "Competing for a Consumer's Identity: Limits to Self-Expression and the Perils of Lifestyle Branding." *Journal of Marketing* 75, 3 (May 2011): 66–82. Investigates the role of transient changes in the need for self-expression on how consumers value brands.

Dickson, Peter R., and Alan G. Sawyer. "The Price Knowledge and Search of Supermarket Shoppers." *Journal of Marketing* 54, 3 (July 1990): 42–53. Survey research conducted on shoppers in supermarkets to determine how well they remember prices of items immediately after selecting them.

Dolan, Robert J. "How Do You Know When the Price Is Right?" *Harvard Business Review* 73, 5 (September–October 1995): 174–183. Lists some of the principles for pricing well.

Fournier, Susan, and Julie Yao. "A Case for Loyalty." Harvard Business School Case 9-598-023. Cambridge: Harvard Business Press, 1998. Discusses some of the foundations and advantages of customer loyalty.

Gourville, John T. "Eager Sellers and Stony Buyers." *Harvard Business Review* 84, 2 (June 2006): 99–106. Reviews the psychological differences between buyers (customers) and sellers (marketers) and the problems this disconnect can lead to.

Haire, Mason. "Projective Techniques in Marketing Research." *Journal of Marketing* 14, 5 (April 1950): 649–656. Details the use of projective research techniques to reveal consumers' feelings about the NESCAFÉ brand.

Hamilton, Ryan, and Alexander Chernev. "Low Prices Are Just the Beginning: Price Image in Retail Management." *Journal of Marketing* 77, 6 (November 2013): 1–20. An investigation of price image, a brand's reputation for pricing, and how to manage it.

Kotler, Philip, and Kevin Lane Keller. *Marketing Management*, 14th ed. Boston: Prentice Hall, 2011. An introductory marketing textbook.

Manzi, Jim. *Uncontrolled: The Surprising Payoff of Trial-and-Error for Business, Politics, and Society*. New York: Basic Books, 2012. The case for using controlled, randomized experiments to make better business decisions.

Shiv, Baba, Ziv Carmon, and Dan Ariely. "Placebo Effects of Marketing Actions: Consumers May Get What They Pay For." *Journal of Marketing Research* 42, 4 (November 2005): 383–393. Research article revealing a price placebo effect: Items purchased on sale are sometimes less efficacious than those purchased at full price.

Underhill, Paco. *Why We Buy: The Science of Shopping*. New York: Simon & Schuster, 1999. Interesting insights about consumer behavior gleaned from observational consumer research methods.

Yankelovich, Daniel, and David Meer. "Rediscovering Market Segmentation." *Harvard Business Review* 84, 2 (February 2006): 122–131. A review of the principles underlying good market segmentation.

Notes